# The Rise of Critical Islam

# OXFORD ISLAMIC LEGAL STUDIES

*Series Editors:*
*Anver M. Emon, Clark Lombardi, and Lynn Welchman*

Satisfying the growing interest in Islam and Islamic law, the Oxford Islamic Legal Studies series speaks to both specialists and those interested in the study of a legal tradition that shapes lives and societies across the globe. Islamic law operates at several levels. It shapes private decision-making, binds communities, and it is also imposed by states as domestic positive law. The series features innovative and interdisciplinary studies that explore Islamic law as it operates at each of these levels. The series also sheds new light on the history and jurisprudence of Islamic law and provides for a richer understanding of the state of Islamic law in the contemporary Muslim world, including parts of the world where Muslims are minorities.

ALSO AVAILABLE IN THE SERIES

*Law, Empire, and the Sultan*
Ottoman Imperial Authority and Late Hanafi Jurisprudence
Samy A. Ayoub

*The Anthropology of Islamic Law*
Education, Ethics, and Legal Interpretation at Egypt's Al-Azhar
Aria Nakissa

*The Legal Thought of Jalāl al-Dīn al-Suyūṭī*
Authority and Legacy
Rebecca Hernandez

*Coercion and Responsibility in Islam*
A Study in Ethics and Law
Mairaj U. Syed

*Islamic Legal Revival*
Reception of European Law and Transformations in Islamic Legal Thought in Egypt, 1875–1952
Leonard Wood

*Shari'a and Muslim Minorities*
The Wasati and Salafi Approaches to Fiqh al- Aqalliyyat al-Muslima
Uriya Shavit

*Domestic Violence and the Islamic Tradition*
Ayesha S. Chaudhry

*Shari'a and Social Engineering*
The Implementation of Islamic Law in Contemporary Aceh, Indonesia
R. Michael Feener

*Religious Pluralism and Islamic Law*
Dhimmis and Others in the Empire Law
Anver M. Emon

*Narratives of Islamic Legal Theory*
Rumee Ahmed

# The Rise of Critical Islam

*10th–13th Century Legal Debate*

YOUCEF L. SOUFI
*University of Toronto*

OXFORD
UNIVERSITY PRESS

OXFORD
UNIVERSITY PRESS

Oxford University Press is a department of the University of Oxford. It furthers the University's objective of excellence in research, scholarship, and education by publishing worldwide. Oxford is a registered trade mark of Oxford University Press in the UK and certain other countries.

Published in the United States of America by Oxford University Press
198 Madison Avenue, New York, NY 10016, United States of America.



CIP data is on file at the Library of Congress

ISBN 978-0-19-768500-6

DOI: 10.1093/oso/9780197685006.001.0001

Printed by Integrated Books International, United States of America

**Note to Readers**

This publication is designed to provide accurate and authoritative information in regard to the subject matter covered. It is based upon sources believed to be accurate and reliable and is intended to be current as of the time it was written. It is sold with the understanding that the publisher is not engaged in rendering legal, accounting, or other professional services. If legal advice or other expert assistance is required, the services of a competent professional person should be sought. Also, to confirm that the information has not been affected or changed by recent developments, traditional legal research techniques should be used, including checking primary sources where appropriate.

*(Based on the Declaration of Principles jointly adopted by a Committee of the American Bar Association and a Committee of Publishers and Associations.)*

# Contents

*Acknowledgements* vii

Introduction: Islamic Law and/as Critique 1

PART I

1. Mourning Loss through Debate: Pious Critique and Its Limits 29
2. The Emergence of Pious Critique: A Genealogy of "*Munāẓara*" 51
3. "Why Do We Debate?": Uncovering Two Discursive Foundations for Disputation 77

PART II

4. Debating the Convert's *Jizya*: How the *Madhhab* Enabled *Ijtihād* 103
5. Forced Marriage in Shāfiʿī Law: Revisiting School Doctrine 125
6. The Mistaken Prayer Direction: Debating Indeterminate School Doctrine 143

PART III

7. The End of Critical Islam?: Shāfiʿism and Temporal Decay 165

*Notes* 193
*Bibliography* 251
*Index* 271

# Acknowledgements

I began writing this book in the summer of 2018. I spent my mornings outdoors on the campus of the University of British Columbia (UBC), sometimes in front of the ocean's waves, sometimes a flower garden. The setting was peaceful. I was grateful. After cancer treatments the year before, I was grateful to God for giving me more time on this earth to discover, compose, and share ideas I thought important. I was grateful to the students at UBC who had supported me when I first became ill and had engaged with my ideas the year prior, in particular Zaid Salman, Alex Garcia, Hussain Khan, Noor Youssef, Rex Ng, and Moneeza Badat. My students taught me more than they knew: every listless expression in a class lecture, every confused question, and every engaged discussion became a means for me to rethink how, why, and what ideas I should present about the Islamic tradition. This book, I told myself, will be written for them, not only for the expert in Islamic law.

The writing of this book has been a long journey. Thank you to the many individuals who accompanied me along the way. There were those of you who shaped the ideas of this book from the very beginning, when it was still in dissertation form: Anver Emon, Amira Mittermaier, Mohammad Fadel, Sadaf Ahmed, Basit Iqbal, Jairan Gahan, and Khalidah Ali. You have continued to engage with the chapters in this book ever since. There were those of you who gave me insightful comments as I developed my ideas: Ahmed El Shamsy, Ayesha Chaudhry, Walid Salih, Ruth Marshall, Ammar Khatib, Jeannie Miller, David Vishanoff, Rumee Ahmed, Aun Hasan Ali, Amal Ghazal, Derryl Maclean, Walter Young, Shahid Rahman, Omar Anchassi, Sohail Hanif, and Kamran Karimullah. There were those of you who made me rethink *ijithād*, *munāẓara*, and critique by engaging with my journal articles: David Powers, Joseph Lowry, Ovamir Anjum, Shuruq Naguib, and Peri Bearman. There were those of you who read and gave me your generous and perceptive comments on the most recent versions of the book: Junaid Quadri, Nada Moumtaz, Saadia Yacoob, Bilal Ibrahim, and James Tully. And there were those of you who have given me invaluable editorial support: Ghaith Qassas, Marya Atassi, Nathalie LaCoste, Philip

Sayers, Mohannad Abusarah, and the editorial team at Oxford University Press. I am also grateful to Eric Chaumont for his foundational scholarship on al-Shīrāzī and to Walter Young for having revived interest in the *munāẓara* in the last decade.

My journey included institutional support and intellectual comradery. Anver must be singled out for giving me the time and the institutional backing that enabled me to see this book to completion during a postdoc at the Institute of Islamic Studies (IIS). The support he continues to give to advancing junior scholars' careers is inspirational. Thank you to my circle of academic friends in Vancouver: Seemi Ghazi, Itrath Syed, Faisal Nahri, Maged Senbel, and Çavlan Erengezgin; and to my colleagues at UBC, particularly Florence Yoon, Leanne Bablitz, and Sara Milstein. From 2019 to 2022, I have had the support of two wonderful academic teams: the University of Toronto's IIS and the Canadian Association for the Study of Islam and Muslims (CASIM), whose members included Catherine Larouche, Sara Abdel-Latif, Madeleine Link, Maysa Haque, Sarah Shah, Moska Rokay, Joud Alkorani, Adil Mawani, Sara Hamed, and Zaid Khan. Even with COVID-19, the IIS and CASIM brought together an exceptional group of scholars willing to collaborate in furthering the study of Islam and Muslims. Thank you also to my academic mentors in my younger and more formative years, particularly Georges Vermette and Ravi Vaithees.

Finally, thank you to my family, both immediate and extended: the Denisets, the Soufis, and the Ahmeds. Thank you to my parents, Rachel Soufi (née Deniset) and Taïb Soufi, for their love and encouragement. My mother will always be my first and most important teacher of the humanities. Thank you to my siblings and especially Salah-Eddin for his kindness during my childhood and to Sofiya, who never fails to make me laugh even on the most difficult of days, for our discussions on Islamic law and for her rigorous editing work. Thank you to my wife's parents, Shahida Ahmed and Naseer Ahmed, for their unwavering support throughout these years of book writing. Alongside Anver, they created the conditions that gave me time to write despite raising a young family.

Thank you to my big boy Abdullah and to my two little ones, Ayesha and Sana, for the light you bring to my days. I hope someday the contents of this book benefit you and the communities that you belong to. May you always stay kind, gracious, and thoughtful. Papa vous aime de tout son coeur.

Most of all, thank you to my partner, Sadaf Ahmed. Your impact on this book cannot be overestimated. More than anyone, you were the dialogical partner that made this book possible. At times, you have been my *sāʾil* and at others my *mujīb*. Thank you for your patience, companionship, and love throughout our lives together.

# Introduction

## Islamic Law and/as Critique

"I just don't understand how he wasn't stoned," Arsalan said, shaking his head. Our eyes had met moments before: he was smiling in disbelief. It was the winter term of 2017, during my first year teaching at the University of British Columbia. That day, our "Modern Islam" class was discussing the famous 19th-century Muslim Indian reformer Syed Ahmed Khan. Khan was a complex man and, in many ways, a controversial figure.[1] His ideas were out of step with those of most Muslims, past and present, so I knew my students would likely be surprised to hear how Khan rejected miracles such as Mary's virgin birth and affirmed that prophets like Muḥammad were nothing more than highly perceptive or intelligent men.[2] There were puzzled expressions and eyes widened in surprise. It was then that I noticed Arsalan and Rod, seated beside each other, and their incredulous smiles. Arsalan saw me trying to decipher his reaction: "I just don't understand how he wasn't stoned."

Though extreme, I knew where Arsalan's comments were coming from. His generation lived in the shadow of three decades of violent episodes pitting Islam against freedom of expression—the Salman Rushdie Affair; the Danish Cartoons; and, most vividly in the minds of my young students, the Charlie Hebdo massacre a mere two years prior. Much of the public discourse in Canada and the West more generally saw Islam as intransigently opposing any and all forms of critical scrutiny. TV personalities like Bill Maher and Sam Harris put forward claims like "[Islam] is the only religion that acts like the mafia, that will fucking kill you if you say the wrong thing, draw the wrong picture, or write the wrong book."[3] As many have pointed out, these depictions of Islam are gross caricatures that reflect neither the reality nor the complexity of the Muslim world. They draw upon centuries-old stereotypes that position the Orient and Muslims as irrational and authoritarian. Measured analyses of the *Satanic Verses* and Danish Cartoons affairs have highlighted the breadth of issues far beyond religious dogmatism—immigration and discontent at the US War on Terror, for example—that fuelled the turmoil of these episodes.[4]

*The Rise of Critical Islam*. Youcef L. Soufi, Oxford University Press. © Oxford University Press 2023.
DOI: 10.1093/oso/9780197685006.003.0001

Still, Arsalan's impression of Islam was grounded in more than a mere Western historical bias. He himself came from an Iranian Muslim background: his family had fled Iran's theocratic state and had seen firsthand how men of religion could repress dissenting voices. In fact, many Muslim students in the classroom had similarly witnessed harsh consequences for those who expressed what the Muslim masses or religious authorities in their countries of origin deemed injurious or heretical speech. Those of Pakistani origin, for instance, could point to their country's death penalty for transgressing blasphemy laws.[5] In short, many Muslims in my class felt that contemporary Islam lacked a critical ethos. I have some sympathy with this view. And what I've found especially disheartening is that the violent and dogmatic Muslim fringe does not monopolize this lack of openness to debate. It is also found among the moderate mainstream tradition that celebrates tolerance and pluralism. Take, for instance, the prophetic *ḥadīth* (tradition) in which Muḥammad states, "I promise a house in paradise to the one who leaves debate, even if he/she is correct."[6] I have often heard this *ḥadīth* quoted in Friday sermons and have seldom met a mosque-attending Muslim who has not. It is usually cited in a sincere attempt to foster harmony and brotherly and sisterly bonds between believers. Mosque leaders presuppose that debate leads to bruised egos and conflict, and that keeping the peace necessitates swallowing one's tongue. But there is something troubling about the prevalence of debate's condemnation. Aren't there times when debate is needed? If so, should mosque preachers not be encouraging it? And has it always been this way?

It was a couple of years before the conversation with Arsalan—at a Friday sermon in 2015—that I began to reflect upon the ruptures in the history of Muslim attitudes towards critique. I was attending a sermon at Hart House in the University of Toronto delivered by a well-respected and well-known Toronto imam. The sermon was commonplace, but something caught my attention. My eyebrows furrowed when I heard the imam state that "the great scholars of Islam accepted *ikhtilāf* but not *khilāf*." Many in attendance recognized the statement as witty wordplay: both Arabic words share the same root *kh-l-f*, but whereas *ikhtilāf* refers simply to a difference of opinion, *khilāf* connotes conflict or dissension. The point the imam was trying to make was an important one in this day and age: he sought to convey that religious disagreement and pluralism was a normal part of Islamic thought. The salience of this idea was all the more pronounced at a moment when ISIS's violently dogmatic understanding of Islam was permeating newscasts. The message was dear to this particular imam's heart too, for he had long advocated the condemnation of violence and bigotry, leading the charge in 2007, when over thirty Canadian imams signed a statement denouncing religiously motivated violence.[7] The imam's point was that divergent ideas should not lead to communal turmoil. Though newly urgent, the message was one the audience was familiar with. Virtually any Muslim hears over the course of their life the well-known prophetic statement "*al-ikhtilāf raḥma*" (differences of opinion are a divine mercy).[8] The message also fits well with modern secular liberal sensibilities that view religious choice as a deeply personal and relative matter. And yet there was something about the statement that struck and stayed with me, and it was not its wordplay.

Being at the tail end of my PhD in classical Islamic law, I knew that the terms *ikhtilāf* and *khilāf* were in fact synonyms in the legal vocabulary of a millennium ago.[9] The mistake bothered me: not so much the simple linguistic error, but rather what this historical erasure implied. The statement showed an inability to appreciate what classical Islamic scholars knew at their very core: namely, that different opinions only deserved respect if those opinions had passed through the crucible of debate. Ideas, these jurists knew, needed conflict or *khilāf*. They needed to be tested—in short, to be engaged with critically. To say that the great scholars of Islam did not accept *khilāf*, then, was to miss the fact that respect and pluralism in the world of juristic Islam was something that was earned. Yet the imam was neither the first nor the last to aver that the scholars of Islam accepted *ikhtilāf* but not *khilāf*.[10] That afternoon, as I looked at the opulent, old, wood-panelled structure of Hart House's Great Hall, I pondered the difference between Islamic legal discourse today and during the centuries-ago era I was studying. While pluralism remains a widely embraced good, critique is far less so. More still, I marvelled at how few Muslims were aware of this historical shift.

This book uncovers an Islam that departs from the one featured in media coverage and mosque discourse. It is an Islam that has the potential both to humble advocates of secular reason as a panacea to religious extremism and to uncover for today's diverse range of Muslims the personal quest to understand God's law that animated their legal tradition and made critical debate a revered and pervasive historical practice.

## The *Munāẓara*: Unearthing a Culture of Critique, *Ijtihād*, and Uncertainty

The culture of critique that I examine in this book took shape among Sunni Muslim jurists (*fuqahā'*) in Iraq at the dawn of the 10th century CE.[11] It then quickly spread to Persian lands, including Khurasan and Central Asia. The primary vocation of these jurists was the study of God's revealed law (*al-shar'* or *al-sharī'a*). They trained in legal schools where they were exposed to a series of standard contested questions (*masā'il al-khilāf*) that had divided the legal community over generations.[12] As they acquired the skills to assess the merits of each side of these debates, they were tasked with determining which position was most well founded and why. In doing so, they critically engaged with the views of their predecessors and their peers. This process of critique was understood as a pious pursuit that partook in the task of searching for God's law. Importantly, though, the contested questions were never settled. Nor were they expected to be. It was deemed sufficient that each jurist should come to his own conclusions on the law.[13] A jurist's evaluation of legal arguments made it possible for him to counsel lay Muslims seeking guidance on how to live by God's commands.[14] A jurist was therefore a legislator of sorts, at least for himself and for those who petitioned him.

Jurists' high regard for critique rested upon two other widely held commitments. First was the obligation of *itjihād* (the jurist's effort in searching for God's law). With few exceptions, jurists of this era barred those with legal training from "subscribing to a legal position *without evidence*" (known in Arabic as *taqlīd*).[15] As we shall see, the stakes were high: a jurist's afterlife depended upon the process of finding evidence for his positions.[16] Thus, this classical legal culture was concerned with evidence and justification above all else. Second, jurists saw God's law as largely uncertain.[17] Though God had commanded Muslims to base their legal positions on evidence, he had provided them with very little in the way of clear-cut confirmations. For the vast majority of legal questions, then, a jurist could not definitively claim the correctness of his positions. He could only claim to have examined the law to a degree sufficient to overcome his initial presumptions. Certainty remained out of reach—and this meant acknowledging the possibility of being wrong. More importantly, it meant acknowledging that an opposing jurist might be right. In a legal system in which each jurist must know the evidence justifying a law but no jurist can be certain of what that law truly is, critique comes to hold a place of prime importance.[18] Only through the clashing of ideas could a jurist come to a stronger—though ultimately still uncertain—understanding of the law. Thus, while I call the classical juristic community a culture of critique, it was so because it was a culture of *ijtihād* and a culture of legal uncertainty. All three aspects of this culture—*ijtihād*, uncertainty, and critique—were intertwined, and their analysis serves to explain today what was distinct about this era in Islamic legal history.

To analyze this culture of critique, my study focuses on a particular juristic practice: the disputation (*munāẓara*), also known as "the debate gathering" (*majlis al-naẓar*). Although classical legal critique took different forms, including books featuring lengthy arguments against their authors' detractors, the disputation placed critique in the limelight for all jurists—and now the historian—to see. The disputation brought jurists together for the express purpose of sustained critical examination of the law. Each session would feature two jurists taking opposite roles on a contested legal question, often before an audience of fellow jurists. One jurist was labelled the questioner (*al-sā'il*) and was charged with asking his opponent, the respondent (*al-mujīb*), his position on a contested question.[19] After learning of the respondent's position, the questioner was tasked with raising objections, which the respondent in turn sought to address and overcome. The exchange was to be thorough, detailed, and ruthless. While proper decorum and mutual respect were expected, objections were to be as devastating to the questioner's evidence as possible. Through the exchange, the jurists came to verify sound arguments and discredit false ones.[20] The disputation furthered the jurists' search for God's elusive law. For this reason, disputations were a pervasive practice in Iraq and Persia up until the 13th century. They took place in mosques, homes, and rulers' courts.[21] And though they were often regularly scheduled and mundane affairs,[22] disputations were also held in conjunction with important events in the life of the legal community: the visit of a prominent scholar, the appointment of a new professor, or even the funeral of a loved one. They peppered the landscape of juristic life. In the pages that follow, the practice of disputation is the key mechanism through which I examine the role of critique from the 10th to the 13th centuries.

The prominence of disputation within the classical juristic community is well known. George Makdisi placed the disputation at the heart of his analysis of 11th-century legal colleges. He saw disputation as a pedagogical means of training aspiring jurists and a method for establishing hierarchies within the ranks of a legal school.[23] In the last decade, a number of important studies have examined aspects of the disputation by turning to books of *jadal* (dialectic): a literary genre through which jurists helped prepare their students for disputations.[24] Books of *jadal* dedicate most of their page count to the categorization of arguments and objections that a jurist might deploy to defend his position; a few other passages present the sequence and ethics of the disputation. Studies of *jadal*, while immensely important, have focused on understanding the science of dialectical argumentation among Muslims, remaining largely silent on the social dimension of the disputation. To take an analogy, one can study Aristotle's logic as a science concerned with making claims about correct reasoning, but one can also ask how Aristotle taught logic in his Lyceum, how his teaching shaped his Greek students' practice of philosophy, and what impact it had on Greek society. To ask about the social dimension of the disputation, then, is to recognize it as an act taking place in a context, performed by humans with complex motives, and having far-reaching consequences on other humans living in the same time and place. For such an understanding of the disputation, Makdisi's research remains our best source.

My aim is to revise and extend Makdisi's analysis by studying different aspects of the disputation. A specific set of questions animate my study: How did the disputation emerge? How did jurists justify the practice? What were the limits to their critical aspirations? What impact did disputations have on a jurist's substantive legal thought? How did the legal school a jurist belonged to shape the content and conduct of his disputations? And how in turn did disputations shape the historical evolution of a school's substantive law? Finally, why did disputations wane in prominence around the 13th century? To answer these questions, I treat the literature of the juristic community as an archive that opens a window onto this community's values, disagreements, and practices. This literature includes texts of legal theory, substantive law, historiography, biographical dictionaries, and transcripts of past disputations.

Among my conclusions is that the classical culture's commitment to critique produced the argumentative complexity that other historians have recognized when studying jurists' manuals of substantive law.[25] The complexity of the law was the product of generations critically revisiting, evaluating, refining, and adding their own perspectives to standard legal questions. Over time, the number of arguments supporting different sides of a debate multiplied; so too did the objections. We can gain some semblance of this complexity by examining the large manuals of substantive law which today take up bookshelves in their multi-volume print editions.

Manuals such as Abū Bakr al-Jaṣṣāṣ's (d. 370/980 CE) *Sharḥ Mukhtaṣar al-Ṭaḥāwī*, Abū al-Ṭayyib al-Ṭabarī's (d. 450/1058 CE) *al-Ta'līqa al-Kubrā*, and Abū al-Ḥasan al-Māwardī's (d. 450/1058 CE) *al-Ḥāwī al-Kabīr* list the many arguments and objections that jurists posited in defending their positions.[26] But even the manuals that provide the most elaborate expositions of a legal question present arguments in a much more cursory manner than do jurists engaged in disputations. Indeed, these manuals offer only summary records of the more complex oral examination of the law, the traces of which we can locate in our few extant transcripts of disputations.

But while I emphasize the admirable argumentative complexity produced by classical disputation culture, I also argue that the critical aspirations of jurists were undercut by their exclusivism. The perspectives of groups who were either largely or completely excluded from the juristic community (such as slaves and women) were not heard in this culture of critique. As we shall see through the example of women, the wants, desires, and needs of excluded groups were not disqualified from the debate gathering so much as they were presumed. As a result, the search for God's law sometimes depended on unsubstantiated claims about what would be good for those not party to the discussion.

## The Shaykh Abū Isḥāq and His Disputations

At the heart of this study is the Shaykh Abū Isḥāq, as his contemporaries and later jurists of his Shāfiʿī school affectionately and reverentially called him. His full name was Abū Isḥāq Ibrāhīm b. Yaʿqūb al-Fīrūzābādī al-Shīrāzī. I refer to him as al-Shīrāzī throughout these pages in accordance with contemporary academic conventions.[27] The author of numerous canonical Shāfiʿī books, al-Shīrāzī was born in 1003 CE in the small town of Firuzabad and held the most prestigious professorial position in the Muslim world at the time of his death in 1083 CE.[28] His renown led to the preservation of his copious writings, and most are available today in critical print editions. During his life, al-Shīrāzī's contemporaries most admired him for his unparalleled debating prowess; he was considered a "lion in disputation."[29] Centuries later, the great biographer of the Shāfiʿīs, Tāj al-Dīn al-Subkī (d. 771/1370 CE), would affirm that some rivalled al-Shīrāzī's knowledge of the law but none equalled him in debating contentious legal questions.[30] Al-Shīrāzī's skill in disputation even found itself immortalized in poetry: the poet al-ʿUqaylī uses "Abū Isḥāq's tongue in the debate gathering" (*lisān Abī Isḥāq fī majlis al-naẓar*) as the vehicle of a simile for eloquence.[31] Al-Shīrāzī's life, his writings, and the transcripts of his disputations are the foundation of my analysis of the disputation in the classical era.

Methodologically, the focus on al-Shīrāzī has its virtues. Al-Shīrāzī was a prominent scholar, sought after by students eager to train with him, lay Muslims who requested his *fatwās*, and rulers who respected his learning. We know that he taught not only Shāfiʿī jurists but also famous Ḥanbalīs and Mālikīs. As such, his writings not only shaped his juristic community across school lines but also accounted for its disagreements. Al-Shīrāzī's centrality to the classical legal community and his proficiency in disputation make him a privileged source in seeking to understand this community's practice of disputation. We can get a sense of al-Shīrāzī's place within his legal community by briefly examining his training and rise within the ranks of the Shāfiʿī school.

Al-Shīrāzī's ascent to prominence was gradual. He likely came from humble origins: he had no prestigious lineage or wealth to boast about.[32] In fact, he would struggle financially his entire life. Even into adulthood, he would often visit a generous acquaintance among the marketplace greengrocers to receive food donations. Biographers note that he was too poor to afford the mount needed to make the pilgrimage to Mecca. However, poverty never discouraged al-Shīrāzī from his educational pursuits. He began studying at a young age in his native Firuzabad with a man named Abū ʿAbd Allāh Muḥammad b. ʿUmar al-Shīrāzī.[33] Firuzabad was a small provincial town in the province of Fars in Central Persia that benefitted from fertile land and a temperate climate. Its people had a reputation for piety and were known for their honesty—qualities al-Shīrāzī appears to have exemplified his entire life.[34] Al-Shīrāzī then relocated to Shiraz where he studied under the guidance of a better-known scholar, Abū Aḥmad al-Ghandajānī.[35] It was from his relatively short time in Shiraz that he would later earn the misleading title al-Shīrāzī (the one from Shiraz). Still at a young age, al-Shīrāzī engaged in disputations with members of other schools; he tells us that he frequently debated the Ẓāhirī judge al-Qāḍī Abū al-Faraj al-Shīrāzī.[36]

It would not be long before al-Shīrāzī moved again, first to Basra and then to Baghdad in 1024 CE.[37] For over two centuries, Baghdad had been the centre of Shāfiʿī thought.[38] Jurists from far and wide travelled there to imbibe knowledge from the city's learned class.[39] Unlike Shiraz, Baghdad was a predominantly Arab-speaking land. As a twenty-one-year-old Persian, al-Shīrāzī likely experienced the disorientation foreign travellers feel when entering a new cultural-linguistic space. Nonetheless, his prior study of the Arabic language would have facilitated the transition. Arabic was the shared scholarly language of the 11th-century Muslim world, and many of the great Iraqi scholars either were born in Persian lands or were of Persian stock. The names of historical Iraqi Shāfiʿī leaders collectively provide a lesson in Persian geography—al-Ṭabarī, al-Isfarāyinī, al-Māwardī, al-Shāshī, al-Marwarrūdhī, al-Marwazī, and so on.[40] The *ṭullāb al-ʿilm* (seekers of knowledge) of Baghdad came from a diverse geographical background. Later in life, al-Shīrāzī would attract students from all over the Muslim world seeking to study with him. On one memorable occasion, a prospective student came to introduce himself to the Shāfiʿī master. Al-Shīrāzī inquired about his origins: "Where are you from?" The young man answered, "From Mosul." To this, al-Shīrāzī cheerfully responded, "Welcome, my fellow countryman." The puzzled man pointed out to al-Shīrāzī the obvious fact that Mosul is nowhere near Shiraz. Al-Shīrāzī slyly answered, "Yes, but did we not all descend from Noah's boat?"[41] The anecdote conveys more than al-Shīrāzī's playful sense of humour; it highlights the cosmopolitanism and solidarity of the juristic community.

In Baghdad, al-Shīrāzī attended the lectures of the leading Shāfiʿī professor, a scholar by the name of Abū Ḥāmid al-Isfarāyinī (d. 418/1027 CE). Al-Shīrāzī likely hoped that the famed teacher would take him on as fellow (*ṣāḥib*)—a position equivalent to the modern-day graduate student. It would not be. A few years after al-Shīrāzī's arrival, al-Isfarāyīnī passed away, and al-Shīrāzī found his way to a lesser-known scholar who would take the mantle of the Shāfiʿī leadership after al-Isfarāyinī's death. This teacher, Abū al-Ṭayyib al-Ṭabarī, was already quite elderly, and had spent years in study in different regions of Persia before settling down in Baghdad. More than anyone else, al-Ṭabarī would become al-Shīrāzī's scholarly mentor. Al-Shīrāzī would speak highly of his master's sharp mind.[42] As al-Shīrāzī continued to distinguish himself, al-Ṭabarī made him his teaching assistant, giving him the title of "class repetitor" (*muʿīd*). The position must have provided al-Shīrāzī with a welcomed if modest income. In time, al-Ṭabarī would permit al-Shīrāzī to teach his own lessons within al-Ṭabarī's mosque. Al-Shīrāzī would eventually move on to teach in the mosque of the wealthy Bāb al-Marātib neighbourhood by the Tāj Palace.

Al-Shīrāzī's academic success depended less on his natural intelligence and more on his unmatched work ethic. Fellow students would express surprise at his ability to study continuously for long periods. They even worried that his body might not tolerate the stress he put it through. However, al-Shīrāzī was not without rivals. Abū Naṣr b. al-Ṣabbāgh (d. 477/1085 CE) was another of al-Ṭabarī's star students and in many ways possessed all the resources al-Shīrāzī lacked.[43] Ibn al- Ṣabbāgh was a native of Baghdad and came from a family of prominent jurists. This might partly explain why the two men seemed to dislike each other. It is said that Ibn al-Ṣabbāgh insulted al-Shīrāzī's knowledge of Shāfiʿī substantive law, prompting al-Shīrāzī to write his opus *al-Muhadhdhab* (*The Refinement of Shāfiʿī Doctrine*). When al-Ṭabarī passed away, the two younger men were considered the highest authorities on Shāfiʿī law in Baghdad.[44]

Ultimately, it was political fortune that would change the fate of an aging al-Shīrāzī and raise him to prominence over Ibn al-Ṣabbāgh. In the mid-11th century, the Seljuk Turks swept through the Eastern lands of Islam and took control of Iraq.[45] The Seljuk wazir, Niẓām al-Mulk, was a cunning administrator who recognized the value in courting the scholarly Muslim class of the empire.[46] He decided in 1065 to erect the Baghdad Niẓāmiyya, the most splendid college in his empire, and to appoint al-Shīrāzī to its professorial chair when it opened the following year. The college greatly amplified al-Shīrāzī's fame. Henceforth, students would flock from everywhere to study under his guidance.[47] It also increased al-Shīrāzī's political clout: state rulers consulted al-Shīrāzī as a foremost representative of the learned community of Baghdad.[48]

In 475/1083 CE, al-Shīrāzī undertook a political mission for the caliph to Khurasan, in northeastern Persia. The caliph had had a spat with one of his governors and wished to send word of it to the sultan and wazir, camped with their armies in Khurasan. He entrusted al-Shīrāzī with the task of delivering his letter.[49] When al-Shīrāzī arrived in the Khurasanian city of Nishapur, an intellectual hub rivalling Baghdad for primacy in Shāfiʿī thought, the towering jurist Abū al-Maʿālī al-Juwaynī (d. 478/1085 CE) greeted and hosted his travel party.[50] The two were old friends:[51] Al-Juwaynī had sought refuge in Baghdad decades earlier, when the political leadership of his city was subjecting him and other Shāfiʿīs to persecution for their adherence to Ashʿarī theology. Al-Shīrāzī was still an aspiring student when they had met, and the pair would participate in disputations together.[52] How times had changed. Al-Juwaynī's exile provided him with a newfound reputation among the international Shāfiʿī community. His time in the Hijaz region would grant him his enduring nickname, Imām al-Ḥaramayn (the Imam of the two sanctuaries of Mecca and Medina). When Niẓām al-Mulk had become wazir of Khurasan, al-Juwaynī was invited not only to return to his native city but to do so in triumphant fashion. Before the Niẓāmiyya of Baghdad, the wazir had built the first Niẓāmiyya College in Nishapur; al-Juwaynī was appointed its professor in 1058 CE. Both men were therefore at the top of the academic ladder when they reunited. With Niẓām al-Mulk in attendance, the two of them squared off for a series of disputations.

These debates between the two towering figures of the juristic community would prove to be among al-Shīrāzī's last: he passed away later that year. The academic and political community of Baghdad mourned the passing of one of its greatest thinkers. The caliph prayed over al-Shīrāzī's body, after which he was interred in the Abraz cemetery, a site that would become a well-known shrine for centuries to come.[53]

In short, then, al-Shīrāzī's eighty-year life offers us a lens into the career and social context of arguably the most influential professor in the most prestigious college in the most erudite city of the Muslim world. But there are two additional methodological virtues to placing al-Shīrāzī at the heart of a study on classical disputation. First, al-Shīrāzī has left us extant texts in every field of the Islamic legal sciences (usually more than one): we have detailed access to al-Shīrāzī's thought in legal theory, substantive law, and dialectic,[54] as well as his biographical dictionary of jurists (which sheds light on how he understood the historical evolution and makeup of Sunni legal schools),[55] a short statement of creed, and a manuscript on disagreement (*khilāf*) between the Shāfiʿīs and the Ḥanafīs.[56] I use these texts to highlight different aspects of the disputation. For instance, al-Shīrāzī's legal theory text *Sharḥ al-Lumaʿ* explains the importance of disputation to a jurist's process of *ijtihād*, while his substantive law manuals shed light on the contested legal issues that al-Shīrāzī debated in disputations.

Second, we possess four transcripts of al-Shīrāzī's disputations. This is a rarity because disputations were seldom written down. The reasons are twofold: first, the exploratory nature of disputations meant that they did not always represent a jurist's final position on a matter; and, second, disputations lacked the concision needed for teaching students the lengthy and varied evidence relevant to contested legal questions. Thus, disputations were usually strictly oral affairs, and while jurists in attendance sometimes sought to memorize what they had heard, these oral transmissions have not often reached us. Al-Shīrāzī's four disputation transcripts offer us a rare opportunity to examine the arguments and settings of historical disputations. I use each of these transcripts as the central piece of analysis in four chapters of this book. Each disputation sheds light on a different aspect of al-Shīrāzī's classical culture of critique.

Two of al-Shīrāzī's disputations took place between 1038 and 1041 CE in Baghdad.[57] Both saw al-Shīrāzī debating a prominent jurist from the opposing Ḥanafī legal school named Abū 'Abd Allāh al-Dāmaghānī (d. 478/1085 CE).[58] Al-Dāmaghānī would later become head judge of Baghdad. One of the disputations tackles a question of marriage law: whether a wife has the right to file for divorce if her husband struggles to provide her financial maintenance.[59] The second examines whether a new convert to Islam must pay the *jizya* (a poll-tax for non-Muslims) that accrued before his conversion.[60] The two other disputations see al-Shīrāzī debating al-Juwaynī in 1083 during his travel to Nishapur. The first of this second pair of disputations asks whether a father can force his adult virgin daughter into an unwanted marriage.[61] The second concerns a question of ritual law: Is it necessary to repeat one's prayer when one knows with certainty that one has prayed in the wrong direction?[62]

All four of al-Shīrāzī's disputation transcripts are found in Tāj al-Dīn al-Subkī's *Ṭabaqāt al-Shāfi'iyya al-Kubrā*. The three centuries that divide al-Shīrāzī and al-Subkī raise the question of historical authenticity. But there is compelling reason to believe that the events depicted in the disputation transcripts did take place. A closer examination of al-Subkī's sources show why. Al-Subkī notes that the Mālikī jurist Abū al-Walīd al-Bājī (d. 474/1081 CE) transmitted at least one of al-Shīrāzī's disputations with Abū 'Abd Allāh al-Dāmaghānī.[63] (Al-Subkī never explicitly tells his reader that al-Bājī also transmitted the second, though this is likely since the two disputations follow each other in al-Subkī's text.) That al-Bājī transcribed the disputations accords with what we know of his biography. First, al-Bājī travelled to Baghdad to study with its jurists, including al-Shīrāzī, and he took an interest in disputation. Second, al-Bājī's lost book *Firaq al-Fuqahā'* allegedly recorded disputations.[64] Third, al-Bājī's travels took place when al-Shīrāzī was still in the shadow of his master al-Ṭabarī, a fact attested to in al-Subkī's transcription of al-Shīrāzī's disputation with al-Dāmaghānī.[65] The transmission of al-Shīrāzī's two disputations with al-Juwaynī is also plausible. Al-Subkī notes that al-Shīrāzī himself recorded his disputations with al-Juwaynī. They were then transcribed by one of al-Shīrāzī's students, and eventually a transcription found its way into the hands of the Damascene scholar Ibn al-Ṣalāḥ (d. 643/1245 CE).[66] Other sources corroborate that al-Shīrāzī travelled to Nishapur where he was hosted by and debated with al-Juwaynī.[67] Considering al-Shīrāzī's intense passion for the art of disputation, we can understand his desire to put his disputation with the formidable al-Juwaynī on paper.[68] Nonetheless, our four transcripts cannot be taken as verbatim recordings. For one, al-Bājī explains that those who heard al-Shīrāzī and al-Dāmaghānī sought to memorize the disputation rather than record it in writing. It is therefore plausible that al-Bājī wrote down the disputations he witnessed some time after they took place, perhaps only on his return to his native Andalusia. For another, al-Shīrāzī could not have written down his disputations with al-Juwaynī while engaged in them:[69] he would have therefore written them down sometime after his meeting with al-Juwaynī and before his death later the same year. What we have, then, are likely four reconstructions of disputations relying on human memory and transcribed sometime after their occurrence. While imperfect, though, al-Subkī's transcriptions, coupled with the many legal and historiographical texts of this era, offer us valuable resources in understanding the practice of disputation.

Despite the methodological virtues of focusing on al-Shīrāzī, we must take note of one peril of my method. The focus on al-Shīrāzī in a study that grapples with a culture that spans three centuries and covers the geography of Iraq and Persianate lands risks erasing what was unique about jurists of different times and locales. Put otherwise, there is a risk of assimilating the contexts and ideas of other jurists to those of al-Shīrāzī. To mitigate this risk, I make wide use of other jurists' writings throughout my study. I cautiously extend my conclusions about the culture of critical Islam to other jurists, and I make explicit the divergences between jurists, both within and between legal schools. Still, the focus on al-Shīrāzī means that this study is only a partial view of classical Islam. I grant al-Shīrāzī's Shāfiʿī school more attention than other legal schools. Likewise, I focus on Iraq more than other centres of learning such as Nishapur. The 11th century is also more prominent than other time periods in my study. This is not to say that my claims about the culture of classical Islam are wrongheaded or overstated. But it is important to foreground how my interpretation, like all interpretation, is mediated by my sources. In the end, I see classical Islam and the role of disputation within it largely through the eyes of al-Shīrāzī. My aim is to help my reader do the same.

## Reimagining *Ijtihād* through the Lens of the Disputation

I have noted that the disputation was deeply intertwined with *ijtihād* in al-Shīrāzī's classical culture. But I want to suggest that this intertwinement offers us a means to think differently about *ijtihād*. In particular, I seek to amend two core assumptions in the scholarship on *ijtihād*. The first pertains to how scholars understand the practice and function of *ijtihād* in the classical period. The second relates to accounts of why the obligation of *ijtihād* waned and gave way to a general acceptance of *taqlīd* in the 13th century. To understand these assumptions, we would do well to review the debate around the closing of the gates of *ijtihād*. I present the debate here in cursory form, pointing out four significant shifts in scholarly positions over the last sixty years.

A typical starting point for the debate is Joseph Schacht's 1961 *Introduction to Islamic Law*.[70] Schacht argued that the beginning of the 10th century marked a period in which Muslim jurists no longer exercised *ijtihād*.[71] By this, Schacht meant that jurists no longer saw each other as possessing the freedom of "independent reasoning" on the law.[72] Instead, their legal positions were bound by *taqlīd*, which he translated as "unquestioning following of the doctrines of established legal schools and authorities."[73] Schacht noted that *mujtahid*s of lesser ranks continued for some centuries afterwards and that creativity among jurists continued to manifest both in stabilizing school doctrine and in *fatwā*s to lay-Muslim petitioners. Still, according to Schacht, a general attitude set in among jurists that all the important questions had been tackled by their predecessors and that they should defer to them rather than think for themselves. Scholarship in the next two decades often echoed Schacht's assessment, though not without some dissenters.[74]

Wael Hallaq's 1984 article "Was the Gate of *Ijtihād* Closed?" renewed scholarly interest in understanding the history of *ijtihād*. Hallaq cast doubt on the thesis that *ijtihād* had come to a close, making three particular claims. First, there was no consensus among jurists over the closing of the gates of *ijtihād*. Second, some jurists throughout Islamic history continued to claim the status of *mujtahid* (one who performs *ijtihād*).[75] Third, jurists continued to perform *ijtihād* after the formation of legal schools. Hallaq positioned himself as attacking a long-held dogma in the field, though his claims were less devastating to Schacht's thesis than he made them out to be. For instance, Hallaq acknowledged that by the 11th century, jurists were rarely considered "independent *mujtahids* (*mujtahid muṭlaq*)," distinguished by their capacity to establish their own legal schools.[76] Thus, Hallaq recognized something of the shift that Schacht was gesturing towards. But Hallaq's contribution was nonetheless valuable in pushing back against an Orientalist view that saw Muslim thought as having stagnated.[77] By claiming on the contrary that *ijtihād* had never ended, Hallaq critiqued the idea that Muslims ceased creatively engaging with the law. Indeed, Hallaq largely used the term *ijtihād* as shorthand for "creativity," "innovation," or "originality."[78] Such a use of the term *ijtihād* overlaps with modern Arab reformist thought, which spoke of *ijtihād* as a means to break free from the authority of schools of law by returning to scripture and coming up with new legal solutions.[79]

In the 1990s, fresh scholarship recognized that Hallaq had been too strong in his claims and attempted to posit a middle ground between Schacht and Hallaq. Sherman Jackson concurred with Hallaq that some scholars continued to perform *ijtihād*, but nonetheless argued that a qualitative shift occurred towards a regime of *taqlīd*. Jackson associated this shift with what he called the stabilization of the legal schools (*istiqrār al-madhāhib*) in the late 11th century.[80] He characterized the regime of *taqlīd* in terms of Sunni jurists' deference to the opinions of their legal school (*madhhab*). Jackson deemed "*ijtihād* proper" to have ended, since jurists no longer engaged in "the interpretation of scripture directly with no intermediate authorities standing between the sources and the individual jurists."[81] But he also claimed that *taqlīd* did not signal intellectual stagnation. Rather, *taqlīd* was about upholding the authority of the law by tracing its origins to the labours of past jurists, and it did not prevent Muslim jurists from innovating or bringing changes to the law when social need dictated that they should. Jackson famously used the term "legal scaffolding," borrowed from the American legal theorist Alan Watson, to designate a mode of engagement with the law where changes are made piecemeal, leaving the authority of the legal school unaffected.[82] Mohammad Fadel added to the debate, noting that *taqlīd* provided predictability to litigants about court rulings. Fadel contended that the move to *taqlīd* was therefore a triumph of "the rule of law" over a legal system that privileged the "personal discretion" of jurists.[83] Thus, for both Jackson and Fadel, *taqlīd* was no longer a dirty word casting Muslim legal thought in a negative light. If anything, the emergence of a regime of *taqlīd* was a sign of Islamic legal thought's success in previous centuries in developing laws to serve society. In short, *taqlīd* signalled the maturity of Islamic legal thought.

Following Schacht, Hallaq, and the 1990s defence of *taqlīd*, the fourth development I wish to draw attention to can be traced to Ahmed El Shamsy's 2008 article "Rethinking '*Taqlīd*' in the Early Shāfiʿī School."[84] El Shamsy pointed out that the fundamental problem with the scholarship on *ijtihād* and *taqlīd* is that scholars have tended to posit their own definitions for these terms rather than to examine how jurists themselves understood them. El Shamsy thus drew our attention to jurists' self-understandings of their practice of *taqlīd* and *ijtihād*. He showed that Shāfiʿīs up until the 13th century did not see themselves as engaging in *taqlīd* since they reserved the term for someone who had no evidentiary basis for his position.[85] But El Shamsy also considered that Shāfiʿīs from the 9th century onwards saw themselves as bounded by the constraints of fidelity to the doctrines of their school predecessors, rather than as practicing *ijtihād* themselves. This fidelity permitted the 13th-century jurist Ibn al-Ṣalāḥ to claim that his predecessors were guilty of at least partly engaging in *taqlīd*. Thus, like scholars before him, El Shamsy saw a gradual attenuation of *ijtihād* in the classical period as Shāfiʿīs fleshed out their school doctrine.

Valuable as all of this scholarship is, it nevertheless rests on the assumption that there is a tension, if not an outright contradiction, between *ijtihād* and belonging to a legal school. According to this literature, subscribing to a legal school's doctrine makes one a lesser *mujtahid*. One is merely a *mujtahid fī al-madhhab* (a *mujtahid* working within the framework of a legal school), tasked with fleshing out the details of a law that one's predecessors had left unfinished.[86] But a central contention of this book is that al-Shīrāzī, his Shāfiʿī contemporaries, and the vast majority of his colleagues among Iraqi and Persianate jurists drew a distinction between blindly following the doctrines of a legal school and critically engaging with them. *Ijtihād*, as al-Shīrāzī defined it, was "the effort in finding God's law," and when a jurist used the ideas of his colleagues (*aṣḥāb*), past or present, to learn about a legal question and evaluate possible evidence to arrive at a final determination, this was still "*ijtihād* proper." Analysis of the practice of disputation reveals that jurists like al-Shīrāzī did not defer to the arguments of their legal school authorities so much as they tested them in determining the merits of different legal positions. This was true even when jurists' critical interrogations led them to the same positions as their school predecessors. These jurists used the concepts of *ijtihād* and *taqlīd* to distinguish on an epistemological basis between those who relied on the authority of evidence alone and those who relied on the authority of men. Indeed, the distinction between "independent *mujtahid*" and "*mujtahid* of the *madhhab*" (*mujtahid fī al-madhhab*) only began to emerge at the end of the 11th century, and it took some time to gain ground. In short, *ijtihād* and *taqlīd* ought to be understood as epistemological categories in the classical era. They were used to speak of a jurist's duty to know *why* he upheld a legal position, not his duty to think independently of others.

The second scholarly assumption I tackle gained ground after Jackson's and Fadel's interventions. This assumption is that the emergence of a regime of *taqlīd* signalled the historical maturity of Islamic law. Both Jackson and Fadel see *taqlīd* as serving beneficial ends for Muslim society. For Jackson, *taqlīd* grants the law authority; for Fadel, it provides litigants with predictability. It may indeed be the case that the emergence of a regime of *taqlīd* brought with it great sociolegal benefits, but these benefits do not offer us a causal account of the shift from an era of *ijtihād* to one of *taqlīd* unless we also assume that legal scholars were consciously working towards doctrinal finality within their legal schools. In other words, for Jackson's and Fadel's accounts of the benefits of *taqlīd* to function as explanations of how *taqlīd* came to be dominant, we must assume some sort of teleology in jurists' labours that gradually brought their legal doctrine to completion. Certainly, later Shāfiʿī jurists of the 13th century CE saw their predecessors as doing just this. According to them, Muslim jurists from the 9th century onwards gradually developed the doctrine of their school founder by verifying (*taṣḥīḥ*), extending (*takhrīj*), and weighing conflicting positions (*tarjīḥ*) until it became possible to produce canonical texts summarizing the authoritative doctrines of their school—what Fadel calls "the rise of the *mukhtaṣar*." But this view fits poorly with how al-Shīrāzī saw his own labours.[87] His task was to seek God's law and counsel lay Muslims, not to provide a final version of his legal school. Indeed, through examination of al-Shīrāzī's disputations, coupled with statements in his books of legal theory, it becomes evident that he had no qualms maintaining divergent opinions in his legal school. We must then find another reason for the shift towards *taqlīd* and the canonization of legal doctrine (at least within the Shāfiʿī school).

In the present work, I do not aspire to provide a full account of the shift towards *taqlīd*. Nonetheless, I provide a foundation for future explorations by examining some important shifts in the Shāfiʿī school. I show that we cannot understand the shift from *ijtihād* to *taqlīd* without paying attention to the emergence of a decaying vision of time in the region of Khurasan in the late 11th century. From this perspective, Shāfiʿī jurists were seen as increasingly incapable of matching the labours of their predecessors and, therefore, as having only engaged in an attenuated version of *ijtihād*—a belief that spread throughout the 12th century. By the mid-13th century, Shāfiʿī jurists of Damascus who inherited the mantle of their school after the Mongol invasions of Persia and Iraq saw their task as preserving rather than critically engaging with their legal school doctrine. As the imperative to perform *ijtihād* waned, so too did the need for disputation.

## The Limits of Critique—Islamic and Secular

I have been using the word "critique" frequently throughout this introduction. However, "critique" is a loaded term, and one intimately associated with a European Enlightenment history. It is therefore important to clarify why and how I am using the term. In this regard, I will make tree points. First, I show that while we have reason to be suspicious of characterizing the *munāẓara* as a form of critique, we can nonetheless cautiously extend the term to the classical Islamic context. Second, I use scholarship in political theory to show the limitations of critique as a means of discovering truth. These limitations serve to temper impulses to consider classical Islamic law as a utopian space for the exchange of ideas. Third, I use the ethics of the *munāẓara* to suggest that jurists also have something to teach us about the limits of post-Enlightenment forms of critique. In particular, jurists help us to see how easily critique can delude and mislead a subject, and limit the very autonomy and self-reflexivity that critique purports to produce. I conclude this section by addressing the question of how critique informs our own political lives today.

There are grounds to be cautious about using the term "critique" in connection with the Muslim jurists of the classical era. The word "critique" refers to social practices that may very well be untranslatable between linguistic communities that lack a shared history of ideas. Thus, while we might say that it is appropriate to study modern French and German "critique," since both peoples have also deployed the terms *critique* and *kritik* in similar philosophical and political senses, it may be wrong to use the term to speak about Muslim societies before the 19th century.[88] In support of this contention, the Arabic word "*naqd*," commonly used in Arab countries today to speak about critique, was infrequently used among the jurists who figure in my study.[89] In fact, there is no single term that jurists used in conjunction with the *munāẓara* that can seamlessly be translated as "critique"—though the words "*khilāf*" (disagreement), "*nizā*ʿ" (contestation), "*mujādala*" (debate), "*tadāfuʿ*" (contention), and "*iʿtirāḍāt*" (objections) all gesture towards an activity we can recognize as approximating critique.[90]

But we might make a case that, while it is often difficult to find an equivalent term for "critique" across different cultures, it is possible to find practices in all or many societies that are best characterized by the word "critique." This appears to be Michel Foucault's tactic in his analysis of the practice of *parrhesia* (truth-telling) in ancient Greek society.[91] Foucault identifies Plato's call to his fellow citizens to examine their lives through *parrhesia* as a form of criticism. Following Foucault, we might state that the *munāẓara* was also a critical practice insofar as it shares features connoted by the modern term. But the problem with this approach is that Foucault himself sees *parrhesia* to be the beginning point of *Western* critique. Thus, even while *parrhesia* is not synonymous with critique, Foucault sees the Greek tradition as the beginning point of critique's development in the Western tradition. Talal Asad appears to agree with Foucault, noting how Greek criticism came to play a central role in medieval Christianity.[92] If this is the case, then once again we should be suspicious of extending the term to non-Western contexts unless we can show a shared history of the practice.

Despite this cautiousness, there are two reasons why the use of "critique" to designate the form of reasoning deployed in the *munāẓara* is warranted. The first is convenience. We lack a better English equivalent. The *munāẓara* was a form of testing and disclosing of ideas, and al-Juwaynī speaks of it as the confirmation of truth and the discrediting of falsehood. Such a view maps on to the central premises of the Enlightenment tradition of critique. Kant saw critique as the means of establishing the conditions of possibility for knowledge. He also considered it to be part of moving beyond "dogmatic slumber" to reveal truth.[93] This meaning of critique as testing has remained central to later Western thinkers, even those more interested in social or political critique. For instance, the Marxist understanding of critique tests the ideology of a capitalist society and reveals it as illusory. Moreover, in both the Islamic and the modern Western contexts, the performer of *munāẓara* or critique does not always know what conclusions will emerge from his arguments. One must be brave to engage in critique—even daring, as Kant would say. In this vein, jurists sometimes spoke of the disputation as "the revealing of truth" or "the revealing of what the position of two debaters [truly] entails." Last, both contexts see critique as the product of trenchant and unrestrained arguments. While we might use the words "evaluation," "justification," or "argumentation" to speak of a variety of contexts in which thought is deployed, "critique" has a harder edge to it. It is reserved for thought aimed at discrediting, so that only what withstands critique remains.

The second reason for using "critique" to speak of the mode of argumentation deployed in the *munāẓara* is to allow us to draw insights across disciplines. By juxtaposing the Islamic legal critique of classical jurists with its "Western" or post-Enlightenment counterparts, we can use analyses from both contexts to better understand the nature of critique across space and time.[94] In this study, I refer to critiques of Jürgen Habermas's account of the Enlightenment public sphere to better understand the limits of critique when it comes to producing either truth or a just society. Habermas's history of the European public sphere touted the richness of debate during the 18th-century Enlightenment. He saw in bourgeois print media, cafes, and salons an open exchange of ideas responsible for modern political and social advances.[95] Writing in the postwar 1950s, Habermas sought to explain how capitalistic encroachment on the public sphere had obstructed European progress and taken modernity down a darker path. Media monopoly—evident in the concentrated ownership of newspapers—had closed the public sphere to open debate,[96] saturating it with a constant dribble of product advertisements,[97] and permitting the dissemination of repressive political ideologies—most consequentially, fascism.[98] Habermas's analysis was therefore as prescriptive as it was historical.[99] If modern society could ensure free and open debate, then the continued fulfilment of freedom and scientific progress would be safeguarded. Habermas's later thought built on this insight.[100] His focus on debate emphasized the need for dialogical reasoning: truth-seeking, he held, necessitated a critical confrontation of ideas.

It was not long before others turned their critical gaze towards Habermas's ideal of rational debate. Supporters and detractors alike acknowledged his idyllic depiction of Enlightenment Europe.[101] They noted the exclusion from this bourgeois public of the great majority of the population and doubted its usefulness as a model for thinking about modern democratic politics. More generally, political theorists followed Foucault's scepticism at the possibility of debate free from power relations. The next decades of scholarship witnessed an intense examination of the social factors that have hindered the construction of an inclusive public sphere. Gender, race, and class were identified as historically prominent axes of marginalization.[102] Theorists noted that the problem of inclusion went beyond discriminatory legislation: even if one could ensure that marginalized groups had the time and money to partake in public debate, they would still face the challenge of deeply entrenched social norms. For instance, James Tully, relying on Wittgenstein's epistemological insights, suggested that all rational exchanges depend upon a set of hidden assumptions that inevitably place limits on what is challengeable.[103] William Connolly, for his part, argued that the affective or embodied dimension of all speech made the notion of dispassionate reason illusory.[104] The discomforting conclusion of this post-Habermasian scholarship is that critical debate, contemporary or historical, produces paradoxical results. On the one hand, it often delivers on its promise to transcend limitations of thought and expand horizons of understanding. On the other, this goal of thinking differently is always only partially achieved, limited by historical circumstances that determine who participates and what is heard.

These critiques of Habermas help us temper the impulse to imagine a premodern Muslim utopia of critical reflection. We are no strangers to the line of reasoning that presents an era of Islamic history as a golden age followed by decline.[105] The culture that avidly engaged in the *munāẓara* did produce an impressive legal system where each argument was carefully examined and where jurists came to recognize the merits of minority opinions, but it also had its limits. For one, it was a male culture where women's voices were silenced. For another, it was an elitist culture that excluded the majority of Muslims from contributing to legal reasoning. The topics tackled in al-Shīrāzī's disputations are testament to the power relations within classical Islamic society: for example, debates on women's rights to seek divorce or choose their marriage partners, slaves' rights to food and shelter, or the state's duty to humiliate its non-Muslim population. As we shall see, the exclusion of lay Muslims undercut the jurists' own aspirations to critical rigour. Moreover, as Abū Ḥāmid al-Ghazālī (d. 505/1111 CE) noted, classical jurists formed an incredibly pedantic culture whose dedication to legal reasoning undercut the allocation of resources to other sectors of society.[106]

But I also wish to suggest that Muslim jurists have something to teach us about the limits of a post-Enlightenment tradition of critique that has often dominated both the academy and Western public spheres. This tradition of critique, locatable in the anticlericalism of figures like Diderot and Voltaire and the anti-monarchism of the French Revolution, sought to free the individual from the shackles of inherited authority.[107] With Marx, this tradition turned towards freeing the individual from social and cultural ideology.[108] Today, this critique is often linked to the protection of individual rights and the construction of individual autonomy. Thus, we hear calls to subject "immigrant" religions to critique to guarantee continued freedom of expression. True critique is always secular, proponents of this tradition say, because it must attack even that which is most "sacred."[109] In contrast, the jurists of the classical era did not train their critical faculties towards emancipating the individual from social, political, or religious authority. In fact, they sought to critique *for* God and to bind themselves and their communities more closely to their legal tradition. The jurists' relationship to God helps us see the historical contingency of the post-Enlightenment tradition of critique. The jurists show us that the instrumentalization of critique in the project of human freedom depends on seeing human autonomy as an ever-threatened good.[110]

But the classical jurists do more than simply show us that critique can be religious—a point which I take to be fairly evident from a cursory account of "Western" practices of critique.[111] Their discourse on the ethics of disputation also shows us how the emancipatory promise of post-Enlightenment critique can fail.[112] This discourse posits that critique can shape the subjectivity of its practitioner in one of two ways. Critique can be a means of intellectual growth, permitting an individual to better understand a question before her. However, critique can also be a ploy to feed the ego through domination. Thus, jurists made a distinction between the debater who arrived at a disputation humbly willing to hear his opponents' arguments and the one who simply sought to win. Ibn ʿAqīl (d. 513/1119 CE) states: "If one of the two [debaters] is remiss in his search [for the best position], and meets only to provide a field for his tongue and heart to roam . . . his argument is transformed into the mere attempt to overwhelm and dominate his opponent."[113] Ibn ʿAqīl reminds us that critique can be a form of self-delusion, misleading its practitioner into thinking that his ability to dominate is a sign of superiority—a sign of his greater apprehension of truth. If we bear this possibility in mind, we can see how critique itself may sometimes be an impediment to learning from others. And if we take it that autonomy depends not only on being able to follow any whim, but also on making informed decisions, then it becomes evident that learning from others is essential to human autonomy. In thinking about the trend of critiquing the beliefs and practices of Muslim immigrants, we might ask this: When critique becomes a sign of one's cultural superiority, as it has in the wake of the Rushdie Affair and the Danish Cartoons, does it not become an impediment to learning more about the world? In turn, does this tendency not itself limit human autonomy?

It is well to conclude by remembering Asad's distinction between critique and understanding. Critique has often been seen as a means to greater understanding. This is true for Kant, who spoke about Enlightenment critique as a process leading out of intellectual "immaturity."[114] It is also true for al-Shīrāzī, who believed that critical engagement with the law produced a more cautious jurist. But, as Asad reminds us, critique is not always in the service of greater understanding. Sometimes other tools, like the method of historical genealogy, are needed to increase understanding. Asad's refusal to place his trust in critique reflects his awareness that much more than a "critical ethos" is needed to forge a just society.[115] Elsewhere, Asad has spoken instead of the need for a "democratic ethos," one that is attuned to our living together.[116] In this book, I do not quite give up on critique's potential for understanding or for human solidarity. I show that critique has a venerable place in the Islamic tradition and that it produced a legal culture in which the search for God's law was to be perfected through continual re-examination. I also show that it aimed to prevent any one jurist from claiming a monopoly over God's law, which in turn would prevent him from precipitously judging his fellow jurists for their differences of opinion. Muslims today might benefit from revisiting this tradition of legal critique in fulfilling their own spiritual and communal aspirations. But Asad's interrogation of critique is a sober reminder that analyzing critique in Islam is not the same as celebrating it. Critique, in the end, is an intervention. It can change dominant ideas and restructure affective states, but, perhaps less intuitively, it can also intimidate, injure, reinforce class status, or uphold the status quo. The Islamic *munāẓara* impacted law and society in ways that were both unpredictable and historically enduring.

## Chapter Road Map

The book is divided into three sections. The first part sheds light on the rise of the classical culture of critical debate. It examines the historical antecedents and power relations that structured the formation of a community united around ongoing critique. Chapter 1 offers an examination of a disputation that took place in a period of mourning. My analysis renders legible the pietistic motives of jurists engaging in disputation: motives that provided legitimacy to critical engagement with the law. But the chapter also grapples with the limits to critique that resulted from the exclusion of lay Muslims and particularly women from engaging with the law. Chapter 2 goes back in time, starting with the early Muslim conquests and the formation of juristic communities under the ʿAbbasid caliphate. The chapter offers a genealogy of the concept of *munāẓara* up until the 14th century. By tracing the varied meanings and uses of the concept, we come to see when and how the word *munāẓara* came to designate a highly structured practice of legal debate characterized by particular norms and ethics. Chapter 3 turns to books of *uṣūl al-fiqh* to capture jurists' divergent claims about the purpose of disputation. Despite these divergences, I show that jurists' justifications for the disputation rested upon two discursive foundations: (1) the discourse on the duty of *ijtihād* and (2) the discourse on the uncertainty of the law. Together these discourses legitimated critical engagement with legal opponents in an attempt to better understand the law.

Part II provides a series of explorations of the disputation's impact on the historical development of substantive law. Chapter 4 examines a disputation to show how al-Shīrāzī relied upon, tested, and refined the legal evidence of his Shāfiʿī school through the practice of disputation. The chapter reveals that disputations allowed jurists to examine the consistency of their arguments across different legal questions. A warning to the reader: Chapter 4 is particularly technical. It is likely to interest the specialist in Islamic law, but those less inclined to wade through dense legal topics will find the subsequent chapters much easier to follow. Chapter 5 begins by thinking about contemporary debates on forced marriage in Muslim societies. I then move to asking how an 11th-century disputation on forced marriage might help us think differently about 21st-century feminist critiques of tradition. Chapter 6 asks whether jurists of the Shāfiʿī school in the 11th century sought doctrinal finality within their legal schools, as later Shāfiʿīs claimed they did. Through a reading of a disputation on a contested question of worship, I argue that doctrinal indeterminacy within the Shāfiʿī school was both banal and accepted.

Chapter 6 is preparatory to the third and final part of the book. By showing that 11th-century jurists did not seek doctrinal finality for their Shāfiʿī school, Chapter 6 leads us to contemplate a question of great importance to Islamic historiography: Why did the 13th century witness the writing of canonical texts purporting to contain the final rendition of Shāfiʿī doctrine?

Chapter 7 answers this question by tracing the historical shifts in Shāfiʿī conceptions of historical time. This shift in conceptions of time marked the waning of *ijtihād*. In turn, the waning of *ijtihād* undercut the historical justification for the practice of disputation. The chapter therefore sheds light on the end of an era in which ongoing critique was deemed a religious duty to God, necessary to good functioning of the law.

# PART I

# 1

# Mourning Loss through Debate

## Pious Critique and Its Limits

Abū al-Walīd al-Bājī left his native Andalusia in 426/1035 CE on a revered journey in search of religious knowledge.[1] The Mālikī jurist would spend the next twelve years of his life in various intellectual hubs of the Muslim East, including Baghdad from 1038 to 1041 CE.[2] His good fortune would permit him to study with some of the greatest Muslim jurists of his era. Upon his return, al-Bājī was much sought after and admired for the knowledge he had acquired: the Muslim East had innovated in the religious legal sciences in ways still unknown to North African and Spanish jurists, and many wanted al-Bājī to impart this new knowledge to them.[3] In particular, they wished to learn about the disputation. Al-Bājī transmitted to his fellow Western jurists the debating techniques he had learnt with al-Shīrāzī. His book *al-Minhāj* covered the standard sequences of the disputation and the myriad argumentative forms jurists might deploy in seeking to defeat an opponent.[4] But it is difficult to fully understand a practice without tangible examples. The *Minhāj* was part of an Iraqi literary genre whose intended audience was already immersed in an existing debating community. Students in Baghdad understood what the disputation was and how to take part in it because they themselves had stood and watched countless debates unfold. Spanish and North African jurists lacked this privilege. Al-Bājī therefore took the rare step of transcribing accounts of disputations. In doing so, he conveyed to his fellow jurists a vivid description of what he had witnessed.

One disputation in particular concerns us here. It would have taken place while al-Bājī was residing in Baghdad. The disputation sees al-Shīrāzī debating his Ḥanafī rival Abū ʿAbd Allāh al-Dāmaghānī and tackles the question of a wife's right to demand divorce (*faskh*) on the grounds of her husband's failure to provide financially for her. The value of al-Bājī's account consists not only in its detailed transmission of each party's arguments, but also in al-Bājī's richly contextualized description. Like a modern ethnographer, al-Bājī attempts to translate foreign practices.[5] Though his intended

*The Rise of Critical Islam*. Youcef L. Soufi, Oxford University Press. © Oxford University Press 2023.
DOI: 10.1093/oso/9780197685006.003.0002

audience was the 11th-century Maghreb and Muslim Spain, his account nevertheless also usefully elucidates the disputation practice for modern readers. In this chapter, I use al-Bājī's description to uncover the inextricable link between critical debate and religious piety in classical Islam. Al-Bājī reveals an intellectual community dedicated to finding God's law (*ijtihād*) through rigorous critical engagement. The disputation raised critique to the level of religious devotion—to engage in critique rigorously and unreservedly, to be critiqued, and even to witness critique were all acts of worship—and made critique the single most revered communal practice of the juristic class. And yet such critique had its limitations and shortcomings. It was an exclusive and exclusivist debate. The jurists saw themselves as a specialized elite (*al-khāṣṣ*) among the Muslim masses (*al-ʿāmm*). They arrogated to themselves the social responsibility of guiding lay Muslims who lacked the legal training necessary to discover the law themselves. It was this responsibility that justified their critical investigations of the laws that governed communal Muslim life. The disputation therefore simultaneously depended upon and cemented social hierarchies of religious knowledge. As al-Bājī's transcript shows, the consequences of the exclusion of lay Muslims undercut the jurists' own aspirations towards critical rigour in the search for God's law.

## The Pious Search for God's Law

Abū al-Walīd al-Bājī had no idea what was about to transpire the day that our disputation took place.[6] He was headed towards one of Baghdad's many neighborhood mosques. Customarily, he went to the mosque to partake in study circles, but things were different that day. The occasion was a sad one. The wife of Abū al-Ṭayyib al-Ṭabarī had passed away and her distinguished husband, the uncontested leader of the Baghdad Shāfiʿīs, was in mourning. Baghdad's post-funerary customs stood out to al-Bājī. A Baghdad resident afflicted with the loss of a loved one would customarily isolate himself in his local mosque, where he would receive condolences from friends and neighbours. He would spend a few days there grieving his loss until his intimates convinced him to resume daily life. Since al-Bājī had come to Baghdad specifically to study with juristic luminaries like al-Ṭabarī, he made his way to convey his sympathies to the ageing jurist.

Later recounting the tale, al-Bājī appears to have anticipated his North African readers' surprise at what was to come next in his unfolding narrative.

He therefore began by explaining that when a grieving person found himself with free time in between the condolence giving, the custom in Baghdad was that he should busy himself with pious acts of worship. "To God we belong and to him we shall return," the Qur'an states (*al-Baqara*:156); death throughout Islamic history has served as an occasion to remember one's ephemeral worldly existence and final destiny in an eternal divine realm.[7] Al-Bājī listed two specific devotional acts the jurists of Baghdad encouraged for the period of mourning, stating that the grieving person should "do nothing other than read the Qur'an and engage in juristic disputation."[8] The statement must have initially jarred Maghrebi sensibilities: How could engaging in debate be proper post-funeral etiquette? Structured ritualized disputation was not yet part of Western Muslims' legal culture and they would have been familiar with several prophetic *ḥadīth* in which Muḥammad condemned argumentative wrangling.[9] Al-Bājī consciously placed the disputation side by side with Qur'anic reading—an act that epitomized what was expected of pious mourning—to highlight the social valence of disputation in Baghdad society.[10] The pious dimension of disputation in Baghdad owed everything to juristic reverence for legal knowledge. Al-Bājī's Shāfiʿī contemporary al-Khaṭīb al-Baghdādī (d. 463/1071 CE) extolled legal knowledge as foundational to proper religion in his *al-Faqīh wa'l-Mutafaqqih*. Al-Baghdādī explained that the juristic vocation served as the necessary precondition to all devotion because it distinguished correct from incorrect ritual. In al-Baghdādī's eyes, this made the search for God's law greater than any other act of worship.

Al-Bājī was not the only jurist heading towards al-Ṭabarī's mosque that day. Al-Ṭabarī was over ninety years of age when his wife died and over his long life he had left a profound mark on the intellectual culture of Baghdad. It was thus expected that many would come to pay their respects. Moreover, he was the leader (*ra'īs*) of the Baghdad Shāfiʿīs and proper decorum demanded deference to the senior authorities across legal schools. Al-Bājī entered a mosque in which "every person belonging to the juristic culture of learning"[11]—from novice students to judges and law professors—had come to pay their respects to the widower. And then something happened that shifted the sober tone of the room and stirred excitement.

At the mosque entrance stood none other than the leader of the Ḥanafī school, Abū ʿAbd Allāh al-Ṣaymarī (d. 436/1045 CE).[12] Whispers began to abound. The students had not seen the two master jurists debate for years. As school leaders, they had the privilege and responsibility to represent and defend their school doctrine in disputation gatherings. However, each jurist had for years now delegated that responsibility to their more junior students. The students wondered if this was their chance to witness the legal brilliance of these two giants. They began to beseech al-Ṭabarī and al-Ṣaymarī to "grace them [*al-tabarruk bihimā*]" with a disputation.[13] They characterized the leaders' potential disputation as a charitable act that would bestow upon its audience divine blessings. The devotional dimension of the disputation evidently exceeded its participants and could include the attentive audience seeking to learn from it. In fact, the disputation was undeniably a communal affair. Even less grandiose and mundane disputation gatherings often broke down academic silos by bringing jurists of various school affiliations together.[14]

The ritualistic dimension of the disputation—its rules, conventions, and characteristic behaviours—made it the most public and concrete manifestation of the jurists' hallowed search for God's law. It is perhaps for this reason that some students in attendance spoke of the disputation with reverential language reminiscent of the prophetic *ḥadīth*. The students expressed their wish to memorize the two leaders' words (*hifẓihā*) and to "be beautified [*yutajammal*]" by transmitting what they had heard (*naqlihā*) to others. Likewise, the language of memorization and transmission were staples of the *ḥadīth* sciences. Traditions about the Prophet's words and deeds were a slice of divine guidance that memory had preserved and passed on in a post-prophetic era. The jurists never claimed divine infallibility, but they often invoked the statement that they "were the inheritors of prophets."[15] They had the same prophetic mission of keeping divine guidance alive in contemporary times. In a world devoid of prophetic revelation, a disputation between intellectual giants was the closest the juristic community could get to witnessing an instantiation, an eruption even, of divine guidance, through an unpredictable exchange of conflicting arguments.

## The Ethics of Pious Critique

We now have some sense of the pietistic value ascribed to critical debate among the classical Muslim jurists of Baghdad and Persia. However, we still have a poor grasp of how critical debate unfolded. What exactly was the practice that Muslim jurists recognized as equal to prayer? What conditions rendered it successful and what actions breached its pietistic thrust? The next section of al-Bājī's transcript gives us some sense of the structure of the classical practice of disputation. We begin here by examining the ethical norms grounding this pious debate gathering before moving on in the next section to examine the argumentative rules and conventions that enabled jurists to make and hear their respective claims. As we continue our narrative, the defining features of the jurists' pious debate practice will become clearer.

Al-Bājī tells us that the students waited with high hopes for their leaders' answer. A palpable joy must have surged through the crowd when al-Ṭabarī expressed his willingness to proceed. Al-Ṭabarī was said to have retained his sharp intellect throughout his long life and was ready to put his legal skill on display for the eager students who had respectfully come to give him their condolences.[16] But the crowd's excitement was quickly chilled. Al-Ṣaymarī declined, stating that among his students was one better suited than him to debate: "It is best that one who has Abū 'Abd Allāh al-Dāmaghānī as a student not step forward."[17] Al-Ṣaymarī's motives remain unclear. Did he feel too out of practice to engage in disputation? Had his legal brilliance always been displayed better as a lecturer than a debater? Was he apprehensive that losing to al-Ṭabarī would have unwanted effects on the public reputation of his Ḥanafī school? Or should we take him at face value, that his student had eclipsed him—at least in debate? What is sure is that al-Ṭabarī no longer had a suitable debate partner. Each community has its behavioural norms—whether explicit or tacit—and the jurists spoke of ethical behaviours (*adab*) appropriate in disputation.[18] One of their most deeply held and pervasive ethical norms in the context of disputation was that jurists only debate other jurists of equal rank. The jurists considered it necessary to respect school hierarchies. More advanced jurists were to be shown deference for their acquired knowledge; it was deemed poor conduct to challenge and dispute with them. The consequence of al-Ṣaymarī's refusal to debate was that he would have to delegate the responsibility to defend school doctrine to a less experienced jurist. The jurists justified this hierarchical norm by affirming that a junior jurist could learn more from listening to an advanced scholar than by engaging in what would inevitably be shallow and showy challenges.[19] They would have understood and concurred with contemporary ethical philosopher Alasdair MacIntyre's argument that critical engagement with an inherited tradition necessitates first submitting to an authoritative teacher capable of transmitting it.[20]

"Here is Abū Isḥāq sitting among my students. He represents me," al-Ṭabarī answered.[21] Al-Shīrāzī came forward, assuming the heavy burden of defending the scholarly integrity of the Shāfiʿīs. Al-Bājī tells us nothing of his demeanour, but we can attempt a plausible reconstruction based on the behavioural norms of debate gatherings. Al-Shīrāzī likely stood still, soberly and with gravitas.[22] He would have turned to face his opponent, and he would retain this position throughout the disputation regardless of his internal emotional state.[23] If he felt nervous, he would resist the temptation to fidget or play with his hands or beard.[24] If he felt a sudden rush to correct his opponent, he would nonetheless refrain from any interruptions and stand in silent waiting until his opponent finished speaking. If he felt anger at ridiculous claims or mischaracterized arguments, he would recompose himself quickly before voicing his concern to the audience. Al-Shīrāzī would commence his disputation in a comparable manner to Qur'anic recitation or the Friday sermon: he would seek refuge in God against his lesser passions and would invoke divine peace and blessings upon the Prophet Muḥammad.[25] All this a jurist was to do to ensure he possessed and retained the proper intentions throughout his long and testing critical exchange. Proper intention stood at the heart of devotional acts: "Actions are judged by intentions," the Prophet had stated.[26] The disputation had no justifiable purpose without right intention. The jurists had heard of raucous debates in caliphal courts; one ended with a theologian slapping his opponent in the face. It was the theologian's final riposte and the audience at the time erupted in uncontrollable laughter. Eleventh-century jurists scorned such showmanship. The only admissible intention was seeking truth. Anything else was impudence that fed the ego and led one astray from God.

Al-Dāmaghānī stayed back. A young man from among the Ḥanafīs came forward and spoke.

## Guiding the Lay Muslim Masses

I want to stop our narrative here. We will resume it in the second half of the chapter where we examine the arguments of each party. For now, I want to elaborate on the reasons why this disputation occasioned pietistic sensibilities. As the previous sections established, the disputation was part of a pious search for God's law. By debating the law, jurists could discover what God wanted of His creation. Debate was thus a form of religious devotion to God. The pietistic purpose of Muslim practices—like prayer, fasting, or donning a headscarf—in shaping God-conscious subjects has been well documented in the work of Talal Asad, Saba Mahmood, and Charles Hirschkind.[27] In some ways, the debate gathering followed this logic. Recall that debaters like al-Shīrāzī were expected to stand facing each other with great decorum and gravitas. They were not to fidget or play with their hands or beard. They would listen attentively to each side of the debate and desist from interrupting. They would speak clearly, but not brashly. They would avoid anger and any belligerent behavior. If the jurists abided by these conventions, they would achieve their aims: they would draw nearer to God's mercy and they would hear the disclosure of sound argument. This pious search for God's law could encompass the audience as well.[28] As is obvious from al-Bājī's narration, the intended audience of the debate gathering were fellow seekers of knowledge—fellow jurists. They had occasion to benefit from hearing the two sides' arguments. A certain bodily comportment was also demanded of them. They too were to remain silent and be attentive to the participants' claims.

And yet, despite the insights of anthropologists of Islam like Mahmood, we will still have a poor understanding of the pietistic thrust of Islamic critique unless we pay attention to the way jurists conceived of their labours as a social service to lay Muslims. In fact, most of the laws that jurists researched and examined had little to do with ritual piety. Many had to do instead with organizing a society and ensuring amicable relations between all. Thus, Islamic law examined a variety of topics including business transactions, marriage and divorce laws, slavery law, inheritance rules, taxation law, martial law, and penal law. These and other topics jurists examined and debated in gatherings. They were rooted in scriptural guidance—the Qur'an and prophetic example—and helped ensure that Muslims conformed to what God demanded of them. Many, perhaps most, of the topics were of little relevance to the personal lives of individual jurists. For instance, most were not warriors or statesmen and therefore had little reason to know the laws of war, criminal penalties, or tax rules. Some might never marry, and others might marry but never divorce. And their business transactions might be limited to purchasing basic material goods—like al-Shīrāzī's seem to have been. Thus, their scholarly travails had little to do with figuring out the law for their own benefit or even that of their families. The point of their legal debates was to guide the masses of lay Muslims who did not know—and could not be expected to know—the law.[29]

As al-Shīrāzī explained, the law was a complex discipline, requiring years to master. If God had asked all Muslims to figure out for themselves what they thought the law was, people would forsake their occupation and delay marriage, leaving fields untilled and neglecting procreation—all ultimately leading to the end of civilization.[30] Some jurists fulfilled their communal service by serving as judges. They litigated formal disputes between Muslims with the backing of state authority. Al-Ṭabarī fulfilled this role late in life, as would al-Shīrāzī's debate partner al-Dāmaghānī.[31] For most jurists, however, the task of Muslim guidance was an individual rather than an institutional affair. Lay Muslims would come to a jurist and ask them for a response on a legal question. For instance, biographers speak of a lay Muslim approaching al-Shīrāzī in the marketplace for religious guidance: al-Shīrāzī grabbed a pen, wrote him a ruling on the spot, and, finding ink on them, wiped his hands on his garment. Lay Muslim petitioners were called in Arabic *mustaftī* and a jurist was called *muftī* (lit. those providing a response or *fatwā*).

A lay Muslim petitioner would receive different answers depending on the jurist he consulted. Moreover, no worldly authority imposed upon the lay Muslim conformity to a *fatwā*.[32] Al-Shīrāzī tells us a humorous story that makes this clear. It begins with a lay Muslim facing a profound and difficult marital dilemma. The man had pronounced a statement of divorce to his wife for the third time, which in Islamic law makes their divorce final and irrevocable. The man regretted his action and thus went to consult a Shāfiʿī jurist to see what might be done to keep his family intact.[33] The Shāfiʿī jurist investigated the man's situation and had good news to report: he concluded that the man's marriage contract was witnessed by a man of ill repute (*fāsiq*) and was therefore invalid. The man could now freely marry his ex-wife in a new contract. Our man should have run home, excited by the news, but he had misgivings about the jurist's answer—perhaps he had trouble countenancing that he had been unlawfully married for so long or that his children were born out of wedlock. In any event, he decided to consult a second jurist, a Ḥanafī this time. The man went to see al-Ṣaymarī who listened to his story. When the man was done, al-Ṣaymarī affirmed the complete opposite of his Shāfiʿī colleague, declaring, "Those Shāfiʿīs told you that you were illegitimately married but that your wife is now sexually lawful to you. I, however, tell you that she was lawful to you but now is no longer so." A Shāfiʿī student in attendance heard those remarks and went to consult his teacher, al-Ṭabarī. Al-Ṭabarī answered, "You should have told al-Ṣaymarī that matters are as he says, except that God did not instruct the man to follow al-Ṣaymarī; rather God instructed the man to follow whoever he willed from the among the juristic class."[34]

Not all jurists would have agreed with al-Ṭabarī's claim. Some considered it necessary for a lay Muslim to investigate the qualifications of jurists.[35] But the story nonetheless reveals the dependence of lay Muslims on juristic opinions. Though centuries have passed, anyone familiar with legal circles in the Arab world will recognize a similar tendency for lay Muslims to walk into religious scholars' offices to ask for legal advice on marriage rules.[36] The search for God's law was ultimately meant to guide lay Muslims. Many jurists, including al-Shīrāzī and al-Ghazālī, considered that jurists were discharging a collective religious obligation. So long as they studied the law, the Muslim community could be sure that their actions conformed to scriptural guidance. Thus, they reasoned that if a jurist found himself in a remote locale, alone among the juristic class, he had the solemn obligation to provide religious *fatwā*s to lay Muslim petitioners.[37]

The pietistic thrust of Islamic legal debate was a product of this noble commitment to guidance for lay Muslims. It is important to note that debate gatherings were not parliamentary affairs. The audience did not vote for a favoured debater or declare one position the new law of the land. In fact, when two skilled debaters like al-Shīrāzī and al-Dāmaghānī faced each other, it was typically impossible to consider either party a winner.[38] Rather, both sides would have made impressive claims, enabling both themselves and their audience to become better informed regarding the merits of each position. Audience and debaters alike could then determine individually the position they felt was strongest. Of course, they could always continue to amend their position through further study and further debate.

The debate gathering permitted jurists to engage in this process of refinement through its dialectical method of inquiry. The opposing debating parties would adopt two distinct roles. The first was the *sāʾil*, or questioner. The questioner's task was to introduce the debate topic. He could choose any topic he fancied so long as it had not achieved juristic consensus in prior generations—a rare feat in Islamic history.[39] The *sā'il* would ask his partner, known as the *mujīb* or respondent, for his position on the case and for the evidence that buttressed his position.[40] Common convention held that respondents should provide only *one* piece of evidence for their positions. That way, the two debaters could examine the merits of this single piece of evidence in some detail. Once the *mujīb* had provided his evidence, the debate's preliminaries were over, and the real action would begin. The *sā'il* deployed as many objections (*i'tirāḍāt*) to the soundness of the evidence as possible. He could also invoke a counterargument (*mu'āraḍa*) that defended an alternative opinion. Several exchanges followed. From extant disputation transcripts, it appears that the *sā'il* was entitled to level two rounds of critique and the *mujīb* was allowed three rounds of defence. Each rejoinder aspired to address in sweeping fashion the particular weaknesses of the previous claim. This process of exploration permitted the testing of the potential evidence determining the legal case. It permitted each jurist to see the issue from the other's perspective.

In sum, Islamic critique was pious critique because it fulfilled a communal need. The debate gathering would have been nonsensical without this division of labour between jurists and lay Muslims. However, this same separation of roles also established relations of power between these two Muslim classes. As the story of our troubled married man shows, lay Muslims were at the mercy of the juristic class—they depended on jurists not only for marital advice, but also for a variety of social, ethical, ritualistic, and economic matters that assured a godly life and religious salvation in the afterlife. This dependence underscored the clear division between those who knew the law and those who did not. In fact, as al-Shīrāzī explained, "there was consensus among jurists that lay Muslims did not have real knowledge."[41] This division also conferred upon the jurists a sense of nobility. "Whoever goes out searching for knowledge to replace misguidance with guidance, or falsehood with truth, it is as though he worshipped in the fashion of someone continually worshipping for forty years," said the *ḥadīth*.[42] A fair bit of elitism crept into jurists' self-conception. Another invoked *ḥadīth* stated that one jurist is worth more than a thousand laymen.[43] Such valuations justified the exclusion of lay Muslims from participation in disputations. In the next half of this chapter, I show how this exclusion of lay Muslims undercut the Muslim jurists' aspiration to critically examine God's law.

## The Limits of Islamic Critique

Let us now return to al-Bājī's account of the debate gathering. At this point in our transcript, a significant narrative shift occurs: al-Bājī moves away from a rich description of the gathered jurists to a more straightforward retelling of the arguments between the two parties he heard that day. We must remember, after all, al-Bājī's desire to inform his Andalusian and North African peers about disputational argumentation. With this narrative shift also comes a move away from pietistic language. The debate of the day would not have anything to do with ritual worship. Rather, the focus would be on a mundane matter of marriage law. In fact, God will recede to the background of the disputation until making one more brief but important appearance at the end of the debate. In focusing on the content of the debate, we will come to recognize both the rigour and the limits of pious critique. On the one hand, our jurists will probe an entrenched position within the Shāfiʿī school and subject it to copious arguments. For brevity's sake, I will only deal with a selection of the two jurists' arguments. On the other hand, the jurists' exclusion of lay Muslims, and particularly women, from the debate gathering will limit some of the critical insights they bring to bear on the case.

We might wonder why such an exclusion would be so deleterious to pious critique. Recall that on the surface of things, jurists had good reason to exclude lay Muslims. Lay Muslims had little awareness of the relevant scriptural sources bearing on a case, and they were ignorant of the hermeneutical principles by which scripture should be interpreted. More importantly still, they did not know the legal positions that would permit them to analogize from one legal case to another. Analogical argument was the most important form of legal argument within the juristic repertoire because it forced jurists to examine the underlying reasons why scripture stipulated a law in one specific case, and permitted them to extend this reasoning to all relevant situations. In short, analogical arguments uncovered the true object of God's legislation. None of this would be understood by lay Muslims.

And yet to properly grasp Islamic law, we need to think of the law as having multiple layers. On the surface of things, the law stemmed from divine scripture. This is why the term *shariʿa* originated as a shorthand for *aḥkām al-sharīʿa*, meaning rulings that derived from scripture. However, when one began debating the law as our jurists did, more practical considerations become visible. Law, after all, whether human or divine, cannot lead to social discord and acrimony—at least not if it aspires to long-term viability. In fact, al-Shīrāzī explained that many Muslim jurists thought the law was for human benefit.[44] The debate arena was the perfect setting in which to examine the practical concerns undergirding Islamic law. As jurists invoked comparable cases to the one under review—whether through analogy or to support their point by way of example—they began to make distinctions between cases that ultimately revealed why they thought God's rules were as they were. What is immediately striking to the historian is how little legal training one needs in order to grapple with some of these practical considerations. More striking still is how, when such considerations arose, lay Muslims had more to offer than jurists themselves. Let us turn to our disputation to see how this is the case.

After it was decided that al-Shīrāzī would face al-Dāmaghānī, a young Ḥanafī jurist from the Iraqi people of Kāzarūn took centre stage in the debate gathering.[45] Al-Bājī told his reader nothing of the young man—even his name was insignificant to the story he wished to tell. But this young man is important because he started off our debate. He would assume the title of questioner and try his hand against al-Shīrāzī before al-Dāmaghānī took over. This was an opportunity for the young man to test out his skill against a more senior jurist.[46]

The young man introduced the debate topic, asking al-Shīrāzī his opinion and his evidence for it. Recall that the *sā'il* was entitled to choose whatever contentious legal topic he wished. Yet the young man chose a topic that fitted the occasion. It was not out of the ordinary to debate topics touching on recent events in the jurists' individual or social lives. The young man asked al-Shīrāzī about the rights of a wife whose husband neglected her financially—or, to be more precise, "struggled in providing for her financial maintenance [*al-i'sār bi'l-nafaqa*]."[47] Al-Shīrāzī answered: "She has the right of *khiyār* [*yūjib al-khiyār*]" *Khiyār* in Arabic means choice or option. Al-Shīrāzī was here affirming Shāfi'ī doctrine, which stipulated that a husband's lack of financial maintenance was suitable grounds for divorce.[48] A wife was therefore given the option to file for divorce before a judge or to remain married to her husband. The question was a sly one coming from a Ḥanafī. The Ḥanafīs denied that poverty was a valid reason to break marriage bonds. And furthermore, the young man from Kāzarūn likely knew his challenge would be especially poignant on this occasion. The juristic community was not an affluent community. Many of its members, like al-Shīrāzī, had lived below subsistence level.[49] The question therefore forced the Shāfi'īs to reflect upon the stakes of affirming poverty as a valid reason to break up a marriage—including, implicitly their own. And this on the day that al-Ṭabarī mourned the loss of his wife.

When asked for the evidence for his position, al-Shīrāzī answered by way of analogical argument—which, as we have noted, was the jurists' favoured legal evidence. Al-Shīrāzī analogized the wife to a slave: "marriage is a type of property [*naw' al-milk*] upon which financial maintenance is due; thus, difficulty in providing maintenance must lead to the cancellation [*izāla*] [of the property right]."[50] In other words, just as the state declares null and void the master's ownership of a slave receiving inadequate food or lodging, so too must it declare a neglected wife free from her husband's authority. The comparison between wife and slave will strike many Muslims in the 21st century as an odd one. Copious academic studies of contemporary Muslims highlight the prevalent argument that the Islamic tradition raises the status of women.[51] Comparing a woman to a slave intuitively detracts from this claim. It was nonetheless a common comparison at the time.[52] To be clear, jurists did not believe that wives were slaves or that husbands owned their wives. The point of analogy is comparison between different things, not assimilation into sameness. But the husband did have ownership over his wife in one respect—her sexuality. A husband was deemed to have an exclusive right to sleep with his wife and, moreover, to demand sex from her as he pleased—so long as this did not violate her ritual obligations to God or negatively impact her health. As Kecia Ali has shown, the wife and the slave were both, in this sense, *milk* (under dominion or proprietorship), to husband and master respectively.[53]

The Shāfiʿī position on *khiyār* was intimately related to the husband's proprietorship over his wife. The Shāfiʿīs reasoned that marriage was a contract granting each party rights and obligations. A husband's right to sexual access was dependent upon him fulfilling a certain set of financial duties.[54] Among them were the provision of food, shelter, an allocation of clothes, and hygiene products like a comb and soap.[55] Depending on the social class to which the wife belonged, she might be entitled to other material comforts, including a servant.[56] The Shāfiʿīs reasoned that if a wife did not receive these material objects, the husband was in direct violation of his contractual obligations and she was within her full right to leave her marriage. Why should she honour her obligations if her husband did not honour his? The woman would thereby be entitled to dissolve the contract. The Shāfiʿīs gave a short reprieve of three days to the man, after which the wife could exercise her choice, whether to stay in or to leave the marriage.[57] Should she opt to stay, she might yet revise her decision if her husband's dire financial situation did not ameliorate itself.[58]

In contrast, the Ḥanafīs held that poverty was a central Muslim virtue.[59] Asceticism was part of a pious way of life. Moreover, they examined Islamic history and saw that the early Muslim community suffered great material hardship for their faith. It was inconceivable to believe that Muḥammad and his companions could have had their homes broken up because of this poverty. The early Ḥanafī authority Muḥammad b. al-Ḥasan al-Shaybānī (d. 188/804 CE) relayed reports of the early community to support this claim:

> It has reached us from ʿĀʾisha, may God be pleased with her, that she has said: "The family of Muḥammad never ate their fill of bread three days in a row until he met God"; and it has been reported from Fāṭima, may God be pleased with her, that she complained to ʿAlī about her children's hunger until he went to some of the people of Medina and they gave him a number of baskets that filled his hands. Within each basket were dates which he gave to his family.[60]

The Ḥanafīs used these examples to assert the normalcy of poverty among the pious and to deny that it offered grounds for divorce. The examples also showed the ability of couples to make due and survive when faced with material want.[61] Thus the Ḥanafīs and Shāfiʿīs were long divided on the question and approached it with a different set of assumptions and arguments. The day of their disputation, the Shāfiʿīs and Ḥanafīs of Baghdad were continuing a debate that had begun long ago.

From this opening we can begin to think in more concrete terms about the promise and limits of Islamic critique. On the one hand, we see a concerted effort to re-examine God's law by permitting a well-established position to be subject to critical inquiry. All this is ostensibly done for the religious and social benefit of lay Muslims. By investigating the evidence grounding the wife's *khiyār*, al-Shīrāzī linked scripture to the everyday lives of Muslims. This fulfilled a twofold function of ensuring proper adherence to God's law while simultaneously safeguarding the rights of all. On the other hand, it is difficult to miss the disparaging link between women and slaves. Even while conceding that attitudes towards slaves differ from one socio-historical context to another, we know from jurists' own texts that slaves were at the bottom of the social ladder. We might then wonder if such a comparison would have been made had women themselves partaken in the debate. Of course, this is conjecture that falls outside of what might historically be known. Still, by keeping this question of women's participation in mind, we will better see, in the next two sections, how the exclusions of Islamic critique undercut its own aspiration to rigorously seek out God's law.

## First Objection: The Possibility of Different Forms of Redress

Our young man from Kāzarūn had trouble competing with the skilled debater he found in al-Shīrāzī. The objections he levelled were easily overcome and it came time for al-Dāmaghānī to step in, and for the debate to begin in earnest. As we turn to the first of al-Dāmaghānī's two objections, we would do well to recall the important role legal examples played in substantiating debate claims. Such examples forced one's opponent to grapple with the consistency in his own reasoning, and, as I have already noted, they forced him to posit distinctions between laws. Al-Dāmaghānī's first objection questioned an assumption al-Shīrāzī made in his analogical argument. It was true, al-Dāmaghānī tacitly acknowledged, that a wife and a slave were both entitled to financial rights. It was also true that the husband and the slave master violated those rights if they withheld material goods like food and shelter from them. But why did al-Shīrāzī assume that the law would always treat rights violations the same way? Why might the law not treat one violation by cancelling ownership (i.e., for the slave master) and the other violation through a different form of redress? We will see later what redress al-Dāmaghānī had in mind.

To make his point, al-Dāmaghānī provided the example of two other legal cases in which the violation of two similar rights was treated differently. One of the cases was also drawn from marriage law, the second from business law. Both cases related to the right of *taslīm*.[62] The Arabic term *taslīm* means to hand over authority to or to transfer. Concerning the first case, al-Dāmaghānī explained that a new bride or her guardian has the duty of *taslīm* towards her husband.[63] In other words, she must be placed under her new husband's care so that they could commence marital life, initiated through the consummation of their marriage. Similarly, in the second case, a seller has the duty of *taslīm* towards a buyer.[64] In this case, the transfer pertains to the sold good. In both cases, failure of transfer resulted in a contract violation. However, al-Dāmaghānī explained, Islamic law did not treat the two cases analogously. The seller's failure of *taslīm*, as in the case of a destroyed good, nullified the business exchange in its entirety, which meant that the buyer had the right to recover his money. In contrast, the failure to transfer a woman to her new husband's care did not lead to an end to the marriage contract. We know this because the wife who passes away before making herself available for the consummation of her marriage is still considered the husband's lawful spouse.[65] The husband, for instance, is still subject to the same inheritance rules that apply to couples whose marriage has been consummated. Note that al-Dāmaghānī did not directly show that the wife/slave analogy was mistaken; all he did, and all he needed to do, was show that al-Shīrāzī relied on an unfounded assumption in comparing them. If it is possible for similar rights violations to be handled differently, then al-Shīrāzī's analogy fails to conclusively show that what applies to the neglected slave also applies to the wife of the poor husband.

With these two examples, al-Dāmaghānī threw the ball back into al-Shīrāzī's court. Al-Shīrāzī now had to explain why the law should redress the violated financial rights of the wife and the slave in similar fashion. Al-Shīrāzī turned his attentions to al-Dāmaghānī's *taslīm* examples. The law redressed these two violations differently because marriage and business contracts had fundamentally opposite purposes. The purpose of a business contract was to exchange goods. If a seller did not receive the good, his very purpose in spending money was frustrated. In contrast, if a woman died before consummating her marriage, the purpose of the marriage contract was nonetheless fulfilled—namely joining the couple together (*al-wuṣla*) under new kinship ties (*muṣāhara*) until death separated them.[66] Al-Shīrāzī affirmed that this type of difference did not apply in the case of the wife and the slave. Their rights violations were analogous and thus what applied to one must apply to the other.

Al-Dāmaghānī was not finished yet. He marvelled at al-Shīrāzī's suggestion that marriage's purpose could be fulfilled without consummation. He exclaimed that the purpose of marriage was not kinship ties but sex, because "a husband gets married for sexual pleasure [*al-istimtā*]."[67] For al-Dāmaghānī, no man would get married if not for sexual fulfillment. The response had some bite to it. Al-Shīrāzī and his Shāfiʿī colleagues agreed that sex was a central purpose of marriage, so much so that al-Shīrāzī considered invalid a marriage contract stipulating a strictly platonic spousal relationship within its conditions. He reasoned that such a prohibition on sex directly violated the purpose of the marriage contract. But al-Shīrāzī would not be outdone. He conceded to his debate partner that sex was one primary purpose of marriage, but maintained that marriage also fulfilled other purposes.

Bringing about the union of the couple and the kinship ties between them was one of them.[68]

Let's pause here. By following the thread of this first objection, something becomes clear: complex legal evidence, such as (in this case) analogical arguments, depended upon an empirical exploration of Muslims' social conditions—their wants, needs, desires, and aspirations. Thus the comparison between wife and slave could not be effectuated without considering the purpose of sales and marriage contracts. These purposes were not outlined in the Qur'an or *ḥadīth*. When, for instance, al-Dāmaghānī exclaimed that a man gets married for sexual pleasure, he made no claim to be basing his judgment upon what scripture said. Rather, he based his claim upon what he assumed were typical desires of Muslim men. He would have likely gotten this assumption from diverse sources—social norms, the prevalent legal discourse of the juristic community,[69] and introspection into his own wants. Al-Shīrāzī, for his part, pointed out to his interlocutor that his view of marriage was too narrow. Yes, men marry for sex,[70] but not only sex. This, then, was the promise of critical Islam: namely, to make jurists think more broadly and reconsider their viewpoints. But al-Shīrāzī was only one man, with assumptions and biases of his own. If the debate ultimately turned on the reasons for which men sought marriage, were not lay Muslims in an equally important position to contribute to the legal question? And, more importantly, did not their exclusion undermine the jurists' own aspirations to seek out God's law?

## Second Objection: The *Umm al-Walad*

As we proceed with al-Dāmaghānī's second objection, we will see how the exclusion of lay Muslim women from the juristic community will have the greatest impact in impoverishing the debate conditions of critical Islam. Al-Dāmaghānī claimed that al-Shīrāzī's analogical argument suffered from a significant oversight: a slave is saleable but a wife is not.[71] The poor master unable to provide food or shelter for his slave could sell him and recover his lost wealth. However, the poor husband could not sell his spouse and therefore lost the often-considerable wealth he had spent on her dowry. Al-Dāmaghānī proposed, therefore, that a better analogy would involve the slightly modified comparison between the wife and the *umm al-walad*. The *umm al-walad* was also a slave but a very particular kind of a slave. The *umm al-walad* was a female slave who had given birth to her master's child.[72] As a result, she could not be sold, and, upon her master's death, she became a freed woman.[73] The Prophet Muḥammad reportedly said of his concubine Maryam the Copt who gave birth to his son: "Her son has freed her [*aʿtaqahā waladuhā*]."[74] Al-Dāmaghānī pointed out to his adversary that the state did not compel the insolvent master to free his *umm al-walad*. By analogy, the state should not force a divorce upon a financially struggling husband.

Al-Shīrāzī, however, came prepared for a bitter struggle and was ready to defend his analogy. He began by expressing that the couple's divorce and the sale of the slave shared a common goal that legitimated the analogy. Separating a wife from her husband permitted her to find a new spouse capable of fulfilling his financial obligations to her in the same way that forcing the sale of a slave guaranteed his access to food and shelter. Next, al-Shīrāzī critiqued his adversary's misplaced concern for the husband's economic loss. He reminded al-Dāmaghānī of another situation in which a wife could petition courts for divorce without monetary restitution to her husband: "Don't you see that we separate the wife from her husband because of his sexual impotence?"[75] According to Shāfiʿī doctrine, the wife of an impotent man also possessed the *khiyār* to stay in or exit her marriage.[76] Like poverty, spousal impotence denied her access to a marital right because it prevented her from experiencing sexual pleasure. In his substantive legal text, *al-Muhadhdhab*, al-Shīrāzī explained that a judge should give an impotent husband a year-long reprieve to ensure his impotence is not the temporary product of unpleasant climatic conditions "because his inability to have intercourse could . . . simply be from exposure to warmth or cold, or humid or dry conditions."[77] If his condition showed no amelioration, the judge would confirm a wife's petition for divorce.

Unconvinced, al-Dāmaghānī straightforwardly and insistently protested: "We separate them because a wife cannot obtain sexual pleasure by an alternative means."[78] The Islamic legal norms regulating sexuality prevented a married woman from having a sexual partner other than her husband. The wife of the impotent husband therefore needed a divorce to fulfil her right to sexual intercourse. Al-Dāmaghānī pointed out that the situation was different for the wife of a poor husband because, as Abū Ḥanīfa (d. 150/767 CE) had contended, her husband could contract a loan and relieve the couple's financial hardship.[79]

Al-Shīrāzī, in turn, expressed two objections. First, forcing the husband to take out a loan generated a precarious situation for the wife. If the husband failed to pay his debts, the state might legally imprison him. The wife would then find herself without either a husband or the financial means to cover her basic subsistence. She would be forced to contract a loan in her own name, placing her in an even more adverse situation. Second, al-Shīrāzī claimed that "if we permit a wife *khiyār* for impotence, then we certainly must offer it to her for her husband's monetary insolvency."[80] He reasoned that lack of sexual pleasure was less serious than lack of financial maintenance. According to him, the wife of an impotent husband could adopt patience and sexual abstemiousness in coping with her unfavourable lot, but could not do the same with financial means because, if she did not have sufficient independent wealth or the support of a well-to-do family, the subsistence upon which her life depends would be in jeopardy. As al-Shīrāzī put it, "The body survives because of [these basic material means]."[81] It was, in fact, for this reason that the Shāfiʿī school granted a wife *khiyār* after only three days in contrast to the yearly reprieve for impotence.

Again, we have a debate where jurists' legal knowledge is ultimately dependent upon their empirical knowledge of Muslim communities. In this case, it is women's hardships and desires that matter most to the debate. At first, the decision to separate wives from their husbands without financial restitution appears to depend upon analogical arguments: the *umm al-walad* and the wife whose husband is impotent. But in the end, the suitability of these comparisons depends upon accurately assessing a wife's pain and suffering. Is impotence a suitable comparison to financial hardship? That depends, we are told, on the answers to other questions. Are they analogously difficult for women? Is patiently living without sexual fulfillment for a year more bearable than not receiving one's entitled maintenance? Can women survive on other sources of income if they are not permitted to leave their husbands? Are family debts too onerous for women? Does the Shāfiʿī position of giving a three-day delay before a judge pronounces a divorce ensure that women do not risk their lives for lack of food or shelter?

As in the case of the first objection, all these are questions that lay Muslims could answer better than a juristic minority. But there is a crucial difference between this thread of the debate and the first objection. In the case of men's purpose for marriage, the jurists had some introspective insights. They were men and many, like al-Ṭabarī, had experienced married life. Although they were a small elite, they came from various socioeconomic backgrounds and cultures. They therefore had a variety of personal viewpoints from which to draw when answering the question of a husband's purpose in seeking marriage. In contrast, the exclusion of Muslim women from the debate amplified the knowledge gap that the juristic community suffered when speaking on women's issues. Take, for instance, the question of impotence and financial constraints: Is it more difficult for a woman to patiently wait a year without sexual fulfillment or to live without her husband's financial support? Wouldn't this question elicit a variety of insightful viewpoints from women themselves, depending on their circumstances, social organization, cultural norms, family stability, and individual wealth? And wouldn't these viewpoints add richness and complexity to the process of searching for God's law?

Here we see the extent to which the exclusion of women impoverished Islamic critique.[82] Of course, we may wonder if it is fair to hold jurists, dead a millennium ago, to our modern democratic standards. But my purpose is not to be prescriptive or moralizing about how the jurists *should* have acted according to others' standards. Rather, I seek to be descriptive: My point is simply to draw out the inconsistencies that undercut jurists' own pious aspirations to critical rigour. The jurists in this gathering set up a lofty and complex debate that acknowledges that God's law is determined by the needs and hardships of Muslim women—needs that are empirical and not scripturally determined. But after all that intellectual labour gesturing towards that which can only be accessed through women's voices, women's voices are excluded from the debate. This, then, was the key limitation of critical Islam. In the end, the very power relations that justified debate as a service to lay Muslims impoverished the tenor of Islamic critique.

## Conclusion

The debate ended as those in attendance must have expected: without a clear winner. Rather the two leading students had both made strong arguments for their respective positions. But for us moderns, trying to understand the social function of classical legal critique, dwelling on al-Shīrāzī's final words offer some possibility of closure to our inquiries. According to al-Bājī, the debate ended with al-Shīrāzī stating, "And it is God who grants success in finding the right answer."[83] It is the reappearance of God here that helps us understand the interconnection between piety and knowledge in classical debate. Al-Bājī's entire transcript aspired to demonstrate that classical jurists took al-Shīrāzī's oft-repeated statement to heart. Al-Bājī presented the disputation as a manifestation of jurists' collective search for divine law. Its participants and audience approached debate with seriousness and decorum. God would bless their efforts and grant them immense rewards if they cleansed their hearts and purified their intentions for his sake. Perhaps nothing concretizes more clearly the communal reverence given to critical debate in classical Islam than the fact that it took place during periods of mourning. Al-Bājī likely knew this: he chose to transcribe a debate which in many ways was a let-down—neither al-Ṭabarī nor al-Ṣaymarī displayed their legal skills—because it conveyed the hallowed place Eastern Muslim jurists gave to the critical search for God's law. Death was an occasion not only for Qur'anic recitation, but also for critical reflection: both had the potential to remind Muslims of their ultimate return to the heavenly realm.

But what is also relevant is to whom God granted success. Al-Bājī and his juristic colleagues imagined that God granted success to jurists, and to jurists alone. Their entire vocation was as communal guides in spiritual and worldly matters. Lay Muslims, by contrast, had no legal training and therefore relied upon jurists' expertise. Islamic law was a serious science, and debate was to occur only between equally proficient legal experts. The purportedly humble service the juristic class provided lay Muslims formed the root of the exalted status of debate gatherings. And yet, in the Islamic disputation, service and privilege were difficult to disentangle. Many facets of juristic debate touched upon the desires, pains, and motives of lay Muslims without seeking to include them within the debate gathering.[84] Al-Bājī seemed unfazed by the missing voices of Muslim wives and husbands on a marital rights issue. This then was the paradox of Islamic critical debate: the social hierarchy that created an expert juristic class functioned as a precondition for the existence of critical reflection on the law and, simultaneously, as a limit to its rigour.

# 2

# The Emergence of Pious Critique

## A Genealogy of "*Munāẓara*"

A word's meanings are a social repository of the past. Wittgenstein compared words to an ancient city with a "maze of little streets and squares" in which the "old and new" exist side by side "with additions from various periods."[1] The architectural patterns change but through the amalgam of distinct eras the present comes into being—the old houses are "surrounded by a multitude of new boroughs with straight regular streets and uniform houses." So it is with words. Their meanings constantly change because language users deploy them in disparate social contexts. Older uses are sometimes retained, sometimes amended; but rarely, if ever, is a word—or a city—devoid of a rich historical inheritance.

The word *munāẓara* is no different. The varied and persistent older meanings of the term in al-Shīrāzī's 11th-century gesture towards a long and complex history, which this chapter traces. I show how the term *munāẓara* came to designate the classical disputation described in the previous chapter. To do so, I begin by examining the use of the term in the 8th and 9th centuries, during which it was deployed to designate a variety of situations in which individuals shared their reasoning with one another. One prominent situation involved debates among political antagonists about the merits of their clashing theological commitments—what I call the "theo-political *munāẓara*." I then examine how jurists began using the term to speak of their own intellectual exchanges in the late 8th century. These exchanges had no rules yet, nor did jurists systematically discuss their disputations' purpose: some exchanges appear to have been for showboating, others to refute an antagonist, and still others for intellectual pleasure and truth-seeking. In short, the *munāẓara* had neither its classical form nor its ethics in the 8th and 9th centuries.

The road to the classical form of disputation is complex: its history includes court intrigues, acrimonious intellectual divergences, pedagogical innovations, and the Greek translation movement. But I argue that a

*The Rise of Critical Islam*. Youcef L. Soufi, Oxford University Press. © Oxford University Press 2023.
DOI: 10.1093/oso/9780197685006.003.0003

turning point in the history of juristic *munāẓara* can be located in the first half of the 10th century, when jurists in Iraq began theorizing the disputation in their texts. Within their books of *jadal* (dialectic), jurists discussed the disputation's ethical norms, standard procedures, and possible strategies. The jurists of the 10th century began presenting the *munāẓara* as an indispensable practice in the juristic search for God's law: it became a standard pedagogical tool for Iraq's nascent legal schools and a tool for legal verification that jurists were expected to use throughout their careers. Henceforth, jurists spoke of the *munāẓara* synonymously with *al-jadal al-ḥasan* or *al-jadal al-maḥmūd* (sound or praiseworthy debate). This synonymity marks the final and most enduring semantic shift in the meaning of *munāẓara* among the classical juristic community.

## The Meaning of *Munāẓara*

Within the legal context of classical Islam, the *munāẓara* was a discernible practice involving a questioner and a respondent, respectively charged with defending and critiquing a contentious legal position. But what was the wider meaning of the word *munāẓara* and what other social practices did it designate? A story concerning the first ʿAbbasid caliph, Abū al-ʿAbbās al-Saffāḥ (r. 750–754 CE), gives us a preliminary glimpse into the meaning of the word during the classical period.[2] Al-Saffāḥ gathered a cohort of jurists to give judgment on a Zoroastrian prisoner. The specific circumstances of the man's imprisonment are left out of the narration, though he likely had some role in one of the many Zoroastrian rebellions that marked early ʿAbbasid rule.[3] The caliph asked the jurists for their verdict and they agreed that the man should be executed—that he should face "the sword," as they put it. The caliph responded approvingly but demanded justification for the verdict. He proceeded to interrogate the prisoner, permitting him to account for himself through debate. He probed him on his creed and questioned its soundness. "Describe to me your argument [*ṣif lī shubhataka*]," said the caliph. The man explained that he had witnessed the stark contrast of good and evil in the world and concluded that they each must have originated from one of two distinct and conflicting sources of creation. The caliph proceeded to ask if the good creator could create evil or the evil creator could create good. When the man answered no, the caliph declared, "Woe unto you, then you believe in two weak deities each capable of decreeing some things and not others." The prisoner remained silent. "Do you have any remaining arguments?" "No," he answered. Having determined that the man subscribed to an indefensible heresy, the caliph declared to his entourage, "Now you may execute him."

The 13th–14th century jurist who transcribed this tale, Abū ʿAlī al-Sakūnī (d. 717/1317 CE), labelled the verbal exchange a "*munāẓara*." In fact, it was part of a collection of *munāẓarāt* that al-Sakūnī gathered with the purpose of teaching Islam's monotheistic creed (*al-tawḥīd*) through enjoyable stories.[4] Al-Sakūnī's use of "*munāẓara*" appropriately reflects how jurists understood the term in centuries prior. The 11th-century jurists of al-Shīrāzī's time located its etymological origins in the word *naẓar*, meaning "to reason."[5] However, *munāẓara* differed from *naẓar* in that it was an act that needed a partner. Al-Juwaynī states that the *munāẓara* "is reasoning between two people"; thus, "every *munāẓara* is [a form of] reasoning though not all reasoning is a *munāẓara* [*wa-kull munāẓara naẓar wa-in kāna laysa kull naẓar munāẓara*]."[6] The tale of the Zoroastrian prisoner who provides his reasoning to the caliph and to the court officials is a tale of *munāẓara* in this sense. There are resemblances between this *munāẓara* and the practice of the legal community examined in the last chapter. Al-Saffāḥ questions and critiques, and the Zoroastrian prisoner presents his defence. Yet there are also striking differences: for one, neither the caliph nor the prisoner is part of an intellectual class for whom the exploration of the topic at hand is part of their vocation. For another, the relationship between the men is characterized by its hierarchy: the caliph has the power not only to question but also to judge. And the stakes for the prisoner are high: his life is on the line. The exchange resembles a trial where the Zoroastrian prisoner must justify his religious convictions before an authority.[7] Through tales such as those of the Zoroastrian prisoner, al-Sakūnī teaches us that the term *munāẓara* could be deployed in a wide variety of social or political circumstances where at least one party defended a position.[8]

Al-Sakūnī's capacious understanding of *munāẓara* as referring to a defence in the presence of another depended on an earlier usage of the term among Arab speakers. In particular, Muslim historians from the late 8th century onwards often invoked the term *munāẓara* to refer to debates that took place between political antagonists in the 7th and 8th centuries CE. As in the case of the caliph and the Zoroastrian prisoner, the antagonism between parties often had a theological dimension. For instance, Ibn Aʿtham presents a *munāẓara* that purportedly took place between partisans of ʿAlī b. Abī Ṭālib and Muʿāwiya b. Abī Sufyān during the First Civil War of 656–661 CE.[9]

Ibn Aʿtham relates that a man named Abū Nūḥ from the tribe of Himyar approached ʿAlī to ask his permission to debate a relative of Abū Nūḥ by the name of Dhū al-Kilāʿ. This relative had some clout among the Syrians, and ʿAlī recognized that should Abū Nūḥ convince him to defect, it would be a heavy blow to Muʿāwiya. When Dhū al-Kilāʿ learned of Abū Nūḥ's desire to speak to him, he asked Muʿāwiya to grant him permission to respond to his relative's invitation. Muʿāwiya saw little benefit in such an exchange, but he nonetheless left the matter to Dhū al-Kilāʿ who chose to meet Abū Nūḥ in the midst of the battlefield. Abū Nūḥ presented a series of reasons why Muʿāwiya was wrong to oppose ʿAlī's caliphate: for instance, that ʿAlī was chosen by the people in the capital of Medina after his predecessor's assassination and was therefore the rightful caliph. Abū Nūḥ then demanded to see the military commander of Muʿāwiya's army, ʿAmr b. al-ʿĀṣ, who confirmed the prophetic statement that a man by the name of ʿAmmār b. Yāsir would die a martyr at the hands of a rebellious party (*al-fiʾa al-bāghiya*).[10] Abū Nūḥ proceeded to reveal that ʿAmmār was among ʿAlī's troops that day, confirming the illegitimacy of Muʿāwiya's rebellion. A theo-political *munāẓarāt* like this one is common in historical accounts of the 7th and 8th centuries. Examples include debates in the context of the Prophet Muḥammad's conflict with Jewish tribes in Arabia;[11] the conflict between ʿAlī and the Kharijites;[12] conflicts between Muslim caliphs and Byzantine Christians;[13] and conflicts between caliphs and their army leaders, governors, or a restive population.[14]

Absent from the historical records of the 7th and early 8th centuries are accounts of the practice of *munāẓara* among scholarly communities.[15] For historians like Ibn Aʿtham and al-Ṭabarī, *munāẓarāt* took place in an ad hoc manner among antagonists whose swords were often unsheathed, with death frequently around the corner. How then did legal *munāẓara*—with its emphasis on pious critique rather than life and death politics—emerge? And when did the term become enmeshed with the search for God's law? To answer these questions, we will first have to examine how oral debate became a pervasive practice among 9th-century Muslim jurists.

## The Beginnings of Legal *Munāẓara* in Late 8th-Century Iraq

Already by the turn of the 9th century CE, a few decades after al-Saffāḥ purportedly questioned his Zoroastrian prisoner, the juristic communities of the Muslim world had started deploying the term *munāẓara* for their own purposes. In the juristic lexicon, the term now referred to a type of disputation.[16] Evidence suggests that the practice of *munāẓara* began in Iraq sometime in the second half of the 8th century. Its emergence was the result of the vivacious intellectual culture taking shape in Iraq under ʿAbbasid rule.[17] This culture was made up of theological and legal groups with conflicting opinions.[18] Abū Ḥanīfa, for instance, clashed with his fellow Iraqi jurists, Ibn Abī Laylā and Sufyān al-Thawrī.[19] In this fertile environment of debate, the legal *munāẓara* was only one of many types of disputations, including theological, grammatical, and literary varieties.[20] The Ḥanafīs appear to have been trailblazers in developing the *munāẓara* as a method for verifying the soundness of their positions. Even at this early stage, *munāẓara* was associated with a process of "questioning." Reports use the term *nāẓarahu* (he examined or questioned him) to speak of early Ḥanafī authorities testing fellow jurists.[21] Thus, a Ḥanafī report relays that "if a man examined/disputed Abū Ḥanīfa on a legal matter [*idh nāẓarahu rajul shay' min al-fiqh*], [Abū Ḥanīfa] gave the issue due concern [*hammathu nafsuhu*]."[22] These reports present *munāẓara* as a practice that could take place between antagonistic parties or between intellectual companions.[23] For instance, one report presents Abū Yūsuf (d. 181/798 CE) questioning his fellow Ḥanafī colleague, Zufar b. al-Hudhayl.[24]

Historians have sometimes pointed to the practice of agonistic poetry among pre-Islamic Arabs to explain the origins of disputation among Muslims.[25] Geert Van Gelder notes how the practice of *mufākhara/munāfara* saw two men extol their virtues in an attempt to assert one's superiority over an opponent.[26] There is some merit to claims concerning a continuity between the pre-Islamic period and ʿAbassid Iraq: the 8th-century *munāẓara* could manifest intense competition over participants' intellectual primacy. For instance, a report notes that the Ḥanafī scholar Zufar b. al-Hudhayl not only sought to make an opposing jurist concede, but also attempted to push him towards uttering plain nonsense.[27] However, an emphasis on continuity overlooks how jurists in centres of learning outside Iraq were either ignorant of the Iraqi method of disputation or plainly opposed to it.

For instance, al-Qāḍī ʿIyāḍ's many reports about Mālik b. Anas (d. 179/795 CE), the foremost legal representative of the Hijaz, demonstrate Mālik's unfamiliarity and discomfort with disputation. One report presents the Ḥanafī Abū Yūsuf questioning Mālik before an audience that includes the Caliph Hārūn al-Rashīd. At first, Mālik answers Abū Yūsuf's queries, but the two men are interrupted by the call to prayer. During the ensuing pause in debate, one of Mālik's students comes to see him. The student is distraught by the exchange he has witnessed between his master and Abū Yūsuf, and suspects that Abū Yūsuf is seeking to confuse his master and prove him wrong. He informs Mālik of this and advises him to remain silent rather than debate. When Abū Yūsuf returns to continue the disputation, Mālik refuses to engage, stating that he "believed that [Abū Yūsuf] was seeking guidance through his questions [*yastarshid*] rather than seeking to beat his opponent [*muta'annit^an*]."[28] The report suggests that Mālik saw proper discussion about the law as a process of inquiry (*istirshād*) among established authorities, not as the testing of these authorities' ideas. An even more telling report sees the Caliph al-Rashīd ordering Mālik to debate Abū Yūsuf. Mālik answers, "Knowledge is not like the prodding of beasts and roosters."[29] His statement can be interpreted in one of two ways: either that knowledge is not produced by prodding two jurists towards disputation or, alternatively, that the quarrelsome nature of disputation is not becoming of those seeking knowledge. But al-Rashīd does not understand Mālik and asks him again to debate. Mālik stays silent until his students explain to the caliph that "Mālik is too dignified for disputation [*jalla Mālik 'an al-munāẓara*]." This report suggests that Mālik did not consider disputation a proper way of seeking knowledge. Of course, al-Qāḍī 'Iyāḍ presents other reports where Mālik willingly engages in disputation. But I suspect that these other reports are products of a later era in which Mālikīs like Abū Bakr al-Bāqillānī and al-Bājī held disputations in high regard and imagined their school founder to have excelled in them.

The centrality of Iraq in the emergence of the early *munāẓara* is also evident from a passage within al-Shāfi'ī's *Kitāb al-Umm*.[30] The passage in question involves a disagreement over the wealth of deceased apostates. Al-Shāfi'ī (d. 204/820 CE) pits himself against an unnamed jurist who claims that the wealth of an apostate is inherited by his Muslim heirs. The unnamed jurist represents the position of Abū Ḥanīfa, Abū Yūsuf, and al-Shaybānī (designated by the term *al-musharriqūn*, the easterners). In contrast, al-Shāfi'ī claims that an apostate's wealth is a type of spoil of war (*fay'*) that belongs to Muslims. Al-Shāfi'ī presents several arguments from both sides, one in particular of which is relevant to our understanding of *munāẓara*. Al-Shāfi'ī's opponent mentions that some of al-Shāfi'ī's colleagues (referred to as "*aṣḥābakum*") transmit a *ḥadīth* in which the Prophet executes an apostate named Ibn Khaṭal, pointing out that in this case "we did not hear of the Prophet treating [Ibn Khaṭal's] wealth as spoils of war [*lam nasma' annahu ghunima māluhu*]." Al-Shāfi'ī responds: "I told him: You characterize yourselves as patient and fair in *munāẓara*, and you characterize our colleagues as negligent, [saying] that they do not employ the method of *munāẓara* [*wa-lā-yaslukūn ṭarīq al-munāẓara*], so how can you refer back to the statement of [our colleagues] who you describe as [negligent]?"[31] Moreover, he points out that the *ḥadīth* does not state whether Ibn Khaṭal even had any wealth when he died. Regardless of both sides' merits in the debate, though, three things are clear. First, the term *munāẓara* had become a term of art among jurists to designate a method of examining the law. Second, this method was associated with Abū Ḥanīfa's Iraqi circle of jurists. And third, these Iraqi jurists claimed that al-Shāfiʿī's colleagues did not employ the *munāẓara*. We know that the allusion to al-Shāfiʿī's colleagues here refers to the scholars of the Hijaz, since al-Rabīʿ b. Sulaymān al-Murādī (d. 270/884 CE), the student of al-Shāfiʿī, interjects, stating, "When [al-Shāfiʿī] says 'our colleagues' . . . he means Mālik, God have mercy on him."[32] The reference to Mālik further supports the idea that the Iraqis had championed the *munāẓara* at a time when it remained unknown or controversial in the Hijaz.

In the next section, I examine the early juristic *munāẓara* of the 8th and 9th centuries more closely. My aim is to show that this disputation was far removed from the classical *munāẓara* in both form and ethics. However, before examining this early *munāẓara*, a word is in order about the role of the caliph's court in the formation of the *munāẓara*. Several contemporary studies have highlighted the caliph's role in fostering *munāẓara* between Muslim scholars.[33] At least one Muslim source from the classical era agrees: in his *Iḥyāʾ*, al-Ghazālī traces the origins of legal disputation back to the caliph's patronage of theological and legal disputations.[34] There is certainly some basis for suggesting that the caliphs were instrumental in forging a culture of debate in 8th- and 9th-century Iraq. We have already seen reports of Hārūn al-Rashīd presiding over disputations between Mālik and Abū Yūsuf. Early ʿAbbasid caliphs used their courts for elucidating thorny intellectual questions, as another of al-Sakūnī's tales shows. The story tells of Hārūn al-Rashīd summoning theologians to debate his erudite Christian doctor. Al-Rashīd had great affection for the doctor and ardently wished he would convert to Islam.[35] One day he asked the man, "What prevents you from converting?" The doctor defended his Christian faith, stating that his own theological commitments were reinforced by the Qurʾan: "One of your scriptural verses supports my [existing] religious convictions." "What is it?" asked al-Rashīd. The doctor responded by quoting the verse describing Jesus as "a spirit from him [i.e., God] [*rūḥ minhu*]" (*al-Nisāʾ*:4), adding that this verse conformed to Christian doctrine regarding Jesus's divine nature. Al-Rashīd was deeply affected by the lucidity of the doctor's argument. He thus summoned learned scholars, but none could offer a satisfactory response to the doctor's query. One day, a Khurasanian delegation arrived in Baghdad, and among them was the Qur'anic expert ʿAlī b. Wāfid. Al-Rashīd presented Ibn Wāfid the verse that had until then dumbfounded the learned Muslim elites of Baghdad. Ibn Wāfid initially hesitated, unsure of himself; he withdrew from the heady court environment hoping for calmer surroundings where he could review with a clear head, from beginning to end, the Qur'anic verses with which he had already great familiarity. He landed on verse 45:13: "God has subjugated for you what is in the heavens and the earth; all of it is *from him*" (emphasis mine). Ibn Wāfid noted the linguistic parity between this verse and the one speaking of Jesus being "from God."[36] He returned to the court prepared for a second and decisive encounter with the doctor: "If you consider that Jesus's divine nature is attested in the expression 'a spirit *from* [*God*]' then you are constrained to also accept that the heavens and the earth partake in this same divine nature." The doctor then embraced Islam. The story shows how caliphs were able to promote the production of knowledge through their court. Other sources confirm that a caliph sometimes bestowed honour and wealth upon a debater, adding to the incentive to participate.[37]

Yet, many of the tales of early ʿAbbasid caliphs show that debate in the presence of rulers was perilous. Caliphs had the power not only to reward but also to punish. Several reports of disputations show the Caliph al-Manṣūr threatening Abū Ḥanīfa. As al-Saffāḥ's Zoroastrian prisoner found out, the threat of violence is always looming. On one occasion, al-Manṣūr requested the presence of Abū Ḥanīfa.[38] Upon entering the court, Abū Ḥanīfa saw one of the caliph's close companions, a man named al-Rabīʿ. Al-Rabīʿ was an acrimonious opponent of Abū Ḥanīfa and immediately addressed the caliph: "Oh Leader of the Faithful, this man here contradicts your grandfather, ʿAbd Allāh b. ʿAbbās, who considered it valid to add an exception to an oath a day or two after it was originally uttered. Abū Ḥanīfa deems that exceptions are only valid if stated during the utterances of oaths." Abū Ḥanīfa realized his opponent had placed him in a precarious situation: an angry caliph was a worrying sight. Quick on his feet, he exclaimed, "Oh Leader of the Faithful, al-Rabīʿ claims that your subjects owe you no allegiance." The caliph, puzzled, asked, "How so?" A palpable discomfort flowed through the room. Abū Ḥanīfa continued, explaining that al-Rabīʿ claimed that "after they take their oath of allegiance, they can go home and add exceptions to their statement, thereby invalidating them." The caliph emitted a loud chuckle and, acknowledging Abū Ḥanīfa's terrific mind, told his friend, "You shouldn't oppose Abū Ḥanīfa." As the two jurists left the gathering, a shaken al-Rabīʿ exclaimed to Abū Ḥanīfa, "You were trying to spill my blood!" Abū Ḥanīfa answered, "Rather, you were trying to spill mine, but I saved myself and you too."

Al-Manṣūr's threatening posture was by no means exceptional.[39] Hārūn al-Rashīd is presented similarly in reports.[40] The complex role of rulers as both patrons and threats to the free exchange of ideas continued into the 9th and 10th centuries. For instance, al-Masʿūdī notes that al-Maʾmūn hosted a weekly gathering of disputation on the law, but al-Maʾmūn is also remembered for persecuting scholars who refused the doctrine of the createdness of the Qurʾan.[41] Likewise, al-Bāqillānī is said to have encountered a hostile ruler when debating in the court of the governor of Shiraz.[42] The lurking dangers of rulers' courts provoked lasting suspicions from some among the juristic class. Ibn ʿAqīl, al-Shīrāzī, and al-Juwaynī all stressed that jurists should be cautious of courts where the favouritism of rulers (*ʿaṣabiyya min al-sulṭān*) could lead to the intimidation of one of the parties in a debate.[43] They understood that truth could not emerge if a jurist fearfully constrained his words. In short, while the caliphal court often sponsored disputations from the 8th century onwards, we should also see the emergence and development of the practice of *munāẓara* as a dynamic internal to the juristic community itself.

## What Was the Legal *Munāẓara* in the Early 9th Century? The Example of al-Shāfiʿī

Even though the word *munāẓara* was used to designate jurists' disputations in the 8th and 9th centuries, these disputations were still distant from the classical *munāẓara* exemplified two centuries later during al-Shīrāzī's life. This difference is evident in the several *munāẓarāt* ascribed to al-Shāfiʿī. While al-Shāfiʿī was initially labelled an outsider to the Iraqi tradition of *munāẓara*, no biographer disputes that he soon took to the practice.[44] Moreover, as Walter Young has shown, al-Shāfiʿī's texts often bear the imprint of his disputations.[45] Before examining al-Shāfiʿī's disputations, I should note that there is good reason to doubt the authenticity of al-Shāfiʿī's recorded disputations. Many could have been forged by al-Shāfiʿī's followers to bolster their master's prestige relative to his rivals.[46] However, for our purposes what matters is that the earliest sources that report these disputations are from the late 9th century. Thus, regardless of whether they truly describe al-Shāfiʿī's disputations, the transcripts of these disputations describe common features of disputations in the 9th century. As a result, they provide insight into how the practice of *munāẓara* at this time compared to later centuries.

One of the most famous of al-Shāfiʿī's disputations involves an encounter between three jurists of legendary repute. One, Abū Yaʿqūb Isḥāq b. Rāhawayh (d. 238/853 CE), had recently undertaken a long and arduous travel from the northeastern region of Persia to the sacred city of Mecca.[47] There, he found a city filled with scholarly learning circles. Ibn Rāhawayh had already established a reputation for himself across the Muslim world as a *ḥadīth* collector and juristic authority. He expected to profit from his Meccan sojourn and increase his already profound religious knowledge.[48] In particular, he longed to sit at the feet of the great Meccan *ḥadīth* scholar Ibn ʿUyayna. One day, Ibn Rāhawayh encountered his friend, the pious *ḥadīth* scholar and tireless defender of orthodox theology Aḥmad b. Ḥanbal (d. 241/855 CE). Aḥmad, knowing full well Ibn Rāhawayh's academic commitments, suggested he join the learning circle of a young scholar named Muḥammad b. Idrīs al-Shāfiʿī: "Oh Abū Yaʿqūb, why don't you join this man's gatherings?" Ibn Rāhawayh voiced scepticism: "What do I have to gain from him?" He explained that he preferred spending time with more senior scholars rather than al-Shāfiʿī, who was roughly the same age as him. His friend censured him for failing to recognize that there was something special about al-Shāfiʿī: "Wise up! Others come and go, but not the likes of this man."[49] The statement sufficiently intrigued Ibn Rāhawayh for him to reconsider his earlier dismissal of al-Shāfiʿī. He made his way to meet al-Shāfiʿī but still felt reluctant to submit to his intellectual tutelage. As such, when he reached al-Shāfiʿī, he promptly launched into a legal discussion to test the young jurist's skill.

Al-Shāfiʿī did not know his new interlocutor: all he knew was that he was eager to examine Islamic law. The two exchanged their views on a contentious matter of property law. The juristic community was divided at the time over whether homes in Mecca belonged to their dwellers or whether they were the communal property of the Muslim community. Ibn Rāhawayh was among a coterie of jurists who believed that these homes were part of the holy land around the sacred temple—the Kaʿba—and, as such, belonged to all Muslims collectively. Al-Shāfiʿī subscribed to the opposing view that granted Meccans property rights over their dwellings.[50] After a few exchanges, Ibn Rāhawayh curtly turned to a fellow Khurasanian jurist who had accompanied him to meet al-Shāfiʿī and uttered a few words in Persian. Al-Shāfiʿī, despite his ignorance of Persian, suspected that he was being slighted. He increased his resolve: "Are you debating? [*A tunāẓir*?]," he asked Ibn Rāhawayh, who, without missing a beat, quipped, "It is for debate that I came [*li'l-munāẓara ji'tu*]."[51]

Al-Shāfiʿī then quoted a Qur'anic verse dealing with Muḥammad's migration alongside his early followers from Mecca to Medina in 622 CE: "To the poor among the *muhājirīn* [the migrants], those who have been forced to leave *their* homes" (*al-Ḥashr*: 8; emphasis mine). Al-Shāfiʿī rhetorically asked his opponent if the verse did not imply that the Muslims who fled to Medina owned their homes. He then presented a second piece of evidence. Had the Prophet not said during his conquest of Mecca in 630 CE that "whoever locks *his* door [among] the Meccans is protected" against military reprisals? Had he not also specified that "whoever takes refuge in the house *of* Abī Sufyān is protected"? Again, the Prophet's words showed that Meccans like Abū Sufyān owned their homes. Ibn Rāhawayh responded, "The evidence for my position is that some of the *Tābiʿīn* [successors to Muḥammad's companions] subscribed to it." So al-Shāfiʿī asked those present, "Who is [this man]?" to which they replied, "Isḥāq b. Ibrāhīm al-Ḥanẓalī [i.e., Ibn Rāhawayh]." Al-Shāfiʿī had clearly heard this name before and exclaimed with astonishment, "You are the one that the people of Khurasan claim as their most learned?" Ibn Rāhawayh answered: "That is what they claim."[52] Al-Shāfiʿī then addressed a wider methodological point: "I tell you 'the Prophet said so-and-so' and you refer me to 'Aṭā', Ṭāwūs, al-Ḥasan, and Ibrāhīm [i.e., famous jurists of the generation succeeding the companions of the Prophet]? Is there anyone that equals the Prophet?" Changing tactics, Ibn Rāhawayh quoted a Qur'anic verse: "The resident [of Mecca] and the Bedouins are equal." But al-Shāfiʿī responded, stating: "Read the beginning of the verse: 'The sacred mosque for which we have made the resident and the bedouins equal.' So this verse is only in regard to the mosque [and not the houses of Mecca]."[53]

Let us stop here to make a few points about the characteristics of the *munāẓara* in the 9th century. There are three points of similarity between this *munāẓara* and al-Shīrāzī's classical *munāẓara*. First, the disputation takes place in a setting free from the threat of imminent violence. Unlike the theo-political *munāẓara* where debate served to determine the political primacy of one party over the other, the two jurists meet as equals in a context where a debate's outcome has little consequence for their lives. Like al-Shīrāzī's *munāẓara*, no authority sits in judgment of the two debaters, and neither man is constrained to follow the views of his opponent. Second, the *munāẓara* takes place between two members of an intellectual class. The men debate as part of their learning of the law. Aḥmad, to recall, tells Ibn Rāhawayh he has something to gain from attending al-Shāfiʿī's classes. Ibn Rāhawayh discovers through his exchange that Aḥmad is correct.[54] Both disputations are therefore recognized as part of the refinement of thought and the search for God's law. Third, the process of *munāẓara* is a process of testing through questioning: in this instance, Ibn Rāhawayh and al-Shāfiʿī are engaged in examining each other's views ("*tanāẓarnā*") on the sale of homes in Mecca.

However, the *munāẓara* between Ibn Rāhawayh and al-Shāfiʿī also displays significant differences from al-Shīrāzī's classical *munāẓara*. In terms of form, there is no firm distinction between questioner (*sāʾil*) and respondent (*mujīb*). Rather, the two men take turns providing evidence for their positions. In contrast, the classical disputation depended on the identification of a single respondent whose position was the object of sustained critique.[55] Such a lack of distinction between questioner and respondent is consistent throughout al-Shāfiʿī's recorded disputations: jurists tend to switch between the positions of respondent and questioner.[56] This interchangeability is related to another difference in form: Al-Shāfiʿī's disputation with Ibn Rāhawayh lacks a sustained engagement with a piece of legal evidence. Instead, one piece of evidence is presented after another. Moreover, there are few objections to this evidence. Again, the lack of sustained inquiry into the soundness of a piece of evidence is consistent throughout al-Shāfiʿī's recorded *munāẓarāt*.[57] In contrast, the examination of a piece of evidence's soundness was *the focus* of the classical *munāẓara*. Jurists of al-Shīrāzī's time would deploy the question "*mā dalīluka*" (what is your evidence) to present an opponent with objections or counterarguments.

In fact, the very word *munāẓara* could refer to debates of extreme brevity between 9th-century jurists. Thus, the transcript of an exchange in which al-Shāfiʿī outlines the merits of Mālik over Abū Ḥanīfa is termed a *munāẓara* despite consisting simply of three questions followed by a conclusion stating Mālik's superiority. This brevity is also evident in an exchange that begins with al-Shāfiʿī lying sick in the mosque.[58] Al-Shāfiʿī's quiet rest is disturbed by the entrance of Bishr al-Marīsī, a figure whom Islamic literature often depicted contemptuously for his espousal of heretical ideas.[59] Al-Shāfiʿī hears al-Marīsī starting to debate a Medinan jurist over a question pertaining to prayer.[60] Al-Marīsī contends that the statement of *iqāma* (which calls Muslims to stand in rows for prayer) should be uttered twice before prayer. This position departs from that of the Medinan jurist, who holds that the *iqāma* remains valid if only uttered once. Al-Marīsī defends his claim by stating that Muslims should abandon controversial positions in favour of those that are agreed upon: since jurists agree on the permissibility of repeating the statement of *iqāma* but disagree on the permissibility of uttering it once, jurists must champion its repetition. Al-Shāfiʿī, sick and lying down, is in no debating state, and yet he evidently finds his Medinan colleague's silence deafening. He therefore musters the little strength he has, sits up, and addresses al-Marīsī by invoking a similar legal case involving the call to prayer (*adhān*). The *adhān*'s purpose is to call people to the mosque, whereas the *iqāma* serves to let worshippers present know that prayer is about to begin. Al-Shāfiʿī states, "If what you say was true, you would be constrained to abandon your view on the impermissibility of raising one's voice and repeating the testimony of faith during the *adhān* (*al-tarjīʿ*), because we agree on the legal permissibility of uttering the testimony of faith once, but repetition is a controversial issue." Having put al-Marīsī in his place, al-Shāfiʿī lays back down to continue his much-needed rest. Throughout this transcript, al-Shāfiʿī only utters a sentence, yet his biographers consider him to have engaged in a disputation with al-Marīsī.

But there is also another distinction between 9th-century and classical *munāẓara* worth paying attention to: the disputation between Ibn Rāhawayh and al-Shāfiʿī lacks the ethical rules of the classical disputation. Instead of showing gravitas in the debate gathering, we find Ibn Rāhawayh slighting al-Shāfiʿī. Of course, we must countenance the possibility that the narrators of the debate consciously showed Ibn Rāhawayh in a negative light, wanting to elevate al-Shāfiʿī's status. Alternatively, perhaps Ibn Rāhawayh did not fully know the norms of proper disputation as he was a Khurasanian and belonged to the *ahl al-ḥadīth*.[61] But it is al-Shāfiʿī himself who falls short of ethical norms in other disputation transcripts. Take, for instance, a disputation where an Iraqi man named al-Faḍl b. al-Rabīʿ comes to see al-Shāfiʿī, asking him to debate al-Ḥasan b. Ziyād al-Luʾluʾī, a student of Abū Ḥanīfa.[62] Al-Shāfiʿī states that al-Luʾluʾī is not good enough ("*laysa al-Luʾluʾī fī hādhā al-ḥadd*") but that he will find a student to debate him. When al-Luʾluʾī arrives, al-Shāfiʿī has him debate a Kufan student who has defected from Ḥanafism to join al-Shāfiʿī's camp. The Kufan interrogates al-Lu'luʾī about the case of man who sexually slanders a chaste woman during his prayer, asking whether the man loses his ritual purity (*ṭahāratuhu*). Al-Lu'luʾī responds that the man does not. The Kufan then asks al-Lu'luʾī if a man loses his ritual purity if he laughs in prayer. Al-Lu'luʾī affirms that he does. At this point, the Kufan has al-Lu'luʾī exactly where he wants him: "Slandering a chaste women in prayer is less serious than laughing?" Al-Lu'luʾī then takes his sandals and heads out of the mosque amidst al-Faḍl's laughter. Al-Shāfiʿī, rather than restraining himself, joins in the mockery of al-Lu'luʾī, telling al-Faḍl, "Didn't I tell you he wasn't good enough?" If this story is authentic, then al-Shāfiʿī at least sometimes failed to conform to the later ethics of disputations.[63] Of course, al-Shāfiʿī's derision of al-Lu'luʾī does not suggest that no sense of ethics existed. Later Shāfiʿīs often quote al-Shāfiʿī as affirming that he debated in a spirit of counsel (*naṣīḥa*), seeking good for the other person, and that he did not care whether the truth was revealed on his tongue or the tongue of his opponent. Moreover, al-Bayhaqī has al-Shāfiʿī lament the ill conduct of an opponent who insults him.[64] But we can nonetheless conclude that the ethics of the classical disputation had yet to fully take shape during al-Shāfiʿī's time.

In sum, the practice of *munāẓara* in al-Shāfiʿī's generation included any and all oral debates between jurists. Some of these debates resembled the later classical *munāẓara* more than others, but even these debates lacked the sequence and ethical norms that would characterize the disputation in al-Shīrāzī's time. When and how did the shift that the practice of disputation underwent in the two centuries between al-Shāfiʿī and al-Shīrāzī take place? I will make a case for the beginning of the 10th century in Iraq, paying close attention to the intellectual, social, and political milieu in the late 9th and early 10th centuries. But before turning to this period of formalization, I wish to examine a final semantic turn in the word *munāẓara*, one that ushers in the meaning of *munāẓara* in the classical era.

## A Final Semantic Turn: The Classical *Munāẓara* as "Commendable *Jadal*"

Jurists of the 11th century emphasized that their use of the term *munāẓara* departed from the word's original linguistic meaning. To recall, they located the linguistic roots of the word *munāẓara* in the concept of "reasoning" (*al-naẓar*). These jurists also sometimes linked *munāẓara* to "seeing"—another translation of "*al-naẓar*." Thus, al-Baghdādī notes that "*naẓar*" could be done with the eye (*al-baṣar*) or with the heart (*al-qalb*) or mind (*al-ʿaql*).[65] But in the specialized language of these 11th-century jurists, the word "*munāẓara*" had become synonymous with "*jadal*." In previous chapters, I have translated *jadal* as the science of dialectical argumentation. This translation is sound when speaking of the manuals that Muslim jurists authored elaborating strategies of debate. But linguistically, the term *jadal* is better translated as "debate," "argumentation," or even "critique." Eleventh-century jurists themselves define the term along these lines. Al-Khaṭīb al-Baghdādī defines *jadal* as "the back and forth between two debaters [*al-taraddud bayna al-khaṣmayn*] that occurs when each of them seeks to strengthen his discourse [*iḥkām qawlihi*] so as to refute that of his opponent [*li-yadfaʿ bihi qawl khaṣmihi*]."[66] Al-Baghdādī explains that the origins of the word go back to the tightening of the arm when holding a rope that controls an animal. The image is one of clashing wills, with one party seeking to pull the other towards their side. Al-Juwaynī also notes that the term has roots in the world of wrestling, where it describes attempts to strike one's opponent to the ground.[67] Thus, linguistically, *jadal* implied the clashing or conflict of ideas and the adversarial character of debate far more clearly than did the term *munāẓara*.

Nevertheless, several 11th-century texts attest to the synonymity between *munāẓara* and *jadal*. Al-Juwaynī states that "there is no difference between '*al-jidāl*,' '*al-munāẓara*,' '*al-mujādala*,' and '*al-jadal*' in the customary speech [*al-ʿurf*] of the scholars of theology and law [*al-uṣūl wa'l-furūʿ*] even though the two terms are linguistically distinguishable."[68] He thus characterizes *munāẓara* as involving "mutual refutation and negation."[69] Al-Shīrāzī also notes the synonymity of the terms, stating that what jurists call a *majlis al-naẓar* (lit. a gathering for reasoning) is more accurately *mujādala* (an exchange of *jadal* or debate).[70] Among the Ḥanbalīs, Ibn ʿAqīl speaks of the *munāẓara* as the "type of reflection [*naẓar*] which they [the jurists] customarily [*fī ʿurfihim*] refer to as *jadal*."[71] The jurists' conscious appropriation of the term *jadal* highlights their agreement that legal debates *should* involve the clashing of ideas.

Of course, in practice, the juristic use of the term *munāẓara* had overlapped with the meaning of *jadal* since the 8th century: our sources speak of *munāẓara* in contexts that often involved the clashing of ideas and conflict between parties.[72] But for jurists to equate the term *munāẓara* with *jadal*, they first needed to theorize and justify their practice of mutual critique. The meritoriousness of critique was far from obvious. Al-Baghdādī and al-Juwaynī note several Qur'anic verses and prophetic *ḥadīths* that present critique in an unfavourable light.[73] One Qur'anic verse refers to the Meccans as responding to the Prophet's call to Islam with a "spirit of *jadal*"; the verse rebukes the Meccans as "a people given to contention [*qawm khaṣimūn*]" (*al-Zukhruf*:58). Elsewhere, the Qur'an affirms that those who debate (*yujādilūna*) have no escape from God. Likewise, the Qur'an rebukes humans as being "argumentative [*jadal^an*]" (*al-Kahf*:54). Jurists also knew of prophetic statements that suggested the impermissibility of *jadal*: "A people will not go astray after attaining guidance unless they adopt *jadal*." Other prophetic statements used terms similar to *jadal* to discourage argumentation: "Leave wrangling [*al-mirā'*] even if you are correct [in your views]." Jurists were therefore obliged to defend the critical dimension of the *munāẓara*. Several 11th-century texts suggest that they did so by positing a distinction between two types of *jadal*. The first they termed blameworthy debate (*al-jadal al-madhmūm*): debates engaged in with improper motives.[74] In particular, debaters who defended positions they knew to be false or who persisted in their claims after being shown their indefensibility were said to engage in blameworthy debate. The same could be said of one who debated for the sake of winning, showing off, or gaining a reputation. The jurists interpreted the several Qur'anic verses and *ḥadīths* rebuking those who engage in *jadal* as referring to this blameworthy type of *jadal*.

Against this type of *jadal* stood *al-jadal al-maḥmūd* or *al-jadal al-ḥasan* (commendable or good debate). *Al-jadal al-maḥmūd* showed a concern with faithfully evaluating evidence. In support of this type of *jadal*, jurists quoted the Qur'anic verse ordering the Prophet to "debate with them in the best of ways" (*al-Naḥl*:125).[75] Al-Juwaynī also justifies commendable debate by attributing its practice to previous generations of pious Muslims: he states that it is the "way [*sīra*] of the prophets of the past, the Prophet Muḥammad, the Prophet's companions, and their successors until the present." Al-Juwaynī then claims that since Muslims have a communal obligation (*farḍ 'alā al-kifāya*) to know God's law (*al-sharī'a*), they also have an obligation to engage in debate. In fact, he continues, debate is one of the most "certain of obligations [*ākad al-wājibāt*]" because without it, Muslims would not be able to verify (*taḥqīq*) the truth in either theology or law.

It is likely that these jurists' distinction between commendable and blameworthy debate was a product of their attempts to defend the *munāẓara* in the face of antagonistic *ḥadīth* scholars. Christopher Melchert has argued that the Iraqi *ahl al-ḥadīth* opposed the *munāẓara* in the 9th century.[76] The evidence for this assertion is mixed. On the one hand, we find a report where Aḥmad b. Ḥanbal advises a questioner against debating with an innovator (*mubtadiʿ*). The narrator of the report notes that Ibn Ḥanbal's advice conforms to a statement of the Prophet: "if God wants evil for a people he places *jadal* between them and locks from them good works [*al-ʿamal*]."[77] The narrator then notes Mālik's opposition to *jadal*, positioning Ibn Ḥanbal as following Mālik's example. In contrast, some Shāfiʿī and Ḥanbalī sources describe Aḥmad engaging in disputations (a point Melchert himself notes).[78] Ibn ʿAsākir finds a way to partially reconcile these discrepancies by stating that Ibn Ḥanbal had avoided disputation until the *miḥna* (inquisition) under the reign of al-Maʾmūn made him realize its necessity for defending orthodox religion.[79]

Regardless of these conflicting reports about Ibn Ḥanbal, three points about the historical opposition to disputation are certain. First, we know from al-Baghdādī that some used the Qurʾan and *ḥadīth* to invalidate the religious legitimacy of debate (*ibṭāl al-jidāl*). Second, *ḥadīth* scholars did circulate reports that condemned disputations. Some *ḥadīth* scholars even transmitted a prophecy in which Muḥammad claimed that in the year 135 AH a group of devils would escape from islands where King Soliman had imprisoned them; nine-tenths of these devils would travel to Iraq to engage in debates with its people (*yujādilūnahum*).[80] Third, some Ḥanbalīs of the late 9th and early 10th centuries showed far more vociferous opposition to *munāẓara* than any previous coterie of Muslim scholars. In particular, the populous rabble-rouser, Abū Muḥammad al-Barbahārī (d. 329/941 CE) reportedly gave a warning: "be careful, in *munāẓara* there is wrangling [*al-mirāʾ*], debate [*al-jidāl*], attempts at defeating one's opponent [*al-mughālaba*], argumentation [*al-khuṣūma*], and anger [*al-ghaḍab*] and you have been forbidden from all of this; [*munāẓara*] leads to abandoning the path of truth, and we have not heard [reports] that any of our jurists or scholars of the past debated [*jādala*], disputed [*nāẓara*], or argued [*khāṣama*]."[81] It is thus likely that Ḥanbalī opposition to the *munāẓara* reached its apogee in al-Barbahārī's lifetime. Evidently this opposition waned soon thereafter, such that several 11th-century Ḥanbalīs are said to have excelled in *munāẓara*.[82]

In short, to understand the meaning of *munāẓara* among classical jurists, we must pay attention to the synonymity between *munāẓara* and *jadal*. In doing so, we begin to see how jurists defended the critical thrust of *munāẓara* by distinguishing it from a blameworthy form of debate that disregarded the search for truth in favour of self-aggrandizement. At this point in our narrative, we have seen a slow evolution of the term *munāẓara* from its use in theo-political conflicts to its deployment in a practice of commendable debate on contested legal positions. We have also seen from the last chapter that this commendable debate conformed to a particular sequence and depended upon following a set of ethical injunctions—an evolution of the disputation I have termed the "classical *munāẓara*" to distinguish it from the legal disputation of the 9th century. We know beyond doubt that this classical *munāẓara* was common by the 11th century. Both disputation transcripts and jurists' own statements attest to the pervasiveness of the classical *munāẓara* among 11th-century jurists. But can we locate a moment, a turning point, between the lifetimes of al-Shāfiʿī and al-Shīrāzī at which the early *munāẓara* morphed into the classical *munāẓara*?

## The Emergence of the Classical *Munāẓara*

In this section, I argue that Ibn Surayj's early 10th-century circle in Baghdad was responsible for establishing standard sequences for disputation, positing ethical rules for participants' conduct, and theorizing dialectical strategies that would become widespread in Baghdad and beyond. The evidence for this contention begins with a description of Ibn Surayj (d. 306/918 CE) by the Shāfiʿī historian Abū Ḥafṣ al-Muṭṭawwiʿī (d. 440/1048 CE): "Ibn Surayj is the master of his generation . . . he is the great leader [*al-ṣadr al-kabīr*] and the second [version of] al-Shāfiʿī; he is a complete *imām* [*muṭlaq*], so far ahead of his colleagues that they could not match him, he was the first to have opened the gates of disputation [*al-naẓar*], and the first to teach [his students] the science of dialectical argumentation [*jadal*]."[83] Although al-Muṭṭawwiʿī's statement is terse, it attributes to Ibn Surayj a foundational role in teaching jurists the disputation. At first blush, al-Muṭṭawwiʿī's statement might appear anachronistic, since reports of jurists employing *munāẓarāt* as early as the lifetime of Abū Ḥanīfa abound. We must then conclude either that al-Muṭṭawwiʿī's statement is false or, alternatively, that Ibn Surayj taught his students a *munāẓara* that was qualitatively different from what came before. I make a case here for adopting the second option: that Ibn Surayj should be credited for formalizing the *munāẓara*—for providing it with a conventional sequence in which a questioner engages in the sustained critique of a respondent's position, moving quickly from the preliminary questions "what is your position?" and "what is your evidence?" to the elaboration of a set of objections, which the questioner then seeks to overcome.

The claim that Ibn Surayj formalized the disputation is perfectly consistent with what we know about him. Ibn Surayj was a systematizer of knowledge. Wael Hallaq claimed in 1993 that Ibn Surayj was the true founder of *uṣūl al-fiqh* (legal theory) based on the number of his students who went on to author books within the genre.[84] Hallaq's contention has been critiqued for neglecting the gradual development of *uṣūl al-fiqh* in the century before Ibn Surayj, but there can be little doubt that Ibn Surayj helped shape the discipline of *uṣūl al-fiqh* into a more mature science.[85] Ibn Surayj also further developed Shāfiʿī substantive law: Al-Shīrāzī notes the influence of Ibn Surayj's substantive legal positions in the 11th century.[86] And beyond systematizing the legal sciences, Ibn Surayj was a master pedagogue. In fact, Christopher Melchert argued that Ibn Surayj should be considered the founder of the Shāfiʿī school insofar as he was the first to gather around himself a faithful circle of students and train them according to a set curriculum.[87] Melchert's claim has also been critiqued for overlooking al-Shāfiʿī's relationship to his students in the 9th century,[88] but the point stands that Ibn Surayj trained the generation of Iraqi Shāfiʿīs after him and, as al-Shīrāzī notes, "it is through him that the Shāfiʿī school spread."[89] It makes sense that someone like Ibn Surayj, striving to train a fresh crop of jurists, would seek out pedagogical tools to produce better students. Thus, Ibn Surayj could very well have used the *munāẓara* as part of the training of his students, teaching them dialectical argumentation (*jadal*) to refine their debating skills.

The evidence for Ibn Surayj's role in ushering in the classical *munāẓara* is further supported by two claims that al-Shīrāzī makes about Ibn Surayj's students. First, al-Shīrāzī states that Ibn Surayj's student al-Qaffāl al-Shāshī (d. 365/976 CE) was the first to author a text of dialectic: "he was the first author of 'good *jadal*' [*al-jadal al-ḥasan*]."[90] Second, al-Shīrāzī states that Abū ʿAlī al-Ṭabarī (d. 350/961 CE), another of Ibn Surayj's star students and the eventual head (*raʾīs*) of the Baghdad Shāfiʿīs, wrote the first text purely on "*khilāf* [disputed matters]."[91] This new focus on disputed legal matters reflects a growing 10th-century interest in understanding jurists' ideas so as to better refute potential opponents. (Al-Ṭabarī also, like al-Shāshī, authored a text of *jadal*.) These statements strongly suggest that Ibn Surayj had taught his students strategies and ethics of debate that some of them would later elaborate upon in book form. Indeed, texts of *jadal* would soon become commonplace among the Shāfiʿīs.[92] Other schools followed their example.[93] Ibn

Surayj's formalization of the disputation also helps us understand a statement Makdisi noted as far back as 1981: Ibn 'Imād writes in *Shadharāt al-Dhahab* that Abū 'Abd Allāh al-Thaqafī (d. 328/940 CE) brought "disputation and dialectic [*al-naẓar wa'l-jadal*]" to Nishapur from Baghdad.[94] It is unlikely that the people of Khurasan would not have deployed the term *munāẓara* to speak of their oral debates prior to al-Thaqafī—after all, Ibn Rāhawayh was a Khurasanian. What is more likely is that al-Thaqafī brought to Nishapur the new innovations in disputation that Ibn Surayj and his colleagues were developing, including standardized sequences, ethics, and modes of argumentation. Further supporting this possibility is the fact that Ibn Surayj was not only a contemporary of al-Thaqafī but also seems to have known him well; in fact, Ibn Surayj reportedly stated that "none have come to us from Khurasan more knowledgeable than [al-Thaqafī] [*afqah minhu*]."[95]

It is relevant that Ibn Surayj himself appears to have highly valued and frequently engaged in *munāẓara*. Al-Subkī notes that Ibn Surayj frequently debated Dāwūd al-Ẓāhirī and his son Muḥammad b. Dāwūd al-Ẓāhirī. In fact, Ibn Surayj expressed great sadness after Ibn Dāwūd's death, stating, "My only sorrow is that the earth has consumed the tongue of Muḥammad b. Dāwūd."[96] That Ibn Surayj would eventually formalize the practice of disputation and teach his students debate strategies is therefore consonant with his own appreciation of *munāẓara*. Yet as much acknowledgement as Ibn Surayj ought to receive for beginning to formalize the *munāẓara* and for institutionalizing it within school pedagogy, we should be careful not to grant him excessive credit. The evidence we have from Ibn Surayj's disputations suggests that the ethics and sequence of the *munāẓara* continued to be refined after him. Take, for instance, a heated exchange in which Ibn Surayj squared off against another leading Shāfi'ī scholar of the time, Abū Sa'īd al-Iṣṭakhrī (d. 328/940 CE). Ibn Surayj stated, "You have been asked about a legal matter but your position is mistaken. You are a person who eats a lot of greens; perhaps this has caused you to lose your brains."[97] Al-Iṣṭakhrī then answered, "And you eat a lot of vinegar and *murrī* [a seasoning for food]; perhaps this has caused you to lose your religion." It is possible that in a heated moment, Ibn Surayj lost his composure and violated his own ethical teachings on the disputation; al-Iṣṭakhrī's comment can be interpreted as a reminder that such insults are not becoming of a religious person. But it is equally possible that Ibn Surayj and the jurists with whom he debated had not fully adopted the ethics that would characterize the *munāẓara* in later generations—either because they had yet to fully formulate these ethics or because the ethics had not gained the importance that they would in al-Shīrāzī's time. In any case, we should assume that the ethics of legal disputations were further elaborated after Ibn Surayj.

Likewise, the standard sequence of the *munāẓara* is not fully attested to in Ibn Surayj's recorded disputation with Ibn Dāwūd al-Ẓāhirī. Al-Subkī informs us of Ibn Surayj's regularly scheduled disputations with Ibn Dāwūd at the home of a judge named Abū 'Umar.[98] One day, Ibn Surayj arrived late and found a younger Shāfi'ī jurist questioning Ibn Dāwūd on the topic of *ẓihār*. *Ẓihār* is one of those cases in Islamic law that needs some contextual unpacking to understand.[99] The laws governing *ẓihār* go back to an incident during the Prophet's time when a man made an oath never to sleep with his wife again.[100] He did so by invoking a customary practice among pre-Islamic Arabs in which a man compares his wife to his mother—or more precisely, to his mother's back. What did a man mean by this? In short, he meant to say that just as it was repugnant to have sexual relations with his mother, so too would it be repugnant to sleep with his wife. This practice was naturally demeaning to the wife, and the woman in our story complained about it to the Prophet. The Qur'an narrates the complaint in the chapter *al-Mujādala* (*The Complaint*), and rebukes those who engage in the practice.[101] Most legal schools interpreted the Qur'an as saying that men who had pronounced *ẓihār* and wished "to go back [*ya'ūdūn*] on what they said" should perform an expiation by freeing a slave, feeding sixty needy people, or fasting for two months. However, when Ibn Surayj arrived that day, he found Ibn Dāwūd arguing for an unusual interpretation of the Qur'anic verse. Ibn Dāwūd argued that the word *ya'ūdūn* should be interpreted as "repeating," such that only those men who repeat their *ẓihār* pronouncement a second time should perform an expiation. Though Ibn Dāwūd's interpretation was highly unusual, it was nonetheless consistent with a plausible meaning of the term *ya'ūdūn*. After getting caught up on what had transpired, Ibn Surayj entered the arena of disputation. He critiqued Ibn Dāwūd, stating that his position had no precedent in Islamic history: "Oh Abū Bakr [Ibn Dāwūd], may God strengthen you, who among Muslims has said this before you?"[102] The rhetorical question accused Ibn Dāwūd of breaking the consensus of the juristic community. Ibn Dāwūd would have none of it. With an annoyance bordering on anger, he answered, "Do you really think that I see consensus on the matter?" In response, Ibn Surayj told his opponent that he displayed more skill in his collection of love poems than in the present disputation. Ibn Dāwūd, unfazed, began to quote from his poetry book to show the profundity of his thought. Ibn Surayj then recited his own poetry, before concluding the debate with a methodological point. We see in this disputation that neither man felt bound to explore the question of *ẓihār* in a sustained manner: they moved from examining Ibn Dāwūd's evidence for his position to reciting poetry and then on to a separate methodological point. Though it is possible that Ibn Surayj standardized the disputation after this instance, or that this disputation was exceptional in its failure to provide a sustained engagement with one party's evidence, it is also possible that Ibn Surayj had, to quote al-Muṭṭawwiʿī, only "opened the door" to formalizing disputation and that his students should be credited with continuing his initial labours.

## Two Causes for the Emergence of the Classical *Munāẓara*

Why then was the early 10th century a turning point in the formation of the classical *munāẓara*? Here, I present two reasons. The first is the increased interest in the science of dialectic (*jadal*) among theological circles in Iraq. The development of dialectical theory among Iraqi theologians is well-trodden ground among historians. Larry Miller has shown that the theologian Ibn al-Rāwandī (d. 245/860 or 298/910 CE) wrote a text of dialectic of considerable influence titled *Adab al-Jadal*.[103] Ibn al-Rāwandī was first a Muʿtazilī but then became one of the Muʿtazila's most vociferous critics. During his anti-Muʿtazila phase, Ibn al-Rāwandī spent time with Muslim and non-Muslim (e.g., Manichean and Jewish) thinkers. It is unclear whether he returned to the ranks of the Muʿtazila before death or died as a sceptic.[104] In any event, Ibn al-Rāwandī's engagement with thinkers across sectarian and religious affiliations provides evidence that dialectical theory was taking shape among theological (*kalām*) and other philosophical circles. In fact, our earliest extant text of dialectic was authored by the 10th-century Karaite Jew al-Qirqisānī, who reproduced much of Ibn al-Rāwandī's thought.[105] Moreover, the Muʿtazilī Abū al-Qāsim al-Balkhī al-Kaʿbī (d. 319/931 CE) wrote a refutation of Ibn al-Rāwandī's text of *jadal*.[106] Abū al-Ḥasan al-Ashʿarī (d. 324/935–936 CE), in turn, wrote a refutation of al-Kaʿbī's critique of Ibn al-Rāwandī. My point is not that Ibn al-Rāwandī is the origin of dialectical theory, but rather that he represents the growing interest in dialectic among late 9th-century theologians. Ibn Surayj likely frequented these theological circles. The evidence for this is that Ibn Surayj is reported to have been the "most skillful of al-Shāfiʿī's followers in theology [*kalām*]."[107] Though biographers have given conflicting dates for the year of Ibn al-Rāwandī's death, Ibn al-Rāwandī either was Ibn Surayj's contemporary or had shaped the theological environment of Ibn Surayj's generation. Either way, it is inconceivable that Ibn Surayj would not have known of new developments in dialectical theory. It is also telling that al-Qaffāl al-Shāshī, the first jurist to have authored a text of "good dialectic," was the most theologically distinguished of Ibn Surayj's students.[108] All this suggests that Ibn Surayj found inspiration in the new theorizations of dialectic being developed in theological circles.

What is less clear is whether the interest in dialectic in the late 9th century was the product of engagement with Greek thought or whether it emerged organically among Muslim theologians. The Caliph al-Mahdī (d. 785 CE) presided over an early translation of Aristotle's principal text on dialectical argumentation, *The Topics*.[109] Within Aristotle's Lyceum, dialectic referred to a practice that trained students to critique popularly held beliefs in Greek society.[110] Aristotle would pit two students against each other, and one would be charged with undoing his opponent's position by asking a series of questions. The questioner's aim was to trap an opponent by showing the gaps or inconsistencies in his position. *The Topics* became the subject of a commentary by al-Fārābī in the middle of the 10th century, aptly titled *Kitāb al-Jadal*. Both Hallaq and Abdessamad Belhaj have attributed juristic interest in dialectic to the influence of Greek thought.[111] For his part, Young has pushed back against attributing excessive importance to Aristotle.[112] He has convincingly shown that the argumentative strategies in 11th-century books of *jadal* are already found in al-Shāfiʿī's writings. Young sensibly concludes that the Greek translation movement supported the further development of an already existing dialectical practice.

The second cause for the formalization of the *munāẓara* is the competition between nascent schools of law in 10th-century Baghdad. The increasingly rigid boundaries between schools in this period created inter-school competition. Prior to this moment, Melchert notes, scholars had tended to move more freely from one learning circle to another.[113] But after the 10th century, they showed greater fidelity to their *aṣḥāb* (colleagues). In this context, the Shāfiʿīs and Ḥanafīs increasingly came to compete and butt heads on a number of legal topics. Later biographers spoke about them as "the two parties."[114] Al-Ghazālī speaks of them as the main participants in *munāẓara*, and traces of their debates are rife in a text as early as al-Jaṣṣāṣ's 10th-century *Sharḥ Mukhtaṣar al-Ṭaḥāwī*.[115] We saw in the last chapter how the prospect of debate between the leaders of these schools could stir excitement among Baghdad's jurists. It is reasonable to assume that Ibn Surayj and his students saw in the elaboration of dialectical theory an opportunity to better train their faction against opposing jurists. Two points lend support to this view. First, Young has recently discovered that Ibn Surayj's Ḥanafī contemporary Abū al-Ḥasan al-Karkhī (d. 340/951–952 CE) used his text *Uṣūl al-Karkhī* to prepare his students for disputation with their school's detractors. Young highlights a passage in which al-Karkhī tells his students how they should respond when a questioner critiques them. Second, the extent to which al-Shīrāzī uses the Ḥanafīs as examples throughout his texts of dialectic makes clear that the two schools' rivalry animated his preoccupations with theorizing the disputation. Al-Shīrāzī likely inherited a tradition that had begun in the 10th century in which dialectic was at least partly aimed at defending a school's doctrine against detractors.

## Conclusion

The word *munāẓara* had a long and complex history on its way to designating the practice of disputation that al-Shīrāzī and his peers engaged in. The word's usage at the dawn of Islam in 7th-century Arabia remains obscure. Nonetheless, we know that in the vibrant intellectual milieu of ʿAbbasid Iraq, the word came to refer to a variety of different intellectual exchanges. Included among these exchanges were the debates of political rivals, whose antagonism often bore a religious dimension (for this reason, I have termed this type of debate a "theo-political *munāẓara*"). But by the late 8th century, Iraqi jurists had also begun using *munāẓara* to refer to a method for examining the views of fellow jurists. The Iraqis claimed that those who did not perform *munāẓara* were negligent in their legal reasoning. With al-Shāfiʿī's appropriation of the *munāẓara* and his deployment of it in Egypt and Mecca, we see the practice spreading across Muslim territories, including among Persianate scholars of Khurasan such as Ibn Rāhawayh. Still, this "early *munāẓara*" departed from al-Shīrāzī's "classical *munāẓara*" because of its lack of standardized sequences, roles, or ethics.

The 9th century very likely saw a gradual refinement of the practice of *munāẓara*. Nonetheless, a watershed moment can be located in the 10th century, when the *munāẓara* became an object of conscious theorization within Ibn Surayj's learning circle in Iraq. This conscious theorization led to the formation of the science of dialectic (*jadal*), which elaborated strategies for defeating an opponent, enumerated the standard questions and roles of the *munāẓara*, and gave deliberate attention to the proper ethics of debate. Part of this conscious theorization involved justifying debate in response to those who considered it impious. The result was the equation of juristic *munāẓara* with "praiseworthy debate" (*al-jadal al-maḥmūd*). Henceforth, when jurists used the term *munāẓara*, they did not designate any and all intellectual exchanges; rather, they had in mind a critical practice with a particular sequence and ethics, which would allow them to perform their revered search for God's law. The synonymity between *munāẓara* and "praiseworthy *jadal*," the sequence of the *munāẓara*, and its expected ethics would all remain features of the specialized juristic understanding of *munāẓara* long after the classical legal culture waned in the 13th century.[116]

But while tracing the semantic changes in the term *munaẓara* provides a genealogy of the practice of debate among Sunni jurists from the 8th to the 11th centuries, it barely scratches the surface of jurists' discursive justification for the disputation. In the next chapter, I turn to texts of *uṣūl al-fiqh* to uncover a rich archive of arguments about the function of the disputation. In doing so, I show how jurists' justifications for the disputation shaped the frequency and pervasiveness of the practice itself.

# 3

# "Why Do We Debate?"

## Uncovering Two Discursive Foundations for Disputation

In this chapter, I examine how jurists justified the practice of *munāẓara*. At first blush, it may appear as though I have already provided an account of their justifications in Chapters 1 and 2. There, I showed that the *munāẓara* served to test the merits of legal arguments. This testing was necessary in order to correctly apply God's law and counsel the community of lay Muslims. Critique, when done with proper motives, was therefore a pious act that enabled living by God's law. But if we leave matters here, we are faced with two lingering questions about the *munāẓara*. The first relates to the *munāẓara*'s pervasiveness. Even if we grant that the disputation served to discover God's law, we must still ask the following: Why were all jurists expected to participate in disputation? Why was it not sufficient for the likes of al-Ṭabarī and al-Ṣaymarī to engage in disputations, use their findings to elaborate upon the law, and expect their students to conform to their arguments?

Second, why did jurists tackle well-trodden legal topics in their disputations? When we examine disputation transcripts, we notice that jurists continued to debate the same contested issues as their predecessors. This is true of al-Shīrāzī's disputation with al-Dāmaghānī on the wife's *khiyār*, which al-Shāfiʿī and al-Shaybānī had already debated in their respective books of substantive law, and it is true of the other disputations we will examine in later chapters. If disputations were meant to discover God's law, then we might expect that they would be used only when new cases arose. After all, we would find it odd if our contemporary legislators met to discuss matters for which sensible solutions have already been offered. Were disputations then a lavish waste of time? Were they merely pedagogical? A pastime? Or perhaps a means to defend a school's reputation? If so, then we must commit ourselves to rejecting jurists' claims to be piously seeking God's law.[1]

George Makdisi and Wael Hallaq have sought to provide an account of why jurists re-examined well-known controversial legal issues, though their

*The Rise of Critical Islam*. Youcef L. Soufi, Oxford University Press. © Oxford University Press 2023.
DOI: 10.1093/oso/9780197685006.003.0004

endeavours ultimately prove unsatisfying. Both scholars imagine that the disputation aimed to achieve juristic consensus on the law (within and across legal schools). Makdisi writes: "When the determination achieved consensus, it became the madhab, 'the way to go,' the objections being resolved; failing solution, it remained in the realm of khilāf; whence the term for those questions, problems, still in dispute: al-masā'il al-khilāfiya, 'the disputed questions.'"[2] Hallaq explains this desire for consensus by referencing jurists' commitment to finding a single truth, adding that "At least on the theoretical level—and presumably in practice—dialectic served to minimize legal pluralism in Islam." According to this view, disputations tackled the same topics because jurists sought to weed out differences of opinion, even if this goal of consensus was rarely achieved. In what follows, I will not deny that in some cases disputations might have led to doctrinal consolidation (even as I have yet to find an instance of such consolidation). But, as I will show, this interpretation's emphasis on minimizing differences squares poorly with jurists' own descriptions of their disputation. At best, it gives us an understanding of how only one subsection of jurists saw the function of disputation—but even in this best case, it is a partial understanding.

My contention in this chapter is that justifications for the classical *munāẓara* rested upon two discursive foundations. These discursive foundations gave distinct shape to the practice of *munāẓara*, thereby accounting for its pervasiveness among jurists and for jurists' interest in re-examining well-trodden legal questions. The first foundation was the obligation of *ijtihād* (the juristic effort to search for God's law); the second was the uncertainty of the law. By affirming the obligation of *ijtihād*, the jurists of the classical period enjoined each other to take responsibility for reaching greater confidence (*ghalabat al-ẓann*) in the soundness of legal positions, regardless of the views of the leading authorities of their school. And by promoting a view of the law as an uncertain enterprise, jurists elevated the importance of critique as the means for properly assessing the subtle and complex evidence for different legal positions. Only by engaging in critique could a jurist hope to fully examine the law and successfully fulfil his obligation of *ijtihād*. Both foundations were the product of epistemological debates in 9th-century Iraq on which widespread juristic agreement coalesced by the early 10th century.

To support my contention, I turn to a protracted debate between jurists, preserved in their texts of *uṣūl al-fiqh*. This debate relates to the question of juristic infallibility (*taṣwīb*), with one group of jurists affirming the pluralistic truth of God's law and another asserting that God's law is singular. In the course of this debate, jurists asked each other why, if all jurists are correct, they would engage in disputation. The answers to this question varied. Yet, as will become clear, jurists' conflicting justifications nonetheless reveal agreement on one point: the necessity of disputation in seeking out God's uncertain and ever-tentative law. This will become particularly evident when we pay attention to the distinction that jurists drew between the purpose of disputation in theology (*kalām*) and its purpose in law.

The chapter is broken down into several interconnected sections. I begin the analysis by providing an account of the two discursive foundations of disputation, showing (1) that *ijtihād* had become an imperative across legal schools in Iraq and Persia by the 10th century, and (2) that jurists saw the possibility of reaching certainty on legal positions as a rarity. I then examine jurists' competing justifications for the *munāẓara*. I lay out the differences between the infallibilists (Muṣawwiba) and the fallibilists (Mukhaṭṭi'a) before showing that both camps agreed on the necessity of disputation for *ijtihād*. Finally, I address two potential objections to taking jurists' claims about the obligation of *ijtihād* and legal uncertainty at face value. In particular, I draw upon a claim in al-Shīrāzī's *Sharḥ al-Luma'* that shows that al-Shīrāzī saw his juristic community as possessing a *habitus*, or an embodied sensibility, of uncertainty. I conclude by considering the following question: What is the importance of discursive justifications for the continued viability of social practices and what does this importance tell us about the relationship between discursive justifications and the practice of disputation in the classical period?

## Foundation 1: The Obligation of *Ijtihād*

Modern scholarship has often associated *ijtihād* with innovation or creativity in legal reasoning.[3] If this is an accurate understanding of *ijtihād*, we should expect jurists to have used the disputation as a mechanism for *ijtihād* when innovation was needed: when new questions arose or when they wished to overturn the positions of their predecessors. But the contrary is true: jurists debated questions that had been well-trodden for generations. Why was this the case? Al-Shīrāzī provides us with some guidance. To begin, we ought to note that al-Shīrāzī does not define *ijtihād* as "original" or "creative" thought.[4] Rather, *ijtihād* for him is the "expenditure of effort in searching for God's rule on a legal question [*al-ḥukm*]."[5] Nothing in this definition prohibits one jurist's *ijtihād* from being exactly the same as another's. In fact, al-Shīrāzī assumes that a jurist's *ijtihād* on disputed legal topics (*masāʾil al-khilāf*) will begin by examining the arguments of his predecessors. Al-Shīrāzī sees no need to reinvent the wheel: if a jurist finds one of the arguments of his predecessors satisfactory and reproduces it after careful review of evidence, he has successfully performed *ijtihād*.[6] But this clarification about the meaning of *ijtihād* does not yet answer our initial question: Why should a jurist perform *ijtihād* on questions for which his legal school has already developed a standard answer? Addressing this concern helps reveal the importance of critique to the juristic community.

Al-Shīrāzī provides a solution to the question of *ijtihād* necessity that has little to do with the practical needs of a legal system.[7] In fact, from the perspective of a modern state concerned with an efficient judiciary, jurists spent an inordinate amount of time and resources debating questions that would hardly affect legal *responsas* (*fatwā*s) or court rulings.[8] School positions on most contested legal matters had already been sufficiently standardized. Al-Shīrāzī's answer is rather the product of a theological commitment to the rational justification of one's religious beliefs and practices. Al-Shīrāzī claims that Muslims are generally prohibited from adopting "a position without evidence [*qubūl al-qawl min ghayr dalīl*]"—a practice known in Arabic as *taqlīd*.[9] Al-Shīrāzī quotes the Qur'anic condemnation of the polytheists who committed such a transgression ("We have found," they said, "that our forefathers agreed upon a path and we will surely follow in their footsteps").[10] The verse serves to remind Muslims they are no more secure in their religious convictions than Muḥammad's antagonists were if they follow custom or authority rather than rationally defensible evidence.

However, al-Shīrāzī makes a distinction between *taqlīd* in matters of theological belief and in matters of legal practice. He states that all Muslims must know the justification for basic points of creed (*uṣūl al-dīn*).[11] In particular, they must know the justification for the existence of God, his creation of the world, the possibility of prophethood, and the truthfulness of Muḥammad's claims to prophethood.[12] Al-Shīrāzī grounds this obligation to know the existence of God and the truth of prophethood in the radical equality of human rationality, stating that all human beings are equal in their abilities to understand the rational evidence (*al-ʿaqliyāt*) for theological positions. He writes: "The means by which these [theological] positions are understood is the intellect [*al-ʿaql*] and all rational beings [*al-ʿuqalāʾ*] share in this intellect.

It is impermissible that some should follow others without evidence since one person possesses the same evidence as his fellow human when seeking to comprehend these positions."[13] Al-Shīrāzī follows two principles here in imposing an obligation of religious knowledge: (1) rational ability and (2) accessibility of evidence.

In contrast to his position on theology, al-Shīrāzī accepts that lay Muslims defer to jurists in legal matters. In his estimation, legal evidence is more complex than theological evidence, and performing *ijtihād* in legal matters therefore requires extensive training.[14] Obliging all Muslims to undergo this training would be impractical, causing an undue burden on society. Thus, al-Shīrāzī considers that the *fatwā* of the *mujtahid* acts as a sufficient justification for a lay Muslim's actions.[15] The *fatwā* substitutes for "evidence," acting as an equivalent to the jurists' use of scriptural sources. Nonetheless, al-Shīrāzī applies the same two principles of rational ability and accessibility of evidence to render *taqlīd* impermissible for jurists.[16] Jurists share sufficient equality of rational abilities to prohibit following each other's positions without first investigating their soundness. Al-Shīrāzī states: "Acting without evidence has no place when there is equality in [understanding] evidence [*lā yadkhuluhā al-taqlīd maʿa al-tasāwī fī al-adilla*]." Thus, even as al-Shīrāzī recognizes that some jurists are more gifted than others,[17] he also affirms their fundamental equality in being able to understand and determine for themselves which evidence is strongest in a contested case. This rejection of *taqlīd* means that each jurist needs to understand the law for himself through the process of *ijtihād*.

Already, we can see how critique as a mechanism of *ijtihād* would matter for al-Shīrāzī. If *ijtihād* is an individual obligation, then critique becomes a necessary mechanism, not only for establishing proper laws for the Muslim community but also for the jurist to be able to fulfil his duty to seek out God's law. The pervasive practice of disputation among the juristic community and the examination of well-trodden topics become the means through which each jurist can examine the arguments of his colleagues on a contested legal question. But al-Shīrāzī was not alone in making *ijtihād* an individual obligation between the 9th and 12th centuries. In fact, the obligation of *ijtihād* had become a widely held Shāfiʿī position by the 10th century, such that al-Shīrāzī's anti-*taqlīd* position can be understood as the culmination of Shāfiʿī debates on the subject in centuries prior. Al-Shāfiʿī had prohibited *taqlīd* for a scholar (*ʿālim*) of the law.[18] Al-Muzanī writes at the beginning of his *Mukhtaṣar* that al-Shāfiʿī prohibited his followers from "following him or another without evidence [*nahyihi 'an taqlīdihi wa-taqlīd ghayrihi*]."[19] In the early 10th century, Ibn Surayj added a qualification to al-Shāfi'ī's position, claiming that if a jurist was faced with a legal question for which an answer was needed before he could complete his *ijtihād*, he was permitted to follow the position of another jurist.[20] For instance, if the jurist was confused about how to perform a prayer the time of which was soon ending, necessity demanded that he follow another scholar's position. Some accepted Ibn Surayj's position on *ijtihād*, claiming that the jurist in this case is analogous to a lay Muslim incapable of properly performing his religious duties without consulting a jurist.[21] Others, like al-Shīrāzī, rejected Ibn Surayj's position, saying that the jurist is not like a lay Muslim because he possesses the ability to find the correct legal position if given the necessary time.[22] In any event, Ibn Surayj's qualification was only for exceptional situations: the Shāfi'īs generally obliged each jurist to complete *ijtihād* before acting or counselling others about the law.

The Shāfi'īs asserted that they alone among the legal schools rejected *taqlīd*. They sometimes made this claim in order to disparage members of other schools, characterizing their *ijtihād* as insufficiently rigorous.[23] In the *Sharḥ al-Luma'*, al-Shīrāzī singles out Aḥmad b. Ḥanbal and al-Shaybānī as permitting *taqlīd* among jurists.[24] Despite Shāfi'ī claims, an anti-*taqlīd* ethos had become prevalent among the Sunni legal schools of Iraq and Persia by the 10th century. This is true of the Ẓāhirī school, whose founder Dāwūd al-Ẓāhirī rejected *taqlīd*, authoring a book titled *The Invalidation of Taqlīd* (*Kitāb Ibṭāl al-Taqlīd*).[25] Likewise, 10th- and 11th-century Iraqi Mālikī and Ḥanbalī sources are staunchly anti-*taqlīd*. The Mālikī Ibn al-Qaṣṣār (d. 397/1006 CE) affirms that the "opinion of Mālik" is that *taqlīd* is prohibited.[26] Like al-Shīrāzī, Ibn al-Qaṣṣār quotes the Qur'anic verse rebuking the Meccans for following their forefathers. And like al-Shīrāzī, he justifies the obligation of using individual reason (*al-naẓar*) to understand God's law, quoting the Qur'anic verse, "If you are in disagreement about something, then refer [the matter] back to God and his Prophet."[27] As for the Ḥanbalīs, Abū Ya'lā (d. 458/1066 CE) denies that Ibn Ḥanbal supported *taqlīd*. Like al-Shīrāzī, Abū Ya'lā rejects juristic *taqlīd* because "[the jurist] possesses the tool [*āla*] through which to reach the object of his search [*al-maṭlūb*] [i.e., the law]."[28] In fact, all extant Ḥanbalī *uṣūl al-fiqh* texts of the 11th century prohibit one trained in the law from practicing *taqlīd*.[29] The Mu'tazilī Abū al-Ḥusayn al-Baṣrī (d. 436/1044 CE) and the Ash'arī Abū Bakr al-Bāqillānī (d. 403/1014 CE) also prohibit a jurist from engaging in the *taqlīd* of another jurist.[30]

The Ḥanafīs alone showed reluctance to conform to the post-10$^{th}$-century anti-*taqlīd* consensus. This reluctance was likely the product of reports about early Ḥanafī authorities legitimating *taqlīd*. Some reports indicate that Abū Yūsuf, Abū Ḥanīfa, and al-Shaybānī permitted jurists to engage in *taqlīd*.[31] Other reports affirm that all three prohibited the practice. Despite their reluctance, by the 10th century, some Ḥanafīs found a solution that would permit them to uphold the obligation of *ijtihād* while accepting reports that their school founders had permitted *taqlīd*. Al-Karkhī allegedly affirmed that a jurist can only follow the position of another jurist on a given legal question if he has evidence that the other jurist's position is sounder than his own. Al-Karkhī explained that this search for evidence is itself a type of *ijtihād* (*ḍarb min al-ijtihād*) and that the jurist cannot therefore be accused of acting without knowledge.[32] It is not clear from our sources what evidence could grant a jurist confidence in the superiority of his colleague's reasoning on a given matter but perhaps al-Karkhī had in mind the views of renowned early Ḥanafī authorities for which little to no evidence could be found. In any event, the position became popular among the Ḥanafīs of Baghdad such that al-Ṣaymarī restates it in his 11th-century book of legal theory.[33] Moreover, prominent Ḥanafī *uṣūlīs* in Central Asia such as ʿAlā' al-Dīn al-Samarqandī (d. 539/1144 CE) unequivocally adopted the position that a qualified jurist was barred from following the opinion of another jurist.[34]

We should not minimize the differences of opinion among jurists over *ijtihād* and *taqlīd* in the classical period. Jurists differed on what constituted *taqlīd*: for instance, some debated whether following the Prophet's statements or the opinions of the Prophet's companions was a form of *taqlīd*.[35] They also differed on the cause of *taqlīd*'s prohibition. Al-Bāqillānī, for example, rejects al-Shīrāzī's claim that the equality of rational capacities and the accessibility of evidence are the basis of the prohibition of *taqlīd*, presenting other arguments to support the same position.[36] And certainly the number of arguments that al-Shīrāzī presents in favour of *taqlīd*—either without qualification or in particular instances—gestures towards the historical existence of camps that spent considerable effort legitimating some form of *taqlīd* between jurists.[37] Yet the fact remains that extant *uṣūl al-fiqh* texts from the 10th to the 12th centuries display a remarkable agreement around the jurist's obligation to perform *ijtihād*. There is an almost Protestant quality to this commitment: like the Protestant imperative to let the individual's conscience determine his reading of scripture, jurists affirmed their members' individual prerogative in evaluating legal evidence. Each jurist had a duty to follow the conclusions of his own reasoning on the law. Al-Shīrāzī summarizes this adherence to individual reasoning:

> there is scholarly consensus that when a jurist engages in *ijtihād* on a matter and his *ijtihād* leads him to a conclusion, he must [continue to] espouse the [conclusion] to which his *ijtihād* has led him and [he must] act according to it; if he departs from the position dictated by his *ijtihād*, then he is blameworthy [*istaḥaqqa al-dhamm*].[38]

It is easy to see how the commitment to *ijtihād* is consistent with support for critical engagement and disputation. *Ijtihād* demands that the jurist expend his "utmost effort" to find God's law, and critique can play an important part in this effort. As al-Juwaynī reminds us, the disputation is a means of confirming (*taḥqīq*) and discrediting (*tamḥīq*) different legal arguments.[39] Thus, it helps the jurist fulfil his duty before God. But though we have begun to sketch out an account of the disputation's justification, we will not have a full picture of its importance to the classical legal culture unless we also pay attention to the practice's second discursive foundation. After all, while it would make sense for jurists to use the disputation to examine new legal questions, it is not so clear why they used it for well-trodden issues. Would not the arguments of past generations offer the individual jurist sufficient guidance to perform *ijtihād* monologically? To put things more concretely, what more did al-Shīrāzī and al-Dāmaghānī have to contribute to the question of the wife's *khiyār* given that it had been examined by formidable minds within their schools since the time of al-Shāfiʿī and al-Shaybānī? To answer this question, we must turn to the second discursive foundation of the disputation.

## Foundation 2: The Uncertainty of the Law

The jurists of the 10th–13th centuries not only saw themselves as obligated to perform *ijtihād*, but they also saw their *ijtihād* as an uncertain enterprise in which their arguments were always tentative and subject to revision. As in the previous section, I turn to al-Shīrāzī's *Sharḥ al-Lumaʿ* for guidance on this point. I explain al-Shīrāzī's discourse of legal uncertainty and show its importance in justifying critique. Al-Shīrāzī's position on legal uncertainty is best understood by comparing it to his statements on the possibility of theological certainty. To recall, al-Shīrāzī states that theological positions are based on evidence accessible to all rational humans (i.e., sane adults).[40] He claims that humans who examine this evidence correctly should arrive at the same conclusions.[41] This is because the evidence (*adilla*) used to derive conclusions in theology is strong enough to produce certainty (*al-qaṭʿ*).[42] The affirmation that theological arguments could produce epistemic certainty led al-Shīrāzī to deny the acceptability of differences of opinions on the fundamentals of religion: "These principles [of theology] are based on evidence that produces knowledge [*ʿilm*] and thus bar any excuse [*qāṭiʿa li'l-ʿudhr*]."[43] To take a concrete example, al-Shīrāzī denies that the existence of God is subject to doubt. He believes that the rational evidence (*dalīl ʿaqlī*) for the existence of God is sufficiently clear that all fair-minded people can agree on it. Al-Shīrāzī says of the one who subscribes to an opposing theological position that "his belief is ignorant and deceitful [*iʿtiqāduhu jahlan wa-kadhiban*]."[44]

But matters are different when it comes to the law. Al-Shīrāzī sees the law as a product of scripture (*al-sharʿ*), and few scriptural sources from the Qurʾan and *ḥadīths* can produce legal positions that are objectively certain. Why is this so? Is not God omniscient? Is not his Prophet infallible? Should scripture not then be taken as the pinnacle of certainty? In theory, yes, it should: God and his Prophet's words should be followed with the utmost certainty. But there are two impediments to knowing God and his Prophet's commands. First, scripture is conveyed through language, and the meaning of language is not always evident.[45] According to al-Shīrāzī, all language can be categorized in terms of its clarity. One category applies to utterances that are completely clear or "perspicuous" (*al-naṣṣ*) because they have only one possible meaning. Al-Shīrāzī gives the example of a *ḥadīth* regarding the *zakāt*: "For every forty sheep, one sheep [is due]."[46] He notes that the word "forty" would be understood without interpretative effort by any Arab listener. As a result, the jurist possesses the highest epistemic certainty about the meaning of the statement. But very few statements can be ranked as perspicuous: much of scripture falls instead within a second category, where the listener can detect at least two possible meanings but one is more likely or "apparent" (*al-ẓāhir*) than the other.[47] Finally, some statements are impossible to understand without further context. These statements are considered ambiguous (*al-mujmal*). Al-Shīrāzī notes that there are many causes of ambiguity in language. For instance, some words are too vague to mean much without more specification. Al-Shīrāzī gives the example of the word "*ḥaqq*," often translated as "right." The statement "Give the *ḥaqq* (right) [owed upon the land] on the day of the harvest]" (*al-An'ām*:141), leaves the listener unsure about what the "*ḥaqq*" in question refers to. Context, not pure language, permitted some jurists to claim that *ḥaqq* here referred to the right of the poor to the alms-tax (*zakāt*), while other jurists contended that it referred to a different and additional charity to be given to the poor after harvest.[48] In short, the Qur'an and the *ḥadīth* are seldom clear enough for the jurist to consider them definitive legal evidence. The jurist must often use his own interpretative capacities to arrive at the correct meaning of scripture—an endeavour in which he may very well stumble and fall.

The second impediment to knowing God and his Prophet's commands is that much of the law is not based on a direct application of scripture. Rather, many legal questions are determined through analogical arguments (*qiyās*). Analogical arguments depend on identifying the attribute (*al-waṣf*) that, when present, causes a law to come into effect.[49] But certainty about the relevant attribute to a legal question can rarely be achieved. Only if a clear scriptural text identifies the relevant attribute or jurists reach consensus (*ijmā'*) on the attribute can an analogical argument produce epistemic certainty.[50] For instance, if a jurist finds a scriptural statement saying "sugar is prohibited because of its sweetness" or if he discovers that all jurists agree that sugar is prohibited because of sweetness, then he can prohibit honey with certainty, since honey is also sweet.[51] But barring such clear statements or consensus, the jurist must use his rational faculties to find the cause of a given law. Several methods for discovering legal causes are possible, but all are fallible.[52] These two impediments to certainty meant that most legal evidence was labelled *ẓannī* (presumptive).[53] This *ẓannī* evidence might allow a jurist to escape *al-shakk* (doubt) but, as al-Shīrāzī explains, it left open the possibility that a position different from the one the jurist favoured might be correct.[54]

Al-Shīrāzī was not alone in seeing the legal system as dependent upon uncertain legal evidence. Jurists of the classical era displayed considerable agreement about the uncertainty of the law. Aron Zysow's influential text *The Economy of Certainty* aptly notes that the epistemic status of legal sources is the most pervasive concern of Islamic legal theory texts.[55] Zysow shows that among Sunnis, the Ẓāhirī school was an outlier in seeking to ground the law in certainty.[56] In contrast, jurists from other schools did not believe that their legal system could achieve such certainty.[57] They asserted that the *mujtahid*'s task is not to reach objective knowledge (*'ilm*) about the law but rather to "overcome mere presumption [*ghalabat al-ẓann*]" by assessing the evidence and coming to a conclusion on the matter.[58] According to their texts of legal theory, only if they thought a scriptural source was perspicuous or there was consensus on a matter did they deny the validity of another jurist's *ijtihād*.[59]

We can now begin to see how the obligation of *ijtihād*, coupled with an understanding of the law as an uncertain science, heightened the importance of critique in classical Islam. The idea that legal arguments are subtle and demand great consideration suggests that the critique of fellow jurists could facilitate a jurist's assessment of the law and help him fulfil the obligation of *ijtihād*. It also explains the pervasiveness and the repetition of topics of disputation. Since the evidence for the law is uncertain, it stands to reason that different minds might evaluate evidence differently.[60] Thus, no matter how many generations examined a legal question, every new generation of jurist had the responsibility to examine the law again.

But how do we know that jurists themselves linked the discourses on the obligation of *ijtihād* and on the uncertainty of the law to the disputation? Thus far, I have only shown that these two discourses *could* justify critique. I have yet to show that they did do so. At most, I have shown that paying attention to these two discourses can help us make sense of the pervasiveness of disputation among jurists and their practice of revisiting well-trodden questions. Is my attention to these two discourses warranted, then? In what follows, I show that jurists spilt considerable ink answering the question "why do we debate?" As I proceed, it will become evident that their justifications are discursively intertwined with the twin assumptions that *ijtihād* is a juristic obligation and that the law is unavoidably uncertain.

## "Why Do We Debate?": The Justifications for the Disputation

Jurists would provide their justifications for the disputation in their texts of legal theory (*uṣūl al-fiqh*). These justifications are not accorded their own independent chapters in these books of legal theory but rather tucked away in a subsection of one particular chapter on the debate over juristic infallibility (*taṣwīb*).[61] We must therefore linger briefly on this debate. Its origins are traceable to Basra, roughly five hundred kilometres south of Baghdad, at a time when Abū ʿAlī al-Jubbāʾī (d. 303/915 CE) stood at the head of the formidable Basran Muʿtazilī school of theology.[62] Al-Jubbāʾī reputedly championed the idea that "All *mujtahid*s are correct [*kull mujtahid muṣīb*]."[63]

The slogan offered a means to make sense of the daunting patchwork of divergent legal opinions circulating around the Muslim world by affirming that all juristic opinions on contentious matters were equally valid. Those who came to adopt this slogan would be known across Muslim history as al-Muṣawwiba (those affirming infallibility). Fakhr al-Dīn al-Rāzī (d. 606/1210 CE) explains the position of the Muṣawwiba by saying that they believed a legal rule (*ḥukm*) only came into being after a jurist engaged in *ijtihād*.[64] In other words, God's law is not something that exists waiting to be found; rather, God creates rules to be followed through the intermediary of his jurists and their efforts to weigh the strength of evidence on a legal question.

Al-Jubbāʾī's position quickly provoked hostile reactions. An opposing camp arose who emphatically negated juristic infallibility, insisting instead that God prescribed a single answer for any given legal question. The camp's partisans, who included the Iraqi Ḥanbalīs and Shāfiʿīs, came to be known as al-Mukhaṭṭiʾa (those affirming juristic fallibility).[65] They began to muster trenchant arguments to discredit the thesis of the Muṣawwiba. In doing so, they rhetorically asked the opposing camp, "if all positions are correct, why then do we hold debate gatherings?"[66] The Mukhaṭṭiʾa believed that debate gatherings would be a superbly elaborate waste of time if all jurists were correct. Does disputation not by its very nature, so the logic went, aim to convince an opposing side to abandon its position? The Ḥanbalī Abū Yaʿlā writes: "If all the *mujtahids* are correct then the *munāẓara* would be a misguided and foolish practice. When each person sees the other as correct, [engaging in] disputation becomes senseless."[67] Al-Shīrāzī similarly states:

> What proves our position [on the singularity of legal truth] is the consensus [*ijmāʿ*] of the Muslim community [*al-umma*] that reasoning [*al-naẓār*] [on the law] and *ijtihād* are obligations. . . . For if all positions were equally correct, then there would be no point in engaging in reasoning or *ijtihād*. Put otherwise, people have agreed upon the goodness of reasoning [on the law] and have agreed to establish gatherings of disputation within which reasoning on the law takes place. If all [positions] were true . . . there would be no reason for interlocutors to debate each other over legal positions [whose validity] they have already agreed upon.[68]

Thus, for the Mukhaṭṭiʾa, disputation functioned as a way to find the singular truth about God's law. Already, we can see how the obligation of *ijtihād* figured prominently in the background of the Mukhaṭṭiʾa's justification for the disputation. The Mukhaṭṭi'a saw disputation as a clashing of positions from which the strongest emerges.[69] Through disputation, a jurist can discover the truth about God's law and therefore fulfil his duty of *ijtihād*.

But the discourse of legal uncertainty is also key to understanding why the Mukhaṭṭi'a saw the disputation as a means of fulfilling *ijtihād*. What undergirds the Mukhaṭṭi'a's justification for disputation is their agreement that legal evidence is "subtle" (*khāfiya*) and "concealed" (*ghāmiḍa*).[70] Some Mukhaṭṭi'a, of course, considered the evidence to be more uncertain than others. At one extreme, Abū al-Ṭayyib al-Ṭabarī reportedly stated, "I know that [our party] is correct and that those who oppose our positions are wrong."[71] In contrast, Abū Ya'lā quotes Aḥmad b. Ḥanbal as teaching that a jurist should never say to his opponent, "You are mistaken."[72] The reason, Abū Ya'lā explains, is that although "truth is singular, a man does not know if he is correct in identifying it or not." Abū Ya'lā further supports this position with a report concerning the second Caliph 'Umar who, after examining a legal issue, uttered, "By God, 'Umar does not know whether he has reached the truth [*aṣāba al-ḥaqq*] or is mistaken." But even al-Ṭabarī affirmed that though he was certain of the correctness of the Shāfi'īs' positions, he did not "fault his detractor" because all jurists dealt with uncertain legal evidence.[73] In fact, it was a standard position of the Mukhaṭṭi'a that a jurist who was mistaken in his *ijtihād* was nevertheless rewarded for his considerable efforts in grappling with complex evidence.[74]

## The Response from the Muṣawwiba

The Mukhaṭṭi'a's claim that disputation aims to find a singular truth was soon contested by the Muṣawwiba of the 10th and 11th centuries. This contestation has been obscured by the undue attention given to the Mukhaṭṭi'a camp in analyzing the history of disputation.[75] Take, for instance, Hallaq's mirroring of the Mukhaṭṭi'a's position in his contention that the purpose of the disputation was to weed out differences of opinion: "In the Islamic context, juridical dialectic was viewed as an efficient means to reach the truth about a particular legal question. . . . Minimizing differences of opinion on a particular legal question was of utmost importance, the implication being that truth is one, and for each case there is only one true solution."[76] The problem with Hallaq's contention is that it misses the perspective of the Muṣawwiba camp, who by the early 10th century had already developed responses to the claim that the disputation aims to find the singular truth of God's law. I present these responses in this section. They are responses that help demonstrate that, despite their disagreement with the Mukhaṭṭi'a, the Muṣawwiba also saw disputations as a mechanism for performing *ijtihād* in the face of law's uncertainty.

Al-Jubbā'ī's most gifted student, Abū al-Ḥasan al-Ash'arī, reportedly opposed the Mukhaṭṭi'a by arguing that the purpose of legal disputation was as an exploratory mechanism in seeking divine law: "The disputation on legal matters [*al-furū'*] is beneficial . . . despite the principle that all *mujtahid*s are correct, because it allows the jurist to search for *al-ashbah* [the strongest opinion]."[77] "*Al-ashbah*" is a technical term that the Muṣawwiba coined, and for which they offered different definitions. For the Basran Mu'tazila following al-Jubbā'ī, *al-ashbah* referred to a purely subjective legal position.[78] In contrast, the Iraqi Ḥanafīs invoked *al-ashbah* to refer to the juristic position supported by the strongest evidence. But both factions used the concept to clarify that jurists have something to aim for (*al-maṭlūb*) in performing *ijtihād*, even though God's law itself does not exist until the jurist's *ijtihād* is complete. In claiming that jurists used the disputation to find *al-ashbah*, al-Ash'arī countered the claim that disputation is about finding the singular truth of God's law. For him, disputation was instead about weighing the strength of evidence in one's personal search for God's law.

In the generations following al-Ash'arī, the Muṣawwiba elaborated their justifications for disputation. We can locate this elaboration in the *uṣūl al-fiqh* of al-Jaṣṣāṣ,[79] al-Bāqillānī, and al-Baṣrī.[80] At the beginning of the 12th century, al-Ghazālī would summarize these arguments in his text *al-Mustaṣfā*. His summary makes plain the importance of *ijtihād* and legal uncertainty to the Muṣawwiba's justifications for *ijtihād*. Al-Ghazālī argues that there are two reasons why disputation is an obligation (*wājib*) for the juristic community. The first is to ensure that a legal question *should* continue to be a matter of disagreement. To recall, jurists only accepted disagreement so long as there was no perspicuous text on the matter. A perspicuous text was a rare occurrence, but jurists nonetheless had the moral obligation to debate each other to ensure they had not overlooked one. The second reason is to permit a jurist to weigh evidence on a thorny legal question about which he finds himself undecided.

Al-Ghazālī then presents a series of reasons why disputation is, if not obligatory, then at least recommended (*mandūb*).[81] First, he claims that disputations serve to dispel suspicions of bad faith within the legal community by revealing the soundness of different legal positions. Al-Ghazālī notes that, without debate, jurists would fall into sin by thinking poorly of their colleagues: that they would be inclined to claim that their colleagues hold their positions out of obstinacy rather than a sincere consideration of evidence. Second, disputations allow a jurist to dispel his colleagues' claims about the existence of definitive evidence on a given legal question. In doing so, a jurist rehabilitates the validity of a marginal position. Thus, against Makdisi and Hallaq's contestation that the disputation aimed at eliminating dissenting legal opinions (*khilāf*), al-Ghazālī shows here that the disputation also served to preserve and legitimate dissent.

Third, disputations are recommended because they permit a jurist to revise his position: each jurist uses the disputation to "inform [*yunabbih*] his opponent" of an alternative way of thinking about the law, allowing his opponent to reassess the soundness of his position.[82] Fourth, along similar lines, al-Ghazālī recommends disputation as a way to help an opponent move from a legitimate but weak position to a stronger one (*min al-fāḍil ilā al-afḍal*).[83] In short, jurists should use the disputation to mutually refine their thinking on a legal question. The fifth and sixth recommended uses of disputation touch upon the form's pedagogical purpose.[84] Al-Ghazālī notes that disputations benefit their audiences by helping them to gain an "understanding of the means of conducting *ijtihād* [*maʿrifat ṭuruq al-ijtihād*]."[85] Last, al-Ghazālī characterizes the disputation as a "type of training [*nawʿ min al-irtiyāḍ*] and a sharpening of the mind [*tashḥīdh al-khāṭir*]" for both debaters.[86]

Like the Mukhaṭṭiʿa, then, the Muṣṣawiba also saw the disputation as a mechanism for *ijtihād*. From al-Ghazālī's six reasons to recommend disputation, most aim at enriching jurists' thoughts and enabling them to better evaluate the evidence on a legal question. The disputation could accomplish this either indirectly (through pedagogical training to help jurists become competent legal thinkers) or directly (by revealing the merits of different evidence on a question). Moreover, the Muṣṣawiba's justifications for disputation were also intimately tied to the uncertainty of the evidence under review. In fact, al-Ghazālī makes legal uncertainty a precondition for the legitimacy of disputation: he notes that a disputation cannot take place once it becomes evident that a perspicuous text (*naṣṣ*) on the matter exists. If there is already certainty, there is no need to hold a disputation. In short, then, the discourses on the obligation of *ijtihād* and legal certainty shaped the thinking of both the Mukhaṭṭiʾa and the Muṣawwiba. Without them, the jurists' justification for the disputation would have looked very different. These twin foundations help us understand why jurists were expected to participate in disputation and why they tackled well-trodden subjects over multiple generations.[87]

## The Relationship between Theory and Reality: Two Objections

At this point, we have established that jurists' justifications for the disputation depended upon the discourses of *ijtihād* and the uncertainty of the law. We might wonder, however, if these juristic discourses reflect reality. Were jurists really committed to the individual obligation of *ijtihād*, and did they truly see the law as uncertain? In particular, two objections must be countenanced. First, if *ijtihād* was truly a universal obligation for all jurists, then why did jurists typically end up defending their school doctrine, both in their books and in their disputations? Second, if jurists claimed the law was uncertain and that disputations helped them in their search for God's law, why do we find textual evidence that jurists obstinately sought to prove their points and gain fame through disputations? I take each objection in turn.

### *Ijtihād* and School Doctrine

The claim that each jurist must perform *ijtihād* might appear difficult to square with jurists' commitment to defending school doctrine. If, as al-Shīrāzī contends, jurists were in agreement about their individual duty to follow the strongest evidence in deriving the law, then why does al-Shīrāzī throughout his disputations and his books consistently champion Shāfiʿī positions?[88] Are we to presume that it is mere coincidence that his *ijtihād* overlaps with those of his school predecessors and colleagues (*al-aṣḥāb*)? This is a difficult coincidence to accept, especially when we see that other Shāfiʿīs like Abū al-Ṭayyib al-Ṭabarī, al-Juwaynī, and al-Māwardī also follow their school doctrine closely. When Schacht claimed that *ijtihād* had ended by the early 4th century, it was doubtless because he recognized that jurists had begun abiding by school doctrine.

Ahmed El Shamsy has tried to offer a solution to this problem by turning to the discussion on the *ijtihād* of the *qibla* (prayer direction) within Shāfiʿī books of substantive law.[89] A bit of background on this discussion is in order: for Shāfiʿīs, a worshipper who found himself out in the wilderness would be considered to have performed *ijtihād* insofar as he expended the utmost effort in deciphering the signs of nature, like the wind or the stars, to determine the proper prayer direction. The jurists saw an analogy between their efforts to find God's law and this worshipper's efforts in finding the *qibla*.[90] But Shāfiʿīs contended that not all worshippers should perform *ijtihād*. For instance, a blind person should engage in *taqlīd* because he has no means of performing *ijtihād* without eyesight. The blind person's *taqlīd* in the case of the *qibla* mirrors the lay Muslim's *taqlīd* in legal matters. El Shamsy suggests that the discussion on the *ijtihād* of the *qibla* reveals a position between *ijtihād* and *taqlīd* that al-Māwardī calls *tafwīḍ* (deference).[91] Al-Māwardī invokes *tafwīḍ* in a situation where a traveller arrives in a city and discovers a *miḥrāb* (prayer niche) in a mosque revealing the direction in which the city dwellers pray. Al-Māwardī affirms that in such a situation it is impermissible for the traveller to pray in a different direction than the city dwellers because it is highly unlikely that a multitude of Muslims over generations have been wrong.[92] Rather, the traveller must "defer" (*yufawwiḍ*) to the city dwellers for his prayer direction. El Shamsy sees this discussion on *tafwīḍ* as offering an argument for the authority of precedent among classical Shāfiʿī jurists. El Shamsy therefore concludes that 10th- to 12th-century Shāfiʿī jurists were not fully dedicated to *ijtihād*, despite their claims in texts of *uṣūl al-fiqh*.

However, there are two problems with El Shamsy's conclusion. First, the *tafwīḍ* of a traveller is a poor analogy for Shāfiʿīs' engagement with their legal school. *Tafwīḍ* in the case of a traveller involves accepting the prayer direction of a community *without* seeking to understand their justifications for doing so. In contrast, the Shāfiʿīs only accepted following school doctrine *after* studying their predecessors' evidence. Thus, *tafwīḍ* would only characterize the labours of Shāfiʿī's correctly if the traveller in al-Māwardī's writings sought to learn *why* the city dwellers prayed in the direction of their *miḥrāb*. Second, we have reason to consider that al-Māwardī's notion of *tafwīḍ* is instead analogous to a jurist's use of a prophetic report passed on by a multitude (*al-khabar al-mutawātir*).[93] The evidence for this is in al-Shīrāzī's statements in the *Muhadhdhab*: "if [the traveller] finds prayer niches of Muslims in a locale, he is to pray towards them, because they are equivalent to a report [*al-khabar*]."[94] Elsewhere, al-Shīrāzī and al-Māwardī both explain that the report of a trustworthy person on the direction of the *qibla* is to be trusted. Thus, in Shāfiʿī thought, prayer niches serve as the equivalent of the reports of several city dwellers affirming the prayer direction.

Rather than claiming that Shāfiʿī jurists of the 10th to 12th centuries were not truly engaging in *ijtihād*, we ought to try to understand why they believed they could simultaneously perform *ijtihād* and follow their school doctrines. To begin, we should pay attention to the pedagogical training of a jurist from the 10th century onwards. Take a jurist like al-Shīrāzī who first trained in Firuzabad and in Shiraz. When learning the law, al-Shīrāzī would have confronted a legal system in which a high degree of pluralism existed. Most legal questions admitted of several potential answers. Al-Shīrāzī would have also learnt that one of these answers was correct because the Prophet had asserted that his community would never agree upon error. The problem for al-Shīrāzī was that no one knew with certainty what the correct answer was.[95] Al-Shīrāzī could have attempted to determine the correct position by opening the Qurʾan or books of *ḥadīth* and reading them cover to cover in search of evidence for the right position, but such an approach would have been methodologically unsound. It would have been equivalent to a physicist today refusing to read Newton, Einstein, or Niels Bohr and beginning instead with independent empirical experiments to arrive at his own conclusions.[96] A more sound methodology—one that would have ensured al-Shīrāzī had a full grasp of contested evidence—was to begin by learning the arguments of his predecessors.[97] Since al-Shīrāzī was training with Shāfiʿī jurists, he began by examining the merits of Shāfiʿī claims and testing whether they were defensible in the face of other schools' criticisms.

According to standard Shāfiʿī teachings, our young al-Shīrāzī would have been bound to abandon the Shāfiʿī position if he found it weak. But there are two reasons why a young Shāfiʿī jurist would typically have stuck with a Shāfiʿī position. First, the past centuries had produced an immense repository of impressive arguments for standard Shāfiʿī positions. It was therefore vanishingly unlikely that a jurist of al-Shīrāzī's generation would find none of the Shāfiʿī evidence compelling. Second, if a young jurist did not find the evidence compelling, he was at liberty to posit a new argument to refine the thought of his predecessors—not unlike the physicist who might improve upon the ideas of his predecessors after studying them. In doing so, he would be able both to uphold school doctrine and to fulfil the duty of *ijtihād*.

Later Shāfiʿī jurists like Ibn al-Ṣalāḥ would see al-Shīrāzī and his peers as performing *ijtihād* within the parameters of their legal school or *madhhab* (*mujtahid fī al-madhhab*) in contrast to jurists who performed *ijtihād* independently of school authority (*mujtahid mustaqill*).[98] This is not a mistaken description, but it is worth understanding why 11th-century Shāfiʿīs did not see themselves in this light. In their minds, they performed the same *ijtihād* as the master of their legal school since they too had done their utmost to find the strongest evidence in answering a legal question. What differed were the conditions in which they performed their *ijtihād*. Whereas their predecessors had fewer arguments and methodological principles to consider, they had to countenance all the different arguments that their predecessors had left them. As we saw with al-Shīrāzī and al-Dāmaghānī's debate on the wife's *khiyār* in Chapter 1, this difficult labour of seeking out God's law was rendered easier by making use of the disputation.

In the next chapter, we will have occasion to see in practice how al-Shīrāzī used the arguments within his legal school to facilitate his search for God's law. But for now, I emphasize that the overlap between *ijtihād* and the following of school doctrine does two things for our understanding of the function of disputation in the classical period. First, it allows us to make sense of jurists' own claims that the disputation fulfilled the obligation of *ijtihād* regardless of their commitment to school doctrine. And second, it allows us to see why a commitment to school doctrine did not mean a commitment to settling juristic disagreement once and for all. We have seen how the Muṣawwiba were explicit that it would be wrong to ask a fellow jurist to abandon his position. And though the Mukhaṭṭi'a claimed that the disputation was a means to find truth, they acknowledged that a fellow jurist may nonetheless arrive at divergent positions.

## Embodying Uncertainty: The Story of the Persecuted Jurist

Skepticism about jurists' commitment to the uncertainty of the law is also justifiable. Al-Ghazālī's *Mustaṣfā* critiques those jurists who think that their legal positions are truth. He thus gestures towards the presence of a cohort of jurists who acted as though their legal evidence were immune to uncertainty.[99] Moreover, in his opus *Iḥyā' 'Ulūm al-Dīn*, al-Ghazālī accuses jurists of engaging in disputation to gain prestige.[100] He contends that if jurists were sincere in serving God they would abandon their legal careers in order to fulfil less socially respected occupations for which there is a pressing demand, such as medicine.[101] Thus, a critical historian might conclude that the egos of the juristic community were far too inflated for them to take seriously the idea that they were using disputations to sift through difficult evidence. But I would caution against reading al-Ghazālī in this light. After all, al-Ghazālī is following here a familiar script in which classical jurists warn each other not to fall into the trap of debating for wrong motives. Take for instance Abū Ḥāmid al-Isfarāyinī's statement to his students nearly a century earlier:

> Write down my speech in debate gatherings sparingly. For verily this speech occurs in a context of cunningness, fault-finding, and the desire to refute and beat one's opponent. Thus, we do not always speak sincerely for God's sake. If that was truly what we sought after we would be quicker to silence than to speech. But although our disputation often invites God's anger, we nonetheless desire his mercy [*wa-in kunnā fī kathīr min hādhā nabū' bi-ghaḍab Allāh ta'ālā, fa-innā ma'a dhālika naṭma' fī sa'at raḥmat Allāh*].[102]

Here al-Isfarāyinī simultaneously acknowledges the peril of disputation and pushes his students towards proper ethical conduct through his negative evaluation of certain debaters' motives. It is the same type of exhortation that we find in books of dialectic where jurists like Ibn 'Aqīl, al-Bājī, and al-Baghdādī remind jurists of the proper intentions of debate.[103] Thus, a more plausible interpretation of al-Ghazālī's critique of disputation is that it was part of a tradition in which jurists would periodically exhort their peers to remember the need for humility and to recognize that they seldom truly know God's law.[104]

Recent anthropological literature helps clarify how uncertainty was embodied in the classical juristic community. This literature speaks of Islam as involving the shaping of a *habitus*. The term "*habitus*" refers to the aptitudes and sensibilities that the body acquires to achieve its social and ethical ends.[105] As Asad notes, the human body is a malleable tool in the pursuit of a person's ends. We can therefore speak of a *habitus* in reference to the way a person unconsciously learns to navigate the busy streets of a city or to a person's conscious training of their fingers on the piano. Al-Shīrāzī's *Sharḥ* indicates that jurists often possessed a visceral and embodied sense of uncertainty as a result of their legal training. The passage is found in his discussion on the definition of knowledge, in which al-Shīrāzī presents the Mu'tazila's definition of knowledge as "the understanding of something as it truly is, *with peace of mind* [*ma'a sukūn al-nafs*]" (emphasis mine).[106] In other words, the Mu'tazila see the possessor of knowledge as immune to doubt. Al-Shīrāzī takes issue with this description. He invites us to imagine two individuals subjected to persecution for their beliefs. One of these individuals is a lay Muslim and the other is a jurist. Both of them are asked to recant their views on the law or meet execution by the sword. Facing this immense trial, the lay Muslim clings ferociously to his views until his death. Now, if the Muʿtazila are correct about their definition of knowledge, then we should expect the jurist to be even more firm in his convictions. After all, he possesses knowledge of the law while the lay Muslim does not, relying only upon legal opinions of jurists. But surprisingly, al-Shīrāzī considers that the jurist would recant without much effort from his persecutors. Why? Is it because he has learnt of God's dispensation to lie about one's faith when under duress?[107] No: rather, al-Shīrāzī believes the jurist would recant because of his constant exposure to conflicting legal arguments. This constant exposure weakens the jurist's conviction regarding the correctness of one position over another.[108] It is the lay Muslim's "ignorance of legal evidence" that makes him defiant in the face of persecution.[109] Thus, even as jurists defended doctrines of their schools, al-Shīrāzī nonetheless saw them as doing so tentatively, always aware that they may be mistaken.

Of course, this story does not provide sufficient evidence to conclude that uncertainty was characteristic of the classical juristic community's lived experience. It falls short in two regards. First, al-Shīrāzī is only one jurist and his perspective might have been mistaken or partial. Second, it is impossible to truly know what jurists felt "on the inside." All historians have access to are written records. Still, al-Shīrāzī was no outlier in the legal community. He was feted during his life and raised to the highest professorial ranks. His view of his community is at least as important as al-Ghazālī's in understanding how the discourse on legal uncertainty manifested itself in the juristic community. And again, one way to reconcile both jurists' views is to see the discourse on uncertainty as a necessary aspect of the ethical goal of properly searching for God's law. As with all ethical goals, jurists sometimes failed: they sometimes lacked humility and refused to recognize when their opponents had something to teach them. And sometimes they succeeded.

## Conclusion: The Social Importance of Discursive Ideals

In this chapter, I have argued that jurists' justifications for the disputation from the 10th century onwards rested upon two discursive foundations. The first was the obligation of *ijtihād*. The near agreement that a jurist must know the evidentiary basis for the law led to the widespread view that all jurists must perform *ijtihād* on contested legal topics. No jurist could follow the position of another before assessing the evidence upon which his position relied. The second foundation was the uncertainty of the law. Excepting the Ẓāhirīs, Sunni jurists' recognition that most legal questions are uncertain led them to accept that their detractors may be right while they themselves may be wrong. Even when they went into a disputation confident about their own position, they had an ethical responsibility both to respect their opponent for his labours and to yield if his arguments proved stronger.

Despite sharing these two discursive foundations, jurists justified the disputation differently depending on their stance on juristic infallibility. The Mukhaṭṭi'a (fallibilists) affirmed that the disputation was a means to find truth in a legal system so complex that the clashing of ideas was necessary for finding God's law. In contrast, the Muṣawwiba denied the permissibility of trying to convince an opposing jurist to abandon his views, maintaining that God had made all jurists' positions correct. But the Muṣawwiba nonetheless recognized that mutual critique would allow each jurist to better understand the issues at hand. The disputation might allow jurists, for example, to discover definitive evidence like a perspicuous text (*naṣṣ*) that would settle a given legal question once and for all; it might allow a jurist vacillating between pieces of evidence to make up his mind; or it might help a jurist discover the weaknesses in his own reasoning. Beyond refining legal reasoning, the Muṣawwiba claimed that the disputation could maintain goodwill between jurists by preventing them from falling into the sin of thinking that their colleagues held on to positions out of obstinacy. Finally, the disputation ensured that later generations of jurists could countenance all possible positions on the law by rehabilitating marginal but still legitimate positions.

Without the two foundations of *ijtihād* and the uncertainty of the law, the disputation would have lost its raison d'être. The question "why do we debate?" would have been met with a very different set of answers. In fact, we can see as much when we compare the legal disputation to its theological counterpart. In the theological context, the practice of disputation was not grounded in a duty to search for God's truth amid uncertainty, and jurists taught that theological disputations aimed merely to dispel confusion about religion or to correct heresy.[110] Jurists therefore lacked the discursive foundations to justify theological disputations as a mutually beneficial mechanism for exploring ideas and promoting communal solidarity.[111]

It should be evident that a social practice does not only depend upon its justification for its existence. Take, for instance, the practice of obtaining a doctorate in the humanities. The motives of students for undertaking the degree will differ: livelihood, prestige, fascination with a research topic, fear of entering the workforce. These motives keep the practice alive, regardless of the loftier justifications that circulate about how the humanities train us to better understand ourselves and the world around us. But discursive justifications do shape a practice over time—if only because time and resources are limited. So as our contemporary society continues to devalue the humanities and to favour "practical" disciplines, we see the slow draining of resources from humanities departments. In the absence of discursive justifications that give social importance to the humanities, and in turn ensure university funding and a stream of fresh recruits, the practice of earning a PhD in the humanities faces real threats.

The same goes for the disputation in classical law. The early practice of disputation among Iraqi jurists of the 8th century predated jurists' discourses on the obligation of *ijtihād* and the uncertainty of the law. But when these discourses gained traction by the end of the 9th century, they gave distinct shape and salience to the practice of disputation within the nascent Iraqi legal schools. The question that then presents itself is this: What happens to the disputation when the justification for its practice no longer exists? We will tackle this question in the last chapter of the book. But first, let us turn to the relationship between the disputation and the development of substantive law.

# PART II

# 4

# Debating the Convert's *Jizya*

## How the *Madhhab* Enabled *Ijtihād*

Schacht famously announced that the beginning of the 900s marked the end of *ijtihād*. He reasoned that if jurists worked within *madhhab*s or legal schools, then they must have deferred to authority and abandoned "independent" thinking on the law.[1] With this assessment, Schacht largely set the terms of scholarship on *ijtihād* up until the present, despite important critiques of his thought.[2] I have already suggested that Schacht and others' view of *ijtihād* is based on a mistaken understanding of the concept itself—one that discounts the fact that, for classical jurists, *ijtihād* also included reaffirmations of school doctrine so long as this reaffirmation included a commitment to understanding and evaluating their predecessors' legal evidence.[3] But I am not the first to claim that commitment to *ijtihād* and allegiance to a *madhhab* are compatible. Makdisi's analysis of disputations led him to reject claims that *ijtihād* waned during the classical era, and to maintain that belonging to schools of law did not prevent jurists from remaining committed to *ijtihād*.[4] Makdisi rightly countenanced that a culture in which disputation was pervasive could not be characterized by deference to authority, still less by stagnation of thought.[5] Unfortunately, Makdisi's claims were made in cursory fashion at the end of *The Rise of Colleges*. He therefore left two salient questions unanswered: What might we learn about the relationship between *ijtihād* and the *madhhab* in the 10th–13th centuries through the lens of the disputation? And relatedly, what impact did disputations have on the historical development of substantive legal thought?

In this chapter, I answer these two questions. I do so by examining the second of al-Shīrāzī's disputations against al-Dāmaghānī. The disputation asks: Does a non-Muslim who converts to Islam still owe the *jizya* (a poll tax for non-Muslims) that accrued while he was a non-Muslim? It is likely that this disputation took place the same day that the two men tackled the question of the wife's *khiyār*, though al-Subkī never confirms this.[6] Analysis of the disputation reveals an intimate interrelationship between the *madhhab*

*The Rise of Critical Islam*. Youcef L. Soufi, Oxford University Press. © Oxford University Press 2023.
DOI: 10.1093/oso/9780197685006.003.0005

and the individual jurist's *ijtihād*. It shows that a jurist drew on the repository of arguments produced by his school predecessors to then make up his own mind about the strongest evidence for any given position. Sometimes the jurist reproduced existing arguments from this repository and sometimes he modified them or posited new ones. In turn, the jurist's *ijtihād* became part of the repository of arguments from which future jurists could draw. In this process of *ijtihād*, the disputation was key in helping the jurist determine his favoured argument. In particular, the disputation allowed the jurist to ensure that his favoured argument was consistent with his reasoning as it pertained to a range of substantive legal questions. Ensuring consistency was vital because the objections and counterarguments of a questioner during a disputation often referenced other matters of ongoing dispute in order to show that a respondent could not hold his position without contradicting himself. Part of the task of a dexterous respondent was to show how his legal reasoning could be compatible across substantive legal questions. As a result, a disputation on one topic might force a jurist to reconsider his position on another.

Methodologically, I use al-Māwardī's *al-Ḥāwī al-Kabīr* to show how al-Shīrāzī both relied upon and departed from the arguments he inherited from his legal school. I employ the *Ḥāwī* for two reasons. First, al-Māwardī was an Iraqi Shāfiʿī scholar and a contemporary of al-Shīrāzī. He trained with Abū Ḥāmid al-Isfarāyinī (d. 418/1027 CE), who dominated the legal intellectual landscape of Iraq in the first decades of the 11th century.[7] Al-Māwardī therefore had insight into the legal arguments that were circulating in Shāfiʿī circles in Iraq during al-Shīrāzī's lifetime. Second, the *Ḥāwī* is a detailed text that aspires to present a comprehensive list of Shāfiʿī arguments on contested questions. Al-Shīrāzī himself considered it an encyclopedic work preserving different Shāfiʿī arguments throughout history.[8] The *Ḥāwī* reveals the labours of Shāfiʿīs who had sought to perfect their school doctrine up until al-Shīrāzī's time.[9] It therefore offers us an essential point of reference in understanding how al-Shīrāzī relied upon his legal school.

## Background to the Disputation: The Convert's Jizya

Al-Dāmaghānī faced al-Shīrāzī and asked him "about a *dhimmī* who converts: is his past *jizya* cancelled?"[10] The question invoked two interconnected terms of art relating to Islamic statecraft: *jizya* and *dhimmī*. The *jizya* was a poll tax levied on non-Muslim populations living within Muslim-governed lands.

A number of historical reports show Muḥammad applying the poll tax upon newly conquered populations.[11] Muḥammad's successors continued the policy as Muslim armies invaded territories outside of the Arabian Peninsula. The poll tax was a useful means of accruing state funds to support an expanding empire's military efforts. It also justified non-Muslim inclusion within a Muslim-governed polity. Anver Emon puts it best: "the *jizya* was a complex symbol which can be viewed as a tool of marginalization or a mechanism of inclusion, but more fruitfully understood as both."[12]

The *jizya* had Qur'anic sanction in a verse that ordered continual warfare against those labelled "People of the Book" until they agreed to pay the *jizya* (*al-Tawba*:29). Although most jurists considered People of the Book to be a shorthand reference to Jewish and Christian communities, they typically found ways to justify the *jizya*'s imposition upon all non-Muslim peoples.[13] The Shāfiʿīs, for instance, coined the neologism "quasi–people of the book" in order to legitimate taking the *jizya* from Zoroastrian communities.[14] They cited a dubious tale of incestuous lust to explain that Zoroastrianism was in its origins a divinely revealed religion on par with the Abrahamic faiths:

> The Majūs [i.e., Zoroastrians] were a nation who possessed a religious book which they used to study. One of their kings one day got drunk and took his sister to a place outside the town. He was followed by four of his priests who witnessed his copulation with his sister. When he sobered up, he was told by his sister that the only way to save himself from being punished to death for what he had done in the presence of the four priests was to declare the act lawful and call it "Adam's law," because Eve was part of the body of Adam. He followed her advice and ordered accordingly, killing all who were against it. He then threatened to put to fire any objector and this brought them to submit to the new law. The Prophet accepted the *jizya* from them for their original religious book but did not allow inter-marriage and sharing of food with them.[15]

Muslim jurists called a *jizya*-paying individual a *dhimmī*. The name derives from the term "ʿ*aqd al-dhimma*," or covenant of protection.[16] Paying the *jizya* imposed upon the state the legal responsibility to protect the *dhimmī* from any internal or external aggression.[17] However, the *dhimmī* was not an equal among Muslim subjects. Muslim authorities of the 8th century increasingly worried about the harmful effects of Muslim exposure to non-Muslim beliefs and customs.[18] A series of discriminatory laws were therefore drawn up to assert Muslim superiority over other religious communities. Examples include prohibitions against riding horses, bearing arms, or erecting buildings that would tower over Muslim neighbours.[19] Even haircuts were imposed, because Near-Eastern Muslim culture associated long forelocks with respect and esteem.[20] Throughout Muslim history, the *jizya* and the discriminatory *dhimmī* rules have been inconsistently applied.[21] Nonetheless, within the juristic imagination, the *jizya* played the important role of enabling the formation of a multi-confessional empire founded upon Muslim dominance.

The convert occupied the liminal position between *jizya*-burdened *dhimmī* and *jizya*-free Muslim.[22] Conversion elevated his legal status and incorporated him within the dominant Muslim population. Muslim jurists agreed on his future exemption from *jizya* taxation, but wondered about his previously owed *jizya*. Did he owe the state a payment portion commensurate with the time he lived as a *dhimmī* prior to his conversion? If so, then the state should include his payment within its yearly poll tax collection. Or, alternatively, did conversion lead to a type of *jizya*-debt forgiveness? This, then, was the disputation topic that al-Dāmaghānī and al-Shīrāzī were to debate. Their founding school authorities had diverged on the question: Abū Ḥanīfa claimed the past *jizya* was cancelled but al-Shāfiʿī upheld its status as a continuing debt obligation.[23] The initial divergence of the two school masters might have had to do with their differing attitudes towards convert populations.[24] Abū Ḥanīfa championed the equality of all believers in his credal statement that "the faith of every Muslim is identical with that of the prophets and the angels."[25] In contrast, Jackson claims that al-Shāfiʿī had lingering worries about the corrupting influence of non-Arab converts on religious belief and practice.[26] In any event, al-Shāfiʿī left little guidance to his future school disciples on how they could defend his position. He produced no sustained argument for his reasoning and appears to have taken for granted that the collection of the convert's past *jizya* was a fair and practical way of dealing with someone in the process of transitioning into the Muslim community.[27] It was therefore left to future Shāfiʿīs to explain the merits of al-Shāfiʿī's position.

## The Shāfiʿī School as an Argumentative Repository for *Ijtihād*

Al-Shīrāzī predictably answered al-Dāmaghānī's query according to Shāfiʿī doctrine, affirming that the convert's past *jizya* remained owing.[28] Al-Dāmaghānī then asked him for evidence. In this section of my analysis,

I focus attention on the resources that al-Shīrāzī's legal school provided him in answering al-Dāmaghānī's request for evidence. We must first note that al-Shīrāzī's *ijtihād* on the convert's *jizya* had begun long before he debated al-Dāmaghānī. In some sense it had begun before he was a *mujtahid*, when he first undertook legal training at a young age in the province of Fars. During his numerous years of training there—and later in Basra and Baghdad—al-Shīrāzī was exposed to contested legal questions (*masā'il al-khilāf*),[29] and at some point, he would have come to learn about the debate between Shāfiʿīs and Ḥanafīs over the convert's *jizya*. He would also have learnt the many arguments that his predecessors, both within and outside of his Shāfiʿī school, had produced to justify their respective positions. By the time al-Shīrāzī had acquired sufficient training to be considered a *mujtahid*, he would have been expected to determine which of the arguments of his predecessors he found convincing. If he did not find any convincing, then he could modify their arguments or produce new evidence to determine the case.[30] As a Shāfiʿī, al-Shīrāzī began his *ijtihād* by seeking to uphold school doctrine: since his Shāfiʿī colleagues held similar methodological and substantive legal commitments to his own, he could presume that their position on the convert's *jizya* would offer him more guidance than his rival Ḥanafī school.[31] In short, when our two men met for disputation, we can suppose that al-Shīrāzī had already investigated the legal arguments of jurists on the question of the convert's *jizya*. How committed he was to a particular piece of evidence is unknown. But what is certain is that through the disputation, al-Shīrāzī would have the opportunity to further test the evidence he considered plausible.[32]

Al-Māwardī's *Ḥāwī*, a text that al-Shīrāzī knew and respected, shows us how the collective labours of Shāfiʿīs over generations provided an argumentative repository from which a jurist could draw in making his *ijtihād*. If al-Shāfiʿī himself had left al-Shīrāzī without argumentative guidance on why he imposed the payment of the convert's past *jizya*, the same could not be said of his disciples. Their assiduous labours had produced numerous arguments that al-Shīrāzī could apply and test out in the arena of disputation.[33] I should note that the *Ḥāwī* only gives us a glimpse into the evidence of the Shāfiʿī school. Al-Shīrāzī himself signals throughout his biographical dictionary of jurists that he also read several different authors of substantive law[34] and found in them valuable arguments about the law. Nonetheless, as a lengthy reporting of Shāfiʿī doctrine, al-Māwardī provides some sense of the many options that al-Shīrāzī possessed when performing *ijtihād* on the convert's *jizya*.

According to the *Ḥāwī*, Shāfiʿīs attempted to ground the school position on the convert's *jizya* in scriptural sources. They invoked the pithy *ḥadīth*, "*al-zaʿīm ghārim.*"[35] Jurists from all legal schools knew this *ḥadīth* well. They commonly interpreted the word "*al-zaʿīm*" as referring to one who assumes financial liability (synonymous with the word "*kafīl*" or "*ḍāmin bi'l-māl*").[36] The word appears in the well-known Qur'anic story of Joseph, the son of Jacob. When Joseph surreptitiously places the king's goblet within his brother Benjamin's satchel, he states that whoever finds the goblet will be handsomely rewarded with a camel-load of provisions, adding the words, "of this, I am *zaʿīm* [i.e., I accept liability]" (*Yūsuf*:72). The Shāfiʿīs invoked the *ḥadīth* to suggest that *dhimmīs* had accepted liability to pay for their year's *jizya* during the tax collection season. *Dhimmī* liability involved a debt obligation that the new convert could not escape.

The scriptural evidence for this Shāfiʿī position was thin. A Ḥanafī could dismiss the *ḥadīth*'s relevance for its ambiguity; after all, no mention of *dhimmīs* is made, and nothing precludes assuming that *dhimmī* indebtedness is forgiven with conversion. The Shāfiʿīs could make no pretense that they relied on perspicuous textual evidence. In fact, their Ḥanafī opponents had stronger scriptural evidence in their favour, since they invoked more relevant *ḥadīth*: "There is no *jizya* for the Muslim" and "[Conversion to] Islam erases what came before it [*al-Islām yajubb mā qablahu*]."[37] Shāfiʿīs sought to overcome this scriptural evidence by offering their own alternate interpretation. For them, the first *ḥadīth* merely meant no *new jizya* could be imposed upon the convert, leaving unaddressed his past *jizya*. As for the second *ḥadīth*, they claimed that it referenced the forgiveness of a convert for his past sins, not his financial obligations.[38]

Given the shaky textual foundation for their position, the Shāfiʿīs began to search their doctrinal corpus for an analogous substantive legal case that could serve as evidence for the convert's obligation to pay his past *jizya*. In fact, as Islamic law developed, juristic arguments were increasingly analogy-based.[39] The reason was partly that few unambiguous texts provided sufficient guidance on legal cases.[40] *Qiyās*-based reasoning could further bolster a given doctrine. Moreover, *qiyās*-based arguments also allowed jurists to explore the true intent of the law. Analogical reasoning depended upon identification of an *ʿilla*, literally meaning "cause" but often translated in Western academic texts as *ratio legis* or reason for legislation. Analogical reasoning applied the *ʿilla* of a base case to a derivative one. Cross-referencing the *ʿilla* of seemingly disparate legal cases permitted jurists to find consistent patterns in divine law.[41] The intensified use of analogical argument created the effect of a pairing game within the juristic community. Jurists both within and across schools debated which two laws were analogous and, as a consequence, which one among many potential legislative causes was correct.

According to al-Māwardī, Shāfiʿīs suggested various possible analogical cases to pair with the convert's *jizya*.[42] Some compared the *jizya* to debts. Conversion did not function like a lottery ticket absolving a debtor from paying his creditors, and neither should it nullify his past *jizya*. Others compared the *jizya* to renting costs: the convert needed to pay his *jizya* just as he needed to pay his rent. Finally, a third possible *qiyās*, one that al-Māwardī himself favoured, compared the *jizya* to the land tax known as the land-*kharāj*. The convert continued to owe his land tax and, therefore, he continued to owe his *jizya*.[43] The Ḥanafīs, in turn, produced critiques of the Shāfiʿīs' analogies. Regarding the debt analogy, they invoked the case of wedding dowries to show that not all debts continued after conversion.[44] They pointed out that a wedding dowry between idolators (*mushrikīn*) was no longer owed if one party converted to Islam before consummating the union (*qabla al-dukhūl*).[45] The Shāfiʿīs had also come up with possible defences to this objection: the wedding dowry was cancelled not because of conversion per se, they maintained, but rather because conversion mandated the couple's divorce (a Muslim being prohibited from remaining married to an idolater).[46] Divorce, then, was the real legal cause cancelling the dowry in this case. Two centuries of debate had created an argumentative back and forth between the two juristic camps.[47]

The Shāfiʿī literature's rich argumentative repository provided al-Shīrāzī with several options to draw on in effectuating his own *ijtihād*. His choice would depend upon what he himself believed to be the strongest arguments.[48] However, school literature alone was often insufficient to give a jurist like al-Shīrāzī a full sense of arguments' strengths and weaknesses. Even detailed books like the *Ḥāwī* often listed an argument without offering insight into opposing schools' objections to it. In instances when such objections were provided, as in the above-mentioned case of a convert's debts, the text at best gave a brief summation of each side. A jurist might therefore struggle to fully assess an argument's strength by study alone. Hence, the disputation was an essential part of his *ijtihād* in that it allowed him to more fully test a potentially strong yet still tentative argument. Al-Shīrāzī would have the opportunity to witness his chosen argument's merit through his disputation with al-Dāmaghānī.[49]

## Modifying Arguments: The Analogy between the *Jizya* and the Land-*Kharāj*

Let us return to our disputation to see how al-Shīrāzī relied upon his legal school's repository of arguments to fulfil his duty of *ijtihād*. Al-Shīrāzī defended the Shāfiʿī position on the convert's *jizya* by drawing upon al-Māwardī's preferred evidence, that is, the *qiyās* comparing the *jizya* to the land-*kharāj*.[50] What is the land-*kharāj*? The term "*kharāj*" itself referred to any tax imposed upon non-Muslims.[51] Jurists identified the *jizya* as one of two types of *kharāj*; the second was the land-*kharāj*.[52] The Shāfiʿīs imposed the land-*kharāj* on conquered non-Muslim peoples whose treaties of surrender stipulated a yearly payment of agricultural goods.[53] The land remained under its non-Muslim population's ownership, while the amount owed depended upon the terms of the treaty, though records suggest that early Muslim conquerors calculated amounts based on population size.[54] The agricultural goods collected secured for the non-Muslim population the protection and residency rights afforded by the *ʿaqd al-dhimma* and the Shāfiʿīs therefore did not impose an additional *jizya*.[55] If a non-Muslim among the population of this land converted, he would become exempt from the land-*kharāj* in the future.[56] However, if a convert had not yet paid his accrued land-*kharāj*, he was still liable for it. On the basis of this continued obligation, al-Shīrāzī contended that the past *jizya* also remained an obligation after conversion.[57]

But al-Shīrāzī nonetheless articulated his analogy slightly differently than al-Māwardī does in the *Ḥāwī*. Al-Māwardī writes: "The *jizya* is wealth that is owed because of disbelief [*māl mustaḥaqq bi'l-kufr*]; therefore what is owed is not cancelled after conversion, just as in the case of the land-*kharāj*."[58] In contrast al-Shīrāzī states: "the *jizya* is one of two forms of *kharāj* [*aḥad kharājayn*]: because [the *jizya*] is owed when one is in a state of disbelief [*kufr*], conversion does not cancel it, by analogy to the land-*kharāj*."[59] The wording of each analogy conveys nearly the same meaning, since *kharāj* itself is a tax "owed because of disbelief." Nonetheless, by drawing attention to the fact that the *jizya* and the land-*kharāj* fall under the same genus (*jins/nawʿ*), al-Shīrāzī created a presumption that cases possessing the same genus were subject to the same laws. Al-Dāmaghānī would therefore need to contest this assumption in his refutation.

The lack of extant legal manuals makes it impossible to know whether al-Shīrāzī was the first to present the analogy between the *jizya* and land-*kharāj* in this manner. It is quite possible that other jurists also deployed it. Regardless, the existence of variations in school arguments reflects jurists' commitment to not only learning from but also improving the thought of their predecessors. We know that al-Shīrāzī was not unique in modifying standard school arguments because al-Māwardī tells us that "some jurists from Khurasan" also presented the analogy between the *jizya* and the land-*kharāj* slightly differently.[60] These slight variations reflect a process of refinement whereby jurists built upon and modified the arguments of their legal school.

## Testing for Doctrinal Consistency

We now know that a jurist's *ijtihād* began with the examination of conflicting evidence on contested legal questions. We also know that his belonging to a legal school shaped but did not ultimately determine the evidence he favoured as he performed *ijtihād*. But we still have a poor sense of how disputation enabled a jurist to test his favoured argument and how this testing impacted his legal reasoning. As we examine al-Dāmaghānī's objections to al-Shīrāzī's analogy, it will become evident that al-Shīrāzī's success in the disputation depended on showing his analogy's methodological consistency with his reasoning across legal cases.[61] In effect, al-Dāmaghānī's critique permitted al-Shīrāzī to determine if he could justify invoking the *jizya*/*kharāj* analogy in light of his remaining doctrinal commitments. In what follows, I provide a concise overview of al-Dāmaghānī's three objections and the argumentative threads ensuing from each. I omit certain claims to avoid a cumbersome reading of the disputation. Each thread reveals the interconnected nature of classical law, wherein a jurist's arguments supporting his position on one legal question could discredit his position on another.

Before turning to these objections, it is well to note that al-Dāmaghānī could not argue against the claim that the land-*kharāj* remained owing after conversion. The Ḥanafīs agreed with the Shāfiʿīs on this point. They imposed the land-*kharāj* on any land whose inhabitants were non-Muslim at the time of its conquest.[62] Ḥanafīs considered that the tax status of a territory did not change once it was established. Thus, territories would continue to be subject to the land-*kharāj* regardless of their inhabitants' conversion or Muslim immigration to the territory. Instead, al-Dāmaghānī would need to undercut al-Shīrāzī's claim that the law on the convert's land-*kharāj* should be extended to the *jizya*.

## The Two *Zakāt*

Al-Dāmaghānī began by raising the possibility that the payment of the *jizya* might be subject to a condition (*sharṭ*) that the land-*kharāj* is not. More specifically, it is possible that only the *jizya* is conditional upon a *dhimmī* remaining non-Muslim until the time the *jizya* is collected. If so, then the analogy between the *jizya* and the land-*kharāj* would be faulty, despite the two sharing a common genus, and al-Shīrāzī would have committed a methodological error. To support his position, al-Dāmaghānī provided the example of two other cases that also share a common genus but are subject to different conditions: the two types of mandatory charity or alms tax, known as *zakāt*. To understand al-Dāmaghānī's argument, let me elaborate upon the two types of *zakāt*s he invoked. The first type is the *zakāt al-māl*. Both Shāfiʿīs and Ḥanafīs stipulated that this mandatory charity ought to be paid based on yearly accrued wealth, affirming that it is levied on various forms of wealth including gold and silver, livestock, agricultural yield, and business goods.[63] The amount owed varies depending on the form of wealth form. The second type of *zakāt*, *zakāt al-fiṭr*, is due at the end of the month-long fast of Ramadan. The *zakāt al-fiṭr* is imposed upon an individual and consists of a small portion of a food staple such as a grain, dates, or grapes.[64]

Al-Dāmaghānī reminded al-Shīrāzī that a necessary condition for the *zakāt al-māl* is the payer's possession of a minimum specified amount (*niṣāb*) of each form of wealth.[65] For instance, al-Shīrāzī states in the *Muhadhdhab* that one cow is to be taken for every thirty cows: if a person owns only twenty-nine cows, she is not obliged to pay *zakāt* on cattle.[66] In contrast, the *zakāt al-fiṭr* is not subject to the condition of a *niṣāb*. Rather, it is an obligation so long as the payer possesses sufficient wealth to meet his family's basic needs over and above the charity amount.[67] Thus even if the two *zakāt*s share the same genus, one is subject to a condition that the other is not. Just as the condition of the *niṣāb* applies to one *zakāt* but not the other, it is entirely plausible that remaining non-Muslim until tax-collection season is a condition of the obligation to pay the *jizya* but not the land-*kharāj*.[68] If this were true, al-Shīrāzī's argument would have failed to prove the *jizya* is still owing after conversion.

Al-Shīrāzī was ready to defend his analogy against accusations of methodological overreach. Al-Shīrāzī explained that the *zakāt al-fiṭr* is not conditional upon a *niṣāb* because its calculation method does not require it. In the case of the *zakāt al-fiṭr*, the law imposes the same monetary amount upon all individuals, becoming a debt attached to their persons (*al-dhimma*). As a result, the *zakāt al-fiṭr* is calculated independently of an individual's various types of financial assets.[69] In contrast, the *zakāt al-māl* is imposed upon an individual's specific or tangible wealth (*al-'ayn*). For instance, a man pays the *zakāt al-māl* from the wealth he holds based on his possession of a specific group of cows. Moreover, the *zakāt al-māl* increases as one possesses more of a given type of wealth. The *niṣāb* functions as a necessary calculation method for determining the amount due on each wealth type. In contrast, al-Shīrāzī claimed, there is no justification for making the payment of the *jizya* and not the land-*kharāj* conditional upon remaining non-Muslim until the tax is collected.

Al-Dāmaghānī was doubtful that the *niṣāb* ought to be considered indispensable to the calculation method for the *zakāt al-māl*. He pointed out that, like the *zakāt al-māl*, financial compensation in injury cases is also calculated based on the tangible wealth of the perpetrator (*'ayn al-jānī*), but it is not based on the condition of a *niṣāb*.[70] Thus, while compensation is calculated differently depending on the wealth type of the perpetrator—whether he owns cows or camels, livestock or textiles, etc.—the calculation does not depend on the perpetrator's possession of a specified amount.[71] Al-Shīrāzī made short shrift of this argument.[72] He rebutted that he never claimed all financial obligations based on tangible property (*al-'ayn*) necessitated a *niṣāb*; rather he only claimed this to be true of the two types of *zakāt*.

Al-Dāmaghānī then presented a stronger argument. He claimed that the *niṣāb* is not essential to the calculation of the *zakāt al-māl* because Shāfi'īs themselves dispensed with it when calculating the charity owed on currency. The Shāfi'īs imposed ½ a *mithqāl* on an initial *niṣāb* of 20 *mithqāls* of gold and 5 *mithqāls* on 200 *mithqāls* in silver (*mithqāl* being a unit of measure used in the Prophet's hometown of Mecca). However, after a person's gold or silver exceeds these amounts, the two metals become subject to a *zakāt*-rate of 2.5 percent, regardless of whether they reach a second *niṣāb* (i.e., an additional 20 *mithqāls* of gold or 200 *mithqāls* of silver).[73] This method of calculation stands in contrast to methods pertaining to other forms of wealth, such as livestock, for which an animal is taken only when an additional *niṣāb* is reached (one cow for thirty, two for sixty, three for ninety). Al-Shīrāzī rebutted: on the surface, he and the Shāfiʿīs seemed to dispense with a second *niṣāb* for currency, but in reality, a second *niṣāb* of 20 dinars and 200 dirhams was still their basis of calculation. Al-Shīrāzī explained that what changes between the calculation of the first *niṣāb* and the second *niṣāb* is that the second *niṣāb* is subject to fractional amounts.[74] Thus, the rate of 2.5 percent is equivalent to imposing ½ a *mithqāl* on an additional 20 *mithqāls* of gold. Al-Shīrāzī claimed that the Shāfiʿīs would have obligated fractional amounts on livestock too if possible, but because animals cannot be divided into fractions without killing them, they dispensed with this requirement.[75]

Al-Dāmaghānī then sought to cast doubt on al-Shīrāzī's claim that the *zakāt al-māl* possesses a *niṣāb* because it is imposed on tangible wealth (*al-ʿayn*), in contrast to the *zakāt al-fiṭr*, which is levied as a personal debt. Al-Dāmaghānī claimed that al-Shāfiʿī himself had two different opinions on the *zakāt al-māl*. According to one opinion, *zakāt al-māl* is indeed an alms tax on tangible goods, as al-Shīrāzī maintained. But according to al-Shāfiʿī's other opinion, *zakāt al-māl* is a personal debt attached to one's legal person or *dhimma*. (The Shāfiʿīs in al-Shīrāzī's day continued to transmit both of al-Shāfiʿī's two opinions on the subject.[76]) Al-Shīrāzī responded by rejecting the validity of the claim that the *zakāt al-māl* is a personal debt, arguing that it makes no sense to calculate the *zakāt al-māl* based on a portion of a person's tangible wealth unless this tangible wealth is also the object of taxation.

Already, two points must be highlighted about this thread of the disputation. First, we see that the viability of al-Shīrāzī's analogy between the *jizya* and the land-*kharāj* depended on his methodological consistency across legal cases. Thus, al-Shīrāzī needed to disprove the possibility that the *jizya* is subject to a condition that the land-*kharāj* is not (namely the payer's continued status as a non-Muslim until tax-collection). To do so, al-Shīrāzī argued that the two *kharājs* are distinct from the two *zakāts*. He accounted for the condition of the *niṣāb* for the payment of the *zakāt al-māl* by showing that *zakāt al-māl* is calculated from tangible forms of wealth like livestock, while the *zakāt al-fiṭr* is calculated as a fixed sum for every individual. He concluded that no such distinctions between the two *kharājs* might account for why the application of the *jizya* would be subject to a condition that the land-*kharāj* is not. Thus, we begin to see how interconnected a jurist's legal reasoning was: the soundness of his reasoning on one aspect of the law could not be divorced from his reasoning on another.

Second, we see that al-Shīrāzī is not committed to school authority so much as to ensuring the soundness of his own thought. This precedence is evident in his rejection of al-Shāfiʿī's position that the *zakāt al-māl* is an individual debt (levied from a person's *dhimma*). I should add that al-Shīrāzī did not simply reject the view that *zakāt al-māl* is a debt obligation for the sake of disputation. We know this because he also rejected the opinion in the *Muhadhdhab*.[77] In short, the disputation reveals how the testing of evidence and the attempt to ensure consistency across one's legal doctrine also meant committing to views that sometimes departed from one's peers. These two observations will receive further support as we move to examining the disputation's subsequent threads.

## Enslavement and Execution

Al-Dāmaghānī's second objection drew on two legal examples from the laws of war, concerning the execution and the enslavement of military prisoners. As in his first objection, al-Dāmaghānī sought to show that al-Shīrāzī's analogical reasoning depended upon unfounded assumptions. Al-Dāmaghānī's examples were intended to show that while conversion sometimes annuls the laws governing non-Muslims, at other times it has no impact on them. If successful, al-Shīrāzī would be constrained to admit that conversion could impact the *jizya* and the land-*kharāj* differently. Al-Dāmaghānī's examples can best be understood if we first explain jurists' prior discourse around prisoners of war. When a population was overrun and captured in combat, Ḥanafī and Shāfiʿī jurists considered a ruler to have several options regarding male prisoners old enough to serve in an army.[78] One was to allow them to continue to live on their lands and to impose the *jizya* upon them. Two other grimmer options were to either execute or enslave the lot of them.[79] However, the ruler's alternatives were constrained if the population converted to Islam, in which case execution would cease to be a viable option,[80] though the ruler could nonetheless keep the captive population enslaved.[81] Al-Dāmaghānī reasoned that if conversion impacts laws on enslavement and execution differently, then the same might be true of the *jizya* and the land-*kharāj*: that is, conversion before payment might cancel the former but not the latter.[82]

In response, Al-Shīrāzī contended that slavery and execution did not share the same genus, unlike the *jizya* and the land-*kharāj*. There was therefore no reason to believe that slavery and execution would be subject to the same laws: "When genera are different, it is permissible for laws to differ as well."[83] Al-Dāmaghānī answered by pointing out that even if enslavement and execution belong to separate genera, all that matters is that they possess the same legal cause (i.e., disbelief); as a result, he suggested, they parallel the dependence of the *jizya* and *kharāj* upon disbelief. Al-Shīrāzī defended his disagreement by presenting the example of the Friday sermon and the Friday prayer.[84] Although both are obligations upon adult male Muslims, they are nonetheless governed by different laws. For instance, ritual purification is necessary for the latter but not the former.

Al-Shīrāzī also posited a distinction between enslavement and execution to explain the varying impact of conversion in these two cases.[85] He claimed that post-conversion enslavement is simply the "continuation of prior captivity [*istidāmat al-riqq*]," whereas execution is a new act that cannot be legitimately imposed upon Muslims.[86] In response, al-Dāmaghānī noted that if execution is to be cancelled by conversion, then so too is the *jizya*, since both are examples of cases in which the ruler has the right to undertake an action against a non-Muslim but has not yet done so. Thus, just as execution can be cancelled by conversion, so too can the *jizya*.[87] Al-Shīrāzī was not ensnared by the move and simply reasserted that the execution of prisoners and the *jizya* do not possess a common genus. As a result, one cannot say that if execution is cancelled after conversion. then so too is the *jizya*.[88]

As with the first objection on the two *zakāt*s, al-Dāmaghānī's second objection leads al-Shīrāzī to consider whether his analogy is consistent with his positions on other legal questions. If al-Shīrāzī treats the impact of conversion differently for enslavement than for execution, then he must recognize that conversion might also impact the *jizya* differently than the land-*kharāj*. Yet this is where al-Shīrāzī's formulation of the analogy helps him overcome his opponent's objection. Al-Shīrāzī retains consistency by claiming that the *jizya* and the land-*kharāj* share the same genus and, as such, can be expected to be impacted by conversion in analogous ways. The same cannot be said of execution and enslavement. Again, we see how the disputation serves to test not only the legal question under review, but also other legal questions that might reveal contradictions in al-Shīrāzī's methodology. In other words, al-Dāmaghānī helped al-Shīrāzī refine his thinking on all legal questions pertaining to conversion, rather than solely on the question of the *jizya*. The final thread, discussed next, reveals still more strongly how the disputation led al-Shīrāzī to revisit the consistency of his reasoning on the convert's *jizya* with his positions on other legal questions.

## The *Jizya* and the *'Ushr*

Al-Dāmaghānī's final objection was more decisive than the first two. Until that point, he had limited himself to pointing out two assumptions in al-Shīrāzī's thought: (1) that the two *kharāj*s are subject to the same conditions and (2) that conversion impacts each of them identically. Al-Dāmaghānī claimed that these assumptions were unfounded, but al-Shīrāzī provided an account of his methodological commitments that justified his analogy. Now, al-Dāmaghānī turned head-on towards explaining why the land-*kharāj* endures post-conversion but not the *jizya*. He began by explaining that the land-*kharāj* has a Muslim equivalent in the *'ushr*. The *'ushr* is a 10% tax imposed on the agricultural product of Muslim-owned lands.[89] It is a type of *zakāt al-māl*. Al-Dāmaghānī explained that, just as the land-*kharāj* is a non-Muslim land tax, the *'ushr* is a Muslim land tax. Moreover, they share roughly the same legal cause: namely, land use and benefit from its crop.[90] In fact, no land-*kharāj* or *'ushr* is due on flooded or destroyed agricultural territory (*al-mustaghdar aw mā yabṭul al-intifā' bihi*).[91] Al-Dāmaghānī reasoned that it is because of this similarity between the land-*kharāj* and the *'ushr* that the law continues to demand payment of the accrued land-*kharāj* after conversion. In contrast, the *jizya* is a non-Muslim tax for which no Muslim equivalent exists, and therefore conversion cancels any owing amount.[92] In effect, al-Dāmaghānī had provided al-Shīrāzī with a methodological principle that purportedly undercut his argument: namely, that when an analogous law exists for both Muslims and non-Muslims, conversion has little effect on the law's continuation.

Al-Shīrāzī provided two rebuttals. First, he denied the similarity between the land-*kharāj* and the *'ushr*.[93] For instance, al-Shīrāzī noted that the *'ushr* is calculated based on agricultural yield rather than the area of the land used.[94] Second, al-Shīrāzī claimed that there is indeed an equivalent of the *jizya* for Muslims: the *zakāt al-fiṭr*. The *zakāt al-fiṭr* resembles the *jizya* in that it is also calculated on a per individual basis, thus acting like a poll tax. Thus, al-Shīrāzī concluded, if it is permissible to impose the payment of the past land-*kharāj* because of the *ʿushr*, then the *jizya* can continue too because of the *zakāt al-fiṭr*.

The three threads that I have analyzed in this section show the deep intertwinement of laws within the complex doctrinal space of Shāfiʿism. Al-Shīrāzī's reasoning on the *zakāt*, *ʿushr*, enslavement, Friday prayer, injury indemnities, and prisoner execution was potentially at odds with the analogy he drew between the *jizya* and the land-*kharāj*. The two *zakāt*s showed that laws sharing the same genus might be subject to different conditions. The examples of slavery and execution showed that conversion impacts laws imposed on non-Muslims differently. And finally, the example of the *ʿushr* allowed al-Dāmaghānī to argue that conversion need not cancel a law directed towards non-Muslims if there is a Muslim equivalent to it. But al-Shīrāzī demonstrated that his positions on these legal cases fit comfortably with his analogy between the *jizya* and the land-*kharāj*. He maintained that the two *zakāt*s are subject to different conditions because they are calculated differently. Likewise, he claimed that conversion could impact two cases differently so long as they do not share the same genus. Last, he denied that the land-*kharāj* and the *ʿushr* are subject to sufficiently similar causes to justify the continued payment of the land-*kharāj* after conversion; and, moreover, al-Dāmaghānī's logic would necessitate the continued obligation of the *jizya*, since it too has its Muslim equivalent in the *zakāt al-fiṭr*.

Notably, al-Shīrāzī's methodological considerations in the disputation are either absent or barely touched upon in books of *jadal* and *uṣūl al-fiqh*.[95] They are too specific to laws dealing with conversion to warrant separate chapters in books of legal theory.[96] This fact leads us to two conclusions. First, the disputation allowed jurists to examine methodological questions at a more concrete level than *uṣūl al-fiqh*, particularly methodological issues that impacted only a subsection of substantive law, like laws dealing with conversion or taxation.[97] Second, the arguments across subsections of substantive law were intertwined such that committing oneself to a position on one legal question could potentially have an impact on another legal question. Put otherwise, the soundness of classical school doctrine depended upon horizontal consistency across laws just as much as upon vertical consistency between the law and principles of legal theory.

In the next section, I show that the greatest challenge to consistency for al-Shīrāzī in determining the question of the convert's *jizya* stemmed from the question of whether or not the *jizya* was meant to humiliate non-Muslims. The analysis shows how the disputation shaped al-Shīrāzī's substantive legal positions and, in turn, the development of Shāfiʿī law.

## Is the *Jizya* Meant to Humiliate Non-Muslims?

Thus far, we have seen how the disputation permitted al-Shīrāzī to test the relative merits of an argument for a long-standing doctrine within his legal school. We have also seen that a crucial part of this testing entailed subjecting the argument in question to objections centering on the charge of methodological inconsistency across legal doctrine. But as the disputation between al-Shīrāzī and al-Dāmaghānī progresses, it becomes clear that one legal question in particular needed to be grappled with in determining whether the convert's past *jizya* ought to be paid: namely, whether the *jizya* should be taken in such a way as to humiliate non-Muslims. By examining this question in greater depth, it will be possible to better see the interconnectedness of legal doctrine in the classical era.

The strongest argument the Ḥanafīs mustered against the Shāfiʿīs in favour of cancelling a convert's past *jizya* was that the tax humiliated its payer. Al-Dāmaghānī quoted a Qurʾanic verse that seemed to attest to this function: "Fight those who do not believe in God or in the Last Day and who do not consider unlawful what God and His Messenger have made unlawful and who do not adopt the religion of truth, from among those who were given the scripture, until they give the *jizya* willingly while they are *ṣāghirūn*" (*al-Tawba* 9:29).[98] "*Ṣāghirūn*" is a derivative of the noun "*ṣaghār*," which means belittlement or humiliation. Al-Dāmaghānī argued that Muslims should not be humiliated and that, therefore, the convert's past *jizya* must be cancelled.[99] His position was common among Ḥanafīs, some of whom affirmed that the *jizya* was a type of punishment (*ʿuqūba*) for non-Muslims. "This is the reason it is called *jizya*," Burhān al-Dīn al-Marghīnānī (d. 593/1197 CE) would assert, "because the *jizya* is synonymous with *jazāʾ* [recompense, oftentimes referring to a penalty]."[100]

Al-Shīrāzī needed to answer al-Dāmaghānī's claim.[101] To do so, he partially followed the lead of other Shāfiʿīs, including al-Māwardī, who answered the Ḥanafī objection by making a distinction between being subject to the *jizya* and paying it.[102] According to these Shāfiʿīs, to be made subject to the obligation (*al-wujūb*) of paying the *jizya* is indeed humiliating, but the payment of the *jizya* (*al-adā'*) itself is not.[103] Al-Shīrāzī elaborated upon this argument in the disputation by stating that if a Muslim were to assume liability for a non-Muslim's *jizya*, the Muslim would not thereby humiliate himself when paying it.[104] But this line of argument had its weaknesses. Part of the problem was that some Shāfiʿī jurists insisted that the *jizya* be taken from non-Muslims "in a position of humiliation [*adhilla*] and defeat [*maqhūrīn*]."[105] It was therefore difficult to sustain a distinction between accruing the *jizya* and paying the *jizya*. To overcome this difficulty, al-Shīrāzī denied that the word "*ṣāghirūn*" meant humiliated: "It is said in the exegesis of the Qur'an [*tafsīr*] that the meaning [of *ṣāghirūn*] is that [the non-Muslims] are subject to Islamic laws [*annahum multazimūn li-aḥkām al-Islām*]."[106] In other words, the verse should be translated as meaning "fight those who disbelieve . . . until they give the *jizya* and they are subject to Islamic laws." The move was a skillful one: if the *jizya* was never meant to humiliate non-Muslims, then the convert's payment of the *jizya* could not be humiliating either.

Al-Shīrāzī was not the first Shāfiʿī to claim that "*ṣāghirūn*" should be interpreted as "subject to Islamic laws." Al-Māwardī notes that there were competing interpretations of the term.[107] But it is also clear from the *Kitāb al-Umm* that al-Shāfiʿī himself did not see these different interpretations as mutually contradictory: non-Muslims, under this logic, could be *ṣāghirūn* in both senses at once: humiliated precisely through subjection to Muslim rule.[108] In contrast, al-Shīrāzī, among other Shāfiʿīs, denied that "*ṣāghirūn*" meant humiliation.[109] The consequences were significant for non-Muslims living under Muslim rule. The Shāfiʿīs who interpreted *ṣāghirūn* to mean humiliation often affirmed that the Muslim ruler should subject non-Muslims to insults and even beatings as they paid the *jizya*. For instance, al-Juwaynī prescribed that the tax collector degrade non-Muslims: "the *dhimmī* is charged with handing over the *jizya* himself, bowing his head [*wa-yuṭaʾṭiʾ raʾsahu*] as he pours what he has with him onto the scale." Al-Juwaynī added that he is to "be grabbed by the beard [*al-akhdh biʾl-liḥya*] and hit on his cheekbones [*lahāzim*]."[110] Some Shāfiʿī texts also instructed the tax collector to chastise the dhimmīs by saying, "Oh enemy of God, give over God's right.'"[111] But al-Shīrāzī rejected claims that the *jizya* is to be collected with cruelty. In the *Muhadhdhab*, he compared the *jizya* to a payment of rent: just as a landlord has no right to insult his tenants, the ruler of a Muslim state should collect the *jizya* with gentleness (*bi-rifq*).[112]

It is plausible that al-Shīrāzī's stance was motivated by some deeper commitment towards the fair treatment of non-Muslims. There are grounds for speculations that al-Shīrāzī knew non-Muslims and developed friendships with them.[113] Alternatively, perhaps al-Shīrāzī's poverty made him sensitive to the plight of fellow humans.[114] But I would caution against such readings, particularly because al-Shīrāzī has no compunctions imposing other rules on non-Muslims that position them as inferior vis-à-vis Muslims.[115] Rather, the more likely historical explanations is that al-Shīrāzī found it logically inconsistent to support both the payment of the convert's *jizya* and the humiliation of non-Muslims through the *jizya*. He thus amended his reasoning on the humiliation of the non-Muslims to fit with his justification for the convert's payment of his past *jizya*.

Once again, then, al-Shīrāzī's justification for the convert's payment led him to revisit his reasoning on other legal questions. Al-Dāmaghānī sought to show that al-Shīrāzī's position on the convert's *jizya* committed him to accepting that non-Muslims be humiliated, a position he assumed al-Shīrāzī would recognize as unsound. In responding to al-Dāmaghānī, al-Shīrāzī needed to clarify his interpretation of the Qur'anic use of "*ṣāghirūn*."[116] He also needed to explain his position on whether the ruler should insult, beat, or demean non-Muslims when taking the *jizya*. The question of non-Muslim humiliation was therefore closely intertwined with al-Shīrāzī's position on the convert's *jizya*. Moreover, in the process of arguing for the convert's obligation to pay his past *jizya*, al-Shīrāzī rejected one Shāfi'ī position on non-Muslim humiliation in favour of another. This is the most prominent example of how a disputation tested consistency across legal cases.

## The Impact of Disputation on Substantive Law

We must now ask in what ways disputations changed the substantive legal doctrine of a school in the classical period. The answer to this question comes in two stages. First, we need to examine how the practice of disputation impacted al-Shīrāzī's substantive legal doctrine. But we lack sufficient information about al-Shīrāzī's life to fully answer this question. We do not know what his thinking on the issue of the convert's *jizya* was before he engaged in his disputation with al-Dāmaghānī. Was he committed to the analogy between the *jizya* and the land-*kharāj* in justifying Shāfi'ī doctrine? Or was he on the fence and wanted to see what objections might be raised against one of many plausible arguments for his school's position? It is also possible that he was committed to a different argument altogether but wanted to nonetheless consider the merits of his new formulation of the analogy between the *jizya* and the land-*kharāj*. Whatever the case may be, we can point to three facts that bear on the question of how disputations figured in the process of jurists' *ijtihād*. First, we know that the disputation created a testing ground for exploring the merits of a potential argument for the payment of the convert's past *jizya*. Al-Dāmaghānī exposed the potential inconsistencies between al-Shīrāzī's analogy and his reasoning on other legal questions, including the calculation of the two *zakāts* or the proscription against executing prisoners of war after their conversions.[117]

Second, we know that the disputation-as-testing-ground facilitated al-Shīrāzī's life-long search for God's law, or *ijtihād*. This *ijtihād* would eventually lead al-Shīrāzī to abandon the analogy between the convert's *jizya* and the land-*kharāj* in favour of another analogy. In his *Muhadhdhab*, written in the decades after his disputation with al-Dāmaghānī, al-Shīrāzī teaches his students that the convert's past *jizya* remains owing because "it is an exchange for the inviolability [of their lives] [*al-ḥaqn*] and residence [in Muslim lands] [*al-musākana*], and [the Muslim state] has fulfilled [their part of the exchange], so the obligation of this exchange is established, just as in the case of rent [*al-ujra*] after its benefit has been fulfilled [*ba'd istīfā' al-manfa'a*]."[118] Thus al-Shīrāzī came to see the analogy between the *jizya* and rent as stronger than the analogy between the *jizya* and the land-*kharāj*.[119] Third, we know that the testing for methodological consistency that al-Shīrāzī's thinking on the matter underwent led him to commit to some contested Shāfi'ī positions over others. For instance, the commitment to taking the *jizya* "gently" (*bi-rifq*) was at least partly the product of al-Shīrāzī seeing that this was the most viable position for a Shāfi'ī wishing to uphold his school's standard doctrine on the convert's past *jizya*.[120]

Having considered how the practice of disputation impacted al-Shīrāzī's own substantive legal doctrine, another question remains: How did the disputation impact other jurists belonging to his Shāfi'ī school? Again, we must begin by acknowledging the limitations of our analysis here. We do not know the extent to which the disputation on the convert's *jizya* shaped other jurists in attendance. We know from al-Bājī that disputations were sometimes transmitted orally. We also know from Ibn 'Aqīl and al-Ghazālī that disputations were intended for the benefit of the audience as much as the debaters. Thus, it is possible that the other jurists who heard al-Shīrāzī and al-Dāmaghānī were shaped by the two men's arguments. But we lack documentary evidence attesting to the impact of this disputation or of others on 11th-century Shāfi'īs. Nonetheless, insofar as al-Shīrāzī's disputations shaped his positions in the *Muhadhdhab* and the *Tanbīh*, they continued to exert a long-term influence on his legal school: these texts were commonly used in the commentaries of Shāfiʿīs long after al-Shīrāzī's death.[121] We can also locate al-Shīrāzī's influence in substantive legal texts that referenced him in the 12th century. In the same way that al-Shīrāzī quoted authorities like Abū Bakr al-Ṣayrafī, Ibn al-Qāṣṣ, and Abū al-Ṭayyib al-Ṭabarī, 12th-century Shāfiʿīs like ʿAbd al-Karīm al-Rāfiʿī later referenced al-Shīrāzī—alongside al-Shīrāzī's contemporaries, including al-Baghawī (d. 516/1122 CE), al-Māwardī, and Ibn al-Ṣabbāgh—in discussing the treatment of non-Muslims and the application of the *jizya*.[122]

Among extant 12th-century texts, al-Shīrāzī's influence is most evident in Abū al-Ḥusayn al-ʿImrānī's *al-Bayān fī Madhhab al-Imām al-Shāfiʿī*. Al-Subkī describes al-ʿImrānī (d. 558/1163 CE) as the most knowledgeable person on al-Shīrāzī's scholarship.[123] In the introduction to the *Bayān*, al-ʿImrānī explains the genesis of his text, stating that he began by studying the *Muhadhdhab* closely and "relied upon it [*ʿalayhi iʿtimādī*]" as the basis of his legal text. Afterward, al-ʿImrānī supplemented his knowledge by "reading other books" from the Shāfiʿī school to see where they disagreed with al-Shīrāzī. The consequence is that al-ʿImrānī reproduces much of al-Shīrāzī's thought from the *Muhadhdhab*, as well as the *Tanbīh*. For instance, al-ʿImrānī states in his *Bayān*: "The *jizya* is taken from [non-Muslims] as all other debts are taken, that is to say without harm either by word or deed."[124] This position would become increasingly rare in subsequent centuries, as Shāfiʿīs typically subscribed to the view that the *jizya* was a form of humiliation.[125]

Other Shāfiʿī jurists of the 12th century drew on different authorities, which in turn shaped their legal positions. Thus, we find al-Ghazālī reproducing al-Juwaynī's claims about the need to humiliate non-Muslims when collecting the *jizya*.[126] In short, the disputation impacted the doctrines of the legal school indirectly: disputations shaped a jurist's *ijtihād*, which, in turn, found its way into his writings, and these writings would be available for future generations to draw upon in the course of their own *ijtihād*.

## Conclusion

How, then, does this disputation help us understand the relationship between belonging to a *madhhab* and performing *ijtihād* in the classical period? To begin, we see that the *madhhab* offered al-Shīrāzī a repository of arguments from which to develop his *ijtihād* on the question of the convert's past *jizya*. Al-Shīrāzī's role as a jurist committed to *ijtihād* was to study these arguments, after which he would use disputations to test their merit. We know that this testing started in his earliest years of study and continued throughout his legal career. In his disputation with al-Dāmaghānī, al-Shīrāzī chose to invoke an amended version of a common analogy between the *jizya* and the land-*kharāj*. In the course of the disputation, al-Shīrāzī assessed whether this analogy fit with his methodological commitments on other legal topics such as the *zakāt*, enslavement, and the *'ushr*. Disputation, then, was a small but vital part of a jurist's *ijtihād* on contested legal questions. A jurist's *ijtihād* in turn made its way into his substantive legal texts like the *Muhadhdhab*, after which it became available for future jurists to draw upon in the course of their own *itjihād*. We can therefore detect a cyclical process in the relationship between classical legal schools and *ijtihād*: a jurist drew on the arguments of his legal school to perform his *ijtihād*, and, if his *ijtihād* had something new to contribute, it was added to an increasingly large corpus of arguments for future jurists to draw upon and test in their own disputations.

# 5

# Forced Marriage in Shāfiʿī Law

## Revisiting School Doctrine

Let us step away momentarily from the classical period and turn towards events closer to our own times. As the 2018 summer vacations approached, one school in the city of Leeds in the United Kingdom resorted to innovative methods in its attempts to prevent the possible forced marriage of teenage pupils. The school administration instructed its student body to discreetly stow spoons in their underwear. The strange plan assumed forced marriage to be a typically immigrant—and in this case largely South Asian—practice conducted through overseas travel in which a British girl was married to a foreign man from her parents' home country. The metal spoons were meant to set off detectors, thereby tipping off airport security who would then rescue the girl from an unwanted fate. Forced marriage cases have increasingly preoccupied Western governments. During the 2015 election campaign, the Canadian Conservative Party suggested implementing a so-called barbaric cultural practices hotline to prevent practices like forced marriage, which it deemed out of step with Canadian social values and norms. The move was part of a larger effort to foment Islamophobia and to position the party as a saviour of the West in the face of Muslim hordes standing at the nation's gates.

Such state ploys could easily be dismissed as part of a colonial legacy of misunderstanding and mischaracterizing non-Western peoples' historical traditions. But non-Muslims in government office are not alone in their strident condemnation of forced marriages. The matter has drawn increasing concern from Muslim circles who have repeatedly and unhesitatingly condemned the practice within their own communities.[1] For instance, the Canadian Council of Muslim Women (CCMW) adopted an anti-forced marriage position statement in 2014: "As a women's organization that is dedicated to the equality, equity and empowerment of Canadian Muslim women and our non-Muslim sister allies, the CCMW opposes forced marriage on the grounds that it infringes upon a girl's or woman's fundamental

*The Rise of Critical Islam.* Youcef L. Soufi, Oxford University Press. © Oxford University Press 2023.
DOI: 10.1093/oso/9780197685006.003.0006

human rights."[2] CCMW cited 219 documented cases of forced marriage in the Canadian province of Ontario. Muslim reformers today, though, face an uphill battle in their efforts to reinterpret centuries of Islamic law. The Shāfiʿī school, for instance, unambiguously asserted a father's right to determine his virgin daughter's spouse regardless of her feelings on the matter.[3] Some reformers choose to ignore this legal history in their anti-forced marriage campaigns, sometimes declaring the practice a cultural rather than a religious one. CCMW for its part, referred back to what it saw as the general scriptural intent of Islamic law, stating that "the Islamic Marriage contract is intended to fulfil both partners' physical, and spiritual needs, which cannot lawfully be entered [into] out of compulsion."[4]

This chapter is concerned with forced marriage and its internal Muslim critique. But it goes back in time, far from today's politically charged environment, to examine the stance of a Shāfiʿī jurist who, nearly a millennium ago, critiqued his school's doctrine on forced marriage in a clash-of-the-titans disputation against al-Shīrāzī. The context and motives of the critique differed considerably from those of today's arguments. In Arabic, the term used to designate forced marriage was *ijbār* (literally meaning coercion) and referred to the act of a woman's guardian contracting her marriage against her will. The debater in question was al-Juwaynī, who, at the time of the disputation, was hosting the newly arrived al-Shīrāzī in the northeastern city of Nishapur on a political mission to transmit caliphal letters to the Sultan Malikshāh and the Wazir Niẓām al-Mulk.[5] The whole of Nishapur's scholarly community must have been abuzz to see them together: here were the two Shāfiʿī professors of the prestigious Niẓāmiyya colleges of Nishapur and Baghdad at the height of their careers. The juristic community expected and possibly encouraged the two jurists to orchestrate what was sure to be a splendid debate gathering. Al-Juwaynī likely chose the topic of forced marriage because al-Shīrāzī was charged with arranging the marriage of the sultan's daughter to the caliph during his mission. But al-Juwaynī's critique was not motivated by a social urgency to prevent imminent harm to vulnerable women. In fact, outside of the disputation, al-Juwaynī affirmed the lawfulness of forced marriage. His legal opus, the *Nihāyat*, upheld the father's right to determine his virgin daughter's spouse.[6] Thus, his critique was the product of his role as the questioner in the disputation. After all, had he agreed with al-Shīrāzī the disputation would have ended quickly, and neither the two jurists nor those in attendance would have benefitted from the exposition.

But regardless of his own legal commitments, al-Juwaynī's critique was trenchant. What interest me in this chapter are the intellectual consequences of classical jurists' willingness to revisit long-held school doctrine: What happens when jurists like al-Shīrāzī and al-Juwaynī open up their doctrine to internal critique? To doubt? I show that this internal critique produced a re-examination of school doctrine, revealing its weaknesses and the plausibility of an alternative law. It allowed the jurists attending the disputation to imagine their school's history and development differently, to consider the possibility that marginal or rejected positions might be more meritorious than the books of their school predecessors had let on. I end by suggesting that al-Juwaynī's critique is useful to modern reformists in two ways: first, by showing the weaknesses of the position legitimating forced marriage; and second, by showing detractors of reformist thought that the commitment to critiquing the most entrenched legal positions has deep roots in the Islamic tradition.[7]

## Marriage Guardianship in Islamic Law

Understanding the disputation between al-Juwaynī and al-Shīrāzī on forced marriage necessitates some background knowledge on the concept of guardianship. Books of Shāfiʿī law record an amusing discussion topic referred to as "bridal specification" (*taʿyīn al-zawjayn*) that sheds light on what a marriage guardian (*al-walī*) is and does.[8] In a manner reminiscent of the tale of Jacob, Rebecca, and Rachel in the Hebrew Bible, jurists worried that a newly married husband might get confused about which of a man's two daughters was his new bride. The reason why such a mix-up could be a risk was that the Islamic marriage contract did not necessitate a bride's attendance. Her guardian, typically her father, could give her away alone. Thus al-Shīrāzī, who tackled the topic of *taʿyīn al-zawjayn* within his *Muhadhdhab*, explained that a father giving his daughter away sometimes needed to be circumspect with his words. There was little risk of mishap if the bride was present: he could simply say, "I marry you to her." In fact, even if he embarrassingly named his other daughter—saying, for instance, "I marry you to this one, Fāṭima," when her name was ʿĀʾisha—the marriage pronouncement remained valid because gestures confirming the correct daughter rendered the bride's name legally irrelevant.[9] However, if the bride was absent, her father could not say, "I marry you to my daughter" if he had more than one, because of the lingering possibility of mismatched intentions between the bride's father and the groom.

The discussion topic reveals the guardian's wide power to contract his ward's marriage within Islamic law. The female party to a marriage contract did not need to give her public approval to her union. In fact, the marriage contract was a typically male affair. The essence of the contract—"the only element of marriage uniformly agreed to be absolutely necessary to conclude a valid marriage," as Kecia Ali reminds us—"was the offer and acceptance, *ijāb* and *qābūl*, commonly between male guardian and groom."[10] The Ḥanafī school considered the marriage guardian dispensable, affirming the contractual validity of a union in which the bride represented herself.[11] Even they, however, took for granted male representation as a preferred practice.[12] Al-Juwaynī's Shāfiʿī school, for its part, was adamant on the necessary condition of male guardianship. Shāfiʿīs had many textual pieces of evidence within their argumentative arsenal. One prophetic *ḥadīth* pithily stated, "There is no marriage without a *walī*" (*lā nikāḥ illā bi-walī*).[13] Another asserted emphatically, "A woman who marries without her guardian's approval, her marriage is void, her marriage is void, her marriage is void . . ."[14] They also relied on Qurʾanic verses—among them the general statement that "men are the overseers of women" (*al-Nisāʾ*:34)—and on the story of one of the Prophet's companions who prevented his sister from remarrying her former spouse, saying to her ex: "I gave her in marriage to you and I preferred you over other potential suitors, but you divorced her. I will never give her in marriage to you again";[15] Shāfiʿīs concluded from this story that males had a right in the spousal determination of female relatives.

The main purpose of marriage guardianship was to preserve the honour of a woman and her family. Al-Māwardī noted that male guardianship offers protection against a husband who brings shame to a family.[16] A family avoided shame by evaluating the groom's suitability (*kafāʾa*) for the bride and her family. This concern with *kafāʾa* is found across the Sunni schools of law; however, each school posited differing standards of suitability. The Mālikīs, for instance, were known for embracing minimal and easily attainable standards.[17] The Shāfiʿīs, in contrast, provided the guardian with an expansive set of criteria on which to bar a potential suitor. Al-Juwaynī posited six Shāfiʿī standards of *kafāʾa*.[18] The first was religious reputation: although al-Juwaynī acknowledged the impossibility of knowing the internal spiritual state of a human being, he nonetheless affirmed that the public recognition of a man's religious rectitude (*ṣalāḥ fī dīn*) was a measure of his suitability.

The second was family lineage. Historically, this category of suitability was based on a presumption of Arab superiority: the Baghdad Shāfiʿīs asserted that "the non-Arab is not equal to the Arab" and therefore ranked a non-Arab man below an Arab woman.[19] They justified their position by pointing to the Arab origins of the Prophet Muḥammad. Unsurprisingly, this did not sit well with al-Juwaynī and his Persian colleagues. The Khurasanian Shāfiʿīs therefore undercut Arab racialism by affirming that the scholarly class also possessed noble lineage since Muḥammad had asserted that "The jurists are the inheritors of the prophets."[20] Thus a juristic family had legal grounds to refuse a suitor from a lay-Muslim family, whether Arab or non-Arab. The third standard related to the man's status as enslaved or free because, as al-Shīrāzī wrote, "there is shame for a free woman to obey her enslaved husband."[21] The fourth was profession: the Shāfiʿīs provided a hierarchical ordering of trades, affirming for instance the professional superiority of the cloth merchant or tailor over the less dignified cupper or weaver.[22] The fifth standard was physical integrity, that is, the possible physical and psychological defects of a groom. Relevant defects included leprosy, impotence, castration (*majbūb*), and insanity. Finally, some Shāfiʿīs included wealth as a final standard, but both al-Shīrāzī and al-Juwaynī dismissed this as an irrelevant worldly consideration.[23]

Regardless of juristic differences over standards of suitability, guardianship laws across schools were inextricably tied to patriarchal and patrilineal norms that jurists took for granted. They assumed that a marriage placed a woman under the authority of her husband and that therefore, if this husband was of lower social rank, the marriage would bring shame to the woman and her family. The reverse was not true, and thus most Shāfiʿīs applied suitability standards only to a groom. Al-Juwaynī considered that "a noble woman humiliates herself and debases her lineage by marrying the lowly, but there is no dishonour for a noble man in marrying a lowly woman."[24] Shame also passed on to all members of her paternal line (*al-ʿaṣabāt*). It was their good name, rather than the reputation of a groom's agnates, that would be sullied if the woman in question married someone of ill repute. Hence, they all had a stake in guardianship and an absent or deceased father would be replaced by another male representative from her father's side, based on a predetermined order.[25] Shāfiʿīs held that a bride without agnates should receive state representation, since "the sultan is the guardian of those without a [biological] guardian."[26] Thus, beyond scriptural arguments establishing the need for male guardianship, jurists were concerned about the honour of the patrilineally defined family. These concerns contextualize the arguments over the rights of marriage guardians that will figure within al-Shīrāzī and al-Juwaynī's disputation.[27]

All schools granted a marriage guardian the right to prevent a potential couple's union on suitability grounds.[28] Even the Ḥanafīs, who allowed for a woman's self-representation during the marriage contract, granted her guardian the right to petition a court to dissolve her marriage on the grounds of unsuitability.[29] But jurists also debated whether guardians were entitled to *decide* their ward's spouse. Could male guardians disregard bridal consent in contracting a marital union? The schools answered in both the affirmative and the negative: each one theorized both instances of valid forced marriage and instances where female consent was a precondition to the marriage contract. Among the most contentious cases was that of the "forced marriage of an adult virgin woman" (*ijbār al-bikr al-bāligh*—lit. the coercion of a postpubescent virgin). Whereas the Ḥanafīs prohibited the practice, the Shāfiʿīs allowed it. In questioning al-Shīrāzī on the validity of coercing the adult virgin into marriage, al-Juwaynī set the conditions for the Shāfiʿīs in attendance to revisit their long-held doctrine.

## Al-Shīrāzī's Arguments for Forced Marriage

### The Virgin Child vs. The Virgin Adult

Al-Shīrāzī commenced the disputation with a standard argument deployed by Shāfiʿīs against their Ḥanafī opponents to legitimate the forced marriage of an adult virgin.[30] The argument compared an adult virgin to a child (i.e., prepubescent) virgin: the adult woman in question, this argument maintained, "has remained in a virginal state, and therefore her father can force her into marriage in like manner to the virgin child."[31] The argumentative efficacy of the comparison depended upon the view—shared between Ḥanafīs and Shāfiʿīs—that a father could give away his virgin child without her consent (marriage consummation being postponed until each partner was of sufficient physical maturity).[32] Their agreement on the matter depended upon divergent rationales. Ḥanafīs believed all minors, boys and girls, could legally be forced into marriage, but not adults.[33] The Shāfiʿīs, in contrast, sanctioned forced marriage for all virgin females, child or adult. Al-Shīrāzī's comparison between the virgin adult and the virgin child could therefore have cornered a

Ḥanafī jurist arguing against the validity of forced marriage for adults, since a Ḥanafī would have been unable to attack al-Shīrāzī's base case in the analogy (the virgin child forced into marriage) without jeopardizing his own school doctrine.

But al-Juwaynī was not a Ḥanafī, and he was shrewd enough to point out to al-Shīrāzī that his reasoning was circular when deployed against a fellow Shāfiʿī.[34] How so? Al-Shīrāzī had assumed rather than proven virginity's causal relationship to forced marriage in the case of a minor. For a Shāfiʿī jurist like al-Juwaynī, to question the forced marriage of the adult also meant questioning the forced marriage of the minor, since both were allegedly the product of virginal status. Al-Juwaynī thus constrained al-Shīrāzī's options, making it necessary for him to withdraw his analogy and to present evidence for why virginity rendered bridal consent to a marriage unnecessary. Al-Shīrāzī then presented a prophetic statement as his evidence.

Before examining al-Shīrāzī's prophetic statement, I want to emphasize the relevance of al-Juwaynī's use of Shāfiʿī doctrine in the arguments he deployed in the disputation. Had al-Juwaynī drawn on Ḥanafī doctrine, in this case accepting the premise that minors could be forced into marriage, the usefulness of the disputation to both participants and attendees would have been very different. Al-Juwaynī's critique would have permitted al-Shīrāzī to sharpen his arguments against detractors outside of his school. But because al-Juwaynī drew on Shāfiʿī doctrinal positions, he presented al-Shīrāzī with an internal critique of forced marriage, one which allowed al-Shīrāzī to revisit the evidence in question from the standpoint of the Shāfiʿī school. Put otherwise, intra-*madhhabic* disputations provided a means of re-examining Shāfiʿī doctrine in light of the school's own claims across legal doctrine. In future sections, we will see over and again how al-Juwaynī's critique of al-Shīrāzī takes for granted and draws upon his Shāfiʿī doctrine.

## Coercion and Virginity

"The *ayyim* has a greater right over herself than her guardian [has over her]."[35] This was the prophetic statement al-Shīrāzī cited as evidence in favour of the forced marriage of virgins. But what was an *ayyim* and how did this concept relate to forced marriage? The term "*ayyim*" typically referred to an unmarried woman.[36] The Prophet's statement—which was, in fact, part of a longer *ḥadīth*—therefore affirmed an unmarried woman's superior right relative to her guardian. At first blush, the *ḥadīth* might appear to empower all women over their marriage guardians.[37] But al-Shīrāzī took two interpretative steps that made it possible for him to use the *ḥadīth* to justify the adult virgin's forced marriage. The first was to redefine "*ayyim*" to mean a sexually experienced woman. He explained to al-Juwaynī that "*ayyim*" here could not mean all unmarried women because the *ḥadīth* subsequently invokes the virgin (*al-bikr*): "The *ayyim* has a greater right over herself than her guardian; and the virgin is to be consulted."[38] Al-Shīrāzī explained that the juxtaposition of *ayyim* and virgin elucidated the speaker's intent. According to his reasoning, *ayyim* here excluded virgins from among unmarried women.[39] Thus the statement could be rephrased as "sexually experienced women have a greater right over themselves than their guardians [have over them]." The second interpretive step invoked a well-known though not uncontroversial methodological principle within books of legal theory known as the *a contrario* argument.[40] The *a contrario* argument assumed that when a legal ruling addresses only some within a group, then those in the group who are unaddressed are subject to the opposite ruling. A classic example was the mandatory charity (*zakāt*) on pasture-grazing sheep: the prophetic statement "On sheep grazing in open fields, *zakāt* is due [*fī sā'imat al-ghanam zakāt*]" was used to infer a charity exemption on stable-fed sheep.[41] In the context of the current *ḥadīth*, al-Shīrāzī reasoned that if the sexually experienced woman had a greater right over herself than her guardian, then the virgin necessarily had lesser right over herself, and her guardian could therefore decide her spouse without her consent.

## Al-Juwaynī's Alternative Interpretation

There were many ways to attack al-Shīrāzī's *ḥadīth* interpretation. For one, the method of *a contrario* argument was not without its critics.[42] Some jurists thought it wrong to use commands addressing some within a group to make conclusions about others. Accordingly, these jurists would have reasoned that a statement about sexually experienced women left virgins unaddressed. They would have therefore affirmed that no conclusive position on the forced marriage of virgins could be drawn. But even if one accepted the *a contrario* argument, the *ḥadīth*'s meaning remained ambiguous. For instance, the Ḥanafī scholar Jamāl al-Dīn al-Zayla'ī (d. 762/1361 CE) argued that applying the *a contrario* to virgins did not necessarily mean that the Prophet had intended to reference all virgins; perhaps the Prophet intended only to designate virgins of minority age, whose forced marriage Ḥanafīs accepted.[43] Al-Zaylaʿī also gestured towards the second part of the *ḥadīth*—"the virgin is to be consulted"—pointing out that "consultation is incompatible [*munāfⁿ*] with coercion."[44]

Al-Juwaynī, however, exploited another of the *ḥadīth*'s textual ambiguities. The statement "The sexually experienced woman has a greater right over herself" left one wondering what exactly was meant by "greater right." It was far from obvious that the right in question referred to coercive marital authority. Could it not refer to another guardianship-related right? Al-Juwaynī argued that the "greater right" of the sexually experienced woman in the *ḥadīth* referred to her right not to be married without first giving her verbal consent. Applying the *a contrario* to this interpretation of "greater right" did not mean that the virgin could be forced into marriage; rather it meant that a guardian could obtain a virgin's consent to the marriage *tacitly*—that is, she would be considered to have consented if she declined to explicitly reject the marriage. Al-Juwaynī's interpretation made sense according to a doctrine widely held within legal schools that distinguished between the necessary verbal consent of a sexually experienced woman and the tacit approval of a virgin.[45] No legal school demanded a virgin woman's verbal consent as a condition for the validity of her marriage contract. Juristic thought countenanced her possible shyness (*istiḥyāʾ*) in expressing sexual preferences and deemed that her tacit consent could be discerned through lack of explicit disapproval. But what evidence did al-Juwaynī have for his interpretation?

Al-Juwaynī presented two pieces of evidence. The first was that the *ḥadīth* speaks of the marriage guardian in an unqualified manner. This, according to al-Juwaynī, was a clue in discerning the prophetic intent behind the expression "greater right": had Muḥammad truly meant to refer to forced marriage, he would have specified that "the sexually experienced woman has a greater right over herself than *her father or grandfather*."[46] Al-Juwaynī explained that this specification would have been necessary because only a father or grandfather wielded the power to coerce a woman in marriage, according to Shāfiʿī doctrine. The Shāfiʿīs did not permit brothers, uncles, or other agnates to coerce their female relatives into marriage. Shāfiʿīs deemed that the father and grandfather alone could be trusted to exercise "complete care" (*kamāl al-shafaqa*) and concern for his daughter or granddaughter's well-being in choosing a marriage partner for her.[47] Since the *ḥadīth* referenced all potential marriage guardians when speaking about the relative rights of guardians and brides, its topic of concern could not be forced marriage.

Al-Juwaynī's second piece of evidence was the concluding part of the *ḥadīth*. The *ḥadīth* ends, "The virgin is to be consulted, and *her approval is her silence*."[48] According to al-Juwaynī, the mention of silence as tacit approval provided the contextual indicator that revealed the intent behind the Prophet's use of the expression "greater right." It showed that he was concerned with identifying the means by which approval is obtained, rather than establishing whose consent matters and whose consent can be disregarded.

Al-Juwaynī's interpretation in some ways mirrored Ḥanafī arguments. This is clear from al-Zaylaʿī's interpretation of the same *ḥadīth* in his text *Naṣb al-Rāya*. Al-Zaylaʿī writes, "the sexually experienced woman is proposed to directly and orders the guardian to give her away, but as for the virgin, it is her guardian that receives the proposal and he thereafter asks her consent . . . the sexually experienced woman's consent is her speech [*kalām*] and the virgin's is her silence."[49] But al-Juwaynī arrived at this conclusion in a distinctly Shāfiʿī way. His claim that the *ḥadīth* did not address the validity of forced marriage because neither the father nor the grandfather was specified as intended guardians would not have found favour with Ḥanafī jurists. Ḥanafīs could not have made this argument because they affirmed that any and all guardians—brother, uncle, or even state authority—had the right to coerce a prepubescent girl into an unwanted marriage.[50] Again, we see that al-Juwaynī drew on the Shāfiʿī tradition to critique one of his school's most entrenched doctrines. His use of specifically Shāfiʿī positions is important in showing how disputations allowed jurists to revisit school doctrine. In particular, disputations revealed both the weaknesses of standard Shāfiʿī positions and the possible merits of alternative positions, according to the school's own interpretive standards. As the disputation comes to a close, we will again see how al-Juwaynī drew on Shāfiʿī doctrine to question his school's long-standing commitment to forced marriage.

## Al-Shīrāzī's Rebuttal: The Laughing Bride and the Need for Verbal Consent

Al-Shīrāzī found farfetched al-Juwaynī's interpretation of the phrase "greater right *over herself*"[51] as referring to anything other than the marriage contract itself; he considered interpretations that linked "greater right" to verbal consent (*nuṭq*) to be a departure from the customary usage of the Arabic language. It would be like imagining an Arab using the word "camel," instead of using the common idiom "donkey," to designate an imbecile.[52]

Al-Shīrāzī also argued that the guardian's right to contract a virgin bride's marriage without her *verbal* consent was a sign that he did not need her *tacit* consent either. A sexually experienced woman, he contended, needs to vocalize her consent for her marriage contract precisely because she has the final say on whether the union will materialize; in contrast, a virgin can be silent because her consent is immaterial to the marriage contract's validity. Although al-Shīrāzī's claim relied upon an analogical survey of other legal contracts, there was also something commonsensical about his position.[53] A bride's verbalization of her consent prevented a situation where a guardian wrongly assumed consent. The Ḥanafīs gestured towards this possibility of mistaking consent in their discussion on when and how a guardian knows he has received consent from a virgin. They agreed that silence indicated consent, but what about a woman who laughed when her guardian told her of her future spouse? How was the guardian to interpret her sentiments? The Ḥanafī jurist Abū al-Ḥusayn al-Qudūrī thought that laughter was usually a sign of joy and therefore indicated consent.[54] But he cautioned the guardian to look out for derisive or mocking laughter indicative of the woman's displeasure. Likewise, crying made the guardian's assessment more difficult. Tears could indicate either sadness or joy. Al-Qudūrī reminded the guardian that silent tears, the type that come from feeling overwhelmed, should not necessarily be interpreted as displeasure.

In short, al-Shīrāzī contended that the requirement of verbal consent only applies to parties who have the right to accept or reject a marriage contract. Since the virgin did not need to verbalize consent, her consent was irrelevant to the validity of marriage. Al-Shīrāzī followed al-Shāfiʿī in viewing the virgin's consultation as a recommended, rather than obligatory, act. Al-Shāfiʿī had expressed praise for the guardian who consults his virgin daughter. He noted that it is a sign of prudence (*iḥtiyāṭ*) and good manners, and permits the guardian to assess the woman's likes. He also counselled the guardian "not to rush in giving her away except after informing her of her potential spouse, and it is reprehensible [*yukrah*] that her father marry her to someone he knows she dislikes."[55] But this recommendation could still legally be dispensed with.

## Paternalism and Female Autonomy

Before presenting al-Juwaynī's final objection to the forced marriage of virgins, I want to linger on two widely held Shāfiʿī assumptions about women's capacities. I do so via an examination of al-Shīrāzī's *Muhadhdhab*. The first assumption was that virgin women lacked sufficient experience to make proper marriage choices. Al-Shīrāzī considered virginity in marriage laws to stand in for inexperience with men—sexual inexperience, to be sure, but also a lack of experience with conjugal relationships more generally.[56] This is evident in his discussion of the word "virgin." The Arabic word that Shāfiʿīs used to denote virginity was "*bikāra*," which they defined as an intact hymen (*jildat al-ʿudhra*).[57] Al-Shīrāzī maintained that a sexually inexperienced woman with a broken hymen, although not literally a virgin according to the Arabic language, could also be subject to a forced marriage.[58] His reasoning was that her sexual inexperience legitimated paternal guidance. He concluded that a benevolent father knows better than his inexperienced daughter the type of match that could lead to a fulfilling and socially respectable married life. A sexually experienced woman, in contrast, was assumed to possess the requisite maturity and wisdom that made forced marriage both unnecessary and undesirable.[59]

The second assumption was that women—whether or not they were virgins—were "intellectually deficient [*nuqṣān ʿaqlihā*]."[60] Al-Shīrāzī tied the obligation of guardianship to this intellectual deficiency. He claimed that women can be "easily tricked [*surʿat inkhidāʿihā*]." As a result, guardianship was necessary to prevent women from making bad choices that could affect their happiness and the reputation of their agnates. This guardianship applied to all women, though only virgins could be coerced into an unwanted marriage. For al-Shīrāzī, then, the question of the virgin's forced marriage was shot through with assumptions concerning her capacity for autonomous choice.

In contrast, al-Juwaynī claimed that all sane adult women, virgins and non-virgins alike, were rationally capable of making independent choices about their marriage partners. "A woman," al-Juwaynī contended, only "requires guardianship when lacking the capacity for autonomy [*li-ʿadami istiqlālihā*] because of minority age or insanity."[61] He maintained that an adult woman "possessed all the requisite factors [*ijtamaʿa fīhā al-asbāb*]" that would legally permit her to choose her spouse, presumably so long as her union did not harm her family's honour.[62]

Like al-Juwaynī, the Ḥanafīs critiqued the Shāfiʿī position on forced marriage by pointing out that the law considered adult women financially independent and entitled to spend their wealth as they saw fit (*al-taṣarruf fī al-māl*).[63] They therefore drew an analogy between marriage law and property law in order to affirm an adult woman's legal autonomy in the marriage contract. In both cases, the age of majority, determined through the onset of her first menses, marked the end of a woman's "intellectual immaturity [*quṣūr ʿaqlihā*]" and permitted her to accede to the full legal rights afforded to her by adulthood.[64] Moreover, the Ḥanafīs also justified female intellectual independence by pointing out that women were "addressed within Qur'anic scriptural injunctions [*tawajjuh al-khiṭāb*]." If God thought them responsible enough to carry the burden of the religious law and the obligation to perform deeds like prayer and fasting, then there could be no doubt about their intellectual capacities.[65]

Al-Juwaynī, however, did not invoke an analogy from property law. Rather, he relied upon the concept of *maṣlaḥa* or human benefit to uphold a woman's autonomy in marriage. This concept is known to many contemporary Muslims because of its wide impact on modern Muslim thought.[66] Modern reformers have often invoked *maṣlaḥa* to justify changes to long-established Islamic laws. Ebrahim Moosa compares the modern use of *maṣlaḥa* to a utilitarian approach in which public benefit justifies overriding the textual injunctions of scripture.[67] For example, the 19th-century Egyptian reformer Muḥammad ʿAbduh once argued in favour of usury or interest-based financial transactions because of the Egyptian government's need to compete in increasingly interconnected global markets. ʿAbduh considered that Muslims who invoked Qur'anic verses about the prohibition of usury placed Muslim society in harm.[68] Little surprise then, that the concept has sometimes provoked unfavourable responses from Muslims fearing a preference for Western values over God's commands.[69]

But for al-Juwaynī, *maṣlaḥa* was not a reformist tool for overriding textual commands.[70] In fact, it was just the opposite. *Maṣlaḥa* was first and foremost a hermeneutic method of *discovering* the true intent and meaning of Qur'anic verses and *ḥadīth*s. Al-Juwaynī championed the view that scriptural commands were to be read through the lens of human benefit.[71] His reasoning was that God, out of his infinite mercy, had designed a legal system that, if faithfully followed, would lead to human flourishing.[72] A jurist contemplating various possible scriptural interpretations should therefore gravitate towards the one conducive to human benefit. He should deem a purported legal cause as suitable (*munāsib*) only if he could reasonably find within it a justifiable good for individual and society. Once a jurist discovered the human benefit invoked, he could declare it the legal cause of the case in question and employ it as the basis of analogical arguments in other legal derivations. Al-Juwaynī was by no means the first Shāfiʿī to invoke *maṣlaḥa* in identifying legal causes. In the *Burhān*, he explicitly aligned his use of *maṣlaḥa* with the Shāfiʿī-Ashʿarī legal theorist Abū Isḥāq al-Isfarāyinī;[73] Al-Juwaynī justified his use of *maṣlaḥa* by claiming that it was the practice of the first generations of Muslims (*al-awwalūn*).[74]

Al-Juwaynī concluded that the forced marriage of an adult virgin promoted no human good. "Virginity," he explained to al-Shīrāzī, was "an unsuitable legal cause" for forced marriage. He continued, "The mention of an attribute [in the utterance of a rule] only identifies a *ratio legis* if [the attribute] is suitable [*munāsib*]" as an object of legislation.[75] Thus, the Prophet's statement about the rights of women relative to their guardians could not refer to forced marriage. Al-Juwaynī's critique contrasted al-Shīrāzī's textualist approach to Muḥammad's statement.[76] Al-Shīrāzī contended that an Arab speaker would only mention an attribute when uttering a rule if the attribute is the rule's cause. In the case at hand, the Prophet would only mention a woman's sexual experience if this sexual experience was the cause of a woman's "greater right" over her guardian (and by extension, if virginity was the cause of a woman's lesser right).[77] Al-Shīrāzī's response shows that the use of *maṣlaḥa* to find the legal cause was not uncontroversial among Shāfiʿīs. Al-Juwaynī recognized the validity of invoking Arab linguistic conventions in some cases,[78] but he refused to accept that a jurist should identify a legal cause in a contested question that is detrimental to Muslims.[79] Therefore, regardless of certain Arab linguistic conventions, al-Juwaynī rejected virginity as the legal cause of forced marriage.

Again, in the final thread of the disputation, we find al-Juwaynī drawing on a prominent doctrine among some Shāfiʿīs, namely that all laws must serve human benefit. By deploying this argument in his critique of forced marriage, al-Juwaynī does two things: First, he makes al-Shīrāzi requestion his commitments to a hermeneutic model based on the customary speech patterns of Arab speakers in favour of a model that takes seriously God's graciousness in providing a legal code that benefits his human creation. Second, as a consequence of his critique of al-Shīrazī's hermeneutics, al-Juwaynī summons al-Shīrāzī to rethink the validity of a law that renders forced marriage lawful despite its failure to secure benefit to God's creation.

## Conclusion: A Tradition of Self-Critique

After carefully analysing al-Juwaynī's critique of forced marriage, it is jarring to find him not only justifying forced marriage in the *Nihāyat*, but doing so with the same *ḥadīth* as al-Shīrāzī. Al-Juwaynī writes that a father and a grandfather "possess a coercive right over the virgin . . . based on the prophetic statement 'the sexually experienced woman has greater right over herself than her guardian' and it is understood from this that the guardian has greater right over the virgin than she has over herself, regardless of whether she is a minor or an adult."[80] But it is precisely al-Juwaynī's willingness to critique a position he deemed correct that should interest us. As historians of classical law, we are accustomed to reading manuals in which jurists tenaciously uphold the doctrines of their schools. Certainly, the commitment to upholding school doctrine could take place in the disputation as well, as was evident in Chapter 1 where al-Shīrāzī and al-Dāmaghānī represented the Shāfiʿī and Ḥanafī schools before the audience of Baghdad. But justifying school doctrine was not always the only concern of classical jurists. Rather, al-Juwaynī and al-Shīrāzī debated the question of forced marriage in a context where an eager audience wanted to better comprehend the merits of the evidence for the Shāfiʿī position. To recall, al-Shīrāzī had just been tasked with arranging the marriage of the daughter of the sultan to the caliph. The question of the rights of the sultan's daughter therefore preoccupied the men in attendance. The matter could not be adequately elucidated without one of the two men taking on a posture of critique. The tradition needed to be dissected if the merits of different positions were to be understood properly. To this end, al-Juwaynī avoided invoking standard Ḥanafī arguments against forced marriage, since Shāfiʿīs started from a different set of legal assumptions and commitments.[81] Al-Juwaynī's willingness to critique established Shāfiʿī doctrine reflects a commitment to treating tradition as an ongoing object of scrutiny, regardless of how entrenched a legal position might at first appear. This commitment is not only pedagogical but also consistent with the affirmation in books of *uṣūl al-fiqh* that jurists had a responsibility to use disputations in searching for God's law. In the end, the doctrinal agreement of the Shāfiʿīs masks a history of Shāfiʿī self-critique.[82] Drawing on the case of forced marriage, I have argued in this chapter that intra-*madhhabic* disputations were an occasion to rethink long-held legal positions and to consider the possibility that rejected positions were perhaps more meritorious than the historical books of one's school had presumed.[83]

I want to conclude by arguing for the value of al-Juwaynī's critique to Muslim reformers today. First, al-Juwaynī offers reformers a cogent critique of forced marriage. His argument against reading the prophetic statement "the non-virgin has greater right over herself than her guardian" as referring to coercion in marriage is well-reasoned. How could the Prophet have intended to speak of coercion when he did not specify the father or grandfather as the guardian in question in his statement? And how could the Prophet have intended to legitimate forced marriage when an adult woman is fully capable of making rational choices about her marriage partner? The adult virgin's capacity for making independent choices undercuts the suitability of virginity as a cause for forced marriage. Of course, al-Juwaynī's critique also has its limits. For one, taking al-Juwaynī as an authority opens reformers up to the counterclaim that al-Juwaynī nonetheless embraced forced marriage. For another, one may wonder why al-Juwaynī deserves more respect and deference than contemporary Muslim women's critiques of forced marriage. Granting al-Juwaynī deference reinforces the often implicit and sometimes explicit bias that men merit greater authority in making religious pronouncements. As Saadia Yacoob notes, one strand of Muslim feminist thought sees little benefit in drawing on the ideas of premodern jurists.[84] For instance, over three decades ago, Fatema Mernissi famously pitted the Prophet's commitment to social justice against the subsequent usurpation of authority by a male elite. A decade later, Leila Ahmed spoke of a female oral Islam that is distinct from the male jurists' literate culture. Being highly attuned to how the marginalization of women's voices shaped the Islamic legal tradition, feminist reformers belonging to this strand caution us about championing the ideas of jurists like al-Juwaynī, despite their discursive merits.[85]

Second, al-Juwaynī's commitment to critiquing entrenched doctrine serves to legitimate the labours of Muslim reformers against accusations that they either depart from or violate the Islamic tradition. The problem of reformist legitimacy is one that Ayesha Chaudhry tackles directly in her study of the Qur'anic verse 4:34. Chaudhry shows that verse 4:34 has historically been read as sanctioning a husband's physical violence against his spouse. Chaudhry contends that premodern jurists inhabited a hierarchical cosmology in which men stood above women. She claims that this cosmology is deeply at odds with most modern Muslims' commitment to egalitarianism.[86] But Chaudhry's study also shows that the critique of tradition comes at the cost of lost authority.[87] Critique of tradition can often be seen as faithlessness. It is in response to this loss of authority that al-Juwaynī's critique of forced marriage is most valuable to reformers today. Al-Juwaynī's critique reveals that the Islamic tradition was less a set of stable doctrines than a method of legal enquiry. This method of enquiry presupposes that Islamic laws should be the object of continual critique and dissent.[88] Modern reformers denouncing forced marriage are therefore not violating tradition so much as recovering its lost critical method. Put otherwise, critique, including feminist critique today, has deep roots in the Islamic legal tradition. One may reasonably claim that there are striking similarities between al-Juwaynī's willingness to revisit, critique, and reassess long-held school doctrine and feminist critiques of the law today. Both are committed to a project of re-examining inherited and long-accepted positions. This is particularly the case for the critical feminist legal scholars whose methods focus on a close reading of historical juristic debates to both understand and re-evaluate their merits today.[89]

It is telling that according to the theory of *ijmāʿ* (consensus) that both al-Shīrāzī and al-Juwaynī subscribed to a question that produced legal disagreement could never again be closed.[90] For these classical jurists, dissent was to perdure. God's law was not only uncertain; it also lacked finality. The classical jurists' method of self-critique acknowledged the possibility—ever latent in Islamic law—of new futures by revisiting the merits of dissenting views. There is a parallel here with Anglo-American law's long-held judicial tradition of writing minority reports. Susanna Lee eloquently explains how judicial dissent, even if non-binding on future judgments, is part of a project of imagining an alternate but consequential reality:

> In the forever-unfolding story of the law . . . a would-be narrator or character displeased with the outcome may not only envision an alternate story but also, at a future time, a politically different time, substitute that alternative story for the present dominant narrative. That potential is always there, subtextual in all dissents: wishing it had been otherwise, arguing that other interpretations should have dominated, and insinuating that in a better world they would dominate and will dominate.[91]

If al-Juwaynī himself did not seek this alternative future in the case of forced marriage, he nonetheless kept its possibility alive for the juristic community that heard him debate. For most contemporary Muslims, grappling with aspects of their tradition that violate their vision of God as merciful, al-Juwaynī left not only a means to delegitimize forced marriage as textually dubious and founded on untenable assumptions about female incapacity; he also left them a case study in how well-established laws can and should be the object of ongoing critique.[92]

# 6

# The Mistaken Prayer Direction

## Debating Indeterminate School Doctrine

Scholars of classical Islamic law commonly assume that 11th-century jurists' primary vocation was to consolidate school doctrine by tackling those legal issues that continued to divide them.[1] This view concords with how Shāfiʿīs of the 13th century thought about their legal school. They presented their 11th-century colleagues as having been engaged in tying up loose doctrinal ends via the process known as *tarjīḥ*: that is, weighing the relative merits of different Shāfiʿī jurists' opinions on a legal question and choosing the opinion they considered strongest and therefore most worthy of possessing the official stamp of Shāfiʿī doctrine.[2] By contrast, I am not at all convinced that 11th-century Shāfiʿī jurists cared much about resolving the indeterminacy that was rife within their school opinions. As we shall see, the entire structure of regional school authority made continued plurality of opinions a tolerable fact of belonging to the Shāfiʿī school. But perhaps the strongest piece of evidence indicating their acceptance of continued doctrinal indeterminacy is the customary openness that characterized the ending of a debate gathering. The lack of declared winners reveals classical Islamic culture's willingness to leave things unsettled. What mattered was not the construction of school doctrine but rather the continued individual exploration of divine law. This, at least, is what I aim to show in this chapter.

I focus on the transcript of the final debate between al-Shīrāzī and al-Juwaynī. Their disputation tackled a topic pertaining to ritual worship (*ʿibāda*), asking what a Muslim is to do after discovering with certainty that she has prayed in the wrong direction. This was a topic that had long divided Shāfiʿī opinion, with some arguing for the necessity of prayer repetition and others defending the validity of her original prayer. It might have therefore been expected that al-Shīrāzī and al-Juwaynī would purposefully instrumentalize their debate to attempt to settle their school disagreements. Instead, though, the disputation played out as a means for both participants to freely examine the evidence underlying each position without the

*The Rise of Critical Islam*. Youcef L. Soufi, Oxford University Press. © Oxford University Press 2023.
DOI: 10.1093/oso/9780197685006.003.0007

expectation of definitive conclusions. Their attempts at finding the right opinion—their *tarjīḥ*—was part of a personal quest between jurist and God, and neither jurist expected deference from the other.

I proceed in four stages. First, I provide an account of the regional differences between al-Shīrāzī's Iraq and al-Juwaynī's Khurasan. Doing so will explain the doctrinal divergences between the two men. Second, I explain the historical differences of opinion among Shāfiʿīs of the two regions on the topic of mistaken prayer direction. Next, I show how these differences played out in the context of their disputation: I conclude this third section by showing that the jurists neither reached agreement in their disputation nor did they pronounce themselves unequivocally in favour of one position over the other in their texts of substantive law. Fourth, I explain why indeterminacy in the legal school was both banal and valued, revisiting the division between Iraqis and Khurasanians: I argue that 11th-century jurists saw the regional division in their school as unexceptional and that the unity of the legal school did not depend upon establishing doctrinal consensus. Rather, unity was the product of recognizing how the legal school could provide a framework with which to understand legal discourse and, as a result, to search for God's law.

## Doctrinal Indeterminacy in the Legal School: Between Iraq and Khurasan

As their disputation on a matter of ritual law began, al-Shīrāzī stood just a short distance away from al-Juwaynī. Their spatial proximity on that day mirrored the close relationship between the two men: years prior, they had met, debated, became friends, and now espoused a deep respect for one another.[3] And yet a great divide nonetheless stood between al-Shīrāzī and his erudite challenger. The distance al-Shīrāzī had travelled to meet al-Juwayni exceeded 1,500 kilometres—a separation that made Khurasan an alien and strange culture to al-Shīrāzī. The Persian from Firuzabad had spent the last six decades of his life assimilated among Iraqi Arabs. Moreover, Khurasan was not Fars. Al-Shīrāzī's distant memories of his native Fars province did not prepare him for the peculiar customs of Khurasanian Persians. Upon arrival in Khurasan, al-Shīrāzī witnessed *ʿajamī* (non-Arab) customs that he found exceedingly confounding.[4] Reports speak of his astonishment at being greeted by Khurasanian locals literally showering him with sundry goods: fruits, sweets, and even clothes rained down upon him and his travel companions. Good-natured al-Shīrāzī laughed even as he asked them unsuccessfully to stop. Once they left, he jovially turned to his companions and asked them if they had kept any of the thrown goods. As far as al-Shīrāzī was concerned, Khurasan might as well have been the other end of the earth.

Adding to the geographical and cultural divide between the two men was their educational lineage. Al-Juwaynī and the Khurasanian Shāfiʿīs were no longer deferentially following Baghdad's intellectual leadership in the manner of previous generations.[5] The Shāfiʿī primacy that Ibn Surayj and his students in 10th-century Baghdad once held over the region had gradually given way to an independent juristic tradition among Khurasanian Shāfiʿīs. The intellectual status of native Khurasanian teachers was now more than sufficient for an aspiring jurist to reach the highest level of academic prestige. Al-Juwaynī's teacher was his very own father, Abū Muḥammad,[6] and his educational pedigree in no way depended upon travelling to Iraq. Later in life, al-Juwaynī continued to consider his father his foremost intellectual authority even though he had come to learn of the Iraqi doctrines developed by his contemporaries in Baghdad.[7]

Later Shāfiʿī historians would even speak of al-Shīrāzī and al-Juwaynī as representing two separate branches of 11th-century Shāfiʿī law. Their tone gives the impression of a near schism within Shāfiʿī thought. For instance, Ibn al-Mulaqqin, in his *al-ʿAqd al-Mudhhab fī Ṭabaqāt Ḥamalat al-Madhhab*, speaks of the "division" (*inqisām*) and "splintering" (*tafarruq*) of the Shāfiʿīs between the regions of Iraq and Khurasan.[8] Shāfiʿī historians would locate the doctrinal break within early 11th-century chains of knowledge transmission. An unlikely scholarly prodigy by the name of al-Qaffāl al-Marwazī (d. 417/1026 CE) was identified as having been responsible for the emergence of the Khurasanian branch of Shāfiʿī doctrine.[9] Al-Qaffāl—often called al-Qaffāl "the younger" (*al-Ṣaghīr*) to distinguish him from the towering Shāfiʿī theologian-jurist of the century prior, al-Qaffāl al-Shāshī—was a latecomer to legal studies. As his name indicates, he lived his young adult life as a locksmith in the Khurasanian city of Marv, west of al-Juwaynī's Nishapur. Al-Qaffāl then developed a thirst for legal knowledge. Marv boasted a prominent Iraqi-trained jurist named Abū Zayd al-Marwazī (d. 372/982 CE).[10] Abū Zayd had been a diligent disciple of Abū Isḥāq al-Marwazī (d. 340/952 CE): one of Ibn Surayj's students, who had since become the respected leader of the Baghdad Shāfiʿīs.[11] Al-Qaffāl carefully studied under Abū Zayd's guidance until he had absorbed Shāfiʿī doctrine.[12] But he never undertook the voyage to Baghdad for his training as his master had. The trek was likely too arduous, and besides, what need was there? Abū Zayd was a sufficiently erudite teacher. Al-Qaffāl soon assumed a teaching position in Marv. Having dispensed with the customary trip to Baghdad, al-Qaffāl would refine and systematize Shāfiʿī doctrine in directions that differed from the labours of his Iraqi colleagues. Shāfiʿī historians would speak of him as the head of the Khurasanian branch, or the Marv branch (Marwazī), of Shāfiʿism.[13] But al-Qaffāl's teachings might not have caused as great a rift as later Muslim historians would describe if not for the generation of Khurasanian scholars who studied under his watchful eye.

Al-Qaffāl attracted three eminent disciples whose names would continue to inspire and shape future Shāfiʿī generations. These three jurists—al-Qāḍī al-Ḥusayn al-Marwarrūdhī (d. 462/1069 CE), Abū ʿAlī al-Sinjī (d. 427/1036 CE), and Abū Muḥammad al-Juwaynī (al-Juwaynī's father; d. 438/1046 CE)—produced legal rulings that Khurasanian Shāfiʿīs would regularly cite in later generations.[14] Moreover, their training was removed from the legal developments happening miles away in Baghdad. As they carefully expounded and systematized their renderings of Shāfiʿī doctrine, so too did the Iraqis. Both regional groups of scholars extended their school doctrine in new, innovative, and consequently different directions. Later Muslim historians gave pride of place to Abū Ḥāmid al-Isfarāyinī among the expositors of Iraqi Shāfiʿī doctrine.[15] He was praised as nearly equalling al-Shāfiʿī himself in skill for his rigorous and laborious elaboration of legal thought. When speaking of the two branches of Shāfiʿī thought, these historians would identify al-Isfarāyinī as the head of the Iraqi Shāfiʿīs, just as al-Qaffāl was dubbed the head of the Khurasanian branch.

The question that al-Shīrāzī and al-Juwaynī would tackle in their disputation was one that the two Shāfiʿī branches had expounded upon differently.[16] There was thus a sense in which al-Juwaynī and al-Shīrāzī each represented the intergenerational regional scholarly divide that had taken shape over the 11th century. Each had imbibed the doctrines of their respective teachers, and each displayed full confidence in their scholarly pedigree. In the next two sections, we shall see how the divergences between the Khurasanian and Iraqi Shāfiʿīs played out on the question of the mistaken *qibla*.

And yet it is important to bear in mind that, in another way, each scholar in the disputation represented himself and only himself. Both al-Juwaynī and al-Shīrāzī espoused in their *uṣūl al-fiqh* the view that God had charged them with finding what they each personally saw to be the strongest evidence on any given question. As will eventually become clear, doctrinal divisions on difficult cases were therefore expected and, in many ways, welcomed.

## Finding the Right Prayer Direction—Twice?: Debating a Matter of School Divergence

Al-Juwaynī and al-Shīrāzī took turns as *sā'il* (questioner) and *mujīb* (respondent) in their debate gathering. Al-Shīrāzī had been the respondent in the two men's disputation on forced marriage; now he had the less onerous task of questioning al-Juwaynī on a topic of al-Shīrāzī's choice. He presumably chose the topic because of its relevance to the journey he had just undertaken: al-Shīrāzī's party had travelled through the Persian countryside, during which they had often stopped for prayers. During these prayers, the travel party would have needed to determine the correct prayer direction (*qibla*), that is, the direction of the sacred temple called the Kaʿba in Mecca. Al-Shīrāzī thus asked al-Juwaynī about a scenario in which a worshipper tried his utmost to find the right prayer direction; after completing his prayer, the worshipper came upon epistemically certain proof that he had prayed in the wrong direction. Should the worshipper rest content that God had mercifully accepted his devotion despite his mistake, or should he repeat the prayer? The question had divided the Shāfiʿīs for generations.

The Shāfiʿīs agreed that the worshipper who merely doubted himself after striving to find the correct direction should categorically not redo his prayer. Their argument was simple: they drew on the practice of juristic *ijtihād* to show the validity of the worshipper's search for the prayer direction.[17] Just as a jurist's *ijtihād* on the law is valid regardless of plausible alternative legal interpretations, they explained, the worshipper's *ijtihād* on the prayer direction remains valid despite his later doubts. In other words, a second performance of *ijtihād* would not overturn the validity of the first—whether in the case of God's law or the prayer direction. This is the case because both *ijtihād*s are fallible and there is thus no reason to privilege the conclusions of one over the other. But al-Shīrāzī's question did not ask al-Juwaynī about a situation of doubt. Rather, he asked al-Juwaynī what a worshipper is to do if he has *certainty* about his mistake. Certainty typically trumped *ijtihād* on the law. For instance, if a jurist found irrefutable evidence, like a perspicuous scriptural source, all dissenting views were to be considered mistaken. In the case of the prayer direction, something like seeing the Kaʿba itself could produce such certainty.[18] The question then presented itself to the Shāfiʿīs: Should such certainty force a worshipper to repeat his prayer? On this question, they presented conflicting arguments.[19]

## Al-Juwaynī's Use of the Khurasanian Analogy between Direction and Time

Al-Juwaynī affirmed the obligation of prayer repetition. He knew several possible analogical arguments to present to al-Shīrāzī. For instance, he knew of his Khurasanian colleagues' analogy between praying in the wrong direction and praying while wearing clothing sullied by ritually impure substances like urine or excrement. The Khurasanians noted that a mistake about the ritual purity of clothes bound one to repeat one's prayer.[20] Following his Khurasanian peers, al-Juwaynī could have invoked this case to argue that a mistaken direction also necessitated prayer repetition. In the end, though, he decided to pursue another route, drawing inspiration from a different but equally popular analogy invoked among Khurasanians that compared prayer direction to prayer time.[21] Al-Juwaynī told al-Shīrāzī that the prayer direction "is a condition among the conditions of prayer," and just as with the time of prayer, failure to fulfil this condition necessitates repetition.[22] Al-Juwaynī had in mind here the prescribed times of the five daily prayers, each of which must be calculated; the time for the dawn prayer, for instance, lasts from the first appearance of morning light until sunrise. Al-Juwaynī held that a person who attempted to find the right prayer time but later became certain of his error would need to repeat his prayer. If this were true, then surely the mistaken prayer direction would also, by analogy, necessitate repetition. Or would it?

Al-Shīrāzī answered pithily that prayer direction could not be properly compared to time because "prayer direction is of lesser importance [*akhaff*] than time." On what basis did al-Shīrāzī make this claim? Prayer direction, he went on to explain, was a dispensable prayer condition in a way that time was not. Had not al-Juwaynī considered that Islamic law permitted Muslims in the battlefield to abandon the *qibla* and to knowingly face other directions so as to avoid bodily harm from incoming armed troops? The same was true of optional prayers in travel:[23] a traveller could face any direction in his optional prayers in order to permit his mount (his horse or camel, etc.) to continue upon its steady voyage uninterrupted.[24] These two examples showed that facing the Kaʿba in Mecca was not an absolute rule over which God would always and without exception hold Muslims to account. Perhaps, then, God would accept the prayer of a worshipper who mistakenly but sincerely attempted to find the right prayer direction.

Al-Juwaynī seemed caught off guard. He understood al-Shīrāzī's argument but did not understand why he would make it. It seemed too simple and easy to overcome. He exclaimed, "There is agreement among the community of verifiers [of the law] [*al-muḥaqqiqūn*] that two cases do not need to be identical in all regards."[25] In other words, the relative importance of each prayer condition—and al-Shīrāzī's claim that time was a more important condition than direction—was immaterial to the analogy's effectiveness. In fact, the point of an analogy, al-Juwaynī explained, was to make a comparison between two *different* things. Analogy would be impossible if it demanded the two cases be identical in all respects. All that analogy required was that two cases share the same legal cause (*ʿilla*). After all, the legal cause was the real object of legislation. Time and direction shared the presumed legal cause of the ruling by virtue of being prayer conditions.[26] Moreover, al-Juwaynī explained, their Shāfiʿī legal school was replete with analogies between acts of varying religious and social weightiness. Examples could be found among both ritual laws and laws regulating the rights of individuals.

For good measure, al-Juwaynī added that he also denied the lesser importance of direction. He contended that similar dispensations as those for direction could be found for time. Al-Juwaynī pointed out that the worshipper could lawfully join his prayers together during travels.[27] The joining of prayers paralleled the traveller's right to abandon the *qibla*. If anything, al-Juwaynī reasoned, prayer direction was more important than prayer time. His evidence? God outright refused the prayer of a worshipper who knowingly abandoned the prayer direction, and yet God rewarded a worshipper who intentionally prayed before the prayer's correct time, considering it a pious act of devotion (even if the worshipper was still required to perform his obligatory prayer again at its correct time).[28]

Al-Shīrāzī agreed with al-Juwaynī that the validity of an analogical argument depended upon the two cases' shared legal cause. However, the validity of an alleged legal cause depended on more than simply finding a common trait between two cases, in his estimation. He contended that "it is a condition of *qiyās* that an analogized case be matched to its pair [*naẓīr*]."[29] By this, al-Shīrāzī did not mean that both cases needed to resemble each other in all respects, but that it was necessary that God's laws apply in the same manner to both. If different laws applied to each—which was clearly the case for time and direction in both war and travel—then a comparison between the two was a hazardous and dubious operation. It jeopardized the project of consistently pairing like cases and risked arbitrarily extending rulings from one case to another. Moreover, al-Shīrāzī denied al-Juwaynī's claim that the Shāfiʿīs often analogized cases of lesser and greater significance. He at least did not: Al-Shīrāzī's own legal method had no place for such analogical arguments.[30] Whatever the cases al-Juwaynī had in mind, they were to be resolved otherwise.

The tables had now turned. Al-Juwaynī's last rebuttal had merely stated the obvious point that analogies depended upon difference. His erstwhile puzzlement gave way to an earnest attempt to overcome a plausible and legitimate objection. Al-Juwaynī's defence avoided a direct refutation of al-Shīrāzī's methodological claim about the need for parity between cases in analogies. Instead, he turned his attention to showing that time and direction were indeed pairs—at least in ways that mattered to their debate. Al-Juwaynī could not deny that different laws governed time and direction on the battlefield and in travel. He could, however, try to explain the underlying cause of these differences and show its irrelevance to the question of mistaken prayer direction. Al-Juwaynī's strategy was to explain the dispensations in travel and battle as cases of excessive hardship (*ʿajz* or *mashaqqa*).[31] Battling troops could not seriously be expected to turn away from their foes and invite their destruction. Likewise, to force a traveller to dismount his animal to pray was an undue hardship.[32] The law therefore did away with the requirement of praying to the Kaʿba.

In contrast, hardship was nowhere present for the worshipper who had become certain of his mistake in determining the prayer direction. The worshipper's doubts about the validity of his prayer were not a question of hardship—after all, praying anew was not an excessively demanding or onerous obligation—but of confusion (*ishtibāh*). It was confusion about the prayer direction that had led him to his dilemma, and in this respect, al-Juwaynī argued, time and direction could be treated as pairs subject to the same rulings. Since confusion about time obligated the worshipper to redo his prayer, so too did confusion about direction. Moreover, al-Juwaynī continued, confusion in general is not a valid excuse for neglecting obligations: "do you not see that if someone who prayed while menstruating or with urine on his garment [both of which are impermissible in Islamic law] thought they were ritually pure, their confusion does not free them from their prayer obligation [i.e., they must repeat their prayers]?"[33] In short, confusion was not an excuse to jettison prayer conditions, whether time, ritual purity, or direction.

Al-Shīrāzī had a final chance to frustrate al-Juwaynī. He seized upon al-Juwaynī's distinction between hardship and confusion to bring his argument back to its original contention that direction mattered less than time. "Your statement, 'The leaving of the *qibla* in optional prayer and war is because of weakness or hardship,' is not correct," Al-Shīrāzī exclaimed. Hardship was only part of the reason, al-Shīrāzī claimed. If all that mattered was hardship, then surely men on a battlefield would be permitted to delay their prayers until the burdens of combat had subsided and they found themselves in safe surroundings. Instead, they were obliged to stick diligently to their prayer schedules in contrast to their dispensation from the prayer direction. Al-Shīrāzī believed that this obligation could only be accounted for if time was more important than direction. Al-Shīrāzī thus added support to his claim that the lesser importance of direction relative to time prohibited the analogy between the two.

But what of al-Juwaynī's argument that prayer times could also be abandoned during travel? And what of his claim that an early prayer was still an accepted pious act in contrast to a prayer made intentionally in the wrong direction? Did these two claims not show that direction was equal to if not more important than time? Al-Shīrāzī sought to answer the second claim by explaining why God accepted prayers performed at the wrong time. A prayer during a mistaken time was still a valid devotional deed in his view because it was performed during the prescribed time of *optional* prayers.[34] In contrast, the *qibla* was the correct direction of prayer for optional *and obligatory* prayers, and thus intentionally deviating from it resulted in a prayer's nullification. Regarding the claim that prayer times could be abandoned during travel, al-Shīrāzī denied that combined prayers amounted to a dispensation (*'udhr*) from ritual practice. Rather, he claimed that combining prayers was the proper way to perform them during travels, based on the Prophet's example. In his opinion, the combination of prayers in no way indicated time's lesser weight; rather, God had simply changed the proper time of prayers during travels.[35]

The debate ended. It had been a long and intricate one—worthy of transcription. Our two jurists explored the question of the mistaken *qibla* with great care, but ultimately with no resolution. Let us now explore the consequences of this indeterminacy for the classical Shāfiʿī school.

## Was Doctrinal Indeterminacy Really Something to Fix?

If we are to subscribe to both Makdisi's and Hallaq's view of the disputation as a mechanism of doctrinal resolution, our current debate would be deemed an unfortunate failure. There is no indication that the pair succeeded in solving the problem of mistaken prayer direction. Quite the contrary: the participants made points that plausibly both defended and critiqued the case for prayer repetition. Shāfiʿīs would continue to agree to disagree. Historians have identified three ways in which this type of indeterminacy might undermine the good functioning of the Islamic legal system. First, the law would lack authority.[36] Shāfiʿīs would be unable to provide lay petitioners with *fatwās* that possessed the stamp of approval of their legal school. Second, indeterminacy would threaten the predictability any legal system needs.[37] Shāfiʿī judges would give discordant and contradictory rulings in cases where they possessed divergent positions within their legal school. Although a case of ritual law like the mistaken *qibla* would not typically appear before judges, indeterminacy in areas of family or business law could create serious problems for litigants. Third, jurists would have failed to find the truth of God's law.[38]

But there does not seem to be any evidence that Shāfiʿī jurists were perturbed by doctrinal indeterminacy. In fact, doctrinal indeterminacy within the Shāfiʿī school was an expected and normal part of juristic life in the 11th century, and had existed since the school's inception. The case of the mistaken *qibla* illustrates this clearly. Indeterminacy about the mistaken *qibla* did not begin with the Khurasanians and Iraqis. It had begun way back when al-Shāfiʿī's students began interpreting their teacher's legal positions. The students' foremost problem was that al-Shāfiʿī had sometimes changed positions on a legal question over the course of his scholarly career. So common was this that al-Shāfiʿī's successors would coin the technical terms "*qadīm*" (old) and "*jadīd*" (new) to speak of their master's conflicting positions.[39] Which position, then, were they to champion as authoritative? Another no less serious problem was that al-Shāfiʿī's reasoning across different legal questions sometimes contradicted itself. One of al-Shāfiʿī's star pupils, al-Muzanī, contemplated these twin problems when addressing the question of the wrong *qibla*. Al-Muzanī noted that al-Shāfiʿī's original position affirmed the validity of the prayer performed by one having diligently but mistakenly sought out the proper direction.[40] In contrast, al-Shāfiʿī later deemed prayer repetition imperative. Complicating matters further, al-Muzānī noted that al-Shāfiʿī had continued to champion the position for non-repetition in his reasoning on the laws of pilgrimage.[41] Al-Shāfiʿī had claimed that a pilgrim who tried to determine the proper day to spend on Mount ʿArafa (the 9th of *Dhū al-Ḥijja*) but failed to do so (instead spending the day there on the 8th or the 10th) was not obliged to repeat his pilgrimage.[42] This suggested that an earnest mistake did not invalidate a devotional action, and on this basis al-Muzanī championed the position of non-repetition. Other Shāfiʿīs were not so quick to jettison their master's alternate view. For instance, Abū al-Ṭayyib al-Ṭabarī championed al-Shāfiʿī's position favouring repetition.[43] It therefore became customary for Shāfiʿīs to pass down both positions to their students.[44]

Later Shāfiʿīs made resolving such hard legal debates even tougher. As with a game of telephone, the transmission of teachings on a wide variety of legal topics from generation to generation eventually gave rise to different historical accounts of what al-Shāfiʿī had actually taught.[45] For instance, later Shāfiʿīs like al-Shīrāzī and al-Juwaynī inherited divergent reports about whether al-Shāfiʿī subscribed to two different positions or just to one on a variety of legal topics.[46] So common were contradictory accounts that the Iraqis used the specialized terminology of *ṭarīqa* (i.e., a different "account" of transmission) to speak about them, saying, for example, that "there are two *ṭarīqas*" on a given legal issue. Adding to these discordant views, Shāfiʿīs also had to grapple with the myriad positions that al-Shāfiʿī's successors had theorized after his death—either because al-Shāfiʿī did not anticipate an issue or because of new social circumstances.[47] Shāfiʿīs employed the concept of *wajh* (position) to distinguish these later jurists' opinions from the *qawl* (statement) of their founder.[48] However, more than all else, the growing discursive complexity of Shāfiʿī law was a product of the new arguments that later Shāfiʿīs developed while examining and defending their school doctrines. A series of minutely thought-out arguments were posited and passed on to posterity. For instance, should the case of the mistaken *qibla* be solved by recourse to comparisons between direction and time? Or perhaps between direction and ritually pure clothing? Or should Shāfiʿīs refer to the two Qur'anic verses that speak to the issue? Or again, should they use a report about the Prophet and his companions praying in the wrong direction?[49] All these potential pieces of evidence were part of the Shāfiʿīs' argumentative repertoire. In the end, the legal school or *madhhab* was often characterized by a mishmash of stridently clashing views. It contained layers upon layers of increasingly complicated discourse formed over generations.

To seek closure in these debates would have been to erase centuries of hard intellectual work and to do violence to the intellectual edifice of the legal school.[50] More importantly still, it would have made it harder for future jurists to perform their duty of *ijtihād*, since closure would deny them access to the different viewpoints necessary for them to make up their minds on the correct position.

But beyond the banal fact of its ubiquity, there is also reason to consider that doctrinal indeterminacy was actively valued. Authors of 10th- and 11th-century Shāfiʿī texts did not regard the continued existence of two (or more) positions on a legal question negatively.[51] They disparaged neither their school master nor his successors for their ambivalent pronouncements on the law. Al-Shīrāzī himself went into some detail to explain that scholarly ambivalence was a sign of necessary cautiousness and a tempered judicious mind.[52] He explained that a jurist like al-Shāfiʿī sometimes posited more than one position as a means of narrowing down the issue for his future consideration.[53] Unfortunately, a human life is short and the law was complex: death often overtook a jurist before he could finalize his position on a question. In response to the criticism that only weak juristic minds would remain unsure of a legal position for an extended period of time, al-Shīrāzī argued the opposite.[54] Only a legal mind capable of grasping the subtle nuances of the law could identify and appreciate the merits of myriad pieces of evidence bearing on different sides of an issue. Ambivalence and tentativeness were the product of a cautious mind working within a complex legal system; only fools rushed to declare themselves on the law. Al-Shīrāzī invoked a well-known tale illustrating this point. A man among the juristic class once came to Ibn Surayj telling him that he used to respond to legal inquiries swiftly and without hesitation. Now, the man explained, when he received similar petitions, he required some time to reflect upon the matter. The man felt disappointment at his lost ease in legal thinking, but Ibn Surayj saw the situation differently. "Only now," he exclaimed, "have you truly understood the law"; only now "has your [knowledge] of legal evidence multiplied."[55] A good jurist, in sum, needed to be exposed to the messiness of the classical *madhhab*. Without it, he did not really understand God's law and was little better than an uneducated layperson.

One might nonetheless wonder why jurists did not find the means to collectively decide upon and canonize the best legal positions. The law might be complex, but two heads are better than one and a few thousand heads could surely come up with an authoritative doctrine for their school. Canonization would eventually take place within the 13th-century Shāfiʿī tradition, so why not start earlier than later? The disputation seemed exceptionally well-suited to a role in weeding out discordant positions and establishing the foremost evidence for the law. Jurists could have creatively organized grand debating tournaments with participants representing different positions jostling against each other until one was canonized, like a modern-day parliament of sorts. So, if they had the brains and the means to set their school doctrines in stone, once and for all, why did they choose not to do so?

The answer to this question was not worldly but spiritual. The Shāfiʿīs very early on developed an individualistic understanding of the relationship between human and God. They believed that each human stood before God responsible for following their interpretation of the law.[56] Every person had to make up their minds about what God wanted of them. The Shāfiʿīs used the example of seeking out the prayer direction to drive their point home. They believed that two men in the desert both had the individual responsibility to determine the direction of the Meccan temple.[57] If both men's' judgments coincided they could pray together in congregation, but if one diverged from the other they each had the religious duty to pray apart. Al-Muzanī writes, "If the *ijtihād* of two men [on the prayer direction] differ, it is not possible for one of them to follow his companion."[58] Al-Shīrāzī elaborates, writing that this is because "both believe that the other is mistaken, and that the other's prayer is therefore mistaken."[59] Likewise, a man seeking out God's law could not blindly follow the position of another. Thus al-Ṭabarī writes, "If their *ijtihād* leads to two different directions, then they are like two jurists whose *ijtihād* differs, such that it is not permissible for either to follow his companion."[60]

There are, however, three points about the *ijtihād* on prayer direction to keep in mind if we are to fully understand how Shāfiʿīs envisaged divergence within their legal system. The first is that the two travellers could consult each other.[61] Suppose one man was an avid camper and nature expert capable of orienting himself with ease and the other was a city dweller who had never set foot outside a residential area with clearly demarcated prayer directions. In this case, the city dweller could ask the nature expert how to read the signs of nature.[62] This process of learning was equivalent to the pedagogical process a jurist underwent within the legal schools. An individual like al-Shīrāzī had learnt to read the signs of scripture from his teachers, like al-Ṭabarī. Second, in the scenario just laid out, the nature expert could tell the city dweller why he thought he knew the correct direction, but the city dweller was still bound by God to investigate the issue and determine for himself whether this direction seemed right or not. Likewise, jurists could learn their predecessors' positions and trust that they had put time and effort into formulating them, but they nonetheless had the responsibility to verify them themselves, to see whether or not they considered them correct. It was for this reason that 11th-century jurists gave so much care to examining the various arguments of their legal schools. Third, there was a possibility that the city dweller simply did not have the requisite intellectual skills to understand the method for calculating the right prayer direction. In this case, Shāfiʿīs gave the person a pass and permitted him to blindly follow the nature expert.[63] This last scenario mapped on to the situation of lay Muslims who lacked the time to dedicate themselves to the legal sciences. They would arrive before God in the afterlife able to claim that they had sought out the opinions of trained scholars to ensure legal conformity in various aspects of their lives.

The individual responsibility to search for God's law meant that each jurist had his own personal understanding of his school doctrine. In effect, there were as many versions of Shāfiʿī doctrine as there were Shāfiʿī jurists. Some jurists were clearly more influential in shaping the positions of colleagues than others, but none could claim to have the final say on the law. All they could do was leave for posterity their explanation for why God's law was as they believed it to be. In the end, future jurists—much like the city dweller learning from the nature expert—would decide whether their illustrious forerunners had posited satisfactory positions or not.

On the question of the mistaken prayer direction, neither al-Juwaynī nor al-Shīrāzī ended up pronouncing themselves with authority in their books of substantive law. In the *Nihāyat*, al-Juwaynī explained that at the heart of the issue of the mistaken *qibla* was the consideration of what God truly demanded from jurists performing *ijtihād*.[64] Did God simply demand that jurists try their best in weighing legal evidence, or did God demand that they find the right answers? If the former was the case, then conscientiously seeking out the proper time or direction was sufficient for a valid prayer. However, if God demanded the right answers from his jurists, then prayer repetition in the correct direction became necessary. Al-Juwaynī gave no further elaboration concerning which of these two positions he favoured.[65] Perhaps he was still unsure. He would leave it to future students and readers to make up their minds. At the very least, though, he had provided them with what he took to be a firmer argumentative foundation than his predecessors. Al-Shīrāzī, for his part, was no more certain of the correct position in his

*Muhadhdhab*.[66] But he too attempted to provide his reader with the best case for both positions. He argued that the position favouring repetition relied upon an analogy with a judge's ruling. Just as a judge should overturn a previous ruling if he finds a perspicuous source text (*al-naṣṣ*) that irrefutably revealed God's will, so too should a worshipper redo his prayer if he has certainty about his error. And he argued that the position favouring non-repetition found support in the original legitimacy of the worshipper's prayer: since the worshipper's *ijtihād* had made the prayer direction legitimate before the discovery of his mistake, the prayer ought to continue to be accepted. Thus, both men continued to see the question of the mistaken *qibla* as an open one, amenable to different positions.

To say that Shāfiʿīs did not actively seek out a consensus on school doctrine is not to say that jurists did not share common doctrinal positions with other members of their school. The Shāfiʿīs' positions examined in previous chapters (the wife's *khiyār*, the convert's *jizya*, and the forced marriage of adult virgins) had been standard since the time of their school master. Nor do I mean to suggest that later Shāfiʿīs did not sometimes largely settle on a question that had once divided them. For instance, 11th-century Shāfiʿīs overwhelmingly affirmed that only a traveller could abandon the *qibla* for his optional prayers. When affirming this position, they tended to critique their 10th-century predecessor Abū Saʿīd al-Iṣṭakhrī for arguing that a non-traveller, or resident, could also abandon the *qibla* for optional prayers (*al-nawāfil*).[67] But the point remains that doctrinal divergences between Shāfiʿīs such as the one between al-Shīrāzī and al-Juwaynī were not problems to be fixed. Their disputation had little to do with weeding out different opinions and building an authoritative school doctrine.[68] Each spoke for himself, and each sought to build his own rendering of the Shāfiʿī school. None had the expectation that the disputation would reveal a final position, thereby closing debate. Debate did not function to settle a matter but to help each party discharge their God-given duty by facilitating a better understanding of a question so that they might inch forward towards a personal resolution on the matter.

## If it Wasn't Broke, Why Did They Fix It?: Rethinking the Iraqi-Khurasanian Split

I have claimed in the previous sections that doctrinal division was a banal and even valued fact for 11th-century Shāfiʿīs. However, this is not how later Shāfiʿīs of the 13th century onwards spoke of their legal school. Jurists like al-Nawawī, al-Subkī, and Ibn al-Mulaqqin characterized the doctrinal division between Iraqi and Khurasanian scholars as a momentous event creating a split (*tafarruq/inqisām*) in their school.[69] They claimed that no sooner had the split occurred than Shāfiʿīs attempted to recreate doctrinal unity. They credited Abū ʿAlī al-Sinjī—a star student of the purported founder of the Khurasanian branch—as the first to attempt a doctrinal synthesis of Iraqi and Khurasanian thought.[70] At one level, their characterization of Shāfiʿism conveys the empirical fact that the two locations possessed significantly different arguments and sometimes doctrines. However, it also distorts and hides from view the historical workings of the legal school in the classical era by conveying the impression that Shāfiʿīs attempted to overcome doctrinal differences among themselves. Here, I wish to make two points. First, the alleged split between the Shāfiʿīs of Iraq and Khurasan was not deemed noteworthy by the Shāfiʿīs of the 11th century. Rather, jurists recognized continued regional doctrinal differences as the norm. Second, by examining the regional hierarchies between Shāfiʿīs, I show that the jurists never undertook steps to create the institutional mechanisms that could have unified Shāfiʿī doctrine. I make these two points both to reinforce my prior argument that indeterminacy was acceptable to the Shāfiʿīs of the classical era and to foreshadow a change that would take place in the 13th century.

Four facts suggest that Shāfiʿīs of the 11th century saw the doctrinal differences between the Iraqis and the Khurasanians as unremarkable. First, doctrinal splits of the kind that 13th-century Shāfiʿīs located between al-Qaffāl and Abū Ḥāmid al-Isfarāyinī were widespread across Iraq and Persia. Every region possessed its own great scholars who had systematized school doctrine differently. This was a natural consequence of the institutional organization of legal schools. Even though Baghdad was the intellectual capital of Shāfiʿīs, its authority—embodied in the concept of *riyāsa* (school leadership)—did not extend beyond Iraq. Al-Shīrāzī spoke of several Shāfiʿīs in places like Fars and Tabaristan who were leaders in their respective regions. Each of these regions' leaders gathered students under their wings and spread their own interpretations of Shāfiʿī doctrine. For instance, al-Shīrāzī tells us that the people of Hamadan learnt the law from Abū Bakr b. Lāl al-Hamadhānī (d. 398/1007–1008 CE),[71] the people of Jurjān from Abū Bakr Aḥmad b. Ibrāhīm b. Ismāʿīl (d. circa 370/980–981 CE), and the people of Shiraz from Abū Naṣr b. al-Ḥannāṭ (d. 375/985–986 CE).[72]

Second, if there was a division of significance between Khurasan and Iraq, al-Shīrāzī himself knew nothing about it. He was intimately aware that great scholars resided in Khurasan, eagerly listing them in his biographical dictionary of jurists, but he did not view this cohort as a separate branch of Shāfiʿism or write about them in a manner that distinguished Khurasan from other regions of Shāfiʿī scholarship. Moreover, he did not single out al-Qaffāl as being exceptionally important.[73] In fact, al-Shīrāzī credits Abū al-Ṭayyib Sahl b. Muḥammad al-Ṣuʿlūkī, not al-Qaffāl, as the foremost influence on legal studies in Nishapur.[74] This is not to say that al-Shīrāzī was unaware that certain doctrines and arguments alien to or rare among Iraqis proliferated in Khurasan. Nor is it to say that he and his colleagues would not occasionally speak of the "Khurasanians" in their legal texts. Rather, it is to say that al-Shīrāzī spoke of Khurasan as he did of other regions of Shāfiʿī scholarship.

Third, even within a single region like Iraq, jurists would make distinctions between the doctrines developed in different cities. To take one example, al-Māwardī notes that the Baṣriyyīn (the scholars of Basra) differed from the Baghdādiyyīn (the scholars of Baghdad) on the question of the relative merits of different clans within the Prophet's tribe of Quraysh as they pertained to a potential marriage partner.[75] The Basrans claimed that all members of the tribe shared the same lineage status and therefore that intermarriage between clans happened between equals. In contrast, the Baghdadis made distinctions between the Prophet's clan (the Hashimites and the Muṭṭalibites) and the rest of Quraysh. For instance, al-Ṭabarī explained that "God had chosen [to send his message to] the Arabs from among other nations; and he had chosen the Hashimites among Quraysh." It is therefore difficult to maintain that the divisions between Iraqis and Khurasanians could have concerned 11th-century Shāfiʿīs much when similar divisions existed among Shāfiʿīs of neighbouring cities.

Fourth, regional differences were simply more pronounced manifestations of local differences. This is the reason that rivalries like that between al-Shīrāzī and Ibn al-Ṣabbāgh for primacy among the Baghdad Shāfiʿīs were possible.[76] And even when an uncontested leader like Abū Ḥāmid al-Isfarāyinī showed up on the scene, no one within the Shāfiʿī ranks expected him to pontificate on his views to other Baghdad Shāfiʿīs. For instance, al-Shīrāzī's own master, al-Ṭabarī, had received training from others in addition to al-Isfarāyinī and therefore drew on eclectic sources in coming up with his own doctrines.[77] As we have seen, the discourse of the 10th- and 11th-century Shāfiʿīs was one that supported and indeed mandated the individual interpretive labour of each qualified jurist. This is why Abū ʿĀṣim al-ʿAbbādī (d. 458/1066 CE) begins his biography of al-Shāfiʿī by stating that "the scholars have chosen his *madhhab* [i.e., doctrine] [*ikhtāra al-ʿulamāʾ madhhabahu*] based on evidence establishing its veracity [*li-adillat*$^{in}$ *qāmat ʿalā siḥḥatihi*]."[78] Al-ʿAbbādī then contrasts this scholarly method with the methods of lay Muslims who are bound to *taqlīd*. The priority that Shāfiʿīs gave to individual interpretation would have undercut any deep aspiration towards doctrinal uniformity. The fact that they did not aspire to doctrinal unity is also evident in how Shāfiʿīs put little effort into making one region or institution the centre of Shāfiʿī thought. Rather, they expected every jurist to produce his own doctrinal corpus based on evidence. That al-Qaffāl should differ from al-Isfarāyinī and that al-Juwaynī should differ from al-Shīrāzī was therefore expected, just as two jurists from Baghdad would also differ from each other.[79] If we keep this fact in mind, we will better understand why al-Shīrāzī and al-Juwaynī were plainly satisfied to leave the matter of the mistaken *qibla* inconclusive.

Why, then, did later Shāfiʿīs feel the need to posit a split between Iraqis and Khurasanians of the 11th century? In answering this question, we will begin to understand what changed in classical Shāfiʿism and how this change spelt the end of the classical culture of *ijtihād* and the value it gave to critique. A full exposition of this question will need to wait until the next chapter. For now, it will suffice to say that the historical revision of later Shāfiʿīs was meant to explain to students of the 13th century onwards why their core textbooks were authored by two men, al-Shīrāzī and al-Ghazālī, who provided two very different renderings of Shāfiʿī doctrine. In short, claims about a historical split between Shāfiʿīs were the product of attempts at tracing the intellectual genealogy of two men and their books. Part of the task of explaining the end of the classical Shāfiʿī culture of critique will be to explain why these two men's books gained such popularity. But for now, I simply maintain that doctrinal indeterminacy and divergence were seen as inevitable and banal within the classical Shāfiʿī school.

How, one might wonder, was school unity maintained amidst this diversity? The answer is quite simply a commitment to a shared legal discourse on the basis of which to form one's own legal thought. The Shāfiʿī school resembled a discursive tradition in the sense delineated by Alasdair MacIntyre and Talal Asad.[80] Each Shāfiʿī drew on a common past and argued with their colleagues in hopes of producing the best answers to the historical questions that had preoccupied them.[81] Thus, while they were all primarily trained by their regional teachers, they often took an acute interest in intellectual developments in far-flung regions. Most took an interest in Baghdad since it had long been the centre of the most cutting-edge thought. Yet al-Shīrāzī, even as a leading Iraqi jurist, informs us of the books he read from jurists of other regions.[82] Likewise, al-Juwaynī's *Nihāyat* bears the traces of his encounters with other Shāfiʿīs during his years of exile from Nishapur. In the end, the two men's attempt to study different regional doctrines should be understood as a corollary of their search for the best legal position. The debate gathering was part of this process. By subjecting one's arguments to critique from scholars who had varied perspectives, a jurist could gain greater self-reflexivity and strengthen his arguments. Solidarity came not from doctrine per se, but from a shared commitment to finding God's law.

## Conclusion

In this chapter, I have analyzed a disputation between al-Shīrāzī and al-Juwaynī to show that doctrinal indeterminacy was neither a troubling nor a lamentable fact within the classical Shāfiʿī school. Quite the contrary, it was essential to the school's proper functioning. Upholding doctrinal indeterminacy in the case of mistaken prayer direction reflected each jurist's appreciation of the increasing complexity of their legal system and the tempered cautiousness with which anyone should make legal pronouncements. The debate gathering did not pursue finality or closure but sought to elucidate the relevant aspects bearing upon the case. The legal school, with its argumentative complexities and divergences was meant to be a repository from which the diligent jurist would draw in his search for God's law, and regional variations enriched the discursive resources available for this search. School unity was predicated not on common doctrine but on a shared project of seeking out God's law. Disputation, by permitting the testing of arguments, was an essential part of this project.

I have placed heavy emphasis on the claim that the Khurasanian-Iraqi doctrinal divide was unremarkable to al-Shīrāzī, al-Juwaynī, and their coterie. There was, nonetheless, one significant way in which Khurasan differed from other Shāfiʿī-dominated regions. Khurasan at the time of al-Juwaynī had emerged as the only region capable of rivalling the Iraqi scholarly elites for intellectual primacy within their school. Not since the time of Ibn Surayj had a region outside of Baghdad produced so many influential jurists, free of deference to the historic centre of their school. Khurasanian-trained jurists authored key Shāfiʿī legal manuals that would later be taken up as authoritative representations of the legal school alongside Iraqi texts. The 13th-century emphasis on two distinct school branches was therefore the product of later reception and categorization of these works as belonging to separate intellectual streams. Moreover, the assumption that the two branches needed to be combined depended upon a radically new presupposition about what defined the legal school. For the first time in the history of Shāfiʿism, these 13th-century jurists considered doctrinal unity a possibility and a goal to be pursued. The project of the next chapter is to understand why this shift came about and how it spelt the end of the classical culture of *ijtihād*, uncertainty, and critique.

# PART III

# 7

# The End of Critical Islam?

## Shāfiʿism and Temporal Decay

Three centuries after al-Shīrāzī's death, the historiographer Ibn Khaldūn—writing in his famed *Muqaddima*—had this to say about the art of disputation: "It is neglected [*mahjūra*] in our times, because of the decline in knowledge and teaching in Muslim cities [*al-amṣār al-Islāmiyya*]. Moreover, it is now considered [a way of achieving] perfection [in one's knowledge] rather than a necessity."[1] Ibn Khaldūn's assessment of the decline of the *munāẓara* needs qualifying. Biographical dictionaries and books of historiography from the 13th and 14th centuries continued to characterize jurists as proficient in *munāẓara*. Moreover, Ibn Khaldūn's knowledge of legal learning in Egypt and Syria—the centres of legal scholarship in his time—is questionable; he did eventually travel to these sites, but his first draft of the *Muqaddima* was written prior to residing in Cairo.[2] Still, Ibn Khaldūn seems to have picked up on a shift in the importance of disputation.[3] Whereas disputation was once necessary (*ḍarūrī*), it had now become optional.

In this chapter, I explain both how and why the disputation lost its status as a necessary practice by the 13th century. My explanation will inevitably be partial because I limit my analysis to al-Shīrāzī's Shāfiʿī school. I suspect the other Sunni legal schools experienced similar trajectories, but I leave to another historian the task of examining their particularities more closely. My contention is that the decline of the disputation went hand in hand with the decline in the obligation of *ijtihād*. The duty of *ijtihād* had been the basis for the disputation's discursive justification, and that of critique more broadly. To recall, the classical culture that emerged in Iraq in the early 10th century was not only a culture of critique, but also one of *itjihād* and uncertainty. But by the 13th century, the leading jurists of the Shāfiʿī school increasingly saw *ijtihād* as something that could only be performed to a limited degree. For most legal questions, deference was to be given to the authoritative doctrines of the legal school (the *madhhab*). In theory, the law remained epistemically uncertain, but in practice, the arguments justifying school doctrine were no

*The Rise of Critical Islam*. Youcef L. Soufi, Oxford University Press. © Oxford University Press 2023.
DOI: 10.1093/oso/9780197685006.003.0008

longer objects of re-examination or verification—at least, not to the same extent.

But why did *ijtihād* wane? The short answer to this question is that a particular conception of time slowly gained prominence among the Shāfiʿīs in the late 11th and 12th centuries, one that had been marginal to al-Shīrāzī and his Iraqi colleagues' understanding of the juristic duty of *ijtihād*. The discursive development of this view of time is traceable to Khurasan among jurists who squarely belonged to the classical culture of critique, *ijtihād*, and uncertainty, and we can locate it in the writings of al-Juwaynī and even more so in those of his student al-Ghazālī. These two Khurasanian jurists saw themselves as living in a period in which skilful jurists were increasingly rare. By the 13th century, Ibn al-Ṣalāḥ and al-Nawawī (d. 676/1278 CE) from the Dār al-Ḥadīth College in Damascus had come to embrace a narrative of decay over time in telling the history of their Shāfiʿī school, in which each succeeding generation of jurists was understood to be less capable of performing *ijtihād* than the last. It was this emphasis on a temporality of degradation—a view I refer to as one of decaying time—that gave rise to a new typology of jurists in their writing. In short, Ibn al-Ṣalāḥ and al-Nawawī reimagined the history of their school in ways that obscured the preceding centuries' vibrant thought. They saw figures like al-Shīrāzī as merely filling in the blanks that their predecessors had left unanswered, rather than as scholars of equal responsibility for searching God's law.

I begin by closely examining al-Nawawī's historical narrative of his legal school in the introduction to his opus *al-Majmūʿ*. I use al-Nawawī to show not only the changes that took place in the understanding of juristic competence between the 11th and 13th centuries, but also to show the increasing desire for doctrinal finality among Shāfiʿīs. I therefore turn in the second section to examining al-Nawawī and his colleagues' efforts to determine the authoritative doctrines of their school so as to alleviate students of the burden of sifting through the discordant views of their predecessors. I highlight how the desire for finality diverged from the classical tradition, in which the discordant arguments concerning the law facilitated the training of a jurist by offering him an increasingly rich repository from which to construct his own views. Throughout both these sections, I show how the decline in the obligation of *ijtihād* and the search for doctrinal finality undercut the discursive justification for the disputation. In the final section, I examine Mamluk historiographical sources to draw out a brief snapshot of the disputation among 13th- and 14th-century Shāfiʿīs.[4] These Shāfiʿīs had inherited the mantle of their school in the wake of the Mongol destruction of Iraqi and Persianate lands. The evidence suggests that disputation continued to be practiced, though in attenuated form: its frequency decreased slightly and, most importantly, its function appears to have shifted from serving primarily as a tool for *ijtihād* to being mostly a pedagogical means of testing students. And even though the disputation retained the pedagogical function it possessed in the classical period, it was no longer viewed as an indispensable practice in the training and career of a jurist.

## Time and Decay in al-Nawawī's Thought

In the mid-13th century, al-Nawawī sat down to write what he hoped would be his legal opus. The Syrian ascetic scholar from the small town of Nawa had spent the early part of his life training and then teaching at the prestigious Dār al-Ḥadīth College of Damascus, before retiring to dedicate himself to writing books of law and *ḥadīth*.[5] The scholar had already composed manuals summarizing Shāfiʿī legal doctrine when he turned his attention to al-Shīrāzī's *Muhadhdhab*. The *Muhadhdhab* had become a respected legal text that Shāfiʿī students studied in minute detail. Now, al-Nawawī decided it would form the foundation of his most complete legal commentary yet. The text would be called *al-Majmūʿ* (*The Collection*) because it would gather the legal opinions of the Shāfiʿīs and present the most authoritative of them in one multi-volume work. On the surface, al-Nawawī's text was similar to any other classical legal commentary: it was common for al-Shīrāzī and his colleagues to write commentaries of varying lengths—some as large as al-Nawawī's—and it was also common for them to use a respected legal text like the *Muhadhdhab* as a foundation. During al-Shīrāzī's time, for instance, many used the *Mukhtaṣar* of al-Muzanī. But al-Nawawī's introduction to the *Majmūʿ* reveals a change in the Shāfiʿī jurists' understanding of *ijtihād*, at the core of which was the new ascendence of particular conception of time—one that envisioned Islamic legal history as a story of gradual decline and decay.

Time is a culturally mediated concept and one that is of foundational importance to social life. A people's temporal beliefs about historical progress, stasis, cycles, or decay shape their basic assumptions about the world around them.[6] Human communities, past and present, have been shaped by the dominant conception of time holding sway over them. Take, for instance, the progressive conception of time that has dominated European modernity.

The ascendancy of the view that the passing of time leads to historical progress or positive development is at the foundation of nearly all 19th-century thought: it shaped biological evolutionary theories in the natural sciences; anthropological assumptions about primitive tribes progressing into civilized nations; and philosophical and sociological theories like Marxism that imagined freer, more prosperous, and equitable societies.[7] European linear notions of time have seeped into everyday speech and modern thought—the usage of words such as "civilized," "backwards," "development," "barbaric," or "medieval" in reference to cultures, institutions, economies, and political regimes are persistent legacies of this era.[8] Despite recent critiques, the dominance of the modern progressivist notion of time makes it difficult for many of us to imagine the possibility that alternate conceptions of time might shape a community's ideas and practices. In this regard, we are like fish unable to imagine life without water. And yet, should we wish to understand the end of the era in which juristic critique was indispensable, we must do precisely this. We must pay attention to life on land—to different conceptions of historical time.

The Islamic tradition's deep historical roots and geographical reach means that we should expect to find diverse conceptions of time among Muslims throughout the last fifteen centuries.[9] Relevant to us here is a late 11th- and 12th-century shift that drastically altered Shāfiʿī jurists' perceptions of historical time. This shift is made clearer by noting what came before. Al-Shīrāzī and his Shāfiʿī predecessors understood their legal practice in relationship to three different conceptions of time. Each conception of time related to a different aspect of their community's self-understanding. One conception saw time as decaying: under this framework, al-Shīrāzī saw al-Shāfiʿī and his circle of students as superior to later jurists. This is clear from an anecdote that al-Shīrāzī shares in his *Ṭabaqāt*. He explains that the Shāfiʿī leader Abū Ḥāmid al-Isfarāyinī succeeded in attracting hundreds of students to his lectures in Baghdad through his skilful legal reasoning. As al-Isfarāyinī's reputation soared, the Ḥanafī leader al-Qudūrī made the bold assertion that al-Isfarāyinī had surpassed the legal skill of al-Shāfiʿī himself. Al-Shīrāzī had great esteem for al-Isfarāyinī but the comment went too far: he could not fathom anyone surpassing his school master. He thus condemned al-Qudūrī's comment as an underhanded insult to the Shāfiʿīs born out of school partisanship (*taʿaṣṣub*), concluding that none among al-Isfarāyinī's generation could rival "al-Shāfiʿī or his [immediate] successors."[10] The reverence shown to al-Shāfiʿī was to be expected. After all, al-Shīrāzī and his peers belonged to al-Shāfiʿī's school and the titles of many of their books explicitly mention "the legal thought [*fiqh*] *of the Imām al-Shāfiʿī*" (emphasis mine).[11] They referred back to al-Shāfiʿī's methodological and legal opinions and they understood themselves as collectively continuing his intellectual labours.[12]

Second, al-Shīrāzī also understood Shāfiʿī legal arguments and doctrines through a conception of progressive time. If al-Shīrāzī saw al-Shāfiʿī as a more skilful scholar than later jurists, he nonetheless saw these later jurists as having a more sophisticated legal doctrine than their school master. By standing on the shoulders of al-Shāfiʿī and other school luminaries, they were able to produce legal positions of greater subtlety, nuance, and rigour. This view of doctrinal progress is tacit in al-Shīrāzī's recounting of how Shāfiʿīs embraced Ibn Surayj's legal positions as an improved version of the doctrine of early Shāfiʿīs.[13] It also manifests in other texts by 11th- and even 12th-century Shāfiʿīs: al-Juwaynī, for example, contends that later jurists of the school produced the strongest rendering of school doctrine.[14] Fakhr al-Dīn al-Rāzī sums up this vision of progress, stating: "Though the [intellectual] predecessor has the right to establish and found [his craft], the one who comes later has the right to complete and perfect it."[15] Al-Rāzī even claimed that al-Shāfiʿī's superiority over Mālik and Abū Ḥanīfa resulted from his ability to study and improve on their arguments. In other words, al-Shāfiʿī was the better scholar *because* he came later.

The widespread presence of both these conceptions of time should occasion little surprise for the legal historian. We are accustomed to reading the admiration that jurists had for early school authorities, and we are also accustomed to analyzing legal schools as traditions whose thought is refined with each generation. But it is the third conception of time that we must linger upon if we are to understand the shift that begins to take shape in the late 11th century. This final conception of time is a static one. Stasis has often been associated with the Orientalist insult that Muslim societies do not change in comparison to the progressive West. But a static conception of time is not necessarily a negative one. To speak of a static conception of time is to foreground expectations of stability and continuity across generations. For al-Shīrāzī and his Shāfiʿī predecessors, the capacity and responsibility of each generation of jurists to determine God's law for themselves remained static. In this regard, al-Shīrāzī did not privilege one historical era over another.[16] He saw himself as part of a great chain of knowledge seekers connecting back to the Prophet Muḥammad.[17] Each generation of knowledge seekers had inherited the prophetic role of determining God's law (*ijtihād*) and guiding lay believers in their spiritual and social lives. This juristic role would endure so long as God's community lived on earth.[18]

We can locate this static view of time in al-Shīrāzī's texts of *uṣūl al-fiqh*. These texts give no indication that jurists of later generations were less qualified to perform *ijtihād*. Nor do they describe any Shāfiʿī predecessors who thought that the responsibility of *ijtihād* was waning.[19] The same view of time is observable in al-Shīrāzī's *Ṭabaqāt*, which presents the passing of each generation of scholars as something unremarkable. In fact, al-Shīrāzī's presentation of the great Shāfiʿī scholars in his *Ṭabaqāt*—for example, al-Muzanī, Ibn Surayj, al-Isfarāyinī, al-Ṭabarī—suggests that he saw no rhyme or reason in when a great jurist might be born.[20] He documents the influence of each generation's great Shāfiʿīs up until his own. Al-Shīrāzī's writings thus suggest that he would have agreed with the defence of static time penned by his Ḥanbalī student and the man that prepared al-Shīrāzī's body for his funeral, Ibn ʿAqīl. Ibn ʿAqīl provides his defence while responding to an unnamed opponent who has diminished the abilities of contemporary jurists:

> A man states: "The Prophet said, 'the best generation is my generation, then those that follow them, then those after them.'" So the man places generations in rank, one after the other, claiming that the previous generations are better jurists and more knowledgeable . . . so the Ḥanbalī among the verifiers [of sound doctrine] answers, "know that you have neglected the rights of later generations and their excellence."[21]

Ibn ʿAqīl's response also shows us that at least some 11th-century Iraqi jurists beyond the Shāfiʿī school shared the vision of a community of jurists equally capable and responsible for seeking out God's law across generations.

In contrast, 13th-century Shāfiʿīs made a remarkably pessimistic move away from a static conception of legal capacity. In the writings of Syrian Shāfiʿīs, the vision of decaying time that had been present but marginal in al-Shīrāzī's thought on his legal community gained such prominence that it overshadowed any sense of parity among jurists' capacity for *ijtihād*.[22] These Syrian jurists saw time as moving in an ineluctable downward spiral and situated themselves at the far end of this history of decay. As we shall see in the next section, the roots of this vision of decay can be located in late 11th-century Khurasan. But Ibn al-Ṣalāḥ appears to be the first to have outlined a history of his school in which each generation of Shāfiʿīs was increasingly less capable than its predecessors.[23] Al-Nawawī became Ibn al-Ṣalāḥ's intellectual heir at the Dār al-Ḥadīth in Damascus and appropriated, expanded upon, and further popularized Ibn al-Ṣalāḥ's views within the *Majmūʿ*.[24] Al-Nawawī's historical outline imagined the best jurists of his legal school as having come first and conceived of later jurists as increasingly unable to match their abilities to perform *ijtihād*. This conception of time introduced a hierarchical ranking among jurists that departed from the 11th-century Shāfiʿism that al-Shīrāzī had studied and taught. For al-Shīrāzī and his predecessors, there were *ʿālims* (scholars) and lay Muslims—and nothing in between.[25] A radical equality therefore defined the relationship among all jurists.[26] Al-Shīrāzī and his 11th-century peers disagreed only slightly on the criteria for a jurist's capability in seeking God's law.[27] Typically, a basic knowledge of legally relevant scripture, linguistic interpretative methods, analogical reasoning, and an awareness of past jurists' doctrinal opinions figured within the list of criteria. As Hallaq has pointed out, the standard for becoming a seeker of God's law was not excessively onerous.[28] One did not need to match the outstanding level of brilliance achieved by school leaders or law professors like al-Shīrāzī. What mattered was that one sufficiently understood legal evidence to be able to evaluate the merits of different doctrines. Without attaining this level of capability, one remained a lay Muslim whose duty was to follow the opinion of a qualified jurist.

Al-Nawawī's hierarchical distinctions between jurists swept away the equality among seekers of divine law. He jettisoned the simple binary framework dividing Muslims into legal specialists and common laypersons in favour of distinguishing categories *among* jurists based on their purported intellectual caliber. Al-Nawawī imagined that the passing of each generation of Shāfiʿīs led to the dwindling of juristic skill needed to engage in *ijtihād*. He believed that early jurists of the Islamic faith, that is, the luminaries of the 7th and 8th centuries, were the only real seekers of divine law.[29] They were the only ones who were fully entitled to being called "complete" (*muṭlaq*) and "independent" (*mustaqill*) *mujtahid*s because their legal brilliance had enabled them to independently draw up a complex methodology with which they derived their legal rulings. Only the founder and master of the Shāfiʿī school was therefore a complete and independent *mujtahid* among the Shāfiʿīs.[30] Al-Shāfiʿī's incomparable mind had laid the groundwork of a legal school and all subsequent Shāfiʿīs were beholden to him. Al-Nawawī conceived of all Shāfiʿīs as in some way or other unquestioningly following al-Shāfiʿī and trusting that his positions were well founded.[31] He considered that as time went on and generations of jurists passed, the Shāfiʿīs' tendency to blindly follow their school's doctrine increased still further.[32] The generation that immediately followed al-Shāfiʿī still boasted men capable of employing al-Shāfiʿī's methodology to derive legal rules; their considerable level of dependence upon their master was mitigated by their ability to deal directly with textual and analogical evidence to come up with their own rulings. But the subsequent generation, according to al-Nawawī, were unable to do even this: their juristic abilities were limited to fleshing out new rulings based upon already existing legal doctrine. Next came a generation who only occasionally extended their reasoning to new and still unaddressed cases. This generation sometimes also posited innovative arguments, but they were wholly incapable of understanding legal complexity in the manner of earlier scholars.[33] Finally came al-Shīrāzī's generation. Despite the lofty praise Shāfiʿīs had for al-Shīrāzī, al-Nawawī saw him and his generation as synthesizers rather than critical thinkers.[34] They stood at the end of the tradition and produced books articulating past Shāfiʿī positions. Al-Nawawī and his generation were indebted to al-Shīrāzī and his peers for their understanding of Shāfiʿī legal doctrine, but they did not see them as the equals of their predecessors.

Several historians have given attention to al-Nawawī's typology of jurists in his *Majmūʿ*. Norman Calder and Hallaq have provided the most detailed breakdown of each category.[35] But even before these scholars, Leon Ostroróg and Schacht replicated al-Nawawī's typology of jurists in their explications of the gradual decline in *ijtihād* after the 9th century, though neither referenced him explicitly.[36] These scholars took al-Nawawī's typology as an accurate historicization of the legal school rather than a 13th-century reimagining of the past. Thus, Schacht's tracing of the end of *itjihād* to 900 CE conforms to how al-Nawawī himself saw the history of his legal school. Likewise, Calder states that al-Nawawī "explains and justifies the school loyalty that was in fact, historically, constitutive of the juristic experience of Islam."[37] For his part, Hallaq uses Ibn al-Ṣalāḥ's typology to contend that even early jurists like al-Shāfiʿī should be considered to have engaged in *taqlīd*, since they too learnt from and followed the guidance of previous authorities.[38] What these historians miss is the rupture in the understanding of *ijtihād* between al-Shīrāzī and al-Nawawī. Whereas al-Shīrāzī saw all competent jurists, even those who were part of a legal school, as *mujtahid*s, al-Nawawī saw *ijtihād* as part of a spectrum, with the incomparable originality of al-Shāfiʿī at one end and the merely synthetic work of al-Shīrāzī's generation at the other. His introduction of this hierarchical spectrum in some ways reflected empirical reality. It is true that Shāfiʿīs like al-Shīrāzī were not reinventing the wheel: rather, they refined the Shāfiʿī tradition of their predecessors in ways that conform to al-Nawawī's description of them. For instance, it is true that al-Shīrāzī's contribution to the development of the Shāfiʿī legal tradition was largely limited to improving the arguments of his predecessors. But insofar as his typology suggests that Shāfiʿīs followed school doctrine because of their intellectual *inability*, al-Nawawī also distorted how jurists like al-Shīrāzī saw their own labours as part of an individual duty to re-evaluate and critically engage with the positions of their predecessors.[39] Moreover, al-Nawawī's new understanding of *ijtihād* also shifted the meaning of *taqlīd*. For al-Shīrāzī, *taqlīd* meant following one's opinions "without evidence." A Shāfiʿī jurist who knew why al-Shāfiʿī had subscribed to a legal position, according to this view, could not be said to be a *muqallid*.[40] But for al-Nawawī, *taqlīd* was also something that admitted of gradation, since a jurist who knew the evidence for a law but was not sufficiently skilled to evaluate its merit was also called a *muqallid*.

Already, we can surmise the impact of al-Nawawī's view of decaying time on the value of disputation. If Shāfiʿī jurists were no longer capable of evaluating the arguments of their predecessors and, instead, must conform to their predecessors' doctrinal positions, then much of the need for the disputation would be undercut. Certainly, the pedagogical function of the disputation might remain, but its exploratory function would now seem superfluous. The jurist who seeks to re-examine the evidence of his predecessors might even appear pretentious, claiming a status he does not possess. In such a situation, the disputation might no longer be a necessity to one's juristic craft, as Ibn Khaldūn points out. But we are getting ahead of ourselves here. It is quite possible that al-Nawawī's view of the decaying capacity for *ijtihād* was marginal among the Shāfiʿīs. Thus, we must now ask how al-Nawawī's view of decaying time emerged and how widespread it was in the Shāfiʿī school in Mamluk lands during the 13th and 14th centuries.

## The Rise of Decaying Time in Shāfiʿī Thought

Al-Juwaynī championed the strict dichotomy between *mujtahid* and lay Muslims, particularly in his books of *uṣūl al-fiqh*, and his writings consistently articulate the need for jurists to use disputation to find God's law.[41] And yet we can see the beginnings of al-Nawawī's emphasis on decline and decay in his writings.[42] Al-Juwaynī's *Ghiyāthī* is the earliest extant Shāfiʿī text that affirms a version of the view that *mujtahids* had become scarce. Before examining how this is the case, a word on the *Ghiyāthī* provides useful context. The *Ghiyāthī* is not a legal text but a treatise of political theory, which al-Juwaynī wrote for the Wazir Niẓām al-Mulk.[43] At one level, it resembles other texts on politics, such as al-Māwardī's *al-Aḥkām al-Sulṭāniyya*. But the text is unique for its apocalyptic tone: the *Ghiyāthī* sets for itself the task of asking what the Muslim community should do if a disaster one day does away with the class of jurists who have hitherto acted as the inheritors of the prophets and the guides of lay Muslims. Perhaps the question arose because al-Juwaynī had witnessed the persecution of Shāfiʿī scholars in his hometown of Nishapur.[44] He had seen firsthand how scholars could be banished and exiled.

Of course, the question of what Muslims should do when faced with the disappearance of legal scholars was a hypothetical one.[45] Jurists still existed and could still guide the lay Muslim community during al-Juwaynī's lifetime. Yet in the course of answering this hypothetical question, al-Juwaynī made three discursive moves that would shape future Shāfiʿī thought. First, he made it known that he saw his own time as one in which few genuinely skilful jurists existed. Thus, after stating that it is possible for an era to be devoid of *mujtahids* and for Muslims to rely solely on transmitters (*naqala*) of the "doctrines of past imams [*al-aʾimma al-māḍīn*]" in order to know the law, al-Juwaynī affirms that "this description nearly conforms to this time and to its people."[46] This statement shows that al-Juwaynī considered most of his colleagues not true *mujtahids* but merely transmitters of the labours of past jurists. His assessment in many ways mirrored al-Nawawī's nearly two centuries later. The key difference is that al-Juwaynī never claimed that the decline was linear or that future generations of jurists might not continue to produce jurists of the highest caliber. Indeed, perhaps he saw himself and his father as two jurists still sufficiently skilful to independently assess the worth of legal arguments. Thus, even as al-Juwaynī helped popularize the view that would ultimately reshape the understanding of *ijtihād* and *taqlīd*, he himself still belonged to the classical tradition that affirmed the stark division between *mujtahids* and lay Muslims.

Al-Juwaynī's second discursive move made it possible for future Shāfiʿīs to imagine the continuation of their legal tradition despite the loss of its intellectual luminaries. Al-Juwaynī explained that so long as the transmitters of legal doctrine were trained such that they understood the legal sciences (*istiqlāl biʾl-dirāya*), the Muslim community could continue to practice its religion.[47] This assertion represented a shift from the Shāfiʿī view that lay Muslims needed to consult *mujtahids* for correct religious practice: Al-Juwaynī staked out an intermediate position where correct religious practice could be transmitted by non-*mujtahid* jurists capable of accurately conveying the ideas of past *mujtahids*. In other words, the meaning of "jurisconsult" or "*muftī*" no longer overlapped with that of the *mujtahid* in al-Juwaynī's statement. Al-Juwaynī's last discursive shift was terminological. His *Ghiyāthī* introduced the notion of an "independent jurist [*faqīh mustaqill*]" and set this jurist apart from those who merely transmitted a prior jurist's doctrine. For al-Juwaynī, the paradigmatic example of the independent jurist was al-Shāfiʿī. Al-Juwaynī thus opened the door to thinking of some *mujtahids* as of lesser status than others. Later jurists would speak of the independent *mujtahid* (*al-mujtahid al-mustaqill*) in contrast to the *mujtahid fī al-madhhab* (the *mujtahid* who labours within the parameters set by the legal school).

Al-Juwaynī's pessimistic view of his times became more pronounced in the writings of his student al-Ghazālī. In contrast to al-Juwaynī's assertion that his current era was "nearly" (*takād*) devoid of *mujtahids*, al-Ghazālī categorically stated that *mujtahids* no longer existed. Moreover, al-Ghazālī claimed that the disappearance of *mujtahids* rendered the *munāẓara* nearly futile. He explains in the *Iḥyāʾ*:

> [Another condition of the *munāẓara*] is that the debater should be a *mujtahid* who provides *fatwā*s according to his opinion rather than the opinion of al-Shāfiʿī, Abū Ḥanīfa, or others, such that if he finds the opinion of Abū Ḥanīfa to be correct, he should leave the opinion of al-Shāfiʿī and give *fatwā*s according to it, just as the companions of the Prophet, peace be upon them, used to do and the Imāms [of past times]. Regarding the one who does not attain the rank [*rutba*] of *ijtihād*—and *this is the case for all the people of our times* [*kull ahl al-ʿaṣr*]—who gives *fatwā*s by transmitting the doctrines of his school leader [*nāqil*$^{an}$ *ʿan madhhab ṣāḥibihi*], and who is not allowed to abandon his school leader's position even when its weakness becomes manifest, [I ask] what benefit is there [for him to engage] in disputation? (Emphasis mine).[48]

Al-Ghazālī then explains that weak debaters often try to save face in a disputation by claiming that their school masters could have better defended their positions. They state that these school masters were independent *mujtahids* and therefore more knowledgeable regarding their evidence than their followers. Al-Ghazālī here appropriates al-Juwaynī's terminology concerning independent *ijtihād* and amplifies his teacher's view that it is increasingly rare if not impossible for him or his contemporaries. Moreover, in the *Mustaṣfā*, al-Ghazālī explains that the status of *mujtahid* is attainable incrementally rather than just absolutely, thereby positing a hierarchy between jurists like the one that would characterize al-Nawawī's later typology.[49]

It does not seem that al-Ghazālī's pessimism about the possibility of *ijtihād* had any impact on the practice of disputation in either his lifetime or the 12th century. Al-Ghazālī himself valued disputations. He is said to have "left disputation and teaching to focus on worship" only in the last years of his life, sometime after returning to his native city of Tus.[50] And, as we have seen, his late text *al-Mustaṣfā* still presents many reasons why disputation might be either necessary or recommended. Moreover, Ibn al-Samʿānī characterizes several 12th-century Khurasanian jurists as debaters (*munāẓir*s) of great repute.[51] Among them were students of both al-Juwaynī and al-Ghazālī.[52] In short, the disputation continued to be an essential practice among the Shāfiʿīs of Khurasan, who performed *ijtihād* by examining the evidence their predecessors had left them on diverse legal questions. As we shall see later in this chapter, al-Ghazālī's pessimism around *ijtihād* was still not as pronounced as it would be for al-Nawawī. It would take time for this pessimism to spread.

But the view that juristic skill had gradually begun to wane became commonplace by the late 12th century. In his chapter on the judgeship (*Adab al-Qaḍāʾ*), al-Rāfiʿī departs from the Iraqi Shāfiʿīs who made the capacity for *ijtihād* a prerequisite for judges. Al-Rāfiʿī quotes al-Ghazālī as saying that it is no longer necessary to appoint a judge who possesses the qualities of an independent *mujtahid* since "our era is devoid of independent *mujtahids*."[53] Soon afterwards, al-Rāfiʿī states that it is "as though humankind is in agreement that there are no more *mujtahid*s today" such that it becomes necessary to follow the *ijtihād* of "those who have passed [*al-māḍīn*]."[54] Al-Rāfiʿī also provides a typology of members of the Shāfiʿī school that approximates those of Ibn al-Ṣalāḥ and al-Nawawī, dividing al-Shāfiʿīs' followers into three types. The first are those jurists who reach the level of *mujtahid* but find the methodology of al-Shāfiʿī sound, such that their search for God's law concords (*yuwāfiq*) with his. The second are the lay followers whose lack of legal proficiency obliges them to follow al-Shāfiʿī without knowing the evidence for his positions. The third group are those jurists who belong to an intermediate position between the first two groups. These jurists reach the level of *mujtahid* by virtue of their understanding of the methodology of the law. But their capacity for *ijtihād* is limited and their legal practice depends on transmitting the positions that they find within the texts of a dead *mujtahid* and using analogical reasoning based on these positions when the need arises. In al-Rāfiʿī's estimation, these jurists can therefore also be characterized as *muqallidūn* (i.e., those who engage in *taqlīd*). We can draw three salient points from al-Rāfiʿī's text. First, the view that jurists could no longer reach the level of independent *mujtahid*s had gained traction in al-Rāfiʿī's time. Second, al-Rāfiʿī relegates many of the jurists of the Shāfiʿī school to a status below that of independent *mujtahid*, characterizing them as *muqallidūn* because they cannot independently seek out God's law. Third, al-Rāfiʿī's typology does not present *ijtihād* and *taqlīd* as antonyms: one can engage in *ijtihād* and *taqlīd* in degrees simultaneously. This view of *ijtihād* and *taqlīd* approximates al-Nawawī's, who also thinks one can engage in *ijtihād* and *taqlīd* to varying degrees. Thus, the typology that al-Nawawī posited had begun to take shape in al-Rāfiʿī's late 12th-century.

By the mid-13th century, Ibn al-Rifʿa (d. 710/1310 CE) echoed the idea that there had been a decline in legal capacity in no uncertain terms. Noting how the Khurasanians of the 11th century had claimed that their era was devoid of independent *mujtahid*s, Ibn al-Rifʿa expressed that if such brilliant 11th-century jurists as al-Juwaynī, al-Ṭabarī, and al-Māwardī did not attain the rank of independent *mujtahid*, then the claim that the status of independent *mujtahid*s was impossible to reach was even more evident in his day.[55] Perhaps Ibn al-Rifʿa's views of decline were amplified by the recent devastation of Iraqi and Persianate lands at the hand of the Mongols; that the great Shāfiʿīs of the past largely came from these lands could not have escaped his notice. Regardless, the prevalence of this view of juristic decline among al-Nawawī's Mamluk Shāfiʿī colleagues is manifest in two legal debates. First, several Shāfiʿīs accepted that judges no longer needed to have the capacities of independent *mujtahids*.[56] Thus, Jamāl al-Dīn al-Isnawī (d. 772/1370 CE), Ibn al-Mulaqqin (d. 804/1401 CE), and Ṣāliḥ b. Sirāj al-Dīn al-Bulqīnī (d. 868/1464 CE) all asserted that the lack of existing *mujtahid*s rendered it permissible to appoint a non-*mujtahid* as judge.[57] This was a major departure from Shāfiʿī doctrine, which up until the late 11$^{th}$ century insisted that a judge be capable of performing independent *ijtihād*. For instance, al-Māwardī had affirmed that a judge must follow his *ijtihād* on a case, even if it led him to oppose the doctrine of his school.[58] Second, *uṣūl al-fiqh* texts of the 13$^{th}$ and 14$^{th}$ centuries report the increasing acceptability of non-*mujtahids* providing *fatwās* on behalf of dead jurists, overturning the 9th–11th-century wisdom that demanded from a *muftī* the capacity to engage in *ijtihād.*[59] Thus, the late Ayyubid scholar Sayf al-Dīn al-Āmidī (d. 631/1233 CE) reports that it is the custom in his day for non-*mujtahids* to give *fatwās* on behalf of dead *mujtahids.*[60] Likewise, in his abridgement of al-Rāzī's *Maḥṣūl,* Sirāj al-Dīn al-Urmawī (d. 682/1283 CE) reports the popular position that a non-*mujtahid* scholar (*ʿālim*) can give *fatwās* "because the era is devoid of *mujtahids* by consensus [*ijmaʿ*]."[61] And Nāṣir al-Dīn al-Bayḍāwī (d. 719/ 1319 CE) also expresses the need to follow the *fatwās* of dead *mujtahids* because of the lack of living ones.[62] As Hallaq correctly notes, not all Mamluk Shāfiʿīs agreed that non-*mujtahids* could give *fatwās.*[63] For instance, al-Āmidī insisted that only a *mujtahid fī al-madhhab* could transmit a *fatwā* on behalf of a dead jurist. Nonetheless, the debate testifies to a pervasive sense that *mujtahids* were scarce, particularly those possessing the competences of independent *mujtahids*. In short, the view that jurists were declining in skill was shared by al-Nawawī's 13th-century contemporaries.

But one may wonder why this view of decaying time came about. Some historians have linked the increasing denial of the existence of independent *mujtahids* to the construction of school authority. For instance, Hallaq has argued that school authority was bolstered by jurists' retrospective elevation of their school eponym to an unattainable intellectual status.[64] But there are problems with this view. For one, the classical conception of static time did not undercut the internal authority of the legal school. Al-Ṭabarī and al-Shīrāzī trained and taught *as* Shāfiʿīs and defended their legal school against detractors despite also seeing themselves as part of a community in which all members held the simple title of *mujtahid.* The Shāfiʿī school's internal authority rested upon argumentative intricacy rather than deference to past figures of peerless intellect.[65] Nor were the Shāfiʿīs alone in championing evidence over deference. Ibn ʿAqīl argued that deference to men in determining the law threatened the Islamic religion: "Innovations creep into religions by way of the comportment of commoners . . . [which is characterized by] the deference to men [*taʿẓīm al-rijāl*] and the abandonment of evidence [*tark al-adilla*], that is to say by *taqlīd.* And the first to have travelled this path of *taqlīd* is Satan when he gave preference to his self-adulation over clear evidence [*al-dalāla al-qāṭiʿa*]."[66] Ibn ʿAqīl understood Satan's sin of pride in the Garden of Eden as a form of deference to the individual—in this case to Satan himself—rather than to evidence, just as those who follow scholars without evidence give them unmerited deference.[67] Although a Ḥanbalī,

Ibn ʿAqīl was expressing a sentiment that was likely common among 11th-century Shāfiʿīs, particularly those in Iraq, who for the last two centuries had vociferously denied that following al-Shāfiʿī meant engaging in a form of *taqlīd*.[68] In short, for both Ibn ʿAqīl and the Shāfiʿīs up until al-Juwaynī, authority was undercut by deference without evidence.

Nor is it coherent to claim that the extinction of *mujtahid*s capable of independently assessing legal evidence bolstered the authority of judges. For one, claims about a judge's diminished capacities would be far more likely to undercut than to bolster his authority. Under this new vision of decaying juristic capabilities, litigants must worry about whether the judges before them truly understand the law of the dead jurist they claim to follow. One problem the judiciary did face in the classical era of *ijtihād* was suspicion regarding their impartiality. Thus al-Māwardī alerts us to some Shāfiʿīs claiming that a judge should only rule according to the positions of his legal school to avoid accusations of changing his ruling to favour one litigant over another.[69] Were claims about decaying time a means for Khurasanian Shāfiʿīs to ensure the application of standard doctrine rather than face accusations of bias? It is possible, but other explanations also present themselves. One, which I have already noted, is that al-Juwaynī wished to distinguish himself from the mass of jurists whom he deemed unable to fully grasp the complexity of the law. Al-Juwaynī must have recognized that few could produce a text such as his *Nihāyat*, which sought to countenance the divergences and complexities of his legal school before settling on a position. A second possibility, most clearly visible in al-Ghazālī's thought, is that the view of decaying time explained why jurists rarely if ever abandoned their legal school after they lost a disputation. Lesser jurists seemed to have sometimes affirmed their inferiority as justification for upholding a view they could not satisfactorily defend. As this justification became more common, some—like al-Ghazālī—might have found it difficult to maintain the fiction that all Shāfiʿīs followed legal positions based on the strongest evidence. Instead, it may have been simpler to affirm that they were living in times of intellectual decay.

In short, our sources make it difficult to determine the cause of the Shāfiʿī view of decay in *ijtihād* beyond mere conjecture. But the view of the decaying juristic capacity for *ijtihād* undoubtedly occasioned a rupture in thought—one that would have great consequences for the history of *munāẓara*. Even in Khurasan, the standard view in the early to mid-11th century was that Shāfiʿīs followed the doctrine of their school master only after verifying his positions. This was the line common to al-Sinjī, Abū Isḥāq al-Isfarāyinī, and al-ʿAbbādī.[70] Their positions might have understated the loyalty Shāfiʿīs showed to their legal school, but they also accurately depicted the process wherein jurists like al-Shīrāzī and al-Juwaynī were encouraged to examine the evidence for school doctrine and to modify this evidence when they found it lacking. The rupture that the new conception of time occasioned undercut the need for critical engagement with one's school doctrine. If jurists could no longer perform *ijtihād* to the same level as their predecessors, then the natural instinct would have been to preserve rather than to critically assess the doctrines of the past. In the next section, I examine al-Nawawī's impulse to preserve the doctrines of his predecessors and show how this impulse towards preservation shaped the Shāfiʿīs of his era—and how it undercut the value of disputation among post-classical Shāfiʿīs.

## The 13th-Century Shāfiʿī Search for Doctrinal Finality

Did al-Ghazālī know that his claims about the diminished capacities of jurists would undercut the rationale for disputation? It appears he did, but only to a certain extent. To recall, al-Ghazālī rhetorically asked his reader what benefit there is to the practice of disputation in an era when both participants in any given debate are unwilling to change their positions because of school loyalty. But al-Ghazālī had more to say. He noted that the disputation could still be of benefit if it helped jurists assess discordant opinions in their school of law.[71] To take a concrete example, al-Ghazālī would have applauded al-Shīrāzī and al-Juwaynī for tackling the question of mistaken prayer direction, examined in the last chapter, since it allowed both jurists to assess the two prevalent positions in their legal school. Thus, the view of decaying time did not necessarily lead to a complete disparagement of either *ijtihād* or disputation. Given the many questions that divided members of the Shāfiʿī school, perhaps al-Ghazālī imagined that disputations would remain necessary until the end of time.[72] Perhaps these intra-school divisions were the reason that he chose to reaffirm his predecessors' arguments for the necessity of the disputation in the *Mustaṣfā*. But what if jurists were to start believing that it was possible and even desirable to develop authoritative positions for *all* legal questions that had hitherto divided the Shāfiʿī community? What use would the disputation have should such a universal resolution be realized?

The impulse towards finality in school doctrine appears to have animated al-Nawawī when he began writing the *Majmūʿ*. Al-Nawawī writes that his era is characterized by doctrinal confusion. Shāfiʿī students are faced with a dizzying array of doctrines, which makes it difficult for them to know which ones are correct. "Know," he writes, "that the books of our companions manifest intense disagreement such that it is hard for the student to be confident that what he reads is the authoritative opinion of the school [*madhhab*] until he reads the majority of well-known Shāfiʿī books."[73] Al-Nawawī thus explains that the *Majmūʿ* will reduce the burden that falls on students seeking to know what the *madhhab* truly is and why. Al-Nawawī states that while his text is titled the "Commentary of the *Muhadhdhab*," it is really "a commentary of the *madhhab* or more accurately, of Islamic law as a whole."[74] In some ways, then, al-Nawawī sees the divergent claims of the *madhhab* to be a pedagogical drawback insofar as this abundance of views prevented the Shāfiʿī student from swiftly understanding the authoritative rules of his school. He maintains that access to the *madhhab* should be simplified to help young jurists learn their craft. As a *ḥadīth* scholar, al-Nawawī sets out his aspiration to provide the most authoritative doctrines of his school by subjecting the views of past Shāfiʿīs to *ḥadīth* evidence, and to sift through the many books of Shāfiʿī jurists to find the positions that are most common among the majority (*al-jumhūr*).

In fact, al-Nawawī believed that al-Rāfiʿī had already largely accomplished the task of determining the authoritative positions of his legal school. In his *Rawḍa*, al-Nawawī says of al-Rāfiʿī that "God has permitted one among our later companions to gather these divergent views and to polish them in the best of ways."[75] In his *Minhāj*, al-Nawawī notes that he only diverges from al-Rāfiʿī on a few points.[76] Both the *Rawḍa* and the *Minhāj* were his attempts at condensing al-Rāfiʿī's texts so as to make them more accessible to students. Al-Nawawī suggests that Shāfiʿī students will have great difficulty knowing what the authoritative positions of their school truly are without his and al-Rāfiʿī's texts. In short, al-Nawawī lived in a time when it was possible to imagine the finality of school doctrine—whether by al-Rāfiʿī's pen or his own. On this point, my analysis in the preceding chapters suggests two differences between al-Shīrāzī's and al-Nawawī's understanding of school doctrine. First, it is unlikely that al-Shīrāzī could have imagined that a single book would contain the authoritative doctrines of his school because certain questions were too thorny to be settled and because he recognized each book as a reflection of a jurist's particular interpretations. Second, al-Shīrāzī saw his own summaries of school doctrine as a starting point for a student's *ijtihād*, rather than as a way of transmitting a set of binding rules.[77]

But despite envisioning the possibility of finality in his *madhhab*, al-Nawawī did not entirely disparage the confusing array of divergent doctrines in his legal school. Al-Nawawī also expressed that his intention in the *Majmūʿ* was to encourage the student to study and learn from the numerous books of Shāfiʿīs.[78] As Norman Calder notes, al-Nawawī expressed the hope that students would find intellectual delight in jurists' different viewpoints. Insofar as he evaluated the discordant views in his legal school positively, al-Nawawī was not only a figure of rupture relative to the classical Shāfiʿī tradition but also an inheritor of that tradition.[79] His appreciation of divergence alongside his desire for doctrinal finality reflects the continuation of the classical Shāfiʿī tradition despite his beliefs about the waning practice of *ijtihād*.

In the century following al-Nawawī's work on the *Majmūʿ* (which he never completed), the assumption that doctrinal finality was possible, desirable, and imminent animated Shāfiʿī thought. Two examples will suffice to show the prevalence of this assumption. First, Tāj al-Dīn al-Subkī provides his reader with a simple way to identify the authoritative doctrines of the Shāfiʿī school. Al-Subkī identifies al-Rāfiʿī and al-Nawawī as the authoritative sources for the school's legal doctrines. He refers to them by the shorthand "the two shaykhs" (*al-shaykhayn*) to signal their elevated position among Shāfiʿīs.[80] Al-Subkī explains that any position the two scholars agreed on ought to be understood as the definitive position of the Shāfiʿī *madhhab*. If the two jurists were in disagreement, al-Nawawī's position would be deemed most authoritative because al-Nawawī had carefully studied al-Rāfiʿī's text. A similar position is articulated at the beginning of al-Isnawī's legal text *al-Muhimmāt*, where he notes that al-Rāfiʿī and al-Nawawī had refined the legal opinions of Shāfiʿīs and produced a summation of school doctrine.[81] But despite conceiving of school doctrine as something that could, in theory, reach finality, neither al-Subkī nor al-Nawawī saw the formulation of authoritative school doctrines as a completed project. Thus al-Subkī held that his father, Taqī al-Dīn al-Subkī, could override al-Nawawī and al-Rāfiʿī when he deemed their positions faulty. Taqī al-Dīn was competent to do so because of his "complete qualifications" in assessing legal disagreement.[82] Al-Subkī thus accepted that his father and other *mujtahid*s of his father's rank could depart from the opinions of the two scholars. Likewise, al-Isnawī asserted that one of the aims of his book was to correct what he perceived as the mistakes of the "two shaykhs."[83] In sum, the ideal of finality in school doctrine was widespread but not understood as having been fully achieved during the late 14th century.[84]

Nonetheless, the search for doctrinal finality had succeeded in weeding out most divergences among Shāfiʿīs. By al-Nawawī's time, the dwindling of divergence meant undercutting the justification that jurists had historically posited for the practice of disputation. Classical jurists had defended disputation by pointing to its usefulness in performing *ijtihād* on contested questions (*masāʾil al-khilāf*). Even in the early 13th century, al-Āmidī had made proficiency in disputation a precondition for a jurist's capacity to transmit his predecessors' doctrines. Al-Āmidī appears to have associated proper understanding of legal doctrine with the ability to debate the subtleties of legal evidence.[85] But now, even *ijtihād* on intra-school disagreements was increasingly superfluous. A jurist of al-Nawawī's time did not need to debate in order to discover which opinion of the Shāfiʿīs he found soundest. Instead, he could refer to al-Rāfiʿī's writings. Likewise, a jurist after al-Nawawī could refer to al-Nawawī's texts to determine the soundest opinion of his legal school. Like Taqī al-Dīn al-Subkī and al-Isnawī, this jurist might disagree with "the two shaykhs" on occasion—but only on occasion. The historical justification that the disputation was a tool in the systematic search for God's law could not have made much sense to the 13th-century Mamluk Shāfiʿīs. At most, the disputation could have retained its pedagogical justification: the examination of the law through oral debate could help jurists better understand different laws and, in turn, could help them better apply, extend, and even sometimes modify the law as judges and *muftīs*.

Of course, my claims here are focused on the realm of discourse. That the disputation lost its most salient justification is a fact, but does this mean that the disputation waned in practice, as Ibn Khaldūn claims it did? I turn to this question in the final section of this chapter. But before doing so, I want to briefly tackle the causes that motivated Shāfiʿīs to search for doctrinal finality. Partly, the search for doctrinal finality and the canonization of texts was a product of jurists' vision of decaying time. When they no longer felt capable of performing the feats of their predecessors, the preservation of doctrine became essential to their community's continued religious practice. Al-Juwaynī had already noted that the disappearance of *mujtahid*s created a necessity for the transmission of doctrine, rather than for critical engagement with it.

But there is another cause we should briefly attend to. Institutional changes brought about through the establishment of the Baghdad Niẓāmiyya in the late 11th century created the precondition for Shāfiʿīs to imagine the possibility of doctrinal finality. To recall, doctrinal indeterminacy was an inevitable product of the regional separation between different Shāfiʿīs. The head jurist of Baghdad could not assert his authority over the leader of another city because there was no mechanism for enforcing the doctrines of one region over another. At most, Baghdad needed to content itself with its soft power—the prestige of its scholars, which attracted students from across the Muslim world. This state of affairs continued in the immediate aftermath of Niẓām al-Mulk's establishment of a network of Niẓāmiyya colleges throughout Seljuk lands.[86] Al-Shīrāzī, for instance, was made head of the Baghdad Niẓāmiyya and al-Juwaynī was made head of the Nishapur Niẓāmiyya. Each college was independent from the other and each scholar represented his local legal tradition. But after al-Shīrāzī's death, Niẓām al-Mulk's family took the bold step of inviting a Khurasanian jurist by the name of Abū Saʿd al-Mutawallī (d. 478/1086 CE) to occupy the professorial chair of the Baghdad Niẓāmiyya. This move did not sit well with the Shāfiʿīs of Baghdad. Every leader of the Shāfiʿīs in Baghdad since Ibn Surayj had been one of their own: al-Shīrāzī, Ibn al-Ṣabbāgh, al-Ṭabarī, and Abū Ḥāmid al-Isfarāyinī had all trained and taught in Baghdad before becoming the recognized authorities of their school.[87] In contrast, al-Mutawallī was an outsider to the Baghdad Shāfiʿīs. He was certainly qualified to lead a college, having trained in Khurasan at the hands of the famous al-Qāḍī al-Ḥusayn.[88] But it is likely that the Baghdad Niẓāmiyya students saw the disparity in doctrinal arguments between al-Shīrāzī and his new replacement as excessively pronounced. It was asking too much of them to show deference to a teacher who knew little about the Iraqi way of legal argumentation. Prior to the Niẓāmiyya, al-Shīrāzī's displeased students would have left al-Mutawallī for another local Shāfiʿī. But the Niẓāmiyya was too prestigious a school with too generous a stipend for them to leave. Indeed, even al-Shīrāzī's own students had once threatened to leave him when he expressed reluctance to take up the professorial chair of the Niẓāmiyya.[89] To my knowledge, their ultimatum to al-Shīrāzī was the first time in the history of the Shāfiʿī school that an institution was more successful in attracting students than its teacher. With al-Shīrāzī now deceased and an outsider occupying the Niẓāmiyya's professorship, al-Shīrāzī's former students expressed their displeasure with al-Mutawallī by asking him to sit beneath al-Shīrāzī's usual chair, thereby enjoining him to acknowledge his inferior status relative to their former master.[90] Al-Mutawallī attempted to appease them by stating that one of his greatest pleasures in life was being judged worthy of succeeding "our Shaykh Abū Isḥāq." Al-Mutawallī had not been appointed long to the Niẓāmiyya before he was removed in favour of the Iraqi jurist Ibn al-Ṣabbāgh. But Niẓām al-Mulk and his family were set on appointing jurists from their native land of Khurasan.[91] Al-Mutawallī was eventually reappointed and later, in 1091, Niẓām al-Mulk appointed al-Juwaynī's protégé al-Ghazālī to the chair of the Niẓāmiyya of Baghdad.

In the years after al-Ghazālī's death, a new trend emerged among Shāfiʿī jurists. Three substantive law books became the objects of sustained commentary over the next century, up until the time of al-Nawawī. Al-Shīrāzī authored two of these books—*al-Tanbīh* and *al-Muhadhdhab*[92]—while Al-Ghazālī authored the third, *al-Wasīṭ*. Writing commentaries on famous authors' books was nothing new. For instance, Abū ʿAbd Allah al-Khatan (d. 386/996 CE) is reported to have written a commentary on Ibn al-Qāṣṣ's *al-Talkhīṣ*.[93] But up until the 12th century, the most frequently used text for commentary among the Shāfiʿīs was al-Muzanī's *Mukhtaṣar*. The *Mukhtaṣar* was a useful base text because it was a short, standard reference on al-Shāfiʿīs thought. Thus al-Ṭabarī, al-Māwardī, and al-Juwaynī all used al-Muzanī's *Mukhtaṣar* as a starting point in their elaboration of school doctrine. Eric Chaumont believes that al-Shīrāzī's texts supplanted al-Muzanī's *Mukhtaṣar* because the Shāfiʿīs had exhausted what could be said of al-Muzanī's text.[94] But this explanation is doubtful because al-Muzanī's text was never much more than a springboard for more complex legal thinking. A more plausible explanation for why the texts of al-Shīrāzī and al-Ghazālī supplanted al-Muzanī is that they had come to represent the two streams of thought jostling for primacy within the Niẓāmiyya. It is likely that the appointment of al-Mutawallī caused al-Shīrāzī's students to fall back on al-Shīrāzī's texts to preserve the now threatened Iraqi tradition. But the appointment of a Khurasanian had been inevitable and Iraqis began to learn the Khurasanians' legal arguments too: al-Ghazālī's *Wasīṭ* became the representative text of the Khurasanian branch. The focus on these texts within the most prestigious Shāfiʿī college of the 11th and 12th centuries led later Shāfiʿīs to speak about their school's Iraqi and Khurasanian streams (*ṭarīqa*), tracing them back to the teachings of al-Qaffāl al-Marwazī in Khurasan and Abū Ḥāmid al-Isfarāyinī in Iraq.

The raising of the *Tanbīh*, the *Muhadhdhab*, and the *Wasīṭ* to the status of standard school texts was a precondition for envisioning finality in the *madhhab*. The near canonization of these texts made it possible for Shāfiʿī jurists to imagine that a single book could be a repository for all the school's authoritative positions. Al-Shīrāzī could not have written the *Tanbīh* or the *Muhadhdhab* with the expectation that future Shāfiʿī jurists would be compelled to follow them without violating his own commitments to the juristic duty of *ijtihād*, but his texts had now been invested with an authority he had never envisioned. And whereas al-Muzanī's *Mukhtaṣar* represented a starting point for the elaboration of school doctrine, the *Muhadhdhab*, the *Tanbīh*, and the *Wasīṭ* were now deemed the summation of the last centuries of Shāfiʿī labours. Thus, in the mid-13th century, al-Nawawī's legal training consisted in the study of al-Shīrāzī's and al-Ghazālī's texts. For years, al-Nawawī allegedly spent each day going through two lessons on the *Wasīṭ* and one on the *Muhadhdhab*. Al-Nawawī even once claimed to have studied the *Wasīṭ* four hundred times. These two texts would eventually be the basis of al-Nawawī's own legal manuals. This intense focus on the *Wasīṭ* and the *Muhadhdhab* speaks to how al-Nawawī was taught to see these texts as more refined and therefore more accurate representations of the legal school than other renderings.

## The Practice of Disputation in the 13th and 14th Centuries

How then did the disputation change in the post-13th-century era of *taqlīd*? Here our evidence is limited by the lack of disputation transcripts. But we can nonetheless draw out two conclusions. First, the disputation continued to be practiced among Mamluk Shāfiʿīs as part of the pedagogical training of jurists, but its frequency waned and its importance in college curricula diminished. Second, deference to school doctrine generated among jurists a measure of reluctance to critique the positions of their predecessors: jurists opted instead to engage in disputations that would help them understand the historical evolution of Shāfiʿī doctrine.

The quantitative data from biographical dictionaries reveals no abrupt decline in the practice of disputation in the Mamluk era. At first glance, al-Subkī's biographical dictionary appears to show the contrary: we find a decline in the percentage of jurists noted for their skill in disputation between the 5th/11th centuries and the 8th/14th centuries. Thus, the percentage of jurists noted for disputation in the 11th century is 17.1%, which then drops to 8.8% in the 13th century before rising slightly to 10% in the 14th century.[95] But there are two problems with taking quantitative data from al-Subkī's biographical dictionary. First, al-Subkī drew on other written sources to compile his biographies: some of these sources tend to emphasize the debating skills of a jurist more than others. For instance, I have already noted that Ibn al-Samʿānī often referenced debating prowess in his description of 12th-century jurists. We can therefore expect that mentions of skill in disputation would appear more frequently when al-Subkī relied on Ibn al-Samʿānī than when he relied on some of his other sources. Second, al-Subkī's biographical entries vary greatly in length such that some entries say comparatively little about the life and legal practice of a jurist. As a result, short entries that omit mention of disputation are not indicative of a jurist's abandonment of disputation. Moreover, other biographical dictionaries show that the disputation was alive and well in Egypt and the Levant in the 13th and 14th centuries. Ibn Kathīr (d. 774/1373 CE), al-Ṣafadī (d. 764/1363 CE), al-Sakhāwī (d. 902/1497 CE), and al-Nuʿaymī (d. 927/1521 CE) all note several Mamluk jurists who were recognized for their skill in disputation.[96]

However, from a qualitative perspective, we can locate a slight decline in the value attributed to disputations in the training of jurists, ascertainable by two methods. First, we can compare two manuals delineating the ethics of professors and student-jurists, one composed the 11th century and the other composed in the 13th century. In his 11th-century text *al-Faqīh wa'l-Mutafaqqih*, al-Baghdādī unambiguously asserts the importance of disputations in the training of jurists. Al-Baghdādī devotes considerable attention to defining the disputation and the ethics of its participants. He also provides recommendations to professors about when and how they should encourage their students to debate: "It is recommended that [the teacher] reserve Fridays for his students' revision, during which he presents to them legal problems and commands them to speak and engage in disputations on them."[97] Al-Baghdādī then states that if there is a young boy who shows promise, the teacher should pay him greater attention: "And if this young boy attends a gathering of disputation, he is to listen to the arguments of the debaters, and remain among those [in the audience] who are silent." When the boy attains a sufficient level of knowledge, his teacher must grant him permission to "join the group of debaters in disputation."[98] At this point, the boy is not to hold back in his arguments even if his opponent is a senior jurist (*shaykh*). Finally, al-Baghdādī notes that the teacher must notify his student when his arguments are sound and when they are mistaken.[99] In short, a professor should ensure that his students engage in disputation on a weekly basis at minimum and he should oversee their progress throughout their exchanges. Al-Baghdādī's recommendation is the reflection of a legal culture in which professors encouraged and valued disputations.

In contrast, Ibn Jamāʿa (d. 733/1333 CE) pays very little attention to the *munāẓara* in his 13th-century text *Tadhkirat al-Sāmiʿ wa'l-Mutakallim fī Adab al-ʿĀlim wa'l-Mutaʿallim*. His only mention of *munāẓara* comes when he distinguishes between a college's superior and inferior students. He notes that in cases in which a school benefactor (*wāqif*) requests that students be tested on the memorization of their lessons each month, those capable of undertaking "research, independent thinking, the study of books [*al-muṭālaʿa*], and disputation [*al-munāẓara*]" should have their testing reduced because an overemphasis on memorization can lead to rigidity of thought.[100] The statement shows that disputations were still deemed part of the training of promising students; disputations on the law were likely considered important in providing jurists with the skills needed to tackle new cases. However, Ibn Jamāʿa does not value the disputation to the same extent as al-Baghdādī. Elsewhere, Ibn Jamāʿa explicitly places the science of dialectic among the inferior academic subjects. Thus, he states that a professor should prioritize the teaching of subjects in accordance with their nobility and importance, in the following order: "the exegesis of the Qur'an, *ḥadīth*, the sources of creed, the sources of *fiqh*, school doctrine, inter-school disputes, and then grammar or dialectic."[101] Dialectic is taught, but only if there is sufficient time. The diminished importance that Ibn Jamāʿa accorded to the disputation is likely a reflection of the status quo in colleges of the 13th century.[102]

In addition to Ibn Jamāʿa's text, al-Nawawī's biography reinforces the idea that disputation had become optional to a student's training.[103] Al-Sakhāwī's lengthy biography of al-Nawawī exceeds seventy pages in a modern print edition but has very little to say about disputation. Al-Sakhāwī does, however, address al-Nawawī's dislike of the practice, stating that he "took offense from one who debated [*yataʾadhdhā mimman yujādil*] and recoiled from him."[104] Al-Sakhāwī adds that al-Nawawī "could not stand the commotion of jurists or their clamouring as they examined the law [*fī al-baḥth*] [through disputation]." We know that al-Nawawī did not condemn jurists who engaged in disputation, since his close friend ʿAlāʾ al-Dīn al-Bājī was the foremost Shāfiʿī debater of his time.[105] But al-Nawawī preferred the quiet documentation of Shāfiʿī texts over the confrontation of debating opponents. Al-Nawawī's rejection of disputation might have been exceptional among Shāfiʿīs of his era: for instance, two other prominent Shāfiʿīs, Ibn Bint al-Aʿazz (d. 695/1296 CE) and ʿIzz al-Dīn ʿAbd al-Salām (d. 659/1261 CE), were noted for their debating prowess.[106] Still, that the man often credited with canonizing Shāfiʿī doctrine should shun disputations is a reflection of Ibn Khaldūn's claim that the disputation had lost its status as a necessary practice for jurists.

Beyond the practice's diminished pedagogical value, we can also identify a shift in the subject matter of disputations. In al-Shīrāzī's 11th century, the disputation was meant to serve as a mechanism for evaluating the soundness of contested positions. However, by the 13th century, the disputation was sometimes also used as a mechanism for better understanding the positions of particular figures within Shāfiʿī history. Take for instance the following anecdote: Taqī al-Dīn al-Subkī gave a lesson in which he referenced al-Shīrāzī's opinion on a matter of legal theory. After al-Subkī finished his lesson and left, a jurist by the name of Zayn al-Dīn b. al-Katnānī spoke with another Shāfiʿī jurist in attendance: "tell your companion [*ṣāḥibaka*] that the question he mentioned is not addressed in [al-Shīrāzī's] *Lumaʿ*."[107] The fellow jurist went to see al-Subkī and relayed what al-Katnānī had said. Al-Subkī had a message of his own to pass on: he answered that the question from his lecture is tackled in al-Shīrāzī's commentary of the *Lumaʿ*, the *Sharḥ al-Lumaʿ*, adding derisively that it is a beneficial text that al-Katnānī should read. When al-Katnānī learnt of al-Subkī's response, he fell speechless.

Two points stick out in this anecdote. First, the exchange is described as a *munāẓara* even though neither jurist speaks directly to the other. Linguistically, the term "*munāẓara*" is appropriate since each man is engaged in presenting his reasoning to the other. But it is nonetheless a departure from the typical sequence that characterized disputations in al-Shīrāzī's time. This departure might indicate the increasingly fluid use of the term "*munāẓara*" in speaking of the intellectual encounters of jurists in the Mamluk era. Second, the subject of the disputation is not a contested legal position, but the historical understanding of al-Shīrāzī's ideas. The use of debate to better understand the ideas of past Shāfiʿīs should occasion no surprise in an era in which jurists like al-Ghazālī and al-Shīrāzī were perceived as carriers of the authoritative doctrines of their legal school.[108] Put otherwise, after the locus of legal authority had shifted from arguments to particular texts, Shāfiʿī jurists had an interest in using disputation to better understand the canonical sources of their legal school.

In short, there is reason to believe that Ibn Khaldūn's claims about the diminished status of disputation is correct. Disputations continued, but in attenuated form, shorn of the importance they previously had in the training and practice of jurists.

## Conclusion

In this final chapter, I have sought to explain how the disputation lost its discursive justification among Shāfiʿī jurists between the 11th and mid-13th centuries. First, the view of decaying time undercut the belief that most jurists could competently deal with legal evidence. Second, the belief that canonical texts could serve as a repository of a legal school's authoritative doctrines led jurists like al-Nawawī and al-Subkī to support a project of doctrinal finality rather than the continued open-ended exploration of the law. Jurists of al-Nawawī's generation displayed a preservationist impulse that undercut the need to critically interrogate past authorities through disputation. It is difficult to assess the extent to which this loss of discursive justification impacted the disputation in practice. Disputations continued to take place among Shāfiʿīs during the 13th and 14th centuries, and jurists still valued them for their pedagogical use. They also used disputations to analyze canonical texts like the *Muhadhdhab*, the *Tanbīh*, and the *Wasīṭ*. The disputation continued, but it had become less important and had been cut off from its past function as a mechanism for *ijtihād*.

I have contended that the view of the decaying capacity for *ijtihād* first found expression in al-Juwaynī's *Ghiyāthī*. One might wonder how al-Juwaynī came to be simultaneously both a central figure in the classical culture of critique and an agent of its demise? How could a Shāfiʿī who theorized the disputation, engaged in copious disputations, and affirmed the individual obligation of *ijtihād* also promote a vision of time that would eventually undercut the disputation's raison d'être? Here, we must remember that al-Juwaynī could not have known the consequences of his discursive intervention. *Al-Ghiyāthī* was not a legal text used in the training of students. We have no reason to believe that al-Juwaynī taught his students that they could not become *mujtahid*s and that they could only transmit what *mujtahid*s of the past had stated. Rather, the evidence from Ibn al-Samʿānī's biographical dictionary suggests that al-Juwaynī taught his students what he himself had been taught: to search out the evidence for different legal positions, evaluate it, and then test it in the arena of debate. For this reason, al-Ghazālī's and al-Juwaynī's students continued the tradition of disputation for another generation. But over time, the view of decay took hold until it became dominant among Shāfiʿīs.

I want to conclude by asking how the analysis of disputation in this chapter helps us think differently about the history of *ijtihād* and the rise of *taqlīd*. My conclusions overlap with much of the common wisdom among historians on the subject of *taqlīd*. First, I agree with Jackson that while the door of *ijtihād* was never closed, there was certainly a "triumph of *taqlīd*." Second, I agree with those that have located this shift at the end of the 12th century.[109] Finally, I also agree with Fadel that the "rise of the *mukhtaṣar*"—evident in summaries like al-Nawawī's *Minhāj*—is a sign of this shift towards *taqlīd*. Where I diverge from both Jackson and Fadel is in my emphasis on the discursive rupture that gave rise to the emergence of *taqlīd*. For the Shāfiʿīs, the emergence of *taqlīd* was accompanied by a reimagining of the legal school as a teleological project that slowly culminated in the finalization of school doctrine. This reimagining depended on a new vision of time that masked the importance *ijtihād* had held during the classical era. The Iraqo-Persian legal culture that had placed authority solely on the individual jurists' assessment of evidence could not function without constant and trenchant critical engagement with the law. Jurists of this classical era were deemed radically equal, not because they were all equally skilful, but because they were all equally responsible before God for using their training to seek his law. The rupture occasioned by the spread of a vision of decaying time eventually came to define jurists as "transmitters" (*naqala*) of the law rather than as authorial agents acting on God's behalf.

This book has shown that there was no inherent quality of Islam that made the ascendance of the vision of decaying time or the subsequent acceptance of *taqlīd* inevitable. The classical legal system that prospered before the triumph of *taqlīd* had championed another vision of time in which each generation possessed equal capacity to understand God's law—a vision that promoted indefinite debate over the law. The rupture from a culture that emphasized debate over God's law to one that sought the preservation of God's law marks the end of the culture of critical Islam. By this, I do not mean that Sunni Muslims stopped debating or that they lost their critical faculties. In fact, we know that Sunni Muslims of other times and places have given great importance to disputation up until the present day. They too could be said to belong to cultures of debate. Thus, the story I have told in this book is not the familiar one about how Muslims fell behind a scientific, rational, and progressive West. It is well to point out that Western legal systems have much in common with the Islamic era of *taqlīd* in that legislators are only expected to revisit well-established law when the need arises. Rather, I have sought to illuminate a distinct period in which critique was deemed indispensable to the individual jurist's duty as a seeker of God's law. The belief that doctrinal finality was achievable undercut this indispensability. Those seeking God's law could now find most of it in manuals preserving a school's authoritative doctrines.[110]

At a strictly empirical level, the end of critical Islam marked a loss for Muslims. The vision of the law as open-ended; the vision of the self as solely responsible for evaluating the evidence for God's law; the expectation that one's views will grow, develop, and change through critical engagement; and the acceptance that others will arrive at their own interpretation of God's law were all casualties of the triumph of *taqlīd*. Of course, new forms of religiosity, understandings of the self, and communal relationships emerged that sustained the legal practice of Muslims up until modern times. The moral value of this loss is therefore relative and subject to historians' own values. But I finish with a hope that my labour in disclosing a different form of legal life might provide some benefit to Muslim communities today. Perhaps in coming to see different modes of legal engagement, Muslims will find inspiration to order their lives in ways that better fulfil their aspirations for justice.

# Notes

## Introduction

1. For instance, Khan reproduced the British colonial government's disparaging views about Muslim Indians even as he sought his people's educational and economic advancement; Barbara Metcalf, *Islamic Revival in British India in British India: Deoband, 1860–1900* (Princeton, NJ: Princeton University Press, 1982), 322. See also Naveeda Khan, *Muslim Becoming: Aspiration and Skeptcism in Pakistan* (Durham, NC: Duke University Press, 2012), 77–81.
2. Khan believed that scriptural hermeneutics should be determined through the lens of science. He was fond of saying that the "Word of God and the Work of God . . . were identical." Metcalf, *Islamic Revival*, 323.
3. https://www.youtube.com/watch?v=vln9D81eO60.
4. For instance, Talal Asad's essay on the Rushdie Affair highlights the inextricable link between British Muslim protests and the United Kingdom's colonization and subsequent socioeconomic marginalization of its new, mainly South Asian Muslim, immigrant populations. Talal Asad, "Multiculturalism and British Identity in the Wake of the Rushdie Affair," in *Genealogies of Religion* (Baltimore: John Hopkins University Press, 1993), 239–268. On the Danish Cartoons, see Cindy Holder, "Debating the Danish Cartoons: Civil Rights or Civil Power?," *University of New Brunswick Law Journal* 55 (2006): 179–185.
5. On Pakistan's blasphemy laws, see Shemeem Abbas, *Pakistan's Blasphemy Laws: From Islamic Empires to the Taliban* (Austin: University of Texas Press, 2013).
6. Abū Dāwūd al-Sijistānī, *Sunan Abī Dāwūd*, ed. Shuʿayb al-Arnaʾūṭ and Muḥammad Kāmil Qarah Ballī, 7 vols. (Damascus: Dār al-Risāla al-ʿĀlamiyya, 2009), 7:178. The *ḥadīth* can also be rendered as "whoever leaves wrangling (*al-mirāʾ*)," though the commentators of this of Abū Dāwūd's *Sunan* equate the term *mirāʾ* with *jidāl* (debate); ibid., 7:179.
7. "Canadian Imams Condemn Radical Islam," *National Post*, Aug. 13, 2010. https://postmedia.us.janrainsso.com/static/server.html?origin=https%3A%2F%2Fnationalpost.com%2Fholy-post%2Fcanadian-imams-condemn-radical-islam (last accessed Nov. 18, 2021).
8. A multiplicity of legal schools existed in the 9th century, but their number eventually dwindled to four Sunni schools of law; see Wael Hallaq, *The Origins and Evolution of Islamic Law* (Cambridge: Cambridge University Press, 2005), 168–169. See also Zulfika Amir Hijri, *Diversity and Pluralism in Islam: Historical and Contemporary Discourses amongst Muslims* (London: I.B. Tauris, 2010).

9. George Makdisi, *The Rise of Colleges: Institutions of Learning in Islam and the West* (Edinburgh: Edinburgh University Press, 1984), 128. Scholars differ in their deployment of the use "classical" to speak of a particular era of Islamic law. For the purposes of this study, I speak of the classical era as the period between 900 and 1258 CE. The beginning of this period is marked by the solidification of boundaries between legal schools in Baghdad, the establishment of standard legal sciences in school curricula, and the hierarchy of school leadership, typified in the position of *raʾīs* (school leader); see Christopher Melchert, *The Formation of the Sunnī Schools of Law, 9th–10th Centuries C.E.* (Leiden: Brill, 1997). The end of the classical period is characterized by both the emergence of canonical texts summarizing school doctrine and the Mongol destruction of the historical Iraqi and Persianate heartlands of Islamic legal scholarship. For scholarly debates concerning the periodization of Islamic legal scholarship, see Susan Spectorsky's discussion, *Women in Classical Islamic Law: A Survey of the Sources* (Leiden: Brill, 2011), 3. See also Marion Katz's excellent discussion of the differences between the Classical and Medieval periods in her article "The Age of Development and Continuity, 12th–15th Centuries CE," in *The Oxford Handbook of Islamic Law*, ed. Anver Emon and Rumee Ahmed (Oxford: Oxford University Press, 2018), 437–458.
10. The origin of the statement appears to be Taha Jabir al-Alwani's *The Ethics of Disagreement in Islam*, trans. Abdulwahid Hamid (Herndon: The International Institute of Islamic Thought, 2011), 11, 76–77, though al-Alwani himself recognizes that *ikhtilāf* and *khilāf* were oftentimes used as synonyms.
11. My use of the word culture here is not a technical one. We commonly speak of "a culture of ___" to designate communities that value and frequently engage in particular practices: we thus speak of cultures of food, music, dance, literature, etc.
12. Youcef Soufi, "Why Study *Uṣūl al-Fiqh*?: The Problem of *Taqlīd* and Tough Cases in 4th–5th/10th-11th Century Iraq," *Islamic Law and Society* 28, no. 1–2 (2021): 7. See al-Shīrāzī's comments on the function of *uṣūl al-fiqh* in relation to the science of *khilāf*; Abū Isḥāq al-Shīrāzī, *Sharḥ al-Lumaʿ fī Uṣūl al-Fiqh*, ed. ʿAbd al-Majīd Turkī, 2 vols. (Beirut: Dār al-Gharb al-Islāmī, 1988), 1:161.
13. From the 10th–12th centuries, most jurists rejected that someone trained in the law (an *ʿālim* or "scholar") follow the opinion of another authority without evidence (in Arabic, *taqlīd*); al-Shīrāzī, *Sharḥ*, 2:1012–1013; Ibn al-Qaṣṣār, *Muqaddima fī Uṣūl al-Fiqh*, ed. Muṣṭafā Makhdūm (Riyadh: Dār al-Maʿlama li'l-Nashr wa'l-Tawzīʿ, 1999), 140; Abū al-Maʿālī al-Juwaynī, *Kitāb al-Talkhīṣ fī Uṣūl al-Fiqh*, ed. ʿAbd Allāh al-Nībālī and Shubbayr al-ʿAmarī, 3 vols. (Beirut: Dār al-Bashāʾir al-Islāmiyya, 1996), 3:425; Abū al-Ḥusayn al-Baṣrī, *al-Muʿtamad fī Uṣūl al-Fiqh*, ed. Khalīl al-Mays, 2 vols., 3rd ed. (Beirut: Dār al-Kutub al-ʿIlmiyya, 2005), 3:362; Abū al-Ḥasan al-ʿUkbarī, *Risālat al-ʿUkbarī fī Uṣūl al-Fiqh*, ed. Badr b. Nāṣir al-Subayʿī (Amman: Arwiqa, 2017), 77; Abū Yaʿlā b. al-Farrāʾ, *al-ʿUdda fī Uṣūl al-Fiqh*, ed. Muḥammad ʿAbd al-Qādir ʿAṭā (Beirut: Dār al-Kutub al-ʿIlmiyya, 2002), 2:444.
14. On the lay-Muslim obligation to follow the jurists' *fatwās*, see al-Shīrāzī, *Sharḥ*, 2:1010; Abū Yaʿlā, *al-ʿUdda*, 2:444; al-Khaṭīb al-Baghdādī, *Kitāb al-Faqīh wa'l-Mutafaqqih* (Riyadh: Dār Ibn al-Jawzī, 1996), 292; Ibn al-Qaṣṣār, *Muqaddima*, 154;

Muhammad Khaled Masud, Brinkley Messick, and David Powers, "Muftis, Fatwas, and Islamic Legal Interpretation," in *Islamic Legal Interpretation: Muftis and their Fatwas*, ed. M.K. Masud et al. (Cambridge, MA: Harvard University Press, 1996), 3–4.

15. Al-Shīrāzī, *Sharḥ*, 2:1007: "*qubūl al-qawl min ghayr dalīl.*" Emphasis mine.
16. A jurist's *ijtihād* (effort in seeking the law) was a precondition for his correct performance of the law, and therefore his salvation. See, e.g., Ibn al-Qaṣṣār, *Muqaddima*, 140; al-Shīrāzī, *Sharḥ*, 2:1007, 1012.
17. On the uncertainty of the law, see Aron Zysow, *The Economy of Certainty* (Atlanta: Lockwood, 2013), 1; Bernard Weiss, *The Spirit of Islamic Law* (Athens: University of Georgia Press, 1998), 98; Marie Bernand, *Le problème de la connaissance d'après le Muġnī du cadi 'Abd al-Ğabbār* (Alger: Société nationale d'édition et de diffusion, 1982).
18. Michael Cook calls Islam "a culture of debate"; Michael Cook, "Ibn Qutayba and the Monkeys," *Studia Islamica* 89 (1999): 43.
19. Ibn 'Aqīl, *Kitāb al-Jadal 'alā Ṭarīqat al-Fuqahā'* (Port Said: Maktabat al-Thaqāfa al-Dīniyya, n.d.), 42; al-Khaṭīb al-Baghdādī, *Kitāb al-Faqīh*, 257; al-Bājī, *al-Minhāj fī Tartīb al-Ḥijāj*, ed. 'Abd al-Majīd Turkī, 3rd ed. (Beirut: Dār al-Gharb al-Islāmī, 2001), 34.
20. Al-Juwaynī, *al-Kāfiya fī al-Jadal*, ed. Fawqiyya Maḥmūd (Cairo: Maṭba'at 'Īsā al-Bābī al-Ḥalabī wa-Shurakā'uh, 1979), 24.
21. For the culture of debate among non-juristic circles of the 10th century, see Joel Kraemer, *Humanism in the Renaissance of Islam: The Cultural Revival During the Buyid Age* (Leiden: Brill, 1986), 58; Hava Lazarus-Yafeh et al., eds., *The Majlis: Interreligious Encounters in Medieval Islam* (Wiesbaden: Harrassowitz, 1999).
22. E.g., Tāj al-Dīn al-Subkī, *Ṭabaqāt al-Shāfi'iyya al-Kubrā*, ed. 'Abd al-Fattāḥ al-Ḥulū and Maḥmūd al-Ṭanāḥī, 10 vols. (Cairo: Maṭba'at 'Īsā al-Bābī al-Ḥalabī, 1964), 3:26; Abū al-Ḥasan al-Mas'ūdī, *Murūj al-Dhahab wa-Ma'ādin al-Jawhar*, ed. Kamāl Ḥasan Mar'ī, 4 vols. (Beirut: al-Maktaba al-'Aṣriyya, 2005), 4:17.
23. Makdisi, *Rise of Colleges*, 109–110, 128–132.
24. Recent notable studies on *jadal* include Walter Young, *The Dialectical Forge: Juridical Disputation and the Evolution of Islamic Law* (Cham: Springer, 2017); the publication of Larry Miller's seminal 1984 dissertation, *Islamic Disputation Theory: The Uses & Rules of Argument in Medieval Islam* (Cham: Springer, 2020); Abdessamad Belhaj, *Argumentation et Dialectique en Islam* (Louvain-La-Neuve: Presses Universitaire de Louvain, 2010); Mehmet Karabela, "The Development of Dialectic and Argumentation Theory in Post-Classical Islamic Intellectual History" (PhD diss., McGill University, 2010); Mohammad Syifa Amin Widigdo, "Imām al-Ḥaramayn al-Juwaynī on *Jadal*: Juridical and Theological Dialectic in the Fifth/Eleventh Century" (PhD diss., Indiana University, 2016); for an important article from the 1980s, see Wael Hallaq, "A Tenth-Eleventh Century Treatise on Juridical Dialectic." *The Muslim World* 77, no. 3–4 (1987): 199.
25. E.g., Norman Calder, "Al-Nawawī's Typology of *Muftīs* and Its Significance for a General Theory of Islamic Law," *Islamic Law and Society* 3, no. 2 (1996): 139.

26. Youcef L. Soufi, "The Lost Oral Genesis of Islamic Law: The Case of an Eleventh-Century Disputation (*munāẓara*) on Broken Oaths." *Journal of the American-Oriental Society* 141, no.4 (2021): 823–846.
27. This shorthand is testament to al-Shīrāzī's influence. Like the modern convention of saying Freud or Marx without specifying their first names, members of the Shāfiʿī community knew who the "Shaykh Abū Isḥāq" was. Unfortunately, it is easy to confuse al-Shīrāzī with Abū Isḥāq al-Isfarāyinī who was referred to as the "al-Ustadh (the teacher) Abū Isḥāq." See al-Isfarāyinī's biography in al-Subkī, *Ṭabaqāt*, 4:256.
28. 478 AH.
29. Al-Subkī, *Ṭabaqāt*, 4:222: "*Kāna al-shaykh Abū Isḥāq ghaḍanfar^an fī al-munāẓara.*"
30. Ibid., 5:123. "*Fa-ammā al-mukhtalaf, fa-ma kanā aḥad yuḍāhī Abā Isḥāq fī ʿaṣrihi.*"
31. Ibid., 4:216.
32. For biographical entries on al-Shīrāzī, see Ibn al-Ṣalāḥ, *Ṭabaqāt al-Fuqahāʾ al-Shāfiʿiyya*, ed. Muḥyī al-Dīn ʿAlī Najīb, 2 vols. (Beirut: Dār al-Bashāʾir al-Islāmiyya, 1992), 1:302–310; Taqī al-Dīn Ibn Qāḍī Shuhba, *Ṭabaqāt al-Shāfiʿiyya*, ed. ʿAbd al-ʿAlīm Khān, 2 vols. (Beirut: ʿĀlam al-Kutub, 1987), 1:238–240; Jamāl al-Dīn al-Isnawī, *Ṭabaqāt al-Shāfiʿiyya*, ed. Kamāl Yūsuf Ḥūt, 2 vols. (Beirut: Dār al-Kutub al-ʿIlmiyya, 1987), 2:7–9; al-Subkī, *Ṭabaqāt*, 4:215–256; Ibn Khallikān, *Wafayāt al-Aʿyān wa-Anbāʾ Abnāʾ al-Zamān*, ed. Iḥsān ʿAbbās, 8 vols. (Beirut: Dār al-Ṣādir, 1968–1977), 1:29–31; Muḥyī al-Dīn al-Nawawī, *al-Majmūʿ: Sharḥ al-Muhadhdhab*, ed. Rāʾid b. Abī ʿAlfa, 2 vols. (Amman: Bayt al-Afkār al-Dawliyya, 2009), 1:17–18. For contemporary biographies of al-Shīrāzī, see Eric Chaumont, "al-Shīrāzī" $EI^2$; Ḥasan Hītū, *al-Imām al-Shīrāzī: Ḥayātuhu wa-Ārāʾuhu al-Uṣūliyya* (Damascus: Dār al-Fikr, 1980).
33. Abū Isḥāq Al-Shīrāzī, *Ṭabaqāt al-Fuqahāʾ*, ed. Iḥsān ʿAbbās (Beirut: Dār al-Rāʾid al- ʿArabī, 1970), 134. As was customary for students at the time, al-Shīrāzī would critically reflect and comment upon his master's lessons. The *taʿlīqa*, or commentary, was a standard way of learning under a teacher. The phrase *ʿallaqtu ʿalayhi* was a common one among jurists characterizing their study under the guidance of a teacher. See Makdisi, *Rise*, 126.
34. Ann Lambton, "Shiraz," *EI*; Ḥamd Allāh Mustawfi, *The Geographical Part of Nuzhat-al-Qulūb*, trans. G. Le Strange (Leiden: Brill, 1915), provides information on Shīrāz in the period soon after the Mongol invasion; A.J. Arberry, *Shiraz: Persian City of Saints and Poets* (Norman: University of Oklahoma Press, 1960); John Limbert, *Shiraz in the Age of Hafez: The Glory of a Medieval Persian City* (Seattle: University of Washington Press, 2004).
35. Al-Shīrāzī, *Ṭabaqāt*, 134. Later biographies, including al-Subkī's *Ṭabaqāt*, erroneously assert that al-Shīrāzī studied in Shiraz with two scholars named Abū ʿAbd Allāh al-Bayḍāwī (d. 424/1033 CE) and Ibn Rāmīn. Al-Shīrāzī himself tells us that al-Bayḍāwī lived in Baghdad and Ibn Rāmīn settled in Basra. Al-Shīrāzī did have them as his teachers, but in these two respective cities, rather than Shiraz; al-Sḥīrāzī, *Ṭabaqāt*, 125–126. On al-Shīrāzī's teacher, Abū ʿAbd Allāh al-Jallāb, known as Khaṭīb Shīrāz, see al-Shirāzī, *Ṭabaqāt*, 133.
36. Al-Shīrāzī, *Ṭabaqāt*, 179.

37. His arrival is dated to 415 AH.
38. Al-Shīrāzī would write of Ibn Surayj that it was "through him that the legal school spread (*Wa-'anhu intashara fiqh al-Shāfi'ī*)." Al-Shīrāzī, *Ṭabaqāt*, 109. On Ibn Surayj, see Wael Hallaq, "Was al-Shafi'i the Master Architect of Islamic Jurisprudence?," *International Journal of Middle East Studies* 25, no. 4 (1993): 587–605; Ahmed El Shamsy, "Bridging the Gap: Two Early Texts of Islamic Legal Theory," *Journal of American Oriental Society* 137, no. 3 (2017): 505–536; and Christopher Melchert, *The Formation*, 87–102.
39. On his way to Baghdad, al-Shīrāzī briefly studied in Basra; al-Shīrāzī, *Ṭabaqāt*, 125.
40. On the constructing of a Muslim-Persian identity, see Sarah Bowen Savant, *The New Muslims of Post-Conquest Iran: Tradition, Memory, and Conversion* (New York: Cambridge University Press, 2013).
41. Al-Subkī, *Ṭabaqāt*, 4:224: "*Qāla: yā waladī, a-mā jama'atnā safīnat Nūḥ?*"
42. Al-Shīrāzī notes that even at 102 years of age, al-Ṭabarī's mental faculties remained unchanged: *Ṭabaqāt*, 127.
43. On Ibn al-Ṣabbāgh's life, see al-Subkī, *Ṭabaqāt*, 5:122.
44. Ibid., 5:123.
45. On the Seljuks, see ACS Peacock, *The Great Seljuk Empire* (Edinburgh: Edinburgh University Press, 2015).
46. Richard Bulliet, *Patricians of Nishapur: A Study in Medieval Islamic Social History* (Cambridge, MA: Harvard University Press, 1972), 72–75.
47. In the last year of his life, al-Shīrāzī noted that not one city on the way from Baghdad to Khurasan was devoid of a judge, professor, or *muftī* that had been his student, al-Subkī, *Ṭabaqāt*, 4:216.
48. For instance, al-Shīrāzī was in communication with Niẓām al-Mulk and the caliph over intra-communal riots that had shaken Baghdad; al-Subkī, *Ṭabaqāt*, 4:235.
49. Al-Subkī, *Ṭabaqāt*, 4:219; the context of the voyage was a dispute between the caliph and the Iraqi Governor al-'Amīd Abī Fatḥ b. Abī Layth. The journey is also narrated within Ibn al-Athīr, *al-Kāmil fī al-Tārīkh*, ed. Muḥammad al-Daqqāq, 11 vols. (Beirut: Dār al-Kutub al-'Ilmiyya, 1987), 8:428–429.
50. Al-Shīrāzī arrived in Nishapur to the familiar sight of al-Juwaynī, who took pride in hosting the Baghdad jurist with great care "like a young servant"; al-Subkī, *Ṭabaqāt*, 4:222.
51. Ibid., 5:172, where al-Shīrāzī tells others to "Benefit from this Imam because he is the joy of our times (*nuzhat hādhā al-zamān*)."
52. Abū al-Faraj Ibn al-Jawzī, *al-Muntaẓam fī Tārīkh al-Mulūk wa'l-Umam*, ed. F. Krenkow, 8 vols (Hyderabad: Dā'irat al-Ma'ārif 1938–1940), 9:19–20.
53. Ibn Khallikān, *Wafayāt*, 1:30–31. Al-Subkī reports that al-Shīrāzī was buried in the Bāb al-Ḥarb cemetery. Al-Subkī, *Ṭabaqāt*, 4:229. For more on the topography of Baghdad, see Guy Le Strange, *Baghdad during the Abbasid Caliphate: From Contemporary Arabic and Persian Sources* (Oxford: Clarendon Press, 1900); Jacob Lassner, *The Topography of Baghdad in the Early Middle Ages: Text and Studies* (Detroit: Wayne State University Press, 1970).

54. In substantive law: Muḥammad al-Zuhaylī, ed., *al-Muhadhdhab fī Fiqh al-Imām al-Shāfiʿī*, 6 vols. (Damascus: Dār al-Qalam, 1992); and *al-Tanbīh fī al-Fiqh al-Shāfiʿī* (Beirut: ʿAlam al-Kutub, 1983). In legal theory: ʿAbd al-Qādir al-Ḥasanī, ed., *Kitāb al-Lumaʿ fī Uṣūl al-Fiqh* (Tangier: Dār al-Ḥadīth al-Kittāniyya, 2013); Muḥammad Ḥītū, ed., *al-Tabṣira* (Damascus: Dār al-Fikr, 1980); and *Sharḥ al-Lumaʿ*; in dialectic: *al-Mulakhkhaṣ fī al-Jadal* (MS. Atif Effendi Library, Istanbul, copied 590AH/1194CE); and ʿAbd al-Majīd Turkī, ed., *al-Maʿūna fī al-Jadal* (Beirut: Dār al-Gharb al-Islāmī, 1988).
55. Al-Shīrāzī, *Ṭabaqāt*.
56. In *khilāf*: *al-Nukat fī Masāʾil al-Khilāf*. Manuscript; Arabic M.S. 494 copied 1303/1885, Princeton (also available as part of a series of dissertations undertaken at Umm al-Qurā University). In theology: *ʿAqīdat al-Salaf* (published as ʿAbd al-Majīd Turkī, ed., *Muʿtaqad Abī Isḥāq al-Shīrāzī* in *Sharḥ al-Lumaʿ*(Beirut: Dār al-Kutub al-ʿIlmiyya, 1988), 1:91–116.
57. Al-Bājī traveled from Muslim Spain to Eastern Muslim lands seeking knowledge between 426–434/1034–1043; On al-Bājī, see al-Qāḍī ʿIyāḍ, *Tartīb al-Madārik wa-Taqrīb al-Masālik*, 8 vols, 2nd ed. (Rabat: Wizārat al-Awqāf wa'l-Shuʾūn al-Islāmiyya, 1983), 8:117–127.
58. On the lineage of the Dāmaghānīs, see Ibn Abī al-Wafāʾ al-Qurashī, *al-Jawāhir al-Muḍīʾa fī Ṭabaqāt al-Ḥanafiyya* (Beirut: Dār al-Kutub al-ʿIlmiyya, 2005), 355.
59. Al-Subkī, *Ṭabaqāt*, 4:245–252.
60. Ibid., 4:237–245.
61. Ibid., 5:214–218. Reproduced in al-Subkī, *Ṭabaqāt*, 4:252–256. For a translation of al-Shīrāzī's disputations, see Youcef Soufi, "Pious Critique: Abū Isḥāq al-Shīrāzī and the 11th Century Practice of Juristic Disputation (*Munāẓara*)" (PhD diss., University of Toronto, 2017), 244–276; Siddiqui also translates al-Shīrāzī's disputations with al-Juwaynī; Sohaira Siddiqui, "*Jadal* and *Qiyās* in the Fifth/Eleventh Century: Two Debates between al-Juwaynī and al-Shīrāzī," *Journal of American Oriental Society* 139, no. 4 (2019): 923–944.
62. Al-Subkī, *Ṭabaqāt*, 5:209–214.
63. Ibid., *Ṭabaqāt*, 4:245.
64. Samir Kaddouri, "Refutations of Ibn Ḥazm by Mālikī Authors of al-Andalus and North Africa," in *Ibn Ḥazm of Cordoba: The Life and Works of a Controversial Thinker*, ed. Camilla Adang et al. (Leiden: Brill, 2012), 564; al-Qāḍī ʿIyāḍ, *Tartīb*, 8:122.
65. Al-Subkī, *Ṭabaqāt*, 4:245.
66. Ibid., 5:213–214: "Ibn al-Ṣalāḥ said 'I transmitted it from the handwriting of the Shaykh Abū ʿAlī b.' ʿAmmār, who said 'I transmitted it from the handwriting of a man among the disciples (*aṣḥāb*) of Shaykh Abū Isḥāq [i.e., al-Shīrāzī], who mentioned at the end of the text that he had copied it from the handwriting of the Shaykh al-Imām Abū Isḥāq.' "
67. E.g., Ibn al-Athīr, *al-Kāmil*, 8:428–429.
68. Two other points support the case for authenticity. First, the arguments in the disputation transcripts are consistent with those throughout al-Shīrāzī's written corpus. Second, the transcripts show stylistic differences that suggest they came from

different sources. For instance, the disputations that al-Shīrāzī transcribed sometimes use the first-person verbal conjugation (e.g., "*qultu* (I said)") when referring to al-Shīrāzī's statements; al-Subkī, *Ṭabaqāt*, 5:214. In contrast, the disputations that al-Bājī transcribed use the third-person pronoun to refer to the debaters.

69. Moreover, we have to take seriously the possibility that al-Shīrāzī embellished his performance, though the fact that he does not clearly defeat his opponents in his four disputations mitigates this possibility.
70. For earlier formulations of the thesis on the closure of the gates of *ijtihād*, see Leon Ostroróg, *The Angora Reforms* (London: University of London Press, 1927), 27–31; Robert Brunschvig, "Problème de la decadence," in *Classicisme et déclin culturel dans l'histoire de l'Islam*, ed. R. Brunschvig and G. von Grunebaum (Paris: Besson et Chantemerle, 1957), 35; H.A.R Gibb, *Modern Trends in Islam* (Chicago: University of Chicago Press, 1947), 13.
71. Joseph Schacht, *Introduction to Islamic Law*, reprint (Oxford: Clarendon Press, 1964, 1982), 70.
72. Ibid., 71.
73. Ibid.
74. E.g., Montgomery Watt, "The Closing of the Door of Iğtihād," *Orientalia Hispanica 1*, ed. J.M. Barral (Leiden: Brill, 1974), 675–678. For a review of anglophone scholarship before and after Schacht, see Shaista P. Ali-Karamali and Fiona Dunne. "The Ijtihad Controversy," *Arab Law Quarterly* 9, no. 3 (1994): 241–247; Anver Emon, "Ijtihad," in *The Oxford Handbook of Islamic Law*, ed. Anver Emon and Rumee Ahmed (Oxford: Oxford University Press, 2018), 181–189.
75. Wael Hallaq, "Was the Gate of Ijtihad Closed?," *International Journal of Middle East Studies* 16, no.1 (1984): 4.
76. Ibid., 16–17.
77. N.J. Coulson, *A History of Islamic Law*, reprint (Edinburgh: Edinburgh University Press, 1978), 73.
78. On Hallaq's association of creativity with *ijtihād*, see Sherman Jackson, "*Ijtihād* and *Taqlīd*: Between the Islamic Legal Tradition and Autonomous Western Reason," in *The Routledge Handbook of Islamic Law*, ed. Khaled Abou El Fadl et al. (Abingdon: Routledge, 2019), 255–272.
79. E.g., see the late *muftī* of Syria, Muḥammad Saʿīd Ramaḍān al-Būṭī, *Muḥāḍarāt fī al-Fiqh al-Muqāran* (Damascus: Dār al-Fikr, 1993), 7–8, who critiques *ijtihād* as an innovation that overturns tradition; see also Rudolph Peters, "*Idjtihād* and *Taqlīd* in 18th and 19th Century Islam," *Die Welt des Islams* 20, no. 3–4 (1980): 131–145. Junaid Quadri complicates the view that traditionalists rejected new modes of thinking in their encounter with modernity; Junaid Quadri, *Transformations of Tradition: Islamic Law in Colonial Modernity* (Oxford: Oxford University Press, 2021), 65–67.
80. In a more recent text, Jackson locates the triumph of *taqlīd* sometime during the 12th century; Jackson, "*Ijtihād* and *Taqlīd*," 258.
81. Sherman Jackson, "*Taqlīd*, Legal Scaffolding and the Scope of Legal Injunctions in Post-Formative Theory *Muṭlaq* and *ʿĀmm* in the Jurisprudence of Shihāb al-Dīn

al-Qarāfi," *Islamic Law and Society* 3, no. 2 (1996): 167, fn. 5; see also Sherman Jackson, *Islamic Law and the State: The Constitutional Jurisprudence of Shihāb al-Dīn al-Qarāfī* (Leiden: Brill, 1996), 73–82.

82. Jackson, *Islamic Law and the State*, xl.
83. Mohammad Fadel, "The Social Logic of *Taqlīd* and the Rise of the *Mukhtaṣar*," *Islamic Law and Society* 3, no. 2 (1996): 197.
84. Ahmed El Shamsy, "Rethinking, '*Taqlīd*' in the Early Shāfiʿī School," *Journal of the American Oriental Society* 128, no. 1 (2008): 1–23.
85. See also Ahmed El Shamsy, *The Canonization of Islamic Law: A Social and Intellectual History* (New York: Cambridge University Press, 2013), 173–175.
86. Ahmed Fekry Ibrahim speaks of an "*ijtihād-taqlīd* continuum" where *ijtihād* is tempered to the extent that it follows school doctrine; Ahmed Fekry Ibrahim, "Rethinking the *Taqlīd* Hegemony: An Institutional, Longue-Durée Approach," *Journal of the American-Oriental Society* 136, no. 4 (2016): 803. This view contrasts al-Shīrāzī's in two respects. First, al-Shīrāzī sees *ijtihād* and *taqlīd* as antonyms where one either knows or does not know the evidentiary basis for one's position. Second, *ijtihād* is not lessened by following the positions of one's predecessors so long as one knows the evidence that supports precedent.
87. In speaking of the Ḥanafī school, Talal al-Azem has perceptively noted that later school authorities recast the history of their school in ways that transformed the meaning of *ijtihād* by segmenting the practice in hierarchies. See Talal al-Azem, *Rule-Formulation and Binding Precedent in the* Madhhab-*Law Tradition: Ibn Quṭlūbughā's Commentary on* The Compendium *of Qudūrī* (Leiden: Brill, 2017), 14, 35.
88. Michel Foucault, "What is Enlightenment?," in *The Foucault Reader*, ed. P. Rabinow (New York: Pantheon Books, 1984), 32–50.
89. For a contemporary example of the use of *naqd*, see Sādiq al-ʿAẓm, *Naqd al-Fikr al-Dīnī* (Beirut: Dār al-Ṭalīʿa, 1977). The word is also often used in the context of Arab literature; see Roger Allen, *An Introduction to Arabic Literature* (Cambridge: Cambridge University Press, 2000), 219, 221, 227. Nada Moumtaz alerts us to the use of "*naqd*" among medieval Muslim scholars in the context of poetry and law, where she notes that the term is more appropriately translated as "distinction" rather than "critique"; Nada Moumtaz, "Critique, *Naqd*, Orthodoxy" *Critical Research on Religion* 7, no. 2 (2019): 196.
90. On the etymology of the term "critique," see Reinhart Koselleck, *Critique and Crisis: Enlightenment and the Pathogenesis of Modern Society* (Cambridge, MA: MIT Press, 1998), 103.
91. Michel Foucault, *Fearless Speech*, ed. Joseph Pearson (Los Angeles: Semiotext, 2001), 170.
92. Talal Asad, "Free Speech, Blasphemy, and Secular Criticism," in *Is Critique Secular?: Blasphemy, Injury, and Free Speech* (Berkeley, CA: The Townsend Center for the Humanities, 2009), 48.
93. Kant, *Prolegomena to Any Future Metaphysics*, revised ed., trans. and ed. Gary Hatfield (Cambridge: Cambridge University Press, 2004), 10.

94. My claim is not that the Iraqo-Persianate critique of the 10th–13th centuries is the only form of critique in Islam. For instance, Irfan Ahmad presents another form of critique within Islam, one that is associated with the prophets critique of the religio-political order of their times; see Irfan Ahmad, *Religion as Critique: Islamic Critical Thinking from Mecca to the Marketplace* (Chapel Hill: University of North Carolina Press, 2017), 15
95. Jürgen Habermas, *The Structural Transformation of the Public Sphere: An Inquiry into a Category of Bourgeois Society*, trans. Thomas Burger (Cambridge, MA: MIT Press, 1989), 25, 34.
96. Ibid., see chapter 18.
97. Ibid., see chapter 20, where Habermas documents a shift from a critical to a consumer public.
98. Ibid., 203; The Frankfurt School in general was concerned with explaining how the Enlightenment had ended up producing repressive politics. Habermas does not explicitly mention National Socialism, but it lingered in the background of his thought.
99. Ibid., 226–227.
100. For instance, see Jürgen Habermas, *Between Facts and Norms: Contributions to a Discourse Theory of Law and Democracy*, trans. William Rehg (Cambridge, MA: MIT Press, 1996), 287.
101. *Habermas and the Public Sphere*, ed. Craig J. Calhoun (Cambridge, MA: MIT Press, 1992).
102. Marion Iris Young, "Impartiality and the Civic Public: Some Implications of Feminist Critiques of Moral and Political Theory," in *Feminism as Critique: On the Politics of Gender*, ed. Drucilla Cornell and Seyla Benhabib (Minneapolis: University of Minnesota Press, 1987), 56–76; Nancy Fraser, "Rethinking the Public Sphere: A Contribution to Actually Existing Democracy," in *Habermas and the Public Sphere*, ed. Craig J. Calhoun (Cambridge, MA: MIT Press, 1992), 114; and Joan Landes, *Women and the Public Sphere in the Age of the French Revolution* (Ithaca, NY: Cornell University Press, 1988).
103. James Tully, *Public Philosophy in a New Key*, 2 vols. (Cambridge: Cambridge University Press, 2008), 1: 53.
104. William Connolly, *Why I Am Not a Secularist* (Minneapolis: University of Minnesota Press, 2003), 25.
105. For a mid-20th-century example of the assumption of Muslim decline, see R. Brunschvig and G. von Grunebaum, eds., *Classicisme et declin culturel dans l'histoire de l'Islam* (Paris: Besson et Chantemerle, 1957), particularly R. Brunschvig's contribution, "Problème de la decadence," 29–51. For an example of the period after 9/11, see Bernard Lewis, *What Went Wrong: Western Impact and Middle Eastern Responses* (Oxford: Oxford University Press, 2002), 115.
106. Al-Ghazālī, *Iḥyā' 'Ulūm al-Dīn*, ed. Muḥammad al-Dālī Balṭa, 5 vols. (Beirut: al-Maktaba al-'Aṣriyya, 2015), 1:61–62.
107. Reinhart Koselleck, *Critique and Crisis: Enlightenment and the Pathogenesis of Modern Society* (Cambridge, MA: MIT Press, 1998), 113. See also Wendy Brown,

"Introduction," in *Is Critique Secular?: Blasphemy, Injury, and Free Speech* (Berkeley, CA: The Townsend Center for the Humanities, 2009), 10–12.

108. Karl Marx, "For a Ruthless Critique of Everything in Existence," in *The Marx-Engels Reader*, ed. Robert Tucker, 2nd ed (New York: WW Norton and Company, 1978), 12–15; See also Karl Marx, *Contribution to the Critique of Hegel's* Philosophy of Right, in *The Marx-Engels Reader*, ed. Robert Tucker, 2nd ed (New York: WW Norton and Company, 1978), 17.
109. Edward Said, *The World, the Text, and the Critic* (Cambridge, MA: Harvard University Press, 1983), 26. Hoda El Shakry explains well the assumption that religion lacks a critical edge in contrast to secularism, stating, "If the secular is fundamentally sceptical, religion, or so the argument goes, is inherently speculative." Hoda El Shakry, *The Literary Qur'an: Narrative Ethics in the Maghrib* (New York: Fordham University Press, 2020).
110. Talal Asad, "Response to Judith Butler," in *Is Critique Secular?* (Berkeley, CA: Townsend Papers, 2009), 138–139.
111. John Milbank, *Theology and Social Theory: Beyond Secular Reason*, 2nd ed. (Malden, MA: Blackwell Publishing, 1990), 391.
112. On the possibility of a dialogical engagement with premodern jurists over questions of epistemology and ethics, see Omar Farahat, *The Foundation of Norms in Islamic Jurisprudence and Theology* (Cambridge: Cambridge University Press, 2019), 11.
113. Ibn ʿAqīl, *Kitāb al-Jadal*, 2.
114. Kant, *An Answer to the Question: What is Enlightenment*, in *Practical Philosophy*, trans. and ed. Mary J. Gregor (Cambridge: Cambridge University Press, 1996), 17. On understanding, see also Hans-Georg Gadamer, *Truth and Method*, trans. Joel Weinsheimer (Wiltshire: Continuum, 2004), 305.
115. Michel Foucault, "What is Enlightenment?," 39. See also Michel Foucault, "What is Critique?" (trans. Kevin Paul Geiman), in *What is Enlightenment? Eighteenth-Century Answers and Twentieth-Century Questions*, ed. James Schmidt (Berkeley: University of California Press, 1996), 382–388.
116. Talal Asad, "Thinking about Religion, Belief, and Politics," in *The Cambridge Companion of Religious Studies*, ed. Robert Orsi (Cambridge: Cambridge University Press, 2011), 56.

## Chapter 1

1. Al-Qāḍī ʿIyāḍ, *Tartīb*, 8:178; Vidal-Castro, "al-Bājī, Abū l-Walīd" *EI*[3], ed. Kate Fleet, Gudrun Kramer, Denis Matringue, John Nawas, and Everett Rowson (Leiden: Brill, 2011).
2. Reports affirm that he left Andalusia in 1034/1035 CE, spent three years in the Hijaz, and then three years in Baghdad. ʿAbd al-Majīd Turkī, "*Al-Tamhīd al-Awwal*," in *Sharḥ al-Lumaʿ fī Uṣūl al-Fiqh*, ed. Abū Isḥāq al-Shīrāzī, 2 vols. (Beirut: Dār al-Gharb al-Islāmī, 1988), 1:48.

3. Al-Bājī was particularly sought after for his ability to defend Mālikī doctrine against Ibn Ḥazm's Ẓāhirī challenge. Samir Kaddouri, "Refutations by Mālikī Authors," 564. See also 'Abd al-Majīd Turki, *Munāẓarāt fī Uṣūl al-Sharī'a al-Islāmiyya bayna Ibn Ḥazm wa'l-Bājī* (Beirut: Dār al-Gharb al-Islāmī, 2008).
4. Abū al-Walīd al-Bājī, *al-Minhāj*, 34–42.
5. On ethnographic translation, see Talal Asad, *Genealogies of Religion* (Baltimore: John Hopkins University Press, 1993), 171–199.
6. Al-Subkī, *Ṭabaqāt*, 4:245–246.
7. Abū Ḥāmid al-Ghazālī, *The Remembrance of Death and the Afterlife*, trans. T.J. Winter (Cambridge: Islamic Texts Society, 1989); See also Samira Haj, *Reconfiguring Islamic Tradition: Reform, Rationality, and Modernity* (Stanford, CA: Stanford University Press, 2008), 38, for a modern context.
8. Al-Subkī, *Ṭabaqāt*, 4:245.
9. Al-Juwaynī, *al-Kāfiya*, 22.
10. For instance, the recitation of *Yā-Sīn* to the dead and dying is recommended in *ḥadīth* and has figured prominently in funeral rites up until the present; Muḥammad b. Jarīr al-Ṭabarī, *Jāmi' al-Bayān*, ed. Maḥmūd Shākir, 15 vols. (Beirut: Dār Ibn Ḥazm, 2013), 12:180.
11. Al-Subkī, *Ṭabaqāt*, 4:245.
12. Al-Qurashī, *al-Jawāhir*, 140.
13. Al-Subkī, *Ṭabaqāt*, 4:246.
14. In the early 9th century, the Shāfi'īs and the Ḥanafīs possessed two different scholarly orientations. The Shāfi'īs were part of the *ahl al-ḥadīth* (the people relying largely on *ḥadīth* as legal evidence), and the Ḥanafīs were part of the *ahl al-ra'y* (the people who used reason as legal evidence). However, by the 10th century, a rapprochement had taken place between the two parties such that both used similar textual, hermeneutic, and analogical arguments to justify their legal positions. On this rapprochement, see Melchert, *The Formation*, 68–83.
15. Al-Juwaynī, *Nihāyat al-Maṭlab fī Dirāyat al-Madhhab*, ed. 'Abd al-'Aẓīm al-Dīb, 21 vols. (Jeddah: Dār al-Minhāj, 2007), 12:154: "*fa-innahum warathat al-anbiyā'*."
16. Al-Shīrāzī, *Ṭabaqāt*, 127.
17. Al-Subkī, *Ṭabaqāt*, 4:246.
18. Al-Bājī, *al-Minhāj*, 9–10; al-Baghdādī, *Kitāb al-Faqīh*, 250–256; Ibn 'Aqīl, *Kitāb al-Jadal*, 2; al-Juwaynī, *al-Kāfiya*, 529–541.
19. Ibn 'Aqīl, *Kitāb al-Jadal*, 2, who states "that method of argumentation is not the same as the method of knowledge-seeking (*ṭarīqat al-jadal ghayr ṭarīqat al-'ilm*)." This should not be interpreted as meaning that the debater does not seek knowledge through debate. Rather the point is that the questioner in debate gatherings seeks to critique his opponent, whereas questions from students aim to learn from one's teacher.
20. Alasdair C MacIntyre, *After Virtue: A Study in Moral Theory*, 3rd ed. (Notre Dame, IN: University of Notre Dame Press, 2007), 190.
21. Al-Subkī, *Ṭabaqāt*, 4:246.

22. Al-Bājī, *al-Minhāj*, 9: "And he is to show reverence in his manner of sitting (*wa-yatawaqqar fī julūsihi*), not stirring from his position, in a way that weakness in speech and foolishness might be ascribed to him (*wa-lā yanza'ij min makānihi fa-yunsab ilā al-rikka wa'l-khurq*); and he is not to play his hand or beard (*wa-lā ya'bath bi-yadihi wa-liḥyatihi*)."
23. Al-Baghdādī, *Kitāb al-Faqīh*, 252: "And he is to feel gravitas in the gathering and he is to act calmly."
24. Al-Bājī, *al-Minhāj*, 9.
25. Ibid., 9: "The debater must begin [strengthening his] reverence for God, most high, before his argumentation (*yanbaghī li'l-munāẓir an yuqaddim 'alā jadalihi taqwā Allāh*) so as to purify his reasoning [from base motives]. He should praise God, most high, (*wa-yaḥmad Allāh 'azza wa-jalla*) and send abundant peace upon the Prophet, so as to increase and magnify his blessings and his benefits [in debate] (*barakātuhu wa-fawā'iduhu*)." See also al-Baghdādī, *Kitāb al-Faqīh*, 250–251.
26. This *ḥadīth* is of such importance to the Islamic tradition that al-Nawawī begins his collection of forty essential *ḥadīth*s with it; Ibn Daqīq al-'Īd, *Sharḥ al-Arba'īn Ḥadīth[an] al-Nawawiyya* (Beirut: Dār al-Kutub al-'Ilmiyya, 1983), 1. For a treatment of intent, see Wael Hallaq, *The Impossible State: Islam, Politics, and Modernity's Moral Predicament* (New York: Columbia University Press, 2013), 120–121; Paul R. Powers, *Intent in Islamic Law: Motive and Meaning in Medieval Sunnī Fiqh* (Leiden: Brill, 2006).
27. For more on Asad's understanding of the body and its ethical formation, see *Genealogies of Religion*, chapter 2 where Asad grapples with his understanding of the concept of *habitus*; see also his "Remarks on the Anthropology of the Body," in *Religion and the Body*, ed. Sarah Coakley (Cambridge: Cambridge University Press, 2000), 42–52, where he grapples with Marcel Mauss's understanding of *habitus*. For an application of Asad's theory of *habitus* to modern Muslims, see Talal Asad, *Formation of the Secular* (Stanford, CA: Stanford University Press, 2003), 248–252; Saba Mahmood, *Politics of Piety: The Islamic Revival and the Feminist Subject.* (Princeton, NJ: Princeton University Press, 2005), 26–33; and Charles Hirschkind, *The Ethical Soundscape: Cassette Sermons and Islamic Counterpublics* (New York: Columbia University Press, 2006), 98–102.
28. Ibn 'Aqīl, *Kitāb al-Jadal*, 2: "Everything that disturbs and interrupts, like sluggishness, or not paying attention, and being sleepy is among the comportment that the one in attendance should avoid."
29. Al-Shīrāzī outlines with detail who must ask for a religious response in his discussion of *taqlīd* in *Sharḥ al-Luma'*, starting at 2:1007. For Ḥanbalī sources, see al-'Ukbarī, *Risālat*, 74–77; Abū Ya'lā, *al-'Udda*, 2:448. For the Ḥanafī position, see Abū Bakr al-Jaṣṣāṣ, *al-Fuṣūl fī al-Uṣūl*, ed. Muḥammad Tāmir, 2 vols. (Beirut: Dār al-Kutub al-'Ilmiyya, 2010), 2:371–374; Abū 'Abd Allāh al-Ṣaymarī, "Kitāb Masā'il al-Khilāf fī Uṣūl al-Fiqh," in *Les Problèmes de divergences en méthodologie juridique de Ḥusayn B.'Alî al-Ṣaymarî: Présentation, analyze et édition critique*, ed. Abdelouahad Jahdani (PhD diss., Université de Provence, 1991). For the Mu'tazilī position, see al-Baṣrī, *al-Mu'tamad*, 2:360. For the Mālikī position, see Ibn al-Qaṣṣār, *Muqaddima*, 144. For other Shāfi'ī

texts, see Abū al-Ma'ālī al-Juwaynī, "Kitāb al-Fatwā," in *al-Burhān fī Uṣūl al-Fiqh*, ed. 'Abd al-'Aẓīm Dīb, (n.p., 1979), 2: 2:1505–1511; Abū Ḥāmid al-Ghazālī, *al-Mustaṣfā min 'Ilm al-Uṣūl*, ed. Muḥammad al-Mur'ashlī, 2 vols. (Beirut: Dār al-Nafā'is, 2011), 2:937. See also Abū al-Muẓaffar al-Sam'ānī, *Qawāṭi' al-Adilla*, ed. Muḥammad al-Shāfi'ī, 2 vols. (Beirut: Dār al-Kutub al-'Ilmiyya, 1997), 2:341.

30. Al-Shīrāzī, *Sharḥ*, 2:1008–9.
31. Al-Shīrāzī, *Ṭabaqāt*, 127–128. On the lineage of the Dāmaghānīs, see al-Qurashī, *al-Jawāhir*, 140–141.
32. On debates about whom a lay Muslim should consult, see al-Shīrāzī, *Sharḥ*, 2:1011–1012; Abū Ḥāmid al-Ghazālī, *al-Mustaṣfā*, 2:938–940; al-Jaṣṣāṣ, *al-Fuṣūl*, 2:372–373; al-Juwaynī, *Kitāb al-Fatwā*, 2:1519. On juristic leadership in a time of political uncertainty in Baghdad, see Daphna Ephrat, *A Learned Society in a Period of Transition: The Sunni 'Ulama' of Eleventh-Century Baghdad* (Albany: State University of New York Press, 2000).
33. Al-Shīrāzī, *Sharḥ*, 2:1038.
34. Ibid.
35. See al-Shīrāzī, *Sharḥ*, 2:1037, for a discussion of different points of view on who a lay Muslim should consult.
36. See Hussein Ali Agrama, *Questioning Secularism: Islam, Sovereignty, and the Rule of Law in Modern Egypt* (Chicago: University of Chicago Press, 2012), 160. Agrama sees in the *fatwā* a form of care of the self similar to Foucault's analysis of Hellenistic and Roman philosophical schools; Michel Foucault, *Hermeneutics of the Subject: Lectures at the Collège de France, 1981–82*, trans. Graham Burchell, ed. Frederic Gros (New York: Palgrave Macmillan, 2005). Agrama's framing of the issue is very useful for understanding modern Muslims but from the classical legal perspective, the recourse to jurists was less about ethical self-formation and more about ensuring that lay Muslims possessed justifications for their legal practice: Thus, al-Shīrāzī considered a *fatwā* to be a *dalīl*, or evidence, for the lay petitioner, and thus was among the legal sources (*uṣūl*) of the law (Ar: "*fatwā al-'ālim fī ḥaqq al-'āmmī.*"); al-Shīrāzī, *Sharḥ*, 1:161.
37. Providing *responsas* fell on collective shoulders. Al-Shīrāzī explains a common view that a jurist in "a remote location devoid of other qualified jurists (*fa-in kāna fī iqlīm laysa fīhi ghayruhu min al-'ulamā'*)," then he is morally obligated to provide religious *responsas* to lay Muslim ("*ta'ayyana 'alayhi al-fatwā wa'l-ta'līm 'inda al-ṭalab*"). Al-Shīrāzī, *Sharḥ*, 2:1035.
38. On the notion of defeat, or *inqiṭā'*, see Ibn 'Aqīl, *Kitāb al-Jadal*, 485–88. See also Miller, *Islamic Disputation Theory*, 20.
39. Jurists of one generation could also disagree about whether a previous generation had achieved consensus on a legal question, and their disagreement could itself become the topic of a disputation. See, for instance, a disputation between Abū al-Ṭayyib al-Ṭabarī and Abū al-Ḥasan al-Ṭāliqānī, transcribed in al-Subkī, *Ṭabaqāt*, 5:34. Another example is Ibn Surayj's disputation with Ibn Dāwūd al-Ẓāhirī in chapter two of this study.

40. Al-Bājī counselled against presupposing too much and recommended that the *sā'il* begin by asking not *what* but *whether* an opposing jurist had an opinion on a given topic; see al-Bājī, *al-Minhāj*, 34.
41. Al-Shīrāzī, *Sharḥ*, 1:147.
42. Al-Baghdādī, *Kitāb al-Faqīh*, 18.
43. Ibid., 22.
44. Al-Shīrāzī, *Sharḥ*, 2:799: al-Shīrāzī thinks that there is always a wisdom in God's law, *wajh al-ḥikma*, like in the case of the prohibition of wine, which benefits humans by preserving their mind to pray diligently and remember God. But he also states that sometimes God keeps that wisdom hidden, giving the example of the *ratio legis* for the prohibition of usury on comestibles.
45. Al-Subkī, *Ṭabaqāt*, 4:246. On the Kāzarūn, see J. Calmard, "Kāzarūn," *EI2*, P. Bearman, Th. Bianquis, C.E. Bosworth, E. van Donzel, W.P. Heinrichs. Consulted online Sept. 4, 2018 <http://dx.doi.org.myaccess.library.utoronto.ca/10.1163/1573-3912_islam_SIM_4079>
46. Not all debate gatherings started off with a jurist of lesser skill: al-Dāmaghānī could very well have initiated the debate alone. On this tag-team practice, see Miller, *Islamic Disputation Theory*, 87.
47. Al-Subkī, *Ṭabaqāt*, 4:246.
48. For the Iraqi Shāfi'ī discourse on *khiyār*, see al-Shīrāzī, *al-Muhadhdhab*, 4:614; 'Alī b. Muḥammad al-Māwardī, *al-Ḥāwī al-Kabīr fī Fiqh Madhhab al-Imām al-Shāfi'ī, wa-huwa Sharḥ Mukhtaṣar al-Muzanī*, ed. 'Alī Muḥammad Mu'awwaḍ and 'Ādil Aḥmad 'Abd al-Mawjūd, 19 vols., 3rd ed. (Beirut: Dār al-Kutub al-'Ilmiyya, 2009), 11:458; Abū al-Ṭayyib al-Ṭabarī, *al-Ta'līqa al-Kubrā: Kitāb al-Nikāḥ, Kitāb al-Ṣadāq, Kitāb al-Qasm wa-Nushūz*, ed. Yūsuf 'Abd Allāh al-'Aqīl (PhD diss., University of Medina 2004–2005), 71–93.
49. Al-Subkī, *Ṭabaqāt*, 4:227. See Makdisi's discussion of student stipends and wealth disparities, *Rise*, 58–74. The community of Baghdad jurists included financially comfortable families as well as poor students and professors.
50. Al-Subkī, *Ṭabaqāt*, 4:246.
51. E.g., Lara Deeb presents Muslim interlocutors in Beirut's al-Dahiyya district who see Islam as freeing women from the emptiness of a Western consumerist lifestyle. Her interlocutors also assert that a proper interpretation of Islam leads to a freedom from cultural norms that relegate women to the home; Lara Deeb, *An Enchanted Modern: Gender and Public Piety in Shi'i Lebanon* (Princeton, NJ: Princeton University Press, 2006), 30, 204.
52. On the slave's right to food and drink, see al-Shīrāzī, *al-Muhadhdhab*, 4:636–637; al-Jaṣṣāṣ, *Sharḥ Mukhtaṣar al-Taḥāwī*, ed. Muḥammad 'Abd Allāh Khān (Beirut: Dār al-Sirāj 2010), 5:332–333.
53. Kecia Ali, *Marriage and Slavery in Early Islam* (Cambridge, MA: Harvard University Press, 2010), 7.
54. Muḥammad b. Idrīs al-Shāfi'ī, *Kitāb al-Umm*, ed. Rif'at Fawzī 'Abd al-Muṭṭalib, 11 vols. (Mansoura: Dār al-Wafā', 2008), 6:235: "It is her right upon him to be provided

for, just as it is his right upon her to derive sexual fulfillment from her (*kāna min ḥaqqihā ʿalayhi an yaʿūlahā wa-min ḥaqqihi ʿalayhā an yastamtiʿa minhā*)."

55. Al-Shīrāzī, *al-Muhadhdhab*, 4:608–612.
56. The Shāfiʿīs made the amount of maintenance dependent upon the husband's means, but al-Shīrāzī notes that a servant is due for one "who does not work," either because of status or sickness, the reason being that maintenance is based on custom; al-Shīrāzī, *al-Muhadhdhab*, 4:611. For a Ḥanafī description of spousal maintenance, see ʿAlāʾ al-Dīn al-Samarqandī, *Tuḥfat al-Fuqahāʾ*, 3 vols. (Beirut: Dār al-Kutub al-ʿIlmiyya, 1984), 2:157.
57. Al-Shāfiʿī, *al-Umm*, 6:237.
58. Ibid.
59. Muḥammad b. al-Ḥasan al-Shaybānī, *Kitāb al-Ḥujja ʿalā Ahl al-Madīna*, ed. Mahdī al-Kaylānī al-Qādirī, 4 vols. (Beirut: ʿĀlam al-Kutub, 1983), 3:456–458. Al-Shaybānī declared: "The people of righteousness are a people of financial need and poverty." Ibid., 3:457.
60. Ibid., 3:456–457.
61. On the Ḥanafī position on the wife's *khiyār*, see Abū Bakr al-Jaṣṣāṣ, *Sharḥ Mukhtaṣar*, 5:282–288. Al-Jaṣṣāṣ lists several Qurʾanic verses in favour of the non-separation of spouses, including "Let the man of wealth provide according to his means. As for the one with limited resources, let him provide according to whatever God has given him. God does not require of any soul beyond what He has given it. After hardship, God will bring about ease," *al-Ṭalāq*: 7. He also claims that sex is not conditional on the money owed to a wife, since a couple can have sex before the bride receives her promised dowry. See also Abū Bakr al-Kāsānī, *Badāʾiʿ al-Ṣanāʾiʿ fī Tartīb al-Sharāʾiʿ*, ed. ʿAlī Muḥammad Muʿawwaḍ and ʿĀdil ʿAbd al-Mawjūd, 10 vols. (Beirut: Dār al-Kutub al-ʿIlmiyya, 2003), 3:607; 5:164–166.
62. Al-Subkī, *Ṭabaqāt*, 4:247.
63. Ibid. See al-Shīrāzī, *al-Muhadhdhab*, 4:599–600, for discussions of *taslīm* and how it relates to financial maintenance.
64. Al-Shīrāzī, *al-Muhadhdhab*, 3:158. For the Ḥanafī position on the necessity of *taslīm* in sales, see al-Samarqandī, *Tuḥfa*, 2:40–41.
65. Or being made available by her guardians. Al-Subkī, *Ṭabaqāt*, 4:247.
66. Ibid.
67. Ibid., 4:248: "*al-maqṣūd fī al-nikāḥ huwa al-waṭʾ*."
68. Ibid., 4:250.
69. As we have seen, the notion that the marriage contract gives right to sexual enjoyment was part of early (i.e., 8th century) juristic thought. For more on this, see Kecia Ali, *Marriage and Slavery*, 6.
70. In the *Muhadhdhab*, al-Shīrāzī notes that the wife cannot stipulate in the contract the refusal of sexual access, because this would violate the purpose of the marriage contract; al-Shīrāzī, *al-Muhadhdhab*, 4:162.
71. Pointing out the distinction (*al-farq*) between cases was a standard way to refute an opponent's analogy. On the method of *farq*, see Elias Saba, *Harmonizing Similarities: A History of Distinctions Literature in Islamic Law* (Berlin: De Gruyter, 2019), 81–109.

72. On the political and social role of the *umm al-walad* in the period after the 7th-century Arab conquests, see Elizabeth Urban, *Conquered Populations in Early Islam: Non-Arabs, Slaves and the Sons of Slave Mothers* (Edinburgh: Edinburgh University Press, 2020), 106–139.
73. According to Shāfiʿīs and Ḥanafīs, the *umm al-walad*'s expected emancipation prevented her master from selling her, giving her as a gift, or bequesting her in a will: see al-Shīrāzī, *al-Muhadhdhab*, 4:61.
74. Ibid.
75. Al-Subkī, *Ṭabaqāt*, 4:248.
76. Al-Shīrāzī, *al-Muhadhdhab*, 4:165; for the Ḥanafī position, see al-Jaṣṣāṣ, *Sharḥ Mukhtaṣar*, 4:387; al-Samarqandī, *Tuḥfat*, 2:225–226; al-Kāsānī, *Badāʾiʿ*, 3:592–595.
77. Al-Shīrāzī, *al-Muhadhdhab*, 4:169.
78. Al-Subkī, *Ṭabaqāt*, 4:249.
79. Ibid. The Ḥanafī claim that a husband could contract a loan was an early and standard response to the problem of spousal poverty; al-Shaybānī, *Kitāb al-Ḥujja*, 3:451.
80. Al-Subkī, *Ṭabaqāt*, 4:251.
81. Ibid.: "*bihā yaqūm al-badan wa'l-nafs*."
82. Feminist standpoint theory makes us attuned to the distinct "standpoint" or social positioning of a thinker impacts what might and might not be said. See Sandra Harding's edited volume: *The Feminist Standpoint Theory Reader: Intellectual and Political Controversies* (New York: Routledge, 2004).
83. Al-Subkī, *Ṭabaqāt*, 4:252.
84. On juristic concern for applying the law in ways that promoted social welfare, see David Stephan Powers, *Law, Society, and Culture in the Maghrib, 1300–1500* (New York: Cambridge University Press, 2002), 167–205.

## Chapter 2

1. Ludwig Wittgenstein, *The Philosophical Investigations*, trans. G.E.M. Anscombe (Cambridge: Cambridge University Press, 1986), 8.
2. Al-Sakūnī, *ʿUyūn al-Munāẓarāt*, ed. Saʿd Ghurāb (Tunis: Manshūrāt al-Jāmiʿa al-Tūnisiyya, 1976), 1:206. For an analysis of al-Sakūnī's text, see Saâd Ghrab, "Edition critique du Kitab uyun al-Munazarat (polémiques célèbres) d'Abu Ali Umar as-Sakuni (m. 717 h./1317)," 2 vols. (PhD diss., La Sorbonne, 1970). Al-Sakūnī's family was from Spain, though he lived and taught in Tunis.
3. Patricia Crone, *The Nativist Prophets of Early Islamic Iran: Rural Revolt and Local Zoroastrianism* (New York: Cambridge University Press, 2012). It is unlikely that the prisoner would have been simply persecuted for his religious beliefs. Basing themselves on several *ḥadīth*, jurists from across schools permitted Zoroastrians to pay the *jizya* and live in Muslim-governed lands; see al-Māwardī, *al-Ḥāwī*, 14:282.
4. Al-Sakūnī, *ʿUyūn*, 13–14.

5. Al-Shīrāzī, *Sharḥ*, 153. Al-Shīrāzī defines al-*naẓar*: "It is the reflection upon the state of the object about which one reasons (*huwa al-fikr fī ḥāl al-manẓūr fīhi*)." Jurists often noted how there are two types of *naẓar*, one pertaining to the heart and the other to the eye; Abū Ya'lā, *al-'Udda*, 2:122; al-Juwaynī, *al-Kāfiya*, 18.
6. Al-Juwaynī, *al-Kāfiya*, 19.
7. Al-Sakūnī's collection contains several *munāẓarāt* that would be better defined as trials or interrogations than disputations or debates. For instance, al-Sakūnī speaks of the inquisition of Aḥmad b. Ḥanbal as a *munāẓara*; al-Sakūnī, *'Uyūn*, 211. On the use of "*munāẓara*" in characterizing Aḥmad's defence during the *miḥna*, see also Ibn Qudāma, *Ḥikāyat al-Munāẓara fī al-Qur'ān ma'a ba'ḍ Ahl al-Bid'a*, ed. 'Abd Allāh al-Juday' (Riyadh: Maktabat al-Rushd, 1997). Al-Shāfi'ī's trial for participating in a failed insurrection also gave rise to a defence before the Caliph Hārūn al-Rashīd, followed by a *munāẓara* between al-Shāfi'ī and al-Shaybānī; Abū Bakr al-Bayhaqī, *Manāqib al-Shāfi'ī*, ed. al-Sayyid Aḥmad Ṣaqr, 2 vols. (Cairo: Maktabat Dār al-Turāth, 1970), 105–147; Fakhr al-Dīn al-Rāzī, *Manāqib al-Imām al-Shāfi'ī*, ed. Muḥammad Majāzī al-Saqqā (Cairo: Maktabat al-Kulliyyāt al-Azhariyya, 1986), 88–91.
8. The year of Ibn al-A'tham's death has long been identified as 314/926 CE. Lawrence Conrad has shown this to be untenable and suggests that the *Kitāb al-Futūḥ* was written in 204/819 CE; Lawrence I. Conrad, "Ibn A'tham and His History," *al-'Uṣūr al-Wusṭā* 23, no.1 (2015): 93–94.
9. Abū Muḥammad Ibn A'tham, *Kitāb al-Futūḥ*, ed. 'Alī Shīrī (Beirut: Dār al-Aḍwā', 1991), 3:72.
10. Ibid., 3:74.
11. The trend of using the term *munāẓara* to speak of prophets' contestations with antagonists is repeated in Ibn Kathīr's telling of the story of the Prophet Ibrāhīm and the King Numrūd; Ibn Kathīr, *Qiṣaṣ al-Anbiyā'*, ed. Muṣṭafā 'Abd al-Wāḥid, 2 vols., 3rd ed. (Mecca: Maktabat al-Ṭālib al-Jāmi'ī, 1988), 1:171–172.
12. *Akhbār al-Dawla al-'Abbāsiyya wa-fīhi Akhbār al-'Abbās wa-Waladihi*, ed. 'Abd al-'Azīz al-Dūrī and 'Abd al-Jabbār al-Muṭṭalibī (Beirut: Dār al-Ṭalī'a, 1971), 1:39–40; Ibn A'tham, *Kitāb al-Futūḥ*, 4:263. Likewise, al-Ṭabarī states that those who revolted against the Caliph 'Uthmān engaged in a "*munāẓara*" with the Caliph; Muḥammad b. Jarīr al-Ṭabarī, *Tārīkh al-Ṭabarī*, ed. Muḥammad Abū al-Faḍl Ibrāhīm, 11 vols., 2nd ed. (Beirut: Dār al-Ma'ārif bi-Miṣr), 4:354.
13. Abū 'Abd Allāh al-Wāqidī, *Futūḥ al-Shām*, 2 vols. (Beirut: Dār al-Kutub al-'Ilmiyya, 1997), 2:70.
14. Al-Ṭabarī, *Tārīkh*, 2:175, 8:420, 9:347, 9:421, 9:621; Abū 'Abd Allāh al-Ṣaymarī, *Akhbār Abī Ḥanīfa wa-Aṣḥābihi*, 3rd ed. (Beirut: 'Ālam al-Kutub, 1985), 68–69; Abū Muḥammad al-Miṣrī, *Sīrat 'Umar b. 'Abd al-'Azīz 'alā mā Rawāhu Mālik wa-Aṣḥābuhu*, ed. Aḥmad 'Ubayd (Beirut: 'Ālam al-Kutub, 1984), 1:112.
15. It is unlikely that 7th-century Arabs themselves would have used the term *munāẓara* for such theo-political debates. "*Munāẓara*" is not a prominent term in our early extant texts. The Qur'an does not use the term, nor does Ibn Isḥāq's *Sīra* or Abd al-Razzāq's *Muṣannaf*. Moreover, when later sources use the term, they sometimes

apply it retrospectively to their sources. Thus, the figures in Ibn A'tham's story do not themselves use the term. Instead, other words are used: Dhū al-Kilā' tells Mu'āwiya that "Abū Nūḥ wants to speak to me (*Inna Abā Nūḥ yurīd kalāmī*)" and Abū Nūḥ tells 'Alī that he wishes to cause doubt in Dhū al-Kilā''s political alliances (*ushakkikuhu*). This suggests that the original narrators of the story did not use the term. Rather, Ibn A'tham, embedded in his 9th-century context, found "*munāẓara*" an appropriate term to describe the exchange. Ibn A'tham, *Kitāb al-Futūḥ*, 3:72.

16. Several later sources claim that late 8th-/early 9th-century jurists engaged in disputations. For the disputations of Mālik b. Anas, particularly with Abū Yūsuf, see al-Qāḍī 'Iyāḍ, *Tartīb*, 2:113–129, 3:183, 3:312. For Abū Ḥanīfa and early Ḥanafīs, see al-Ṣaymarī, *Akhbār*, 23, 48, 69, 86, 100–104, 110–111.
17. E.g., *Kitāb al-Futūh*, 8:378.
18. Montgomery Watt, *Islamic Philosophy and Theology*, 2nd ed. (Edinburgh: Edinburgh University Press, 1985), 33–37.
19. Christopher Melchert, "The Early Ḥanafiyya and Kufa," *Journal of 'Abbasid Studies* 5, no. 1 (2014): 28–29; Christopher Melchert, "Basra and Kufa as the Earliest Centers of Islamic Legal Controversy," *Islamic Cultures, Islamic Contexts: Essays in Honor of Professor Patricia Crone*, ed. Christopher Melchert et al. (Leiden: Brill, 2014), 184; Nurit Tsafrir, *The History of an Islamic School of Law: The Early Spread of Hanafism* (Cambridge, MA: Harvard University Press, 2004), 17; Robert Brunschvig, "Polémiques médiévales autour du rite de Mālik," *Al-Andalus* 15 (1950): 377–378. Likewise, Abū Yūsuf's "refutation (*al-Radd*)" of the ideas of the Syrian jurist al-Awzā'ī on the laws of war (*siyar*) highlights the Iraqis' penchant for critique; Abū Yūsuf, *al-Radd 'alā Siyar al-Awzā'ī*, ed. Abū al-Wafā al-Afghānī (Hyderabad: Lajnat Iḥyā' al-Ma'ārif al-Nu'māniyya, 2007), 1–2.
20. A famous example of a grammatical disputation is Sibawayh's disputation against al-Kisā'ī; al-Khaṭīb al-Baghdādī, *Tārīkh Madīnat al-Salām*, ed. Bashshār 'Awwād Ma'rūf, 21 vols. (Tunis: Dār al-Gharb al-Islāmī, 2001), 13:589; for reports of late 8th- and early 9th-century theologians engaged in disputation, see al-Dhahabī, *Siyar A'lām al-Nubalā'*, ed. Muḥammad b. 'Abd Allāh al-Shabrāwī (Cairo: Dār al-Ḥadīth, 2006), 8:537. See Josef van Ess, "Disputationspraxis in der Islamischen Theologie. Eine Vorläufige Skizze," *Revue des Études Islamiques* 44 (1976): 23–60. For literary debates, see Jaako Hämeen Antilla, "The Essay and the Debate (*Al-Risāla* and *Al-Munāẓara*)," in *Arabic Literature in the Post-Classical Period*, ed. Roger Allen et al. (Cambridge: Cambridge University Press, 2006), 134–144.
21. The sense of "*nāẓara*" as "questioning" is found in Abū Yūsuf's *Kitāb al-Kharāj* where the Caliph 'Umar b. al-Khaṭṭāb questions the Persian nobles of newly conquered Iraqi lands on the amounts that they previously paid in taxation; Abū Yūsuf, *Kitāb al-Kharāj* (Beirut: Dār al-Ma'rifa, 1979), 85. Even in the 11th century, jurists would note that the meaning of the *munāẓara* encompassed the notion of questioning (*su'āl*) and inquiry; see, al-Baghdādī, *Kitāb al-Faqīh*, 224, 267. The phrase *nāẓara ma'ahu* (to reason with him) would seem to have become more common in later centuries; see Fakhr al-Dīn al-Rāzī, *Munāẓarāt Fakhr al-Dīn al-Rāzī fī Bilād Mā Warā' al-Nahr*, ed. Fatḥ Allāh Khulayf (Beirut: Dār al-Mashriq, 1967), 15.

22. Al-Ṣaymarī, *Akhbār*, 23. Al-Ṣaymarī's reports (e.g., *Akhbār*, 48, 86) of early Ḥanafīs do not mention the term *munāẓara*, but rather the verbal construct *nāẓara*.
23. Ibid., 48. See also Makdisi, *Rise*, 132, quoting from Ibn 'Imād's *Shadharāt al-Dhahab*, 'Abd al-Qādir al-Arna'ūṭ (Damascus: Dār Ibn Kathīr, 1986), 4:151.
24. Al-Ṣaymarī, *Akhbār*, 111.
25. Belhaj, *Argumentation*, 6–7.
26. Geert van Gelder, "The Conceit of Pen and Sword: On an Arabic Literary Debate," *Journal of Semitic Studies* 32, no. 2 (1987): 329–369; E. Wagner, "Munāẓara," *EI*[2], ed. P. Bearman, Th. Bianquis, C.E. Bosworth, E. van Donzel, and W.P. Heinrichs. Consulted online on 1 October 2021, http://dx.doi.org.myaccess.library.utoronto.ca/10.1163/1573-3912_islam_SIM_5507.
27. Al-Ṣaymarī, *Akhbār*, 110–111.
28. Al-Qāḍī 'Iyāḍ, *Tartīb*, 2:118–119. See also the disputation at 2:116–117.
29. Ibid., 2:119.
30. Norman Calder has famously argued that al-Shāfi'ī's writings were not fixed at the time of his death in 820 CE but evolved organically during the next generation; Norman Calder, *Studies in Early Muslim Jurisprudence* (Oxford: Clarendon, 1993), 84. His claims can no longer be entertained in light of a number of critiques; see Ahmed El Shamsy, "Al-Shāfi'ī's Written Corpus: A Source-Critical Study," *Journal of the American Oriental Society*, 132, no. 2 (2012): 199–220; Sherman Jackson, "Setting the Record Straight: Ibn al-Labbād's Refutation of al-Shāfi'ī," *Journal of Islamic Studies* 11, no. 2 (2000): 122; Murteza Bedir, "An Early Response to Shāfi'ī:'Īsa b. Abān on the Prophetic Report (*Khabar*)," *Islamic Law and Society* 9, no. 3 (2002): 286.
31. Al-Shāfi'ī, *Kitāb al-Umm*, 7:425.
32. Ibid., 7:417.
33. See Lazarus-Yafeh et al. (ed.), *The Majlis: Interreligious Encounters in Medieval Islam*; E. Wagner, "*Munāẓara*" *EI2*; Hugh Kennedy, *The Court of the Caliphs: The Rise and Fall of Islam's Greatest Dynasty* (London: Weidenfeld & Nicolson, 2004), 243–260; Letizia Osti, "Culture, Education and the Court," in *Crisis and Continuity in the Abbasid Court*, ed. Maaike van Berkel et al. (Leiden: Brill, 2013), 191; During the Buyid era, see Erez Naaman, *Literature and the Islamic Court* (London: Routledge, 2016), 1–2; Joel Kraemer, *Humanism*, 4.
34. Al-Ghazālī, *Iḥyā'*, 1:60–61.
35. Al-Sakūnī, *'Uyūn*, 207–208.
36. Ibid., 208.
37. E.g., Ibn Abī Ḥātim al-Rāzī narrates that the Caliph grants al-Shāfi'ī five thousand dinars; Ibn Abī Ḥātim al-Rāzī, *Ādāb al-Shāfi'ī wa-Manāqibuhu*, ed. 'Abd al-Ghanī 'Abd al-Khāliq (Beirut: Dār al-Kutub al-'Ilmiyya, 2003), 125. For other disputations narrated at the 'Abbasid court, see al-Sakūnī, *'Uyūn*, 208–209, 211, 213, 215; Aḥmad b. Sahl al-Rāzī, *Akhbār Fakhkh wa-Khabar Yaḥyā b. 'Abd Allāh wa-Akhīhi Idrīs* (Beirut: Dār al-Gharb al-Islāmī, 1990), 310; al-Baghdādī, *Tārīkh*, 15:116.
38. Al-Sakūnī, *'Uyūn*, 215.
39. For another disputation where al-Manṣūr is featured as menacing, see Al-Ṣaymarī, *Akhbār*, 68–69, where Abū Ḥanīfa and Mālik expect al-Manṣūr to shed the blood of

their companion. To avoid the ire of rulers, jurists often held disputations in their homes; see Makdisi, *Rise*, 133, where al-Ḥusayn b. Ismāʿīl al-Maḥamilī (d. 942 CE) is said in *al-Muntaẓam* to have held a gathering of disputation in his home for sixty years.

40. Al-Qāḍī ʿIyāḍ, *Tartīb*, 2:115–116, 118.
41. Al-Masʿūdī, *Murūj*, 4:17; For instance, Aḥmad b. Ḥanbal (d. 241/855 CE) is described as having regarded the court as polluted; Abū Nuʿaym al-Iṣbahānī, *Ḥilyat al-Awliyāʾ wa-Ṭabaqāt al-Aṣfiyāʾ*, 10 vols. (Cairo: Khānjī, 1932–1938), 9: 205.
42. Al-Qāḍī ʿIyāḍ, *Tartīb*, 7:51.
43. Ibn ʿAqīl, *Kitāb al-Jadal*, 2; al-Bājī, *al-Minhāj*, 10; al-Juwaynī, *al-Kāfiya*, 530; al-Shīrāzī, *al-Mulakhkhaṣ*, 11b.
44. Al-Bayhaqī states that were he to draw on all the books that report al-Shāfiʿī's *munāẓarāt*, his treatment of the subject would lengthen considerably, *Manāqib*, 1:178. For accounts of al-Shāfiʿī's *munāẓarāt*, see al-Rāzī, *Ādāb*, 119–137. Al-Bayhaqī, *Manāqib*, 1:105–147, 1:178–219, 1:173–177; al-Rāzī, *Manāqib*, 88–91, 271–296; al-Subkī, *Ṭabaqāt*, 2:61; For secondary literature, see Melchert, *The Formation*, 182; and El Shamsy, *Canonization*, 24–25. Even the passage from the *Kitāb al-Umm* that I examined on apostasy begins with al-Shāfiʿī describing a scene that resembles a debate gathering. Al-Shāfiʿī states that some jurists invoke a *ḥadīth* to deny that a woman is executed for apostasy, favouring instead her imprisonment. Al-Shāfiʿī then writes: "Some of those who adopt this position invoked the *ḥadīth* in the presence of experts of *ḥadīth*, so I asked them about the *ḥadīth*, and all of them stated about the *ḥadīth*: 'this is a mistake'" (4:417).
45. See Young, *The Dialectical*, 3.
46. E.g., al-Rāzī, *Manāqib*, 273, 91. It is telling that al-Subkī notes that only one narration of al-Shāfiʿī sees the master jurist learning something from his peers. Al-Subkī, *Ṭabaqāt*, 2:159.
47. The story is relayed in al-Razī, *Ādāb*, 136–137; al-Rāzī, *Manāqib*, 272–273; and al-Bayhaqī, *Manāqib*, 1:179. See Melchert's rendering of the disputation, Melchert, *The Formation*, 20.
48. For Ibn Rāhawayh's biography, see Ibn Khallikān, *Wafayāt*, 1:199.
49. Shāfiʿī biographical texts present Aḥmad as a follower of al-Shāfiʿī; see, e.g., al-Shīrāzī, *Ṭabaqāt*, 100.
50. For more on the question of house ownership in Mecca, see al-Ṭabarī, *Jāmiʿ al-Bayān*, 10:174–177.
51. Al-Rāzī, *Ādāb*, 136.
52. Al-Rāzī, *Manāqib*, 272–273.
53. Ibid., 273. See also al-Bayhaqī, *Manāqib*, 1:214–215
54. The narrations of the story in both al-Bayhaqī, *Manāqib*, 1:214 and al-Rāzī, *Ādāb*, 137 present Ibn Rāhawayh embracing al-Shāfiʿī's position.
55. Al-Bājī, *al-Minhāj*, 36; al-Baghdādī, *Kitāb al-Faqīh*, 267–269; Ibn ʿAqīl, *Kitāb al-Jadal*, 42–43.
56. E.g., see the disputation between al-Shāfiʿī and al-Shaybānī on the topic of usurped homes, al-Rāzī, *Ādāb*, 120–122. On al-Shāfiʿī and al-Shaybānī's relationship as

debating partners, see Al-Qārī al-Harawī, al-*Athmār al-Janiyya fī Asmā' al-Ḥanafiyya*, ed. Muḥammad Jawal (Beirut: Manshūrāt al-Jamal, 2012), 138. Only in records of al-Shāfi'ī's short *munāẓarāt* is it possible to identify a single questioner or respondent.

57. Among al-Shāfi'ī's twenty-three disputations in Fakhr al-Dīn al-Rāzī's *Manāqib*, only one resembles the sustained engagement with evidence found in transcripts of classical disputations; see al-Rāzī, *Manāqib*, 280–282. This disputation is so out of place with al-Shāfi'ī's other disputations that it is likely it was composed much later than the others. This possibility is further supported by the fact that neither Ibn Abī Ḥātim al-Rāzī nor al-Bayhaqī record the disputation.
58. Ibid., 275.
59. See Montgomery Watt, *The Formative Period of Islamic Thought*, Reprint (Oxford: Oneworld Publications, 1998), 198.
60. Manuscript sources show discrepancies over whether the jurist in question is a Medinan (*al-Madanī*) or Shāfi'ī's student, al-Muzanī; see al-Bayhaqī, *Manāqib*, 1:199; al-Rāzī, *Manāqib*, 274.
61. Al-Shīrāzī, *Ṭabaqāt*, 94.
62. Al-Rāzī, *Manāqib*, 289; al-Rāzī, *Ādāb*, 129.
63. Early Ḥanafīs indicate a similar disregard for the ethics of the disputation in this era. Al-Ṣaymarī, *Akhbār*, 110–111.
64. Al-Bayhaqī also presents al-Shāfi'ī affirming the need for proper behaviour (*adab*) in the face of Ibn Rāhawayh's loss of temper, *Manāqib*, 216.
65. Al-Baghdādī, *Kitāb al-Faqīh*, 224.
66. Ibid.
67. Al-Juwaynī, *al-Kāfiya*, 21.
68. Ibid., 20.
69. Ibid., 21. Al-Juwaynī gives other definitions of *al-munāẓara* circulating among juristic and theological communities, finding fault with them. Examples include the following: "The search for [an intellectual] position by thinking with another debater," "The reflection that is shared between two debaters," and "The verification of truth and the rejection of falsehood."
70. Al-Shīrāzī, *Sharḥ*, 1:153.
71. Ibn 'Aqīl, *Kitāb al-Jadal*, 1. For a 12th–13th century text that reproduces the synonymity between *munāẓara* and *jadal*, see Sayf al-Dīn al-Āmidī, *al-Iḥkām fī Uṣūl al-Aḥkām*, ed. 'Abd al-Razzāq 'Afīfī, 4 vols. (Riyadh: Dār al-Ṣumay'ī, 2003), 4:89; 4:102; 4:89; 4:74; 4:78.
72. It is possible that *jadal* had a negative connotation among jurists in the 8th and 9th centuries. For instance, al-Ṣaymarī presents a report in which Abū Ḥanīfa is said to have been a person "of great intelligence, of little argumentation (*qalīl al-mujādala li'l-nās*) with people, and of few words"; al-Ṣaymarī, *Akhbār*, 59. In al-Bayhaqī's *Manāqib*, 1:383, we find al-Shāfi'ī using the term "*jadal*," though it is not clear if al-Shāfi'ī is using the term favourably or derisively, saying that whoever is interested in *jadal* should refer to Abū Ḥanīfa.
73. Al-Juwaynī, *al-Kāfiya*, 22–23; al-Baghdādī, *Kitāb al-Faqīh*, 225–227.
74. Al-Juwaynī, *al-Kāfiya*, 22; al-Baghdādī, *Kitāb al-Faqīh*, 227; al-Shīrāzī, *Ṭabaqāt*, 112.

75. Al-Juwaynī, *al-Kāfiya*, 23.
76. Melchert, *The Formation*, 20–21.
77. Abū al-Ḥusayn Ibn Abī Yaʿlā, *Ṭabaqāt al-Ḥanābila*, ed. Muḥammad Ḥāmid al-Fiqī, 2 vols. (Cairo: Maṭbaʿat al-Sunna al-Muḥammadiyya, n.d.), 1:236. Aḥmad is asked by a follower if he should engage in disputation and counsels him against it. Ibn Abī Yaʿlā then quotes Mālik rhetorically asking, "Are we going to change our religion everytime someone is a better debater than another."
78. Melchert, *The Formation*, 21. See also Muhammad Qasim Zaman, *Religion and Politics under the Early ʿAbbāsids: The Emergence of the Proto-Sunnī Elite* (Leiden: Brill, 1997), 68–69, 198.
79. Ibn ʿAsākir, *Tabyīn Kadhib al-Muftarī fī mā Nusiba ilā al-Imām al-Ashʿarī*, 3rd ed. (Beirut: Dār al-Kitāb al-ʿArabī, 1984), 116.
80. Al-Baghdādī, *Kitāb al-Faqīh*, 225.
81. Ibn Abī Yaʿlā, *Ṭabaqāt al-Ḥanābila*, 2:39; see also 2:40, where Ibn ʿUmar and Mālik are both singled out as detesting disputation.
82. Ibid., 2:237; Abū al-Faraj al-Jawzī, *Manāqib al-Imām Aḥmad*, ed. ʿAbd Allāh al-Turkī (Cairo: Maktabat al-Khānjī, 1979), 638, 640, 641.
83. Al-Subkī, *Ṭabaqāt*, 3:22. Al-Muṭṭawwiʿī's non-extant book was *al-Mudhhab fī Dhikr Shuyūkh al-Madhhab*; see al-Subkī, *Ṭabaqāt*, 3:12. I translate the term "*al-naẓar*" here not by its literal meaning of "reasoning," but as meaning *munāẓara*. I do so for two reasons. First, classical jurists often used the term *naẓar* as a synonym for disputation, perhaps because of its use as a shorthand for the expression *majlis al-naẓar* (a gathering of reasoning); e.g., al-Shīrāzī, *Sharḥ*, 1054. See also Makdisi, *Rise*, 130. And second, the adjoining statement that Ibn Surayj was the first to teach his students *jadal* (i.e., strategies for debate) suggests that al-Muṭṭawwiʿī had disputations in mind when he made his comment.
84. Wael Hallaq, "Was al-Shafiʿi the Master Architect?," 595–596.
85. El Shamsy, "Bridging," 515.
86. Abū Ḥāmid al-Isfarāyinī used to say that the Shāfiʿīs ought to follow the general positions of Ibn Surayj, if not the details of his positions; al-Shīrāzī, *Ṭabaqāt*, 109.
87. Melchert, *The Formation*, xxvi.
88. El Shamsy, *The Canonization*, 168–169.
89. Al-Shīrāzī, *Ṭabaqāt*, 109: "*Wa-ʿanhu intashara fiqh al-Shāfiʿī.*" He adds that "it is through Ibn Surayj that Shāfiʿism spread" and most of the next generation of Shāfiʿīs were his students.
90. Ibid., 112.
91. Ibid., 115.
92. For other Shāfiʿīs who were experts in *jadal* and/or *khilāf*, see al-Shīrāzī, *Ṭabaqāt*, 128, 129, 130; al-Subkī, *Ṭabaqāt*, 3:254, 4:121, 5:246, 6:390.
93. For Ḥanafī texts of *jadal*, see Miller, *Islamic Disputation Theory*, 76–77.
94. Makdisi, *Rise*, 131. The original reference is from Ibn ʿImād, *Shadharāt*, 4:151.
95. Ibn ʿImād, *Shadharāt*, 4:150.
96. Al-Subkī, *Ṭabaqāt*, 3:24. "*Mā āsā illā ʿalā turāb akala lisān Muḥammad b. Dāwūd.*"
97. Ibid., 3:231.

98. The judge Abū 'Umar's full name is given as Muḥammad b. Yūsuf; ibid., 3:26–27.
99. For more on the matter, see Ibn Rushd, *Bidāyat al-Mujtahid wa-Nihāyat al-Muqtaṣid*, ed. Mājid al-Ḥamawī, 4 vols. (Beirut: Dār Ibn Ḥazm, 2012), 3:1012–1015.
100. For the historical context of the Qur'anic verses on *ẓihār*, see Ingrid Mattson, *The Story of the Qur'an*, 2nd ed. (West Sussex: John Wiley & Sons, Ltd, 1993), 1–4.
101. Al-Ṭabarī, *Jāmi' al-Bayān*, 14:5.
102. Al-Subkī, *Ṭabaqāt*, 3:26. The disputation between Ibn Surayj and Ibn Dāwūd al-Ẓāhirī is also reported in Abū al-Fahm al-Tanūkhī, *Nishwār al-Muḥāḍara wa-Akhbār al-Mudhākara*, ed. 'Abbūd al-Shālijī, 8 vols., 2nd ed. (Beirut: Dār Ṣādr, 1995), 8:186–188.
103. Miller, *Islamic Disputation Theory*, 1
104. Sarah Stroumsa, *Freethinkers in Islam: Ibn al-Rāwandī, Abū Bakr al-Rāzī, and Their Impact on Islamic Thought* (Leiden: Brill, 1999), 37–38; Sarah Stroumsa, "Ibn Rāwandī's *sū' adab al-mujādala*: The Role of Bad Manners in Medieval Disputations," in Lazarus-Yafeh et al., *The Majlis*, 60–76.
105. George Makdisi, "The Relation between the Texts of Qirqisani and Ibn 'Aqil," *Mélanges d'islamologie: Volume dédié à la mémoire d'Armand Abel par ses collègues, ses élèves et ses amis*, ed. P. Salmon, 3 vols. (Leiden: Brill, 1974–78), 1:201–206; G. Vajda, "Etudes sur Qirqisānī V: Les règles de la controverse dialectique," *Revue des Etudes Juives* 122 (1963): 7–74.
106. Racha el Omari, *The Theology of Abū l-Qāsim al-Balkhī/al-Ka'bī (d. 319/931)* (Leiden: Brill, 2016), 18.
107. Al-Subkī, *Ṭabaqāt*, 3:22. Reinhart has also shown that Ibn Surayj often incorporated theological positions within his legal theory, *Before Revelation: The Boundaries of Muslim Moral Thought* (Albany: State University of New York Press, 1995), 16–17.
108. Al-Subkī, *Ṭabaqāt*, 3:200.
109. For the translation movement, see Dimitri Gutas, *Greek Thought, Arabic Culture: The Graeco-Arabic Translation Movement in Baghdad and Early 'Abbasid Society (2nd-4th/8th–10th Centuries)* (London: Routledge, 1998), 61.
110. Mohammad Syifa Amin Widigdo, "Arab-Islamic or Greek Dialectics? Revisiting the Origins and Development of *Jadal*," *Islam and Christian–Muslim Relations* 32, no. 2 (2021): 203–222; Mohammad Syifa Amin Widigdo, "Aristotelian Dialectic, Medieval *Jadal*, and Medieval Scholastic Disputation," *The American Journal of Islamic Social Sciences* 35, no. 4 (2018): 1–24.
111. Hallaq, "A Tenth–Eleventh Century," 197; Belhaj, *Argumentation*, 15.
112. Young, *The Dialectical Forge*, 26.
113. Melchert, *The Formation*, 87.
114. Al-Subkī, *Ṭabaqāt*, 5:24.
115. Al-Ghazālī, *Iḥyā'*, 1:60; see al-Jaṣṣāṣ, *Sharḥ Mukhtaṣar*, 5:332–333, on the wife's *khiyār* (examined in Chapter 1) for an example of how Shāfi'ī/Ḥanafī disputations get distilled into the *sic et non* method of substantive law texts.
116. See Abdessamed Belhaj, "*Ādāb al-Baḥth wa'l-Munāẓara*: The Neglected Art of Disputation in Later Medieval Islam," *Arabic Sciences and Philosophy* 26 (2016):

291–307; Walter Young, "*Mulāzama* in Action in the Early *Ādāb al-Baḥth*," *Oriens* 44, no. 3–4 (2016): 333; Mehmet Karabela, "The Development of Dialectic."

## Chapter 3

1. Makdisi, *Rise*, 135–136.
2. Ibid., 111; see also George Makdisi, "Freedom in Islamic Jurisprudence: *Ijtihad*, *taqlid*, and Academic Freedom," in *La notion de liberté au Moyen Age: Islam, Byzance, Occident*, ed. G. Makdisi et al. (Paris: Les Belles Lettres, 1985), 83.
3. Shaista Ali-Karamali and Fiona Dunne pick up on the academic use of *ijtihād* as a shorthand for creativity when they say that *ijtihād* "has also been described as a 'rethinking' or, most commonly, as 'independent reasoning.'" Shaista P. Ali-Karamali and Fiona Dunne, "The Ijtihad Controversy," 238. See also, Schacht, *Introduction*, 69–70; Hallaq, "Was the Gate," 10, 11, 16; Mohammad Fadel, "The Social Logic," 193–194. Ahmed El Shamsy notes that studies on *taqlīd* "employ the term as an objective description of practice among Muslim jurists, unaffected by the self-understanding of the jurists themselves." El Shamsy, "Rethinking '*Taqlīd*,'" 1.
4. On *ijtihād* as "independent thought," see, for instance, Lutz Wiederhold, "Legal Doctrines in Conflict the Relevance of *Madhhab* Boundaries to Legal Reasoning in the Light of an Unpublished Treatise on *Taqlīd* and *Ijtihād*," *Islamic Law and Society* 3, no. 2 (1996): 235. This definition is ambiguous: it is unclear if "independent" means that a jurist must search for new evidence to be considered as having performed *ijtihād*, or whether verifying the merits of another jurist's evidence shows sufficient independence to fulfil the requirement of *ijtihād*.
5. Al-Shīrāzī, *Sharḥ*, 2:1043.
6. For Sherman Jackson, "*ijtihād* proper" involves the use of *uṣūl al-fiqh* to come up with new positions. This is a different definition than al-Shīrāzī's, for whom *ijtihād* begins by reviewing the already existing positions of jurists on a given topic. Jackson, "*Taqlīd*," 167. Moreover, there is reason to be sceptical that even the masters of legal schools like Abū Ḥanīfa performed *ijtihād* by going directly to the textual sources of the law, see Sohail Hanif, "A Tale of Two Kufans: Abū Yūsuf's *Ikhtilāf* Abī Ḥanīfa wa-Ibn Abī Laylā and Schacht's Ancient Schools," *Islamic Law and Society* 25, no. 3 (2018): 173–211.
7. See Mohammad Fadel's argument that *taqlīd* is the "triumph of the rule of law over the ideal of discretion." Fadel, "Social Logic," 197.
8. The disputations that al-Subkī transcribes reproduce the standard legal positions of each legal school's representative. Al-Subkī, *Ṭabaqāt*, 4:237–256, 5:24–46.
9. Al-Shīrāzī, *Sharḥ*, 2:1008. See also, al-Juwaynī, *Kitāb al-Ijtihād*, 2:1339; al-Ghazālī, *al-Mustaṣfā*, 2:933; al-ʿUkbarī, *Risālat*, 74; al-Jaṣṣāṣ, *al-Fuṣūl*, 2:177.
10. Al-Shīrāzī, *Sharḥ*, 1:108–109; see also Ibn al-Qaṣṣār, *Muqaddima*, 143, where Ibn al-Qaṣṣār quotes the verse: "And when it is said to them, 'Follow what Allāh has

revealed,' they say, 'Rather, we will follow that which we found our fathers doing.' Even though their fathers understood not, nor were they guided?" [*al-Baqara*:170].

11. Al-Shīrāzī, *Sharḥ*, 2:1007, where al-Shīrāzī explains that there is no permissible *taqlīd* in matters of *uṣūl al-diyānāt*, for anyone, scholar (*'ālim*) or lay Muslim (*'āmmī*). See also *al-Shīrāzī, Mu'taqad Abī Isḥāq*, 1:93. Al-Shīrāzī's position on theology is common across schools of law and theology in 10th–11th-century Iraq. In contrast, the Central Asian Māturīdī-Ḥanafīs claimed that a person who did not know the reasons for his beliefs was nonetheless of sound faith; see Abū al-Mu'īn al-Nasafī, *Tabṣirat al-Adilla*, ed. Husayn Ātāy (Ankara: Diyāneṭ Işleri Başlangi, 1993), 39.
12. Al-Shīrāzī, *Sharḥ*, 2:1043.
13. Ibid., 2:1008.
14. Ibid., 2:1043.
15. Ibid., 1:171.
16. Ibid., 2:1008. Al-Shīrāzī writes that lay Muslims' capacity to know the evidence for the foundations of religion is "like the [jurists' capacity to] use of reason and *ijtihād* for legal cases (*al-ḥawādith*)." See also Abū Ya'lā b. al-Farrā', *Kitāb al-Mu'tamad fī Uṣūl al-Dīn*, ed. Wadī' Ḥaddād (Beirut: Dār al-Mashriq, 1974), 26.
17. Al-Shīrāzī, *Sharḥ*, 2:1008.
18. Al-Shāfi'ī is said to have accepted *taqlīd* in his deference to *ḥadīth* experts and to physiognomists to determine paternity; see El Shamsy, "Rethinking '*Taqlīd*,'" 8.
19. Abū Ibrāhīm al-Muzanī, *Mukhtaṣar al-Muzanī fī furū' al-Shāfi'iyya*, ed. Muḥammad Shāhīn (Beirut: Dār al-Kutub al-'Ilmiyya, 1998), 7; al-Suyūṭī, *Kitāb al-Radd 'alā man Akhlada ilā al-Arḍ wa-Jahila anna al-Ijtihād fī Kull 'Aṣr Farḍ*, ed. Khalīl al-Mays (Beirut: Dār al-Kutub al-'Ilmiyya, 1983), 67–69.
20. Al-Shīrāzī, *Sharḥ*, 2:1012; The position is also attributed to al-Muzanī; see al-Juwaynī, *Kitāb al-Talkhīṣ*, 3:447.
21. Al-Juwaynī, *Kitāb al-Fatwā*, 2:1339.
22. Al-Shīrāzī, *Sharḥ*, 2:1014. According to al-Shīrāzī, the confused jurist is still duty bound to perform *ijtihād*, even after the time of the prayer has lapsed, and he must repeat his prayer in accordance with the conclusions he has reached through his *ijtihād*.
23. Al-Shīrāzī, *Sharḥ*, 2:1013.
24. Ibid., 2:1012–1013, 1015, 1026.
25. Amr Osman, *The Ẓāhirī* Madhhab *(3rd/9th–10th/16th Century): A Textualist Theory of Islamic Law* (Leiden: Brill, 2014), 21. On the Ẓāhirīs, see Ignaz Goldziher, *The Ẓāhirīs: Their Doctrine and Their History: A Contribution to the History of Islamic Theology*, ed. and trans. Wolfgang Behn (Leiden: Brill, 2008).
26. Ibn al-Qaṣṣār, *Mukhtaṣar*, 140. See also Abū al-Walīd al-Bājī, *Iḥkām al-Fuṣūl fī Aḥkām al-Uṣūl* (Beirut: Mu'assasat al-Risāla, 1989), 635.
27. Ibn al-Qaṣṣār, *Mukhtaṣar*, 141–142.
28. Abū Ya'lā, *al-'Udda*, 2:255.
29. Al-'Ukbarī, *Risālat*, 77; Abū Ya'lā, *al-'Udda*, 2:444; Ibn 'Aqīl, *al-Wāḍiḥ fī Uṣūl al-Fiqh*, ed. 'Abd Allāh al-Turkī, 5 vols. (Beirut: Mu'assasat al-Risāla, 1999), 4:244; Abū al-Khaṭṭāb

al-Kalwadhānī, *al-Tamhīd fī Uṣūl al-Fiqh*, ed. Mufīd Abū ʿAmsha and Muḥammad b. ʿAlī b. Ibrāhīm, 4 vols. (Jeddah: Dār al-Madanī, 1985), 4:408. To prohibit *taqlīd*, al-ʿUkbarī also relies on the Qurʾanic statement, "If you are in disagreement about something, refer [the matter] back to God and to his Prophet" (*al-Nisāʾ*:59).

30. Abū Bakr al-Bāqillānī, *al-Taqrīb wa'l-Irshād (al-Ṣaghīr)*, ed. ʿAbd al-Ḥamīd Abū Zunayd, 3 vols., 2nd ed. (Beirut: Mu'assasat al-Risāla, 1998), 3:213; al-Baṣrī, *al-Muʿtamad*, 2:362. On al-Bāqillānī's position, see also al-Juwaynī, *al-Talkhīṣ*, 3:424; Al-Bāqillānī did not consider a *mustaftī*'s deference to a scholar to fall under the category of *taqlīd* since following a *fatwā* is different than following a position without evidence; al-Juwaynī, *al-Talkhīṣ*, 3:436.
31. Al-Jaṣṣāṣ, *al-Fuṣūl*, 2:372–373.
32. Ibid.
33. al-Ṣaymarī, *Kitāb Masāʾil*, 227–228. Al-Dabbūsī articulates the same position; Abū Zayd al-Dabbūsī, *Taqwīm al-Adilla fī Uṣūl al-Fiqh*, ed. Khalīl al-Mays (Beirut: Dār al-Kutub al-ʿIlmiyya, 2001), 391.
34. ʿAlāʾ al-Dīn al-Samarqandī, *Mīzān al-Uṣūl fī Natāʾij al-ʿUqūl*, ed. Muḥammad Zakī ʿAbd al-Barr (Doha: Maṭābiʿ al-Dawḥa al-Ḥadītha, 1984), 1:676. Al-Samarqandī allows a jurist in training (*ṭālib al-ʿilm*) that has not reached the requisite level of *ijtihād* to engage in *taqlīd*. See also ʿAlāʾ al-Dīn al-Bukhārī, *Kashf al-Asrār: Sharḥ Uṣūl al-Bazdawī*, ed. ʿAbd Allāh ʿUmar, 4 vols. (Beirut: Dār al-Kutub al-ʿIlmiyya, 1997), 3:335, who prohibits the jurist from engaging in *taqlīd*.
35. Abū Yaʿlā, *al-ʿUdda*, 2:259; al-Juwaynī, *al-Talkhīṣ*, 3:449–450.
36. For instance, see al-Bāqillānī's position in al-Juwaynī, *al-Talkhīṣ*, 3:435.
37. Al-Shīrāzī, *Sharḥ*, 2:1015–1030.
38. Ibid., 2:1067.
39. Al-Juwaynī, *al-Kāfiya*, 24.
40. Al-Shīrāzī calls theological positions "*al-aḥkām al-ʿaqliyya* (rational rules or positions)"; al-Shīrāzī, *Sharḥ*, 2:1043. Al-Juwaynī writes, "know that from among the forms of knowledge there are those that cannot be attained except through rational evidence . . . [this knowledge] is that which is needed to have a complete knowledge of monotheism and prophetic missions (*Iʿlamū waffaqakum Allāh anna min al-ʿulūm mā lā yutawaṣṣal ilayhā illā bi-adillat al-ʿuqūl . . . fa-ammā mā lā yutawaṣṣal ilayhi min al-ʿulūm al-kasbiyya illa bi-adillat al-ʿuqūl fa-hiya kull ʿilm lā tatimm maʿrifat al-waḥdāniyya wa'l-nubuwwāt illā bihi*)"; al-Juwaynī, *al-Talkhīṣ*, 1:133–134. See also Bāqillānī, *al-Taqrīb*, 3:105.
41. Al-Shīrāzī, *Sharḥ*, 2:1043–1044.
42. Al-Shīrāzī considers knowledge to fall within two categories: the first is necessary knowledge (*al-ʿilm al-ḍarūrī*), which includes sensory knowledge and knowledge of one's psychological states. The second is acquired knowledge (*al-ʿilm iktisābī*), which depends on employing one's rational capacities to arrive at a conclusion. Theological knowledge falls within the category of acquired knowledge. Al-Shīrāzī, *Sharḥ*, 1:148–150. See also Abū al-Maʿālī al-Juwaynī, *Kitāb al-Irshād ilā Qawāṭiʿ al-Adilla fī Uṣūl al-Iʿtiqād*, ed. Aḥmad ʿAbd al-Raḥmān Sāyiḥ (Cairo: Maktabat al-Thaqāfa al-Dīniyya 2009), 20.

43. Al-Shīrāzī, *Sharḥ*, 2:1044.
44. Ibid.
45. Al-Shīrāzī sometimes uses the term *naṣṣ*, which refers to a perspicuous scriptural text, interchangeably with the term *qaṭ'* (that which is epistemically definitive or certain).
46. Ibid., 1:449.
47. Ibid.
48. Ibid., 1:454.
49. Ibid., 2:837; al-Shīrāzī defines the legal cause (*'illā*) of the law as "the intended meaning that necessitates God's law (*al-ma'na al-muqtaḍī li'l ḥukm*)." Ibid., 2:833.
50. Ibid., 2:801. Al-Shīrāzī calls an analogical argument that relies on certainty, *al-qiyās al-jalī* (manifest analogy).
51. Ibid., 2:788.
52. For a list of al-Shīrāzī's methods for deriving a legal cause (*'illa*), see ibid., 2:804–805.
53. Al-Shīrāzī states that substantive law only produces probable knowledge for most cases. Ibid., 2:1009, 1044. For a definition of *al-ẓann* and *al-shakk*, see ibid., 1:150–151.
54. Of note, the law's uncertainty was also the product of the wide use of *aḥādīth āḥād*, i.e., *ḥadīth*s that were transmitted by too few people to be certain that they had not colluded in a lie. Despite recognizing the *ẓannī* character of *aḥādīth āḥād*, jurists accepted that such *ḥadīth*s be used in legal practice. Thus, debates about the use of such *ḥadīth* would have rarely been the object of disputations. See ibid., 1:569, 578.
55. Aron Zysow, *The Economy of Certainty*, 1.
56. Ibid., 3. Zysow calls the Ẓāhirīs "materialists" because of their insistence on certainty.
57. Al-Ṣaymarī, *Kitāb Masā'il*, 319–320; Abū Ya'lā, *al-'Udda*, 2:416; al-Sam'ānī, *Qawāṭi'*, 2:307; Abū al-Ma'ālī al-Juwaynī, *al-Burhān fī Uṣūl al-Fiqh*, ed. 'Abd al-'Aẓīm al-Dīb, 2 vols. (n.p. 1979), 2:1316; al-Baṣrī, *al-Mu'tamad*, 2:396–398; al-Juwaynī, *al-Talkhīṣ*, 3:335, 341–344; al-Jaṣṣāṣ, *al-Fuṣūl*, 2:435.
58. Al-Jaṣṣāṣ also uses the expression "*mā ghalaba fī ra'yihi*"; al-Jaṣṣāṣ, *al-Fuṣūl*, 2:379. See also Anver Emon, "To Most Likely Know the Law: Objectivity, Authority, and Interpretation in Islamic Law," *Hebraic Political Studies* 4, no. 4 (2009): 419.
59. Ibn al-Qaṣṣār, *Muqaddima*, 134–136. Al-Juwaynī begins his book of legal theory, *al-Burhān* by presenting that "Most of the matters of the *sharī'a* are probabilistic (*al-ẓunūn*)"; Al-Juwaynī, *al-Burhān*, 85. Ibn Abī Ḥurayra is an exception among Shāfi'īs in thinking that it is possible to overturn another judge's position; al-Shīrāzī, *Sharḥ* 2:1051.
60. Al-Baghdādī, *Kitāb al-Faqīh*, 254.
61. Aron Zysow, "Mu'tazilism and Māturīdism in Ḥanafī Legal Theory," in *Studies in Islamic Legal Theory*, ed. Bernard Weiss (Leiden: Brill, 2002), 235–265; Khaled Abou El Fadl, *Speaking in God's Name: Islamic Law, Authority and Women* (Oxford: Oneworld, 2001).
62. Abū al-Qāsim al-Balkhī, 'Abd al-Jabbār, and al-Ḥākim al-Jushamī, *Faḍl al-I'tizāl wa-Ṭabaqāt al-Mu'tazila*, ed. Fu'ād Sayyid (Beirut: al-Ma'had al-Almānī li'l-Abḥāth al-Sharqiyya, 2017), 277–288. I attribute the origins of the debate on juristic infallibility to al-Jubbā'ī because reports about scholars' positions on juristic infallibility before

al-Jubbā'ī tend to conflict. For instance, Shāfi'īs often attributed different positions to al-Shāfi'ī on the matter.

63. Al-Shīrāzī, *Sharḥ*, 2:1050; al-Shīrāzī, *al-Tabṣira*, 498.
64. Fakhr al-Dīn al-Rāzī, *al-Maḥṣūl fī 'Ilm Uṣūl al-Fiqh*, ed. Muḥammad 'Aṭā, 2 vols, 2nd ed. (Beirut: Dār al-Kutub al-'Ilmiyya, 2015), 2:438.
65. Among the Shāfi'īs, Ibn Surayj affirmed an intermediate position between the Muṣawwiba and the Mukhaṭṭi'a, stating that truth is singular, but that all jurists were right in their *ijtihād* because God only charged jurists to *try* to discover the truth; al-Baṣrī, *al-Mu'tamad*, 2:370–371. Al-Juwaynī embraced the same position as Ibn Surayj; al-Juwaynī, *al-Burhān*, 2:1322–1328.
66. Al-Shīrāzī, *Sharḥ*, 2:1054.
67. Abū Ya'lā, *al-'Udda*, 2:427. Abū Ya'lā adds: "one does not try to convince another to abandon what they already accept as truth."
68. Al-Shīrāzī, *Sharḥ*, 2:1054.
69. Al-Sam'ānī, *Qawāṭi'*, 2:325.
70. Ibid., 2:308; al-Shīrāzī, *Sharḥ*, 2:1063–1064; Abū Ya'lā, *al-'Udda*, 2:416.
71. Badr al-Dīn al-Zarkashī, *al-Baḥr al-Muḥīṭ fī Uṣūl al-Fiqh*, ed. 'Abd al-Sattār Abū Ghudda, 6 vols. (Kuwait: Wizārat al-Awqāf wa'l-Shu'ūn al-Islāmiyya, 2000), 6:253.
72. Abū Ya'lā, *al-'Udda*, 2:417.
73. Al-Shīrāzī, *Sharḥ*, 2:1048, 1051; Abū Ya'lā, *al-'Udda*, 2:416.
74. Al-Jaṣṣāṣ, *al-Fuṣūl*, 2:423.
75. Makdisi's understanding of the disputation as a mechanism for resolving legal disagreement owed much to his focus on the Ḥanbalī scholar, Ibn 'Aqīl, who belonged to the camp of the Mukhaṭṭi'a; Makdisi, *Rise*, 110; see also "Muslim Institutions of Learning in Eleventh-Century Baghdad." *Bulletin of the School of Oriental and African Studies* 24, no. 1 (1961): 1–56; George Makdisi, *Ibn 'Aqil et la résurgence de l'islam traditionaliste au 11e siècle (5e siècle de l'Hégire)* (Damascus: Institut français de Damas, 1963).
76. Wael Hallaq, *A History of Islamic Legal Theories: An Introduction to Sunnī Uṣūl al-Fiqh* (New York: Cambridge University Press, 1997), 137.
77. Abū Bakr Ibn Fūrak, *Mujarrad Maqālāt al-Shaykh Abī al-Ḥasan al-Ash'arī: Min Imlā' al-Shaykh al-Imām Abī Bakr Muḥammad b. al-Ḥasan b. Fūrak (T. 406/1015)* (Beirut: al-Maktaba al-Sharqiyya, 1987), 293.
78. Al-Shīrāzī, *Sharḥ*, 2:1050; al-Ṣaymarī, *Kitāb Masā'il*, 303–304, 316; al-Baṣrī, *al-Mu'tamad*, 2:370.
79. Al-Jaṣṣāṣ, *al-Fuṣūl*, 2:422–423.
80. Al-Baṣrī, *al-Mu'tamad*, 2:384. Al-Juwaynī, *al-Talkhīṣ*, 3:355. Al-Baṣrī presents two additional reasons that legitimate the practice of disputation for legal relativists. The first is that the jurist is to use disputation to help him make up his mind about which "position he thinks strongest." The disputation in this situation serves as a means to explore the variety of arguments bearing on a case. Second, a jurist uses the disputation to ensure that his opponent has sufficiently examined the contested question at hand. Al-Bāqillānī, for his part, claims that the disputation does not invite an opponent to abandon his position, but rather it is a pedagogical tool to train jurists.

81. Al-Ghazālī, *al-Mustaṣfā*, 2:901–902.
82. Ibid.
83. Ibid., 2:902.
84. Makdisi recognized the pedagogical importance of the disputation in the training of jurists; Makdisi, *Rise*, 109. See also George Makdisi, "The Scholastic Method in Medieval Education: An Inquiry into Its Origins in Law and Theology," *Speculum: A Journal of Medieval Studies* 49, no. 4 (1974): 640–661.
85. Al-Ghazālī, *al-Mustaṣfā*, 2:902.
86. As they debate, the two jurists learn to connect arguments about substantive law to foundational positions on the sources of the law (*uṣūl al-fiqh*) and theology. On the relation between on contested issues (*masāʾil al-khilāf*) and *uṣūl al-fiqh*, see Youcef L. Soufi, "'Why Study *Uṣūl al-Fiqh*?': The Problem of *Taqlīd* and Tough Cases in 4th–5th /10th–11th Century Iraq," *Islamic Law and Society* (2021), 10.
87. Importantly, neither the Mukhaṭṭiʾa nor the Muṣawwiba lamented the inherent uncertainty of the law. See al-Shīrāzī, *Sharḥ*, 2:1071, who claims that legal uncertainty served Muslim piety. See also Khaled Abou El Fadl, *The Search for Beauty in Islam: A Conference of the Books* (Lanham, MD: Rowman and Littlefield Publishers, Inc., 2006), xvii, who speaks of a juristic ethos of knowledge seeking; and Rumee Ahmed, *Narratives of Islamic Legal Theory* (Oxford: Oxford University Press, 2012), 153, who emphasizes the pietistic nature of juristic legal writing.
88. Al-Shīrāzī, *Sharḥ*, 2:1067. One might wonder whether al-Shīrāzī's claims to be engaging in *ijtihād* are sincere: later Shāfiʿīs, like Ibn al-Ṣalāḥ (d. 643/1245 CE) and Yaḥyā b. Sharaf al-Nawawī (d. 676/1277 CE), contended that Shāfiʿīs of al-Shīrāzī's era engaged in a type of *taqlīd*, since they rarely departed from the standard rulings of their school; see Calder, "Al-Nawawī's Typology," 145.
89. Ahmed El Shamsy, "Rethinking '*Taqlīd*,'" 14–15.
90. The metaphor of finding the *qibla* as a form of *ijtihād* comes from al-Shāfiʿī's *al-Risāla*; Muḥammad b. Idrīs al-Shāfiʿī, *al-Risāla*, ed. Aḥmad Shākir (Beirut: Dār al-Kutub al-ʿIlmiyya, n.d.), 34–39; Joseph Lowry, *Early Islamic Legal Theory: The Risāla of Muḥammad ibn Idrīs al-Shāfiʿī* (Leiden: Brill, 2007), 32.
91. El Shamsy, "Rethinking '*Taqlīd*,'" 19.
92. Al-Māwardī, *al-Ḥāwī*, 2:71.
93. Al-Shīrāzī, *Sharḥ*, 2:665–666.
94. Al-Shīrāzī, *al-Muhadhdhab*, 1:227.
95. Al-Shīrāzī, *Sharḥ*, 2:727.
96. Although I have critiqued El Shamsy's interpretation that Shāfiʿīs saw themselves as bound to school authority, I nonetheless follow El Shamsy's useful deployment of the term paradigm to speak about the Shāfiʿī legal school; El Shamsy, *The Canonization*, 173. On legal reasoning in the Ḥanafī school, see Eyyüp Said Kaya, "Continuity and Change in Islamic Law: The Concept of Madhhab and the Dimensions of Legal Disagreement in Hanafi Scholarship of the Tenth Century," in *The Islamic School of Law: Evolution, Devolution, and Progress*, ed. P.J. Bearman, Rudolph Peters, and Frank E. Vogel (Cambridge, MA: Harvard Law School, 2005), 39, who identifies that Ḥanafism is characterized by a

commitment to taking the arguments of one's predecessors as a starting point in one's legal reasoning.

97. At the beginning of the *Sharḥ*, al-Shīrāzī acknowledges that studying the dissenting arguments of jurists, rather than seeking to master *uṣūl al-fiqh*, permits one to master substantive law; al-Shīrāzī, *Sharḥ*, 1:219–220. See also Abū Ya'lā, *al-'Udda*, 1:19.
98. Al-Nawawī, *al-Majmū'*, 1:38. Sherman Jackson states that the *mujtahid* who attempts to justify his school's positions should not be counted as having performed *ijtihād* proper; Jackson, "*Taqlīd*," 167.
99. Al-Ghazālī, *al-Mustaṣfā*, 2:902.
100. Al-Ghazālī, *Iḥyā'*, 1:61–62.
101. Ibid., 1:62
102. Al-Subkī, *Ṭabaqāt*, 4:62.
103. Ibn 'Aqīl, *Kitāb al-Jadal*, 2; al-Bājī, *al-Minhāj*, 9–14; al-Baghdādī, *Kitāb al-Faqīh*, 250–257; al-Juwaynī, *al-Kāfiya*, 529–541.
104. On al-Ghazālī's use of dialectic, see Ahmet Adanali, "Dialectical Methodology and Its Critique: al-Ghazālī as a Case Study" (PhD diss., University of Chicago, 1995).
105. Talal Asad, *Genealogies of Religion*, 75–76; Talal Asad, "Remarks," 42–52.
106. Al-Shīrāzī, *Sharḥ*, 1:147–148.
107. Qur'an *al-Naḥl*: 106, "Whoever disbelieves in [i.e., denies] Allah after his belief . . . except for one who is forced [to renounce his religion] while his heart is secure in faith."
108. Al-Shīrāzī writes: "specious arguments affect the beliefs of the scholar (*al-'ālim ta'tarīhi al-shubuhāt fa-tu'aththir fī i'tiqādihi*)." Al-Shīrāzī, *Sharḥ*, 1:148.
109. Al-Shīrāzī, *Sharḥ*, 1:148.
110. Ibn Fūrak, *Mujarrad*, 293.
111. For examples of theological disputations in Central Asia, see al-Rāzī, *Munāẓarāt*, 14–24; see also Paul Kraus, "The Controversies of Fakhr al-Din Razi," *Islamic Culture* 12, no. 2 (1938): 131–150; Frank Griffel, *al-Ghazālī's Philosophical Theology* (Oxford: Oxford University Press, 2009), 116–120.

## Chapter 4

1. Schacht, *Introduction*, 71. Schacht states: "This 'closing of the door of *ijtihād*,' as it was called, amounted to the demand for *taḳlid* . . . which now came to mean the unquestioning acceptance of the doctrines of established schools and authorities." See also Joseph Schacht, "The Schools of Law and Other Developments of Jurisprudence," in *Origin and Development of Islamic* Law, ed. Majid Khadduri and Herbert J. Liebesny (Clark, NJ: The Lawbook Exchange 2008), 57–84.
2. E.g., Hallaq ("Was the Gate," 15–17) where he characterizes the full *mujtahid* (*mujtahid muṭlaq*) by his abandonment of school authority; Jackson ("*Taqlīd*,"

168) locates the beginning of the era of *taqlīd* with the settling of the *madhāhib* (*istiqrār al-madhāhib*); Fadel, "The Social Logic," 197.

3. Two recent studies have sought to complicate the traditional view of *ijtihād* and *taqlīd* by suggesting that they are not binary opposites, but both studies reproduce the assumption that a jurist necessarily engages in *taqlīd* when he follows school precedent; Ibrahim, "Rethinking the *Taqlīd* Hegemony" 804; Rebecca Gould, "Beyond the *Taqlīd/Ijtihād* Dichotomy: Daghestani Legal Thought under Russian Rule," *Islamic Law and Society* 24, no. 1–2 (2017): 142–169.
4. Makdisi, *Rise*, 290. Elsewhere Makdisi writes: "It is often intimated or implied that the closing of the gates of *ijtihād* and the dwindling of the schools of law to four are two interconnected phenomena. To my mind, these two phenomena are due to two different causes." George Makdisi "Authority in the Islamic Community," in *La notion d'autorité au Moyen Age: Islam, Byzance, Occident*, ed. G. Makdisi et al. (Paris: Presses Universitaires de France, 1982), 121. See also George Makdisi, "The Significance of the Sunni Schools of Law in Islamic Religious History," *International Journal of Middle East Studies* 10, no. 1 (1979): 1–2.
5. Joseph Schacht, "Classicisme, traditionalisme et ankylose dans la loi religieuse de l'Islam," in *Classicisme et declin culturel dans I'histoire de I'Islam*, ed. R. Brunschvig and G. von Grunebaum (Paris: Besson et Chantemerle, 1957), 14; Coulson, *A History*, 73; C. Pellat, "Les Étapes de la décadence culturelle dans les pays Arabes d'Orient," in *Classicisme et déclin culturel dans l'histoire de l'Islam*, ed. R. Brunschvig and G. von Grunebaum (Paris: Besson et Chantemerle 1957), 85.
6. Al-Subkī, *Ṭabaqāt*, 4:237.
7. Al-Shīrāzī, *Ṭabaqāt*, 131; al-Subkī, *Ṭabaqāt*, 5:12–80.
8. Al-Shīrāzī called al-Māwardī "*ḥāfiẓ^an^ li'l-madhhab* (a preserver of the Shāfiʿī tradition)." Al-Shīrāzī, *Ṭabaqāt*, 131.
9. Other Shāfiʿī texts similar in length to the *Ḥāwī* include Abū al-Ṭayyib al-Ṭabarī's *al-Taʿlīqa al-Kubrā*; al-Juwaynī's *Nihāyat al-Maṭlab*; Abū al-Maḥāsin al-Rūyānī, *Baḥr al-Madhhab fī Furūʿ al-Madhhab al-Shāfiʿī*, ed. Ṭāriq Fatḥī al-Sayyid, 14 vols. (Beirut: Dār al-Kutub al-ʿIlmiyya, 2009); and Abū al-Ḥusayn al-ʿImrānī, *al-Bayān fī Madhhab al-Imām al-Shāfiʿī*, ed. Qāsim al-Nūrī, 14 vols. (Beirut: Dār al-Minhāj, 2000).
10. Al-Subkī, *Ṭabaqāt*, 4:237–245.
11. Ziauddin Ahmad, "The Concept of Jizya in Early Islam," *Islamic Studies* 14, no. 4 (1975): 301. Ahmad provides a chronology of the *jizya*'s adoption in early Islamic history. He locates its first application around the time of the battle of Tabūk (9 AH/632 CE).
12. Anver Emon, *Religious Pluralism in Islamic Law: Dhimmīs and Others in the Empire of Law* (Oxford: Oxford University Press, 2012), 99.
13. Al-Māwardī, *al-Ḥāwī*, 14:284; al-Marghīnānī, *al-Hidāya: Sharḥ Bidāyat al-Mubtadī*, ed. Muḥammad Tāmir and Ḥāfiẓ ʿĀshūr Ḥāfiẓ, 4 vols. (Cairo: Dār al-Salām, 2000), 2:862.
14. Al-Shīrāzī, *al-Muhadhdhab*, 5:313; al-Juwaynī, *Nihāyat*, 17:9.

15. The version of the story quoted here is taken from Abū Yūsuf, *Abū Yūsuf's Kitāb al-Kharāj*, trans. A. Ben Shemesh (Leiden: Brill, 1969), 89. Al-Shīrāzī summarizes the story in the *Muhadhdhab* slightly differently: "They [the Zoroastrians] had knowledge which they acted upon, and a book that they studied, but their king became drunk and slept with his daughter or his sister, such that some of his royal entourage surrounded him and were going to apply the prescribed penalty for such a crime, and to avoid this penalty, he decreed the nullity of their book, and thus true knowledge disappeared from their breasts (*Kāna lahum 'ilm ya'malūnahu, wa-kitāb yadrusūnahu, wa-anna malikahum sakara fa-waqa'a 'alā ibnatihi, aw-ukhtihi, fa-aṭṭla'a 'alayhi ba'ḍ ahl mamlakatihi, fa-jā'ū yuqīmūna 'alayhi al-ḥadd, fa-amtana'a, fa-rafa'a al-kitāb min bayni aẓhurihim, wa-dhahaba al-'ilm min ṣudūrihim*)." Al-Shīrāzī, *al-Muhadhdhab*, 5:312.
16. For a historical account of the meaning and semantic shifts in the term "*dhimma*," see C.E. Bosworth, "The Concept of the *Dhimma* in Early Islam," in *Christians and Jews in the Ottoman Empire: The Functioning of a Plural Society*, ed. Benjamin Braude and Bernard Lewis (New York: Holmes and Meier Publishers, 1982), 37–51, 40–41.
17. See Abū Ḥasan al-Māwardī, *Kitāb al-Aḥkām al-Sulṭāniyya wa'l-Wilāyāt al-Dīniyya*. (Mansoura: Dār al-Wafā', 1989), 182: "With the exchange of the *jizya*, the non-Muslims are afforded two rights: first, to be left in peace [i.e. not fought or killed]. And second, to be protected protection [from outside attack] (*Wa-yaltazim lahum bi-badhlihā ḥaqqayn: aḥaduhummā al-kaff 'anhum. Wa'l-thānī al-ḥimāya lahum li-yakūnū bi'l-kaff āminīn wa-bi'l-ḥimāya maḥrūsīn*)." al-Marghīnānī explains the *jizya* as an exchange for two things: (1) the Muslim abstention from "killing or combating" the non-Muslims who pay the *jizya*; (2) the support of Muslim armies, which substitutes for the support that could have been given by participating in the army: Al-Marghīnānī, *al-Hidāya*, 2:863.
18. Milka Levy-Rubin, *Non-Muslims in the Early Islamic Empire: From Surrender to Coexistence* (Cambridge: Cambridge University Press), 113.
19. See Antoine Fattal, *Le Statut Légal Des Non-Musulmans En Pays d'Islam* (Beirut: Imprimerie catholique, 1958), 68. Fattal writes: "La convention de 'Umar, dans sa redaction definitive, est peut-être l'oevre de quelques *muǧtahids* du IIIème siècle qui n'ont pu résister à la tentation de réunir en un même document toutes les restrictions successives aux liberté des *Ḏimmīs*, sans tenir compte des circonstances de temps et de lieu." A.S. Tritton, *The Caliphs and Their Non-Muslim Subjects: A Critical Study of the Covenant of 'Umar* (London: Oxford University Press, 1930); al-Shīrāzī, *al-Muhadhdhab*, 5:326–330. Al-Juwaynī, *Nihāyat*, 18:50–55; al-'Imrānī, *al-Bayān*, 12:275–280; al-Maḥāmilī, *al-Lubāb fī al-Fiqh al-Shāfi'ī*, ed. 'Abd al-Karīm al-Ḥarbī (Medina: Dār al-Bukhārī, 1995), 376; al-Ghazālī, *al-Wasīṭ fī al-Madhhab*, ed. Muḥammad Tāmir, 8 vols. (Cairo: Dār al-Salām, 1996), 7:80–85.
20. Al-Shīrāzī, *al-Muhadhdhab*, 5:328.
21. Shawkat Toorawa, "The Dhimmī in Medieval Islamic Society: Non-Muslim Physicians of Iraq in Ibn Abī Uṣaybi'ah's *'Uyūn al-Anbā' fi Ṭabaḳāt al-Aṭibbā'*," *Fides et Historia: Official Publication of the Conference on Faith and History* 26, no. 1 (1994): 15;

Luke Yarbrough, *Friends of the Emir: Non-Muslim State Officials in Premodern Islamic Thought* (Cambridge: Cambridge University Press, 2019), 1.

22. On post-conquest conversion, Richard Bulliet, *Conversion to Islam in the Medieval Period: An Essay in Quantitative History* (Cambridge, MA: Harvard University Press, 1979).
23. Al-Shāfiʿī, *al-Umm*, 5:437; al-Shaybānī, *Kitāb al-Aṣl*, ed. Muḥammad Būyanūkālin, 12 vols. (Beirut: Dār Ibn Ḥazm), 8:547. Al-Shaybānī writes: "And if he converts, and there remains a part of the *jizya*, it is not taken, and it is cancelled (*wa-baqiya ʿalayhi shayʾ min jizyat raʾsihi, lam tuʾkhadh wa-tasquṭ ʿanhu*)."
24. On the debates over the proselytizing motives of Arab-Muslim conquerors, see Fred Donner, *The Early Islamic Conquests* (Princeton, NJ: Princeton University Press, 1981), 271; see also Donner's more recent *and the Believers: At the Origins of Islam* (Cambridge, MA: The Belknap Press of Harvard University Press, 2010).
25. Wilferd Madelung, *Religious Trends in Early Islamic Iran* (Albany, NY: Persian Heritage Foundation, 1988), 19.
26. Jackson, "Fiction and Formalism: Toward a Functional Analysis of *Uṣūl al-Fiqh*," in *Studies in Islamic Legal Theory*, ed. Bernard Weiss (Leiden: Brill, 2002), 188. See also George Makdisi, "The Juridical Theology of Shâfi'î: Origins and Significance of *Uṣûl al-Fiqh*," *Studia Islamica* 59 (1984): 5–47, who presents al-Shāfiʿī as concerned about speculative theology's contaminating influence on the Islamic faith.
27. Later Shāfiʿīs would disagree on whether a ration of the *jizya* should be taken if the *dhimmī* spent only part of the year as a non-Muslim; al-Juwaynī, *Nihāyat*, 17:32; al-Rāfiʿī, *al-ʿAzīz fī Sharḥ al-Wajīz*, ed. ʿAlī al-Muʿawwaḍ and ʿĀdil ʿAbd al-Mawjūd, 13 vols. (Beirut: Dār al-Kutub al-ʿIlmiyya, 1997), 11:505.
28. Al-Subkī, *Ṭabaqāt*, 4:237.
29. Al-Shīrāzī, *Sharḥ*, 1:171–172.
30. Ibid., 2:665–666. Of note, al-Shīrāzī had the right to produce new evidence (*dalīl*) for the law, but he was barred from affirming a new legal position (*ḥukm*) because, according to his understanding of *ijmaʿ*, the Prophet's community "would not agree upon error," and thus one of his predecessors was necessarily correct in his legal position.
31. Ahmed El Shamsy, *The Canonization*, 173.
32. Al-Ghazālī, *al-Mustaṣfā*, 2:901–902.
33. Al-Baghdādī, *Kitāb al-Faqīh*, 254.
34. Al-Shīrāzī, *Ṭabaqāt*, 111, 114, 120.
35. Al-Māwardī, *al-Ḥāwī*, 14:313–314.
36. Ibn Rushd, *Bidāyat al-Mujtahid*, 4:1339. Some jurists also accepted guarantorship over a person (*al-kafāla bi-nafs*), as, for instance in a guarantorship over a person's court appearance.
37. Al-Māwardī, *al-Ḥāwī*, 14:313. Abū al-Ḥusayn al-Qudūrī, *al-Tajrīd*, ed. Muḥammad Aḥmad Sarāj and ʿAlī Jumʿa, 12 vols. (Cairo: Dār al-Salām, 2006), 12:6251. Al-Jaṣṣāṣ, *Sharḥ Mukhtaṣar*, 7: 211. For a complete view of the Ḥanafī position, see also Muḥammad b. Aḥmad al-Sarakhsī, *al-Mabsūṭ*, 31 vols. (Beirut: Dār al-Maʿrifa,

1989), 10:81; al-Samarqandī, *Tuḥfat al-Fuqahā'*, 3:308; al-Kāsānī, *Badā'i'*, 9:438–440; Zayn al-Dīn Ibn Nujaym, *al-Baḥr al-Rā'iq: Sharḥ Kanz al-Daqā'iq*, ed. Zakariyya 'Umayrāt, 9 vols. (Beirut: Dār al-Kutub al-'Ilmiyya, 1997), 5:188–189; Sirāj al-Dīn Ibn Nujaym, *al-Nahr al-Fā'iq*, ed. Aḥmad 'Ināya, 3 vols. (Beirut: Dār al-Kutub al-'Ilmiyya, 2002), 3:244; Fakhr al-Dīn al-Zayla'ī, *Tabyīn al- Ḥaqā'iq: Sharḥ Kanz al-Daqā'iq*, 6 vols. (Cairo: al-Maṭba'a al-Kubrā al-Amīriyya, 1895), 3:278; Badr al-Dīn al-'Aynī, *al-Bināya: Sharḥ al-Hidāya*, ed. Ayman Sha'bān, 13 vols. (Beirut: Dār al-Kutub al-'Ilmiyya, 2000), 7:249–51; Akmal al-Dīn al-Bābartī, *al-'Ināya: Sharḥ al-Hidāya*, 10 vols. (Cairo: Muṣṭafā al-Bābī al-Ḥalabī wa-Awlāduhu, 1970), 6:54–56.

38. See also al-Juwaynī, *Nihāyat*, 18:31–32; al-Rūyānī, *Baḥr* 13:361–362; al-Ghazālī, *al-Wasīṭ*, 7:77–79; al-'Imrānī, *al-Bayān*, 12:260.
39. On the prominence of *qiyās* to classical substantive law, see Hallaq, "A Tenth-Eleventh," 200.
40. See Mohammad Fadel, "*Istiḥsān* Is Nine-Tenths of the *Furu'*: The Puzzling Relationship of *Usūl* to *Furū'* in the Mālikī *Madhhab*," in *Studies in Islamic Legal Theory*, ed. Bernard Weiss (Leiden: Brill, 2002), 165–167, which addresses the lack of textual evidence for many laws.
41. Al-Shīrāzī, *Sharḥ*, 2:799.
42. Al-Māwardī, *al-Ḥāwī*, 14:313–314. Al-Shīrāzī tersely describes Shāfi'ī/Ḥanafī debates on the *jizya* in his *Nukat* in ways that overlap with al-Māwardī's *Ḥāwī*. See *al-Shīrāzī, al-Nukat fī al-Masā'il al-Mukhtalaf fīhā bayna al-Shāfi'ī wa-Abī Ḥanīfa, min Awwal Kitāb al-Jināyāt ilā Nihāyat Kitāb al-Iqrār*, ed. Ṣabāḥ bt. Akbar Ḥusayn Akbar (MA diss, Umm al-Qurā University in Mecca, 2003–2004), 245–247.
43. Jurists used a standard form for analogical arguments. They started by listing the legal cause—usually a characteristic (*ṣifa*) present in the legal question under review—followed by the ruling, and ending by citing the original case being analogized. For instance, al-Māwardī formulates the *jizya*/debt analogy by stating: "It [the *jizya*] is a wealth obligation owed by the individual, thus conversion does not cancel it, just like [in the case of] debts." Al-Māwardī, *al-Ḥāwī*, 14:314.
44. Al-Māwardī, *al-Ḥāwī*, 14:314.
45. On the Shāfi'ī position, see al-Shīrāzī, *al-Muhadhdhab*, 4:178, 190.
46. Al-Māwardī, *al-Ḥāwī*, 14:314.
47. A century later, Ibn Rushd al-Ḥafīd would speak of a stalemate between the Shāfi'īs and the Ḥanafīs: if the Shāfi'īs had examples of past obligations continuing after conversion, their opponents likewise had examples of past obligations that were cancelled after conversion; *Bidāyat al-Mujtahid*, 3:918.
48. Al-Shīrāzī, *Sharḥ*, 2:1067.
49. I have already pointed out how the disputation permitted the testing of arguments in Chapter 3. Both the Muṣawwiba and the Mukhaṭṭi'a note that the disputation is recommended to help one or both jurists improve their reasoning on the law.
50. Al-Subkī, *Ṭabaqāt*, 4:237.
51. Daniel Dennett notes that in the first century of Islam, the terms "*jizya*" and "*kharāj*" were synonymous; Dennett, *Conversion and the Poll Tax in Early Islam* (Cambridge,

MA: Harvard University Press, 1950), 12. The expression "upon their necks (*'alā riqābihim*)" and "upon their lands (*'alā arḍihim*)" served to distinguish between a tax levied upon every non-Muslim adult male and one levied upon the land. However, Khadduri argues that the term *jizya* rarely referred to a land tax and notes that only Ibn 'Abd al-Ḥakam uses the term *jizya 'alā al-arḍ*, speculating that the expression was unique to Egypt. Majid Khadduri, *War and Peace in the Law of Islam* (Baltimore: The Johns Hopkins Press, 1962), 189–190.

52. The Shāfi'īs applied the land-*kharāj* in two circumstances: (1) upon state-owned lands appropriated from non-Muslims after their original owners fled fearing the approaching Muslim armies. The *kharāj* would be taken from this land in perpetuity (as a *waqf*) regardless of conversion or Muslim migration. (2) upon land stipulated in a conquered people's treaty of surrender, in which case the people's land-*kharāj* fulfilled the obligation of the *jizya*. Al-Māwardī, *Kitāb al-Aḥkām*, 181; al-Maḥāmilī, *al-Lubāb*, 379–380. Al-Shīrāzī clarifies that he only has the second type of land-*kharāj* in mind as the subject of the disputation; see al-Subkī, *Ṭabaqāt*, 4:244.
53. Al-Māwardī, *Kitāb al-Aḥkām*, 188; al-Shīrāzī, *al-Muhadhdhab*, 5:315–16. Al-Shīrāzī writes: "It is permissible to impose the *jizya* upon their livestock and upon fruits and grains that grow from the earth (*Wa-yajūz an yaḍrib al-jizya 'alā mawāshīhim, wa-'alā mā yakhruj min al-arḍ min thamar aw zar'*)."
54. Denett, *Conversion*, 12.
55. The Shāfi'īs stipulated that the land-*kharāj* must be at least 1 dinār for the *'aqd al-dhimma* to be valid. Al-Shīrāzī, *al-Muhadhdhab*, 5:314.
56. On the boundaries between Muslim and non-Muslim lands, see Giovanna Calasso and Giulano Lancion, eds., *Dār al-Islām/Dār al-Ḥarb: Territories, People, Identities* (Leiden: Brill, 2017).
57. The Ḥanafīs imposed the land-*kharāj* on all lands belonging to non-Muslims when these lands were first incorporated into the Muslim empire; al-Marghīnānī, *al-Hidāya*, 2:855. See also Baber Johansen, *The Islamic Law on Land Tax and Rent* (London: Croom Helm, 1988), 7–12.
58. Al-Māwardī, *al-Ḥāwī*, 14:314.
59. Al-Subkī, *Ṭabaqāt*, 4:237: "*fa-istadalla 'alā dhālika bi-annahu aḥad al-kharājayn fa-idhā wajaba fī ḥāl al-kufr lam yasquṭ bi'l-islām, aṣluhu kharāj al-arḍ.*"
60. Al-Māwardī, *al-Ḥāwī*, 14:314.
61. On the juristic search for argumentative consistency in a legal school, see Mairaj Syed, *Coercion and Responsibility in Islam: A Study in Ethics and Law* (Oxford: Oxford University Press, 2017), 18–22; Behnam Sadeghi, *The Logic of Law-Making in Islam: Women and Prayer in the Legal Tradition* (New York: Cambridge University Press, 2013), 2.
62. Al-Marghīnānī, *al-Hidāya*, 2:855.
63. Al-Marghīnānī, *al-Hidāya*, 1:251–273; al-Juwaynī, *Nihāyat al-Maṭlab*, 3:77; al-Shīrāzī, *al-Muhadhdhab*, 1:462, 502, 517, 523; al-Jaṣṣāṣ, *Sharḥ Mukhtaṣar*, 2:229, 280, 287, 305, 336; al-Qudūrī, *Mukhtaṣar al-Qudūrī*, ed. Kāmil 'Awīḍa. (Beirut: Dār al-Kutub al-'Ilmiyya, 1997), 51–59. Al-Shīrāzī also lists buried treasure (*rikāz*) and

mined wealth (*ma'dan*) as assets upon which the *zakāt* is due, both of which were to be given immediately upon discovery (subject to the *khums* obligation (one-fifth)); al-Shīrāzī, *al-Muhadhdhab*, 1:531.

64. The Shāfi'īs stipulated the amount due to be a *ṣā'* of grain (approximately 5 pints) for every Muslim, free or slave, male or female. They disagreed as to whether the grain could be any staple (*qūt*), or whether one should give that which is most prevalent in one's region of residence, or that which one possesses most of; al-Shīrāzī, *al-Muhadhdhab*, 1:543; al-Māwardī, *al-Ḥāwī*, 3:377–378. The Ḥanafīs stipulated one half *ṣā'* of wheat or one full *ṣā'* of dates, raisins, or barley; al-Marghīnānī, *al-Hidāya*, 1:291; al-Qudūrī, *Mukhtaṣar*, 61.
65. Al-Shīrāzī, *al-Muhadhdhab*, 1:467; al-Juwaynī, *Nihāyat*, 3: 77–79; al-Qudūrī, *Mukhtaṣar*, 51. Al-Jaṣṣāṣ, *Sharḥ Mukhtaṣar*, 2:229; al-Kāsānī, *Badā'i'*, 2:404.
66. Al-Shīrāzī, *al-Muhadhdhab*, 1:486.
67. Ibid., 1:538–539. The Shāfi'īs made a man responsible for the *zakāt al-fiṭr* of those to whom he owed maintenance, i.e., his dependents. In contrast, the Ḥanafīs made a man responsible only for paying the *zakāt al-fiṭr* of his young children and his slaves, in addition to his own; al-Qudūrī, *Mukhtaṣar*, 61.
68. Al-Subkī, *Ṭabaqāt*, 4:237.
69. The concept of *dhimma* expressed a person's ability to take on legal obligations: a person's *dhimma* was his or her juridical person over and above a biological self. See Baber Johansen, *Contingency in a Sacred Law: Legal and Ethical Norms in the Muslim Fiqh* (Leiden: Brill, 1999), 192–193, 196–198. Kamali calls a claim imposed on a person's *dhimma* an "asset with no tangible existence." Mohammad Hashim Kamali, *Islamic Commercial Law: An Analysis of Futures and Options* (Cambridge: Islamic Texts Society, 2000), 140.
70. Al-Subkī, *Ṭabaqāt*, 4:240.
71. Ibn Rushd posits different amounts as compensation depending on the type of wealth that the perpetrator possesses, like camels, gold, sheep, or cows; Ibn Rushd, *Bidāyat al-Mujtahid*, 4:1552.
72. Al-Subkī, *Ṭabaqāt*, 4:243. Al-Shīrāzī states, "*Zakāt al-fiṭr* is different than the other types of *zakāt* because it is attached to one's *dhimma* (legal personality). This is the reason that the *niṣāb* is not one of its conditions."
73. Al-Shīrāzī, *al-Muhadhdhab*, 1:519.
74. Al-Subkī, *Ṭabaqāt*, 4:243.
75. Ibid., 4:242.
76. Al-Shīrāzī, *al-Muhadhdhab*, 1:473.
77. Ibid.
78. Al-Qudūrī, *Mukhtaṣar*, 232. Al-Qudūrī writes, "In regards to the prisoners, [a ruler] has options. If he wishes, [the ruler] can: kill them, enslave them, or allow them as free persons and subjects of the Muslims (*Wa-huwa fī al-usārā bi'l-khiyār, in shā'a qatalahum, wa-in shā'a istaraqqahum, wa-in shā'a tarakahum aḥrār*[an] *dhimmat*[an] *li'l-Muslimīn*)." Al-Samarqandī, *Tuḥfa*, 3:301–302; Abū al-Barakāt al-Nasafī, *Kanz al-Daqā'iq*, ed. Sā'id Bakdāsh (Beirut: Dār al-Bashā'ir al-Islāmiyya, 2011), 372.

79. Al-Shīrāzī also lists the option of ransoming the prisoners; al-Shīrāzī, *al-Muhadhdhab*, 5:339. The Ḥanafīs disagreed as to whether prisoners could be ransomed, with Abū Ḥanīfa prohibiting it and Abū Yūsuf and al-Shaybānī permitting it so long as it was to obtain Muslim prisoners of war, rather than wealth; al-Samarqandī, *Tuḥfa*, 3:302.
80. Al-Sarakhsī, *Sharḥ Kitāb al-Siyar al-Kabīr*, ed. Abū 'Abd Allāh Ismā'īl al-Shāfi'ī, 5 vols. (Beirut: Dār al-Kutub al-'Ilmiyya, 1997), 5: 368. Al-Sarakhsī (d. 483/1090 CE) writes: "If a non-Muslim is taken to the Muslim ruler and then utters the statement of monotheism, he is either a free Muslim, if this statement is said before he is defeated, or he is part of the war booty if the statement is said after being defeated, because conversion to Islam protects him from execution but not from enslavement after defeat (*Fa-in akhadhahu wa-jā'a bihi ilā al-imām fa-huwa ḥurr Muslim in kāna takallama bi-kalimat al-tawḥīd qabla an yaqharahu al-Muslim, wa-in qāla ba'damā qaharahu fa-huwa fay', li-anna al-Islām ya'ṣimuhu min al-qatl, lā min istirqāq ba'd al-qahr*)."
81. The ruler also had the right to choose between the options of slavery, execution, freedom, or ransom in other cases than conquest. For instance, al-Shīrāzī explains that if a non-Muslim refuses to pay the *jizya* or refuses to recognize the binding nature of the Muslims' rules (*aḥkām al-Muslimīn*), then the '*aqd al-dhimma* is considered overturned, and the ruler chooses either execution, enslavement, release (with exile), or ransom, as we have said for the [case of the] prisoner"; al-Shīrāzī, *al-Muhadhdhab*, 5:345. Ḥanafīs limited the rescinding of the '*aqd al-dhimma* to the waging of war against Muslims; see al-Marghīnānī, *al-Hidāya*, 2:868.
82. Al-Subkī, *Ṭabaqāt*, 4:237. Al-Dāmaghānī states: "There is no [methodological] impediment to preclude that two duties should exist, one of which is cancelled by conversion and the other not (*lā yamna' an yakūna ḥaqqān muta'alliqān bi'l-kufr thumma aḥaduhumā yasquṭ bi'l-islām wa'l-ākhar lā yasquṭ*)."
83. Ibid., 4:238.
84. Ibid., 4:244.
85. Ibid., 4: 237.
86. On the difference between the initiation and the continuation of a law, see al-Shīrāzī, *Sharḥ*, 2:837.
87. Al-Subkī, *Ṭabaqāt*, 4:241: the wording that al-Dāmaghānī used was "the fulfillment of that which has preceded (*Istīfā' mā taqaddama*)"; see al-Shīrāzī's response at 4:244.
88. Al-Subkī, *Ṭabaqāt*, 4:244.
89. Al-Qudurī, *Mukhtaṣar*, 58; al-Shīrāzī, *al-Muhadhdhab*, 1:507, 513; al-Māwardī, *al-Ḥāwī*, 3:249; al-Jaṣṣāṣ, *Sharḥ Mukhtaṣar*, 2:287.
90. Al-Subkī, *Ṭabaqāt*, 4:237.
91. Ibid., 4:241.
92. The Ḥanafīs considered that land could not be subject to both the '*ushr* and the land-*kharāj*. In contrast, the Shāfi'īs saw no impediment to imposing both taxes upon the same land. See al-Shīrāzī, *al-Muhadhdhab*, 1: 516–517; al-Samarqandī, *Tuḥfa*, 1:319.
93. Al-Subkī, *Ṭabaqāt*, 4:239.
94. For the Ḥanafī account of why the amount of the *land-kharāj* is determined by the land's surface area, see al-Marghīnānī, *al-Hidāya*, 2:855.

95. For instance, discussions of conditions (*shurūṭ*) in books of *uṣūl al-fiqh* do not typically engage with whether cases possessing the same genus are subject to the same conditions: see al-Jaṣṣāṣ, *al-Fuṣūl*, 2:313; al-Shīrāzī, *Sharḥ*, 1:227; al-Ṣaymarī, *Kitāb Masāʾil*, 14.
96. At most, *uṣūlīs* tackled the question of whether certain types of laws could not be subject to *qiyās*; e.g., see al-Shīrāzī, *Sharḥ*, 2:791; al-Ṣaymarī, *Kitāb Masāʾil*, 263.
97. Later Muslim scholars would author books of legal maxims that would deal with principles relevant to different areas of the law; Wolfart Heinrichs, "*Qawāʿid* as a Genre of Legal Literature," in *Studies in Islamic Legal Theory*, ed. Bernard Weiss (Leiden: Brill, 2002), 367; see also Mariam Sheibani, "Innovation, Influence, and Borrowing in Mamluk-Era Legal Maxim Collections: The Case of Ibn ʿAbd al-Salām and al-Qarāfī," *Journal of the American Oriental Society* 140, no. 4 (2020): 927–954.
98. Al-Subkī, *Ṭabaqāt*, 4:239–40.
99. Al-Māwardī, *Kitāb al-Aḥkām*, 181. Al-Māwardī, *al-Ḥāwī*, 14:283.
100. Al-Marghīnānī, *al-Hidāya*, 2:865. "*Wa-li-annahā wajabat ʿuqūbat*$^{an}$ *ʿalā al-kufr, li-hādhā tusammā jizya, wa-hiya waʾl-jazāʾ wāḥid.*"
101. Al-Māwardī notes that there should be no humiliation upon the Muslim. Al-Māwardī, *Ḥāwī*, 14:313.
102. Ibid., 14:312. Al-Māwardī explains that "The purpose of the contract of the *jizya* is to strengthen Islam and to bolster it, and to weaken disbelief and humiliate it."
103. Ibid., 14:314.
104. Al-Subkī, *Ṭabaqāt*, 4: 242–243. In the disputation, al-Shīrāzī also invokes the case of a criminal who is still subject to punishment after repentence. Al-Shīrāzī argues that repentence, like conversion, makes humiliation of a person unlawful. Thus the performance of a punishment (*al-adāʾ*), just like the payment of the past *jizya* cannot be a form of humiliation.
105. Al-Māwardī, *al-Ḥāwī*, 14:283.
106. Al-Subkī, *Ṭabaqāt*, 4:242.
107. Al-Māwardī, *al-Ḥāwī*, 14:283. Alongside humiliation, al-Māwardī explains that another meaning of "*ṣāghirūn*" in the Qurʾan is "that the laws of Islam are applied upon [non-Muslims] (*an tajrī ʿalayhim aḥkām al-Islām*)."
108. Al-Shāfiʿī, *Kitāb al-Umm*, 5:415–416. Al-Rāfiʿī states that there is no greater humiliation for a person than to subject him to rules that are contrary to his beliefs; ʿAbd al-Karīm b. Muḥammad al-Rāfiʿī, *al-ʿAzīz*, 11:492. See also al-Rūyānī, *Baḥr*, 13:346.
109. Al-Māwardī, *Kitāb al-Aḥkām*, 181.
110. Al-Juwaynī, *Nihāyat*, 18:17: "*Al-murād biʾl-ṣaghār al-akhdh biʾl-liḥya waʾl-ḍarb fī al-lahāzim fa-yukallaf al-dhimmī an yūfiya al-jizya bi-nafsihi, wa-yuṭaʾṭiʾ raʾsahu, wa-yaṣubb mā maʿahu fi al-kiffa, wa- yaʾkhudh al-mustawfī bi-liḥyatihi wa-yaḍrib fī lahzamatihi*"; see also al-Ghazālī, *al-Wasīṭ*, 7:70.
111. Muḥammad b. Aḥmad al-Shirbīnī, *Mughnī al-Muḥtāj ilā Maʿrifat Maʿānī Alfāẓ al-Minhāj*, ed. ʿAlī Muʿawwaḍ and ʿĀdil ʿAbd al-Mawjūd, 6 vols. (Beirut: Dār al-Kutub al-ʿIlmiyya, 2000), 6:71: "It is sufficient that [*the dhimmī*] be hit on one cheekbone, and the best position, as al-Bulqīnī said, is that he should be hit with an open palm.

Al-Adhraʿī and others have expressed that the [the collector] should say: 'Oh enemy of God, give over God's right.' (*Yashbah an yakfiya al-ḍarb fī aḥad al-jānibayn wa'l-ẓāhir kamā qāla al-Bulqīnī annahu yaḍribuhu bi'l-kaff maftūḥ*[an]. *Wa-qāla al-Adhraʿī wa-ghayruhu: 'wa-yaqūl: 'yā 'adū Allāh addi ḥaqq Allāh'*)."

112. Al-Shīrāzī, *al-Muhadhdhab*, 5:324. See also, al-Shīrāzī, *al-Tanbīh*, 237
113. See Jackson's discussion of non-Muslim viziers in "Fiction," 196.
114. Al-Subkī, *Ṭabaqāt*, 4:217.
115. Al-Shīrāzī, *al-Muhadhdhab*, 5:326.
116. On the Qur'anic exegesis of "*ṣāghirūn*," see al-Ṭabarī, *Jāmiʿ*, 6:138–139.
117. On the disputation's role in improving a jurist's reasoning, see al-Ghazālī, *al-Mustaṣfā*, 2:901–902.
118. Al-Shīrāzī, *al-Muhadhdhab*, 5:317.
119. See also al-Māwardī, *al-Ḥāwī*, 12:314.
120. Al-Shīrāzī, *al-Muhadhdhab*, 1:473–74.
121. Eric Chaumont, L'autorité des textes au sein du šāfiʿisme ancien: Du *Muḫtaṣar* d'al-Muzanī (m. 264/878) au *Tanbīh* d'al-Šīrāzī (m. 476/1083) et du *Tanbīh* d'al-Šīrāzī au *Minhāǧ al-ṭālibīn* d'al-Nawawī (m. 676/1277), *Mideo: Mélanges de L'Institut dominicain d'études orientales* 32 (2017), 53–62.
122. Al-Rāfiʿī, *al-ʿAzīz*, 11:426, 495, 497, 498, 501.
123. Al-Subkī, *Ṭabaqāt*, 7:336.
124. Al-ʿImrānī, *al-Bayān*, 12:271.
125. Al-Ghazālī, *al-Wasīṭ*, 7:73–75; ʿAbd al-Karīm al-Rāfiʿī, *al-Muḥarrar fī Fiqh al-Imām al-Shāfiʿī*, ed. Muḥammad Ismāʿīl (Dār al-Kutub al-ʿIlmiyya, 2005), 456; al-Nawawī, *Rawḍat al-Ṭālibīn* (Beirut: Dār Ibn Ḥazm, 2002), 1834; al-Shirbīnī, *Mughnī*, 6:71. For 11th- and 12th-century Shāfiʿīs who passed down both the opinion that the *jizya* hould be taken harshly and the opinion that it should be taken with gentleness, see Abū Muḥammad al-Baghawī, *al-Tahdhīb fī Fiqh al-Imām al-Shāfiʿī*, ed. ʿĀdil ʿAbd al-Mawjūd and ʿAlī Muʿawwaḍ, 8 vols. (Beirut: Dār al-Kutub al-ʿIlmiyya, 1997), 7:498; al-Rūyānī, *Baḥr*, 13:346.
126. Al-Ghazālī, *al-Wasīṭ*, 7:73–75.

## Chapter 5

1. https://www.musawah.org/wp-content/uploads/2019/05/Musawah-OHCHR-Submission_Child-Early-and-Forced-Marriage-December-2013.pdf, accessed June 19, 2021.
2. Position Statement: Forced Marriage, Posted August 14, 2014, by CCMW Webmaster & filed under CCMW Position Papers, 1.
3. Al-Shāfiʿī, *Kitāb al-Umm*, 6:47; Abū al-Ṭayyib al-Ṭabarī, *al-Taʿlīqa al-Kubrā, Kitāb al-Ṣadāq, Kitāb al-Qasm wa'l-Nushūz*, ed. Yūsuf b. ʿAbd al-Laṭīf ʿAbd Allāh al-ʿAqīl (PhD diss., Islamic University of Medina, 2005), 177; al-Māwardī, *al-Ḥāwī*, 9:56; al-Qāḍī Ḥusayn al-Marwarrūdhī, *Fatāwā al-Qāḍī Ḥusayn*, ed. Amal Khaṭṭāb and

Jamāl Abū Ḥassān ('Ammān: Dār al-Fatḥ, 2010), 314. Al-Shīrāzī, *al-Tanbīh*, 157; al-Qaffāl al-Shāshī, *Maḥāsin al-Sharī'a fī Furū' al-Shāfi'iyya*, ed. Abū 'Abd Allāh Samaka (Beirut: Dār al-Kutub al-'Ilmiyya, 2007), 270–272. See also Carolyn Baugh, *Minor Marriage in Early Islam* (Leiden: Brill, 2017), 123.

4. CCMW, 1.
5. Al-Subkī, *Ṭabaqāt*, 4:219–222. Ibn al-Athīr, *al-Kāmil*, 8:428–429.
6. Al-Juwaynī, *Nihāyat*, 12:42.
7. See Johnathan Brown's typology of legal interpretive trends in the modern period, "Scripture in the Modern Muslim World: The Quran and Hadith," in *Islam and the Modern World*, ed. J. Kenney and E. Moosa (London: Routledge, 2014), 13–34.
8. Al-Ṭabarī, *al-Ta'līqa al-Kubrā*, *Kitāb al-Nikāḥ*, 324–339; al-Juwaynī, *Nihāyat*, 12:170–174.
9. Al-Shīrāzī, *al-Muhadhdhab*, 4:139: "*wa-in qāla: zawwajtuka hādhihi Fāṭima wa-ismuhā 'Ā'isha, ṣaḥḥa li-anna ma'a al-ta'yīn bi'l-ishāra lā ḥukm li'l-ism fa-lam yu'aththir al-ghalaṭ fīhi.*"
10. Kecia Ali, "Marriage in Classical Islamic Jurisprudence: A Survey of Doctrines," in *The Islamic Marriage Contract: Case Studies in Islamic Family Law*, ed. Asifa Quraishi and Frank E Vogel (Cambridge, MA: Harvard University Press, 2009), 13.
11. Al-Jaṣṣāṣ, *Sharḥ Mukhtaṣar*, 4: 273–274; al-Qudūrī, *Mukhtaṣar*, 145; al-Nasafī, *Kanz al-Daqā'iq*, 1:254.
12. Al-Marghīnānī, *al-Hidāya*, 2:477.
13. Al-Shīrāzī, *al-Muhadhdhab*, 4:119. Al-Māwardī, *al-Ḥāwī*, 9:39.
14. Al-Shīrāzī, *al-Muhadhdhab*, 4:118; For a list of evidence upon which the Shāfi'īs relied, see al-Māwardī, *al-Ḥāwī*, 9:38–40; al-Ṭabarī, *al-Ta'līqa al-Kubrā*, *Kitāb al-Nikāḥ*, 321–323; al-Shāfi'ī, *Kitāb al-Umm*, 6:33.
15. Al-Shāfi'ī, *Kitāb al-Umm*, 6:31–32.
16. Al-Māwardī, *al-Ḥāwī*, 9:45: "[women] are prevented from marriage except with a guardian who is cautious lest she be won over by the desire to place herself in the hand of an unsuitable match such that there enters through [the groom] dishonour into her family (*yumna'na min al-'aqd illā bi-walī yuḥtāṭ li-a-lā taghlibahā farṭ al-shahwa 'alā waḍ' nafsihā fī ghayr kuf fa-yadkhul bihi al-'ār 'alā ahlihā*)." See also al-Shīrāzī, *al-Muhadhdhab*, 4:118; Ibn Qudāma, *al-Mughnī*, ed. 'Abd Allāh al-Turkī and 'Abd al-Fattāḥ al-Ḥulū, 15 vols. (Dār 'Ālam al-Kutub, 1997), 9:345, 356.

    Al-Juwaynī, *Nihāyat*, 12:158. Al-Juwaynī explained that there is shame in being the sexually submissive partner (*ḥukm al-mahāna bi'l-iftirāsh*). See also al-Rūyānī, *Baḥr*, 12:158.
17. Mohammad Fadel, "Reinterpreting the Guardian's Role in the Islamic Contract of Marriage: The Case of the Mālikī School," *The Journal of Islamic Law* 3 (1998): 1–26.
18. Al-Juwaynī, *Nihāyat*, 12:152–153. Shāfi'ī jurists differed among themselves on the number of measures by which potential suitors were to be evaluated: depending on the scholar, the answer ranged between four and seven. Al-Māwardī, *al-Ḥāwī*, 9:101–106; al-Shīrāzī, *al-Muhadhdhab*, 4:131–133. Abū 'Alī b. Abī Hurayra is

credited with positing the five measures of *kafā'a* that were widely accepted among Shāfi'īs; al-Ṭabarī, *al-Ta'līqa al-Kubrā, Kitāb al-Nikāḥ*, 249.

19. Likewise, the Qurayshite woman is superior to the non-Qurayshite Arab man, "*al-'ajamī laysa bi-kuf' li'l-'arabiyya . . . wa-ghayr al-Qurayshī laysa bi-kuf' li'l-Qurayshiyya*"; al-Shīrāzī, *al-Muhadhdhab*, 4:131.
20. Al-Juwaynī, *Nihāyat* 12:154. "*fa-innahum warathat al-anbiyā'.*"
21. Al-Shīrāzī, *al-Muhadhdhab*, 4:132.
22. Ibid.
23. Ibid., 4:132–33; al-Juwaynī, *Nihāyat*, 12:153. See also al-Māwardī, *al-Ḥāwī*, 9:106.
24. Al-Juwaynī, *Nihāyat*, 12:158. Al-Juwaynī's father Abū Muḥammad disagreed with other Shāfi'īs by considering that a man who marries a woman of lower status also dishonours himself.
25. Al-Shīrāzī writes: "If the bride is a freewoman, her guardian is her agnates, and foremost among them is her father, her paternal grandfather, her brother, her nephew, her paternal uncle, and her cousin because the purpose of guardianship in marriage is to repel dishonor from one's lineage, and lineage is a matter that pertains to the agnates." Al-Shīrāzī, *al-Muhadhdhab*, 4:120.
26. Al-Shīrāzī, *al-Muhadhdhab*, 4:120–121; al-Juwaynī, *Nihāyat*, 12:79, 88. The statement "the sultan is the guardian of the one without a guardian" is taken from a *ḥadīth* upon which Shāfi'īs relied for their ruling: "*al-Sulṭān walī man lā walī lahā.*"
27. On *kafā'a* in the Ḥanafī school, see Mona Siddiqui, "Law and the Desire for Social Control: An Insight into the Hanafi Concept of *Kafa'a* with Reference to the Fatawa 'Alamgiri," in *Feminism in Islam: Legal and Literary*, ed. Mai Yamani (New York: New York University Press, 1996), 49–68.
28. According to al-Māwardī, Mālik affirmed that a woman need not a guardian if she is of low-status; al-Māwardī, *al-Ḥāwī*, 9:44. See also Saḥnūn, *al-Mudawwana al-Kubrā*, 5 vols. (Beirut: Dār al-Kutub al-'Ilmiyya, 1994), 2:117–118; On the Ḥanbalī position, see Ibn Qudāma, *al-Mughnī*, 9:387–390.
29. al-Jaṣṣāṣ, *Sharḥ Mukhtaṣar*, 4:247.
30. Al-Marghīnānī, *al-Hidāya*, 2:476–477.
31. Al-Subkī, *Ṭabaqāt*, 4:252: "*bāqiyat 'alā bikārat al-aṣl, fa-jāza li'l-ab tazwījuhā bi-ghayr idhnihā, aṣluhu idhā kānat ṣaghīra.*" Al-Marghīnānī, *al-Hidāya*, 2:476–477. Shāfi'īs often invoked the analogy between the virgin minor and the virgin adult against Ḥanafīs. So much so that it is the argument that al-Marghīnānī's *Hidāya* in support of the Shāfi'ī position.
32. Al-Shīrāzī explains that, "It is permissible for a man to marry off his son if he sees it fit," and states that 'Umar the second caliph, married off his son as a minor, *al-Muhadhdhab*, 4:134. See also al-Juwaynī, *Nihāyat*, 12:43; al-Qudūrī, *Mukhtaṣar*, 146; Ali, "Marriage in Classical Islamic Jurisprudence," 32.
33. Al-Jaṣṣāṣ, *Sharḥ Mukhtaṣar*, 4:292
34. Al-Subkī, *Ṭabaqāt*, 4:452.
35. Ibid., 4:253.
36. *Ayyim* also sometimes meant "a widow." Al-Māwardī, *al-Ḥāwī*, 9:43.

37. The Ḥanafis read the *ḥadīth*, "*al-thayyib aḥaqq min waliyyihā*," as prohibiting the forced marriage of a post-pubescent woman; see Jamāl al-Dīn al-Zaylaʿī, *Naṣb al-Rāya li-Aḥādīth al-Hidāya*, ed. Aḥmad Shams al-Dīn, 5 vols. (Beirut: Dār al-Kutub al-ʿIlmiyya, 2010), 3:238–242.
38. Al-Subkī, *Ṭabaqāt*, 4:253.
39. A variant of the hadith substitutes *al-thayyib* (virgin) for *al-ayyim*. See al-Māwardī, *al-Ḥāwī*, 9:43. See also al-Shāfiʿī, *Kitāb al-Umm*, 6:47. On juristic hermeneutics, see Muhammad Yunis Ali, *Medieval Islamic Pragmatics* (Richmond: Routledge, 2000); David Vishanoff, *The Formation of Islamic Hermeneutics: How Sunni Legal Theorists Imagined a Revealed Law* (New Haven, CT: American Oriental Society, 2011).
40. Al-Shīrāzī, *Sharḥ*, 1:428.
41. Ibid.
42. There were logical and theological reasons for which some jurists rejected the *a contrario* argument. See Felicitas Opwis, "Shifting Legal Authority from the Ruler to the *'Ulamā'*: Rationalizing the Punishment for Drinking Wine during the Saljuq Period," *Der Islam* 86, no.1 (2011): 79–80. See also al-Shīrāzī's response to these critics, *Sharḥ*, 1:428–440.
43. Al-Zaylaʿī, *Naṣb*, 3:241–242. Al-Zaylaʿī argues that an *a contrario* argument does not necessarily apply to all other members of a larger group. All that could be drawn from the *a contrario* was that some within the larger group were subject to the contrary ruling.
44. Al-Zaylaʿī, *Naṣb*, 3:242. "*al-isti'dhān munāf$^{in}$ li'l-ijbār.*"
45. Al-Qaffāl al-Shāshī, *Maḥāsin*, 271.
46. Al-Subkī, *Ṭabaqāt*, 4:254.
47. Al-Juwaynī, *Nihāyat*, 12:42. Ibn al-Qāṣṣ states: "It is known that a father loves for his child better than what he loves for himself." Al-Qaffāl al-Shāshī, *Maḥāsin*, 271.
48. Emphasis mine. Al-Subkī, *Ṭabaqāt*, 4:254.
49. Al-Zaylaʿī, *Naṣb*, 3:242. "*waqaʿa al-tafrīq fī al-ḥadīth bayn al-thayyib wa'l-bikr, li-anna al-thayyib tukhṭab ilā nafsihā, fa-ta'mur al-walī bi-tazwījihā, wa'l-bikr tukhṭab ilā waliyyihā, fa-yasta'dhinuhā, wa-li-hādhā farraqa baynahumā, fī kawn al-thayyib idhnuhā al-kalām, wa'l-bikr idhnuhā ṣumātuhā.*"
50. Al-Jaṣṣāṣ, *Sharḥ Mukhtaṣar*, 4:293.
51. Emphasis mine.
52. Al-Subkī, *Ṭabaqāt*, 4:255.
53. On al-Shīrāzī's use of an inductive survey of the law in analogical reasoning, see *Sharḥ*, 2:809, 860–861.
54. Al-Qudūrī, *Mukhtaṣar*, 336. See also al-Marghīnānī, *al-Hidāya*, 2:477–478.
55. al-Shāfiʿī, *Kitāb al-Umm*, 6:47. "*amruhu an tusta'dhan al-bikr fī nafsihā amr ikhtiyār lā farḍ. Li-annahā law kānat idhā karihat lam yakun lahu tazwījuhā kānat ka'l-thayyib, wa-kāna yushbih an yakūn al-kalām fīhā anna kull imra'a aḥaqq bi-nafsihā min waliyyihā.*" For the definition of a reprehensible act, see al-Shīrāzī, *Sharḥ*, 1:170.
56. Al-Qaffāl al-Shāshī claims that a virgin woman can be coerced into marriage because her lack of sexual experience leads her to become overwhelmed by shyness (*istīlā' al-ḥayā'*) in expressing her preferences; *Maḥāsin*, 272.

57. Al-Juwaynī, *Nihāyat*, 12:43.
58. Al-Shīrāzī explains about a sexually inexperienced woman with a broken hymen: "She should marry as a virgin marries." He elaborates that it is because she still possesses the shyness of a virgin. In contrast, a woman with sexual experience, whether through marital or extramarital relations, can no longer be coerced into marriage; al-Shīrāzī, *al-Muhadhdhab*, 4:127.
59. Al-Shīrāzī also considers unlawful the forced marriage of a woman who has had sexual relations outside of marriage; al-Shīrāzī, *al-Muhadhdhab*, 4:127.
60. Al-Shīrāzī, *al-Muhadhdhab*, 4:118; see also al-Māwardī, *al-Ḥāwī*, 1:435.
61. Al-Subkī, *Ṭabaqāt*, 4:253.
62. In the *Nihāyat*, al-Juwaynī affirms the obligation of guardianship for valid marriage contracts. However, he does not justify this obligation by claiming that women were rationally deficient. Rather, he saw a woman's agnates as having a say in who would enter their family and shape their reputation. Al-Juwaynī, *Nihāyat*, 12:92.
63. Al-Marghīnānī, *al-Hidāya*, 2:477.
64. Ibid. "*wa'l-wilāya 'alā al-ṣaghīra li-quṣūr 'aqlihā, wa-qad kamula bi'l-bulūgh bi-dalīl tawajjuh al-khiṭāb, fa-ṣārat ka'l-ghulām*."
65. Ibid.
66. Tariq Ramadan, *Western Muslims and the Future of Islam* (Oxford: Oxford University Press, 2004), 37; Muḥammad al-Ṭāhir b. 'Āshūr, *Maqāṣid al-Sharī'a al-Islāmiyya*, ed. Muḥammad al-Ṭāhir al-Mīsāwī (Amman: al-Bashā'ir li'l-Intāj al-'Ilmī, 1998), 197; Jasser Auda, *Maqāṣid al-Sharī'ah: A Beginner's Guide* (London: International Institute of Islamic Thought, 2008), 3; Adis Duderja, "Contemporary Reformist Muslim Thought and Maqāṣid cum Maṣlaḥa Approaches to Islamic Law: An Introduction," in *Maqāṣid al-Sharī'a and Contemporary Reformist Thought* (New York: Palgrave Macmillan, 2014), 1–12
67. Ebrahim Moosa, "Ethical Landscape: Laws, Norms, and Morality," in *Islam and the Modern World*, ed. J. Kenney and E. Moosa (London: Routledge, 2014), 35–56.
68. Samira Haj, *Reconfiguring Tradition: Reform, Rationality, and Modernity* (Stanford, CA: Stanford University Press, 2009), 85.
69. Mohammad Hashim Kamali, "Goals and Purposes *Maqāṣid al-Sharī'a*: Methodological Perspectives," in *The Higher Objectives of Islamic Law: The Promises and Challenges of Maqāṣid al-Sharī'a*, ed. Idris Nassery et al. (Lanham, MD: Lexington Books, 2018), 11–12.
70. On al-Juwaynī's use of *maṣlaḥa*, see Anver Emon's *Islamic Natural Law Theories* (New York: Oxford University Press, 2010), 102–103, 124–129; Felicitas Opwis, *Maṣlaḥa and the Purpose of the Law: Islamic Discourse on Legal Change from the 4th/10th to 8th/14th Century*. (Leiden: Brill, 2010), 41–58.
71. Al-Juwaynī, *al-Burhān*, 2:803–804.
72. The Ash'arīs were adamant that God was not constrained to rule in terms of human benefit; see Emon, *Islamic Natural Law Theories*, 32.
73. Al-Juwaynī, *al-Burhān*, 2:803.
74. On the later development of this theory, see al-Ghazālī, *al-Mustaṣfā*, 1:478.
75. Al-Subkī, *Ṭabaqāt*, 4:254.

76. In his commentary of al-Shīrāzī's *Luma'*, Eric Chaumont notes that there are many instances in which al-Shīrāzī's *uṣūl al-fiqh* relies on the linguistic conventions of Arabs in opposition to the rational speculations of theologians. Al-Shīrāzī, *Kitāb al-Luma' fī Uṣūl al-Fiqh*, trans. Eric Chaumont (Berkeley, CA: Robbins Collection, 1999), 43, footnote 21.
77. Al-Shīrāzī, *Sharḥ*, 2:853. Al-Shīrāzī explains: "because if there was another meaning that constituted the legal cause of the ruling, there would be no benefit in mentioning the attribute (*li-annahu law kāna ghayruhā fī ma'nāhā lam yakun li-dhikr hādhihi al-ṣifāt fā'ida*)."
78. Al-Subkī, *Ṭabaqāt*, 4:255.
79. According to al-Juwaynī, only a perspicuous text (*al-naṣṣ*) allows a jurist to dispense with considerations of benefit. Al-Juwaynī claimed that no perspicuous text sanctions forced marriage; ibid., 4:254.
80. Al-Juwaynī, *Nihāyat*, 12:42; see al-Shīrāzī's position in *al-Muhadhdhab*, 4:125.
81. For an early Ḥanafī theory of *maṣlaḥa* to find the *ratio legis* in an analogy, see Opwis, *Maṣlaḥa*, 19; Zysow, *Economy*, 228.
82. Shāfi'īs would continue to affirm the lawfulness of coercing a virgin into marriage. See Abū Sa'd al-Mutawallī, *Tatimmat al-Ibāna 'an Furū' al-Diyāna, min Awwal Kitāb al-Nikāḥ ilā Nihāyat Bāb Nikāḥ Ḥarā'ir al-Kuffār*, ed. Taghrīd bt. Muẓahhir al-Bhukhārī (PhD diss., Umm al-Qurā University, Mecca, 2007), 184; al-Ghazālī, *al-Wasīṭ*, 5:63–65 (the same hadith); al-Rūyānī, *Baḥr*, 9:48–49; al-'Imrānī, *al-Bayān*, 9:179–181; al-Baghawī, *Tahdhīb*, 5:255–256.
83. Al-Nawawī reports Abū Isḥāq al-Isfarāyinī's stating of the Shāfi'ī of the 10th and 11th centuries: "We do not follow al-Shāfi'ī out of blind imitation but because he have found his legal arguments to be the most founded." Al-Nawawī, *al-Majmū'*, 1:36–37. See also 'Abd al-'Aẓīm al-Dīb, "*Muqaddimāt*," in *Nihāyat al-Maṭlab*, by Abū al-Ma'ālī al-Juwaynī, ed. 'Abd al-'Aẓīm al-Dīb (Jeddah: Dār al-Minhāj, 2007), 1:151.
84. Saadia Yacoob, "Islamic Law and Gender," in the *Oxford Handbook of Islamic Law* (Oxford: Oxford University Press, 2018), 83; Fatema Mernissi, *Le Harem Politique: Le prophète et les femmes* (Paris: A. Michel, 1987). Leila Ahmed, *A Border Passage* (New York: Farrar, Straus and Giroux, 1999), 128.
85. For some reformers, then, it is best to bypass the juristic tradition altogether in the quest for social justice. On uses of the Qur'an to rethink the Islamic tradition, see Amina Wadud, *Qur'an and Woman: Rereading the Sacred Text from a Woman's Perspective* (New York: Oxford University Press, 1999); Asma Barlas, *Believing Women in Islam* (Austin: University of Texas Press, 2002); See also Shadaab Rahemtullah, *Qur'an of the Oppressed* (Oxford: Oxford University Press, 2017), 101, 170.
86. Ayesha Chaudhry, *Domestic Violence and the Islamic Tradition: Ethics, Law, and the Muslim Discourse on Gender* (Oxford: Oxford University Press, 2013), 12.
87. Chaudhry speaks of an "egalitarian-authoritative dilemma"; Chaudhry, *Domestic*, 10.
88. Some feminist scholars have taken inspiration from the distinction between *sharī'a* as an ideal and *fiqh* as a fallible human enterprise; see Asifa Quraishi-Landes, "What Is Sharia and Is It Creepy." *The Islamic Monthly*, Fall/Winter 2012, http://onlinedigediti

ons.com/article/What+is+Sharia+and+is+it+Creepy%3F/1006292/104350/article.html; Azizah al-Hibri. "An Introduction to Muslim Women's Rights," in *Windows of Faith: Muslim Women Scholar-Activists in North America*, ed. Gisela Webb (Syracuse, NY: Syracuse University Press, 2000), 51–71. But al-Juwaynī and al-Shīrāzī did not only presuppose that *fiqh* is the product of fallible minds, they also presupposed that *fiqh* should be a discipline open to *critical* scrutiny.

89. Kecia Ali writes: "the scholars are worth studying because of their methodological sophistication, acceptance of divergent perspectives, and their diligence in the pursuit of understanding of the divine will"; Kecia Ali, *Sexual Ethics in Islam: Feminist Reflections on Qur'an, Hadith, and Jurisprudence* (Oxford: Oneworld, 2006), xx; Hina Azam, *Sexual Violation in Islamic Law: Substance, Evidence, and Procedure* (New York: Cambridge University Press, 2015); Asifa Quraishi-Landes, "A Meditation on *Mahr*, Modernity, and Muslim Marriage Contract Law," in *Feminism, Law, and Religion*, ed. Marie A. Failinger, Elizabeth R Schiltz, and Susan J. Stabile (New York: Ashgate Press, 2013), 327–341.
90. Al-Shīrāzī, *Sharḥ*, 2: 726: al-Shīrāzī writes that most Shāfiʿīs affirmed that *ijmāʿ* could only be established by the first generation that encountered a given legal question, with al-Qaffāl al-Shāshī and Ibn Khayrān dissenting from this view. See also al-Juwaynī, *al-Burhān*, 1:714–715, who had a slightly different view than al-Shīrāzī on the *ijmāʿ* of subsequent generations.
91. Susanna Lee, "American Animus: Dissent and Disapproval in *Bowers v. Hardwick*, *Romer v. Evans*, and *Lawrence v. Texas*," in *Dissenting Voices in American Society: The Role of Judges, Lawyers, and Citizens*, ed. Austin Sarat (Cambridge: Cambridge University Press, 2012), 57. Another parallel between to think about dissent in the *munāẓara*.
92. Collins and Skover call judicial dissent a form of institutional opposition to existing norms; see Ronald K. L. Collins and David M. Skover. *On Dissent: Its Meaning in America* (Cambridge: Cambridge University Press, 2013), 1. By engaging in disputations, jurists made opposition to their standard doctrine a central aspect of their legal system.

## Chapter 6

1. E.g., see Fachrizal Halim, *Legal Authority in Premodern Islam: Yaḥyā b. Sharaf al-Nawawī in the Shāfiʿī School of Law* (New York: Routledge, 2015), 80, who provides an excellent study of al-Nawawī, which nonetheless presupposes that indeterminacy was a problem to be fixed; Wael Hallaq, *The Origins*, 156; Fadel, "The Social Logic."
2. See Calder, "Al-Nawawī's Typology," 146.
3. The esteem that al-Shīrāzī held for al-Juwaynī is captured in his statement to his students that they should "Benefit from this Imām because he is the joy of our times (*nuzhat hādhā al-zamān*)." Al-Subkī, *Ṭabaqāt*, 5:172.

4. Ibn al-Athīr, *al-Kāmil*, 8:428; al-Subkī, *Ṭabaqāt*, 4:220–222.
5. On Khurasan's rise as an intellectual hub of Islamic scholarship, see Frederick S. Star, *Lost Enlightenment: Central Asia's Golden Age from the Arab Conquest to Tamerlane* (Princeton, NJ: Princeton University Press, 2013), 194–224.
6. Thus al-Juwaynī often refers to his father throughout his legal texts by the shorthand "*shaykhī* (my *shaykh*)." E.g., *Nihāyat al-Maṭlab*, 2:72.
7. As al-Dīb notes, a scholar's ascription to a locale was a function of where he studied and settled rather than his lands of origin; al-Dīb, "*Muqaddimāt*," 132.
8. Ibn al-Mulaqqin, *al-'Aqd al-Mudhhab fī Ṭabaqāt Ḥamalat al-Madhab*, ed. Ayman Naṣr al-Dīn al-Azharī (Dār al-Kutub, 1997), 215.
9. Al-Subkī, *Ṭabaqāt*, 5:53–62; Ibn Qāḍi Shuhba, *Ṭabaqāt*, 1:182; al-Nawawī, *Tahdhīb al-Asmā' wa'l-Lughāt*, 4 vols. (Cairo: al-Ṭibā'a al-Munīriyya, 1965), 2:210; 3:46.
10. Al-Shīrāzī, *Ṭabaqāt*, 115; Ibn al-Ṣalāḥ, *Ṭabaqāt*, 1:94; Ibn Qāḍī Shuhba, *Ṭabaqāt*, 1:145.
11. Al-Shīrāzī, *Ṭabaqāt*, 112.
12. Al-Nawawī, *Tahdhīb*, 2:193.
13. Al-Subkī, *Ṭabaqāt*, 5:53; al-Dīb, "*Muqaddimāt*," 132.
14. Al-Subkī, *Ṭabaqāt*, 4:344–348 (for al-Sinjī), 5:73–93 (for al-Juwaynī), 4:356 (for al-Marwarrūdhī).
15. On Abū Ḥāmid al-Isfarāyinī's leadership, see al-Subkī, *Ṭabaqāt*, 4:61; al-Nawawī, *Tahdhīb*, 2:208; Ibn al-Ṣalāḥ, *Ṭabaqāt*, 3:373–378; Ibn Khallikān, *Wafāyāt*, 1:72–74; Ibn al-Mullaqin, *al-'Aqd*, 65; Ibn Qāḍī Shuhba, *Ṭabaqāt*, 1:172. Neither Ibn Khallikān nor Ibn al-Mullaqin single out al-Isfarāyinī as being the head of the Iraqi *ṭarīqa*, which indicates that not all historians saw him as the leader of distinct branch of Shāfi'ism.
16. For the Iraqi position, see al-Māwardī, *al-Ḥāwī*, 2:68–72 and 80–84; al-Rūyānī, *Baḥr*, 1:464–470; Abū al-Ṭayyib al-Ṭabarī, *al-Ta'līqa al-Kubrā, min Bāb mā Yufsid al-Mā' ḥattā Nihāyat Bāb Istiqbāl al-Qibla*, ed. 'Ubayd b. Sālim al-'Amarī (PhD diss., Medina University, 1998–1999), 762–768; al-Shīrāzī, *al-Muhadhdhab*, 1:229–230. For the Khurasanian position, see al-Juwaynī, *Nihāyat*, 2:97–99. Al-Qāḍī Ḥusayn al-Marwarrūdhī, *al-Ta'līqa*, ed. 'Alī Mu'awwaḍ and 'Ādil 'Abd al-Mawjūd (Mecca: Maktabat Nizār Muṣṭafā al-Bāz, n.d.), 1:691–692.
17. Al-Shāfi'ī had reasoned that just as a worshipper unable to see the Meccan temple needed to interpret the signs of nature such as the sun, the stars, and the direction of the wind to determine the correct prayer direction, so too did the jurist need to interpret scriptural signs to determine the right religious ruling for any legal case. Al-Shāfi'ī, *al-Risāla*, ed. Aḥmad al-Shākir (Cairo: Muṣṭafā 'Isā al-Bābī al-Ḥalabī wa-Awlāduhu, 1938), 34; see Lowry, *Early*, 32. See also El Shamsy, "Rethinking '*Taqlīd*,'" 14.
18. Al-Māwardī, *al-Ḥāwī*, 2:71; al-Ṭabarī, *al-Ta'līqa al-Kubrā, min Bāb mā Yufsid*, 844. Beyond seeing the *Ka'ba*, other instances of certainty include the report of a trustworthy individual and the finding of a prayer niche; see al-Shīrāzī, *al-Muhadhdhab*, 1:228.
19. Al-Shāfi'ī, *Kitāb al-Umm*, 2:212. Al-Shāfi'ī states that a person who prays in the wrong direction should not repeat his prayer unless he is sure that he is mistaken.

20. Al-Juwaynī, *Nihāyat*, 2:99; al-Shīrāzī, *al-Muhadhdhab*, 1:288. Al-Shīrāzī writes: "If a condition among the conditions of purity are not met, the prayer is invalidated (*idhā qaṭa'a sharṭ min shuruṭihā ka'l-ṭahāra baṭalat ṣalātuhu*)."
21. Al-Juwaynī, *Niḥāyat*, 1:98.
22. Al-Subkī, *Ṭabaqāt*, 5:209.
23. On the dispensation from facing the *qibla*, see al-Juwaynī, *Nihāyat*, 2:71 and al-Shīrāzī, *al-Muhadhdhab*, 1:351.
24. Shāfi'īs predicated the dispensation in travel on difficulty (*mashaqqa*); see al-Shīrāzī, *al-Muhadhdhab*, 1:232; al-Mawardi, *al-Ḥāwī*, 2:73; al-Ṭabarī, *al-Ta'līqa al-Kubrā, min Bāb mā Yufsid*, 748.
25. Al-Subkī, *Ṭabaqāt*, 5:210.
26. Al-Shīrāzī affirms the validity of two types of *qiyās*. First, *qiyās al-'illa* where a jurist has evidence for the legal cause (*'illa*) pertaining to a case (*ḥāditha*). Second, *qiyās al-dalāla* where a jurist does not know the *'illa* but has good reason to believe that two cases share the same *'illa*. One of the ways of knowing that the cases share the same *'illa* is that they are subject to the same rules, i.e., they are *naẓīr*; see al-Shīrāzī, *Sharḥ*, 2:799–814; see also Shahid Rahman et al., *Inference by Parallel Reasoning* (Cham: Springer, 2020), 8. Al-Juwaynī explains how the *qiyās al-shabah* resembles and contrasts the *qiyās al-dalāla*; see al-Juwaynī, *al-Burhān*, 2:852.
27. On the traveller's prayer, see al-Juwaynī, *Nihāyat*, 2:423; al-Shīrāzī, *al-Muhadhdhab*, 1:342; al-Marwarrūdhī, *al-Ta'līqa*, 1:1074; al-Māwardī, *al-Ḥāwī*, 2:358.
28. Al-Subkī, *Ṭabaqāt*, 5:210.
29. For more on concept of *naẓīr*, see al-Shīrāzī, *Kitāb al-Ma'ūna*, 255; al-Shīrāzī, *Sharḥ*, 2:810.
30. Al-Subkī, *Ṭabaqāt*, 5:211.
31. Ibid., 5:213; on the dispensation from facing the *qibla* in the battlefield, see al-Ṭabarī, *al-Ta'līqa al-Kubrā: min Bāb mā Yufsid*, 748; al-Māwardī, *al-Ḥāwī*, 2:72; al-Shīrazī, *al-Muhadhdab*, 1:231; al-Maḥāmilī, *al-Lubāb*, 124; al-Juwaynī, *Nihāyat*, 2:597.
32. Al-Shīrāzī, *al-Muhadhdhab*, 1:232; al-Mawardi, *al-Ḥāwī*, 2:73; al-Ṭabarī, *al-Ta'līqa al-Kubrā, min Bāb mā Yufsid*, 748.
33. Al-Subkī, *Ṭabaqāt*, 5:213.
34. Ibid., 5:212.
35. Ibid. Al-Shīrāzī, *al-Muhadhdhab*, 1:343. Al-Juwaynī exclaimed: "If joining prayers was truly for the reason you suggest, then delaying the afternoon (*al-'aṣr*) prayer until its regular time would be an inadmissible violation of correct ritual law." Al-Shīrāzī finished off by positing a fine distinction in ritual law between the ideal and the permissible. A traveller should ideally combine and perform his prayers at the earliest possible time; such devotional diligence would increase his nearness to God. However, should he choose to delay his second prayer, as in al-Juwaynī's afternoon (*al-'aṣr*) prayer example, he would nonetheless be performing it within its correct ritually prescribed time. An analogy to the *'asr* prayer of the resident is useful here: as al-Ghazālī explains, Shāfi'īs saw the obligation of the *'asr* prayer to begin at its earliest time, but characterized it as a "capacious obligation (*wujūb*[an] *muwassa'*[an])" to explain that it could be prayed within a certain time-frame.

I take al-Shīrāzī to be saying something similar in his disputation; al-Ghazālī, *al-Wasīṭ*, 2:21.

36. Jackson, *Islamic Law*, 79.
37. Fadel, "The Social Logic," 197. Ibrahim, "Rethinking," 808.
38. Hallaq, *A History*, 120.
39. Al-Shīrāzī, *Sharḥ*, 1:177–178; Halim, *Legal Authority*, 88.
40. Al-Muzanī, *Mukhtaṣar*, 23–25. See also al-Māwardī, *al-Ḥāwī*, 2:81–83, where the author presents other arguments supporting al-Muzanī's position.
41. Al-Shāfiʿī, *Kitāb al-Umm*, 3:255.
42. On the necessity of the pilgrim's stay in ʿArafa, see al-Shāfiʿī, *Kitāb al-Umm*, 3:548.
43. Al-Ṭabarī explains that mistaking the day of ʿArafa is different from making a mistake on the prayer direction in two regards. First, there is no guarantee that one would actually be correct the next year if one tried to make up their *ḥajj*. Second, returning for *ḥajj* would be a great burden for many. Al-Ṭabarī, *al-Taʿlīqa al-Kubrā, min bāb mā yufsid*, 768.
44. Al-ʿImrānī, *al-Bayān*, 2:143–144; al-Ghazālī, *al-Wasīṭ*, 2:77–78; al-Ruyānī, *Baḥr*, 4:466–470; al-Baghawī, *al-Tahdhīb*, 2:70–71; al-Mutawallī, *Tatimmat al-Ibāna ʿan Furūʿ al-Diyāna, Awwal Bāb al-Ṣalāt ilā Nihāyat al-Bāb al-Ḥadī ʿAshar: Fīmā Yaqtaḍī Karāhiyat al-Ṣalāt*, ed. Nisrīn bt. Hilāl Ḥamādī (PhD diss., Umm al-Qurā University, Mecca, 2007), 286–287; Ibn al-Qāṣṣ, *al-Talkhīṣ*, eds. ʿĀdil ʿAbd al-Mawjūd and ʿAlī Muʿawwaḍ (Mecca: Maktabat Nizār Muṣṭafā al-Bāz, n.d.), 166.
45. Al-Nawawī, *al-Majmūʿ*, 1:53.
46. Ibid. Al-Nawawī writes: "As for the [term] 'paths,' it refers to the disagreement of our colleagues on what is said about the [history] of the school (*Wa-ammā al-ṭuruq, fa-hiya ikhtilāf al-aṣḥāb fī ḥikāyat al-madhhab*)." For an example of the use of "*ṭuruq*" in discussions on the prayer direction, see al-Māwardī, *al-Ḥāwī*, 1:107.
47. For example, the building of new mosques throughout the Muslim empire led later Shāfiʿīs to address whether or not a traveller arriving in a new town was obligated to perform his own *ijtihād*, or whether he should defer to the prayer niche in the towns' mosques; al-Māwardī, *al-Ḥāwī*, 2:71.
48. Al-Nawawī, *al-Majmūʿ*, 1:53.
49. Al-Māwardī, *al-Ḥāwī*, 2:80–81.
50. El Shamsy characterizes the early Shāfiʿī school of the 9th century as a paradigm, in the sense employed by Thomas Kuhn; El Shamsy, *The Canonization*, 173. Like a paradigm in the natural sciences, the Shāfiʿīs were labouring under certain fairly entrenched assumptions, but much of their opinions manifested the discordance we find in vibrant scientific circles.
51. Al-Shīrāzī, *Sharḥ*, 2:1075. The Shāfiʿī defense of their master's "two sayings (*qawlayn*)" was the subject of a treatise; see Ibn al-Qāṣṣ, *Nuṣrat al-Qawlayn li'l-Imām al-Shāfiʿī*, ed. Māzin Saʿd al-Zabībī (Damascus: Dār al-Bayrūtī, 2009), 54–55: Ibn al-Qāṣṣ informs his reader that the partisans of Abū Ḥanīfa (al-Kūfiyyūn) considered that al-Shāfiʿī was "confused" for having more than one opinion; see also al-Shīrāzī, *al-Tabṣira*, 518, where al-Shīrāzī reports legal cases where al-Shāfiʿī acknowledged the validity of possible opinions other than the ones he explicitly championed.

52. Al-Shīrāzī, *Sharḥ*, 2:1077–1078, where he defends al-Shāfiʿī's ambivalence.
53. The claim that al-Shāfiʿī was narrowing down possible opinions is repeated in al-Samʿānī, *Qawāṭiʿ*, 2:330.
54. Al-Shīrāzī, 2:1079–1080. For the Ḥanbalī critique of espousing two positions at one time, see Abū Yaʿlā, *al-ʿUdda*, 2:451–458.
55. Al-Shīrāzī, *Sharḥ*, 2:1079.
56. Ibid., 2:1012–1014.
57. On prayer direction in the desert, see al-Māwardī, *al-Ḥāwī*, 2:78; al-Rūyānī, *al-Baḥr*, 1:458; al-Ṭabarī, *al-Taʿlīqa al-Kubrā, min Bāb mā Yufsid*, 756; al-Shīrāzī, *al-Muhadhdhab* 1:229; al-Juwaynī, *Nihāyat*, 2:108.
58. Al-Muzanī, *Mukhtaṣar*, 24.
59. Al-Shīrāzī, *al-Muhadhdhab*, 1:229.
60. Al-Ṭabarī, *al-Taʿlīqa al-Kubrā, min Bāb mā Yufsid*, 756.
61. Al-Māwardī thus distinguishes between a man who knows how to perform *ijtihād* and a man who can be taught *ijtihād*, both of whom are responsible for performing their own *ijtihād*; al-Māwardī, *al-Ḥāwī*, 2:78.
62. Al-Ṭabarī writes "As for the one who does not know the evidence used in *ijtihād* (*ṭuruq al-ijtihād*) but can learn them if taught, it is necessary for him to learn them. And if he does not learn them, and prays, then his prayer is not valid. And this is equivalent to one who can learn the chapter '*al-fātiḥa*,' but does not learn it and nonetheless prays"; al-Ṭabarī, *al-Taʿlīqa al-Kubrā, min Bāb mā Yufsid*, 759.
63. Al-Māwardī, *al-Ḥāwī*, 2:78; al-Ṭabarī, *al-Taʿlīqa, min Bāb mā Yufsid*, 759.
64. Al-Juwaynī, *Nihāyat*, 2:98. Al-Juwaynī's formulation of the problem became important to a subsequent generation of jurists; see al-Ghazālī, *al-Wasīṭ*, 2:77–78; and al-Rūyānī, *Baḥr*, 4: 466–467.
65. Al-Juwaynī, *Nihāyat*, 2:99. From the *Burhān*, one would surmise that al-Juwaynī favoured the non-repetition of the prayer, since he states that the *ijtihād* for past deeds is valid even if one later finds a perspicuous text (*al-naṣṣ*); see al-Juwaynī, *al-Burhān*, 2:1329.
66. Al-Shīrāzī, *al-Muhadhdhab*, 1:229.
67. Al-Ṭabarī, *al-Taʿliqa al-Kubrā, min Bāb mā Yufsid*, 750; al-Shīrāzī, *al-Muhadhdhab*, 1:233; al-Juwayni, *Nihāyat*, 2:72.
68. The question of the mistaken *qibla* was not resolved in the 12th century. However, both before and after the disputation, Shāfiʿīs often supported repetition: see Al-ʿImrānī, *al-Bayān*, 2:143–144; al-Ghazālī, *al-Wasīṭ*, 2:77–78; al-Ruyānī, *Baḥr*, 4:466–470; al-Baghawī, *al-Tahdhīb*, 2:70–71; al-Mutawallī, *Tatimmat al-Ibāna ʿan Furūʿ al-Diyāna, Awwal Bāb al-Ṣalāt*, 286–287; Ibn al-Qāṣṣ, *al-Talkhīṣ*, 166; al-Rāfiʿī, *al-Muḥarrar*, 30. See also al-Nawawī, *Majmūʿ*, 1:647.
69. See, for instance, Ibn al-Mulaqqin, *al-ʿAqd*, 215. "*Fa-ʿlam anna aṣḥābanā tafarraqū, faʾl-ʿIrāqiyyūn ahl baghdād wa-mā wālāhā*."
70. On al-Sinjī's alleged consolidation of the *madhhab*, see al-Subkī, 4:344; al-Nawawī, *Tahdhīb*, 2:261; Ibn Qāḍī Shuhba, *Ṭabaqāt*, 1:207; Ibn al-Mulaqqin, *al-ʿAqd*, 82; neither al-Shīrāzī nor al-ʿAbbādī make mention of al-Sinjī as one who "combines between the methods of the Khurasanians and the Iraqis"; al-Shīrāzī, *Ṭabaqāt*,

132, presents al-Sinjī as merely one among many important Khurasanian scholars; Abū ʿĀṣim al-ʿAbbādī, *Ṭabaqāt al-Fuqahāʾ al-Shāfiʿiyya*, ed. Gösta Vitestam (Leiden: Brill, 1964), 65.

71. Al-Shīrāzī, *Ṭabaqāt*, 118.
72. Ibid., 117.
73. Al-ʿAbbādī calls al-Qaffāl "the shaykh of Khurasan *in his time*" [emphasis added], which contrasts later Shāfiʿī historians' designation of al-Qaffāl as the shaykh of the Khurasanians; al-ʿAbbādī, *Ṭabaqāt*, 105.
74. Al-Shīrāzī, *Ṭabaqāt*, 120.
75. Al-Subkī, *al-Ḥāwī*, 9:201.
76. Al-Māwardī, *Ṭabaqāt*, 4:222; 5:123.
77. Al-Ṭabarī trained with scholars in Persia and Khurasan before migrating to Baghdad; al-Shīrāzī, *Ṭabaqāt*, 116, 134; al-Subkī, *Ṭabaqāt*, 5:12–50.
78. Al-ʿAbbādī, *Ṭabaqāt*, 6–7. Al-ʿAbbādī's position concords with the comments of al-Sinjī and Abū Isḥāq al-Isfarāyinī that the jurists did not follow al-Shāfiʿī except after investigating his doctrines and founding them to be sound; see Al-Dīb, "*Muqaddimāt*," 151. See also Felicitas Opwis, "The Role of the Biographer in Constructing Identity and Doctrine: Al-ʿAbbādī and his *Kitāb Ṭabaqāt al-Fuqahāʾ al-Shāfiʿiyya*, *Journal of Arabic and Islamic Studies* 11 (2011): 12.
79. Ibn al-Ṣabbāgh used to debate with al-Shīrāzī and al-Juwaynī; Makdisi, *Rise*, 154.
80. Talal Asad, *The Idea of an Anthropology of Islam* (Washington, DC: Center for Contemporary Arab Studies at Georgetown University, 1986). MacIntyre, *After Virtue*, 222.
81. For different theories of what constitutes a *madhhab*, see Schacht, *Introduction*, 57; Merchert, *Formation*, xvii; Hallaq, *Origins*, 150–177. My own description of the *madhhab* is in line with El Shamsy's characterization of a *madhhab* "as encompassing a distinct group identity, a common literature, and a shared intellectual discourse." El Shamsy, *The Canonization*, 169.
82. E.g., al-Shīrāzī, *Ṭabaqāt*, 114, 120, 126.

## Chapter 7

1. The Arabic term that Ibn Khaldūn in this passage is "*jadal*." Ibn Khaldūn, *Dīwān al-Mubtadaʾ wa'l-Khabar fī Tārīkh al-ʿArab wa'l-Barbar wa-man ʿĀṣarahum min dhawī al-Sha'n al-Akbar*, ed. Khalīl Shaḥāda, 8 vols. (Beirut: Dār al-Fikr, 1988), 1:579.
2. Allen James Fromherz, *Ibn Khaldun: Life and Times* (Edinburgh: Edinburgh University Press, 2011), 84, 98.
3. Ibn Khaldūn taught the *Muqaddima* in Egyptian colleges, which suggests that he considered his assessment of the decline in disputation to be true of even the intellectual centres of Muslims; ibid.
4. On the political patronage of scholars in Mamluk cities, see Nimrod Luz, *The Mamluk City in the Middle East: History, Culture, and the Urban Landscape* (Cambridge: Cambridge University Press, 2014), 156–171.

5. Shams al-Dīn al-Sakhāwī, *al-Manhal al-ʿAdhb al-Rawī fī Tarjamat Quṭb al-Awliyāʾ al-Nawawī*, ed. Aḥmad Farīd al-Mazīdī (Beirut" Dār al-Kutub al-ʿIlmiyya, 2005), 19.
6. For instance, understandings of "secular" time have figured in scholarship on the emergence of nationalism; Benedict Anderson, *Imagined Communities*, revised ed. (London: Verso, 2006), 24; Asad, *Formations*, 194.
7. Dipesh Chakrabarty, *Provincializing Europe: Postcolonial Thought and Historical Difference* (Princeton, NJ: Princeton University Press, 2000), 7; Etienne Balibar, "Marxism and the Idea of Revolution: The Messianic Moment in Marx," in *Historical Telelogies in the Modern World*, ed. Henning Trüper et al. (London: Bloomsbury, 2015), 235–250. For the impact of progressive time on the European categorization of religions, see Tomoko Masuzawa, *The Invention of World Religions: Or, How European Universalism Was Preserved in the Language of Pluralism* (Chicago: University of Chicago Press, 2005), 12.
8. Timothy Mitchell, "The Stage of Modernity," in *Questions of Modernity*, ed. T. Mitchell (Minneapolis: University of Minnesota Press, 2000), 16–17.
9. Shahzad Bashir, "The Living Dead of Tabriz: Explorations in Chronotopic Imagination," *History of Religions* 59 no. 3 (2020): 171.
10. Al-Shīrāzī, *Ṭabaqāt*, 124.
11. E.g., the full translation of the *Muhadhdhab* is "The Refinement of the *fiqh* of the Imām al-Shāfiʿī," despite being replete with positions al-Shāfiʿī never countenanced.
12. As Hallaq points out, some Shāfiʿīs even attributed their own legal reasoning to al-Shāfiʿī because they saw themselves as extending his thought; Hallaq, *A History*, 162.
13. Al-Shīrāzī, *Ṭabaqāt*, 108.
14. Abū al-Maʿālī al-Juwaynī, *al-Ghiyāthī*, ed. ʿAbd al-ʿAẓīm al-Dīb, 2nd ed. (n.p. and n.d.), 413–415, 418.
15. Al-Rāzī, *Manāqib*, 411.
16. Al-Shīrāzī, *Sharḥ*, 2:1033; al-Baghdādī, *Kitāb al-Faqīh*, 378; al-Samʿānī, *Qawāṭiʿ*, 2:303.
17. Shāfiʿīs were not the only legal school who recognized continued intellectual excellence across generations of jurists. For instance, al-Ṣaymarī provides a long list of illustrious Ḥanafī scholars who taught in the Darb ʿAbda Mosque before him, and prays that his successors should be as blessed for their intellectual labours as his predecessors, *Akhbār*, 172.
18. Al-Baghdādī, *Kitāb al-Faqīh*, 375; al-Shīrāzī, *Sharḥ*, 2:1035.
19. See also al-Samʿānī, *Qawāṭiʿ*, 2:302, 355, who like al-Shīrāzī gives no indication that Shāfiʿīs of his or any preceding era considered that jurists capacities to perform *ijtihād* were waning. For an earlier Shāfiʿī text that likewise asserts the Shāfiʿī obligation of *ijtihād* and takes the jurists' ability to undertake this *ijtihād* for granted, see Ibn al-Qāṣṣ, *Adab al-Qāḍī*, ed. Ḥusayn al-Jabūrī (Taif: Maktabat al-Ṣadīq, 1989), 98–99.
20. Al-Shīrāzī's preference for Ibn Surayj over al-Muzanī is all the more significant when one considers the high regard with which he saw al-Muzanī, writing "[al-Muzanī] was an ascetic, a scholar, a *mujtahid*, a debater, who was skillful at positing evidence and immersed himself in finding the subtle reasons for legal cases (*al-maʿānī al-daqīqa*)." Al-Shīrāzī, *Ṭabaqāt*, 97–98, 108.

21. Ibn ʿAqīl, *Kitāb al-Funūn*, ed. George Makdisi (Damhur: Maktabat Līna, 1991), 645.
22. Past historians have also noted the emergence of a pessimistic attitude around juristic capabilities though, to my knowledge, there has yet to be a sustained historicization of this attitude, it's departure from the past, or it's impact on legal thought; see Schacht, *Introduction*, 70–71; Hallaq, "Was the Gate?," 18.
23. Al-Nawawī explicitly references Ibn al-Ṣalāḥ in outlining his typology. See Ibn al-Ṣalāḥ, *Ādāb al-Fatwā wa'l-Muftī wa'l-Mustaftī*, ed. Muwaffaq ʿAbd al-Qādir (Mecca: ʿĀlam al-Kutub, 1986), 95–101.
24. Al-Nawawī never studied directly under Ibn al-Ṣalāḥ's guidance, but his three foremost teachers had been Ibn al-Ṣalāḥ's students; see Halim, *Legal Authority*, 19.
25. Al-Shīrāzī, *Sharḥ*, 2:1015; al-Baghdādī, *Kitāb al-Faqīh*, 292; al-Samʿānī, *Qawāṭiʿ*, 2:431.
26. Al-Shīrāzī's *Ṭabaqāt* does not privilege one group of scholars over another within the Shāfiʿī school; for instance, see page *Ṭabaqāt*, 97, where he simply describes the passing on of *fiqh* from one generation to another.
27. Al-Juwaynī, *Kitāb al-Fatwā*, 2:1330–1333; al-Baghdādī, *Kitāb al-Faqīh*, 378; al-Samʿānī, *Qawāṭiʿ*, 2:303; and al-Ghazālī, *al-Mustaṣfā*, 2:865.
28. Hallaq, "Was the Gate," 7.
29. Al-Nawawī writes: "Abū ʿAmr (Ibn al-Ṣalāḥ) said that *mujtahids* are of two types: independent and everybody else." Al-Nawawī goes on to say that "There have not been independent and complete *mujtahid* for a very long time"; *al-Majmūʿ*, 1:37.
30. Ibid., 1:38.
31. Al-Nawawī explains that Ibn al-Ṣalāḥ denied the claims of earlier Shāfiʿīs to be full and independent *mujtahids*; ibid.
32. Shāfiʿīs sometimes considered that later scholars could be more capable than their predecessors. This comes out most clearly in Fakhr al-Dīn al-Rāzī's argument for the primacy of al-Shāfiʿī over Mālik and Abū Ḥanīfa. Al-Rāzī explained that al-Shāfiʿī owed his intellectual primacy to having lived *later* than other noteworthy jurists. Al-Rāzī, *Manāqib*, 411.
33. Al-Nawawī says that this early 5th/11th century generation's dependence on earlier jurists was oftentimes because of their weak knowledge of Arabic or *ḥadīth*. Both claims merit pause. The claim that earlier generations were weak in *ḥadīth* is curious because al-Shīrāzī and other 11th-century Shāfiʿīs did not grant the study of *ḥadīth* great importance in legal derivation. The claim about knowledge of Arabic is also curious considering jurists' training in Arabic: perhaps al-Nawawī's evaluation is the product of an Arabo-centrism that disparaged Shāfiʿīs of Persian origin like Abū Ḥāmid al-Isfarāyinī. Al-Nawawī, *al-Majmūʿ*, 1:38.
34. Al-Nawawī notes that the jurists were weaker in their ability to extract legal rules than earlier generations: "*Wa-lam yalḥaq man qablahum fī al-takhrīj*"; ibid.
35. Hallaq, *Authority*, 9–14; Calder, "Al-Nawawī's Typology," 162.
36. Schacht, *Introduction*, 71; Ostroróg, *The Angora Reforms*, 27–28.
37. Calder, "Al-Nawawī's Typology," 162.
38. Hallaq, *Authority*, 88.

39. Elsewhere, Hallaq notes that jurists were increasingly pessimistic about the possibility of successful *ijtihād*, but he seems to have missed how this pessimism shaped al-Nawawī's retelling of the past; Hallaq, "Was the Gate," 18.
40. Al-Suyūṭī (d. 911/1505 CE) picked up on the semantic shift in the understanding of *taqlīd* between the classical period and his own. In his *Radd*, he makes a distinction between *al-taqlīd* (following an opinion without evidence) and *al- ittibā*ʿ (following a position after learning the evidence for it), stating that the illustrious Shāfiʿīs of the past engaged in the latter but not the former; al-Suyūṭī, *al-Radd*, 120; on al-Suyūṭī's distinction between an "independent *mujtahid*" and an "unrestricted *mujtahid*," see Rebecca Hernandez, *The Legal Thought of Jalāl al-Dīn al-Suyūṭī* (Oxford: Oxford University Press, 2017).
41. Al-Juwaynī, *al-Talkhīṣ*, 3:355; al-Juwaynī, *al-Kāfiya*, 24.
42. At the time of al-Nawawī, reports circulated that al-Qaffāl al-Marwazī had also asserted that there were no longer any *mujtahids*; see Ibn al-Rifʿa, *Kifāyat al-Nabīh: Sharḥ al-Tanbīh fī Fiqh al-Imām al*-Shāfiʿī, ed. Majdī Bāsallūm, 20 vols. Beirut: Dār al-Kutub al-ʿIlmiyya, 2009, 18:71. See also al-ʿImrānī, *al-Bayān*, 13:19.
43. Intisar Rabb, "Islamic Legal Minimalism: Legal Maxims and Lawmaking When Jurists Disappear," in *Law and Tradition in Classical Thought: Studies in Honor of Professor Hossein Modaressi*, ed. Michael Cook et al. (New York: Palgrave, 2013), 145–166; Sohaira Siddiqui, *Law and Politics under the ʿAbbasids: An Intellectual Portrait of al-Juwaynī* (Cambridge: Cambridge University Press, 2019), 171–172.
44. Perhaps it was also prompted by the Muʿtazilī claim that the earth could never be devoid of *mujtahids*, see Ahmad Atif Ahmad, *The Fatigue of the Sharīʿa* (New York: Palgrave Macmillan, 2012), 57.
45. Both Hallaq and Ahmed Atif Ahmed have examined the historical debate about the possibility of the extinction of *mujtahids*. Wael Hallaq, "On the Origins of the Controversy about the Existence of Mujtahids and the Gate of Ijtihad," *Studia Islamica* 63 (1986), 129–141; Atif Ahmad, *The Fatigue of the Sharīʿa* (New York: Palgrave Macmillan, 2012). While Hallaq is correct to claim that this debate was a theoretical one rooted in theological debates, he obfuscates al-Juwaynī's empirical statement that *mujtahids* had all but disappeared.
46. Al-Juwaynī, *al-Ghiyāthī*, 417.
47. Ibid.
48. Al-Ghazālī, *Iḥyā'*, 1:62.
49. Al-Ghazālī, *al-Mustaṣfā*, 2:872.
50. Al-Subkī, *Ṭabaqāt*, 6:205.
51. E.g., *apud* in ibid., 3:395; 7:190, 240, 307, 309.
52. Ibid., 6:72, 6:390, 7:101.
53. Al-Rāfiʿī, *al-ʿAzīz*, 12:418.
54. Ibid., 12:420–421; Al-Āmidī, *al-Iḥkām*, 4:287. Al-Āmidī adds, at 4:278, that if one is a scholar-in-training (*mutaʿallim*) but doesn't reach the level of *ijtihād*, he must engaged in *taqlīd*. See also Bernard Weiss, *The Search for God's Law: Islamic Jurisprudence in the Writings of Sayf al-Dīn al-Āmidī*, revised ed. (Salt Lake City: University of Utah Press, 2010), 715.

55. Ibn al-Rif'a, *Kifāya*, 18:71; see also Badr al-Dīn Ibn Qāḍī Shuhba, *Bidāyat al-Muḥtāj fī Sharḥ al-Minhāj*, ed. Anwar al-Dāghistānī, 4 vols. (Jeddah: Dār al-Minhāj, 2011), 4:445. Ibn Qāḍī Shuhba maintains that the one who loses his capacity for *ijtihād* should be removed from the position of judgment since it is a condition of appointment. His statement shows the continued importance of *ijtihād* in judgeships for some post-classical Shāfi'īs.
56. For the Iraqi position, see al-Qaffāl al-Shāshī, *Ḥilyat al-'Ulamā'*, ed. Sa'īd 'Abd al-Fattāḥ, 3 vols. 2nd ed. Mecca: Nizār Muṣṭafā al-Bāz, 1998), 3:1159; al-Maḥāmilī, *al-Lubāb*, 407. In the *Wasīṭ* (7:290), al-Ghazālī broke ranks with the Iraqi tradition that prohibited that anyone should serve as a judge except for a *mujtahid*. He defined the *mujtahid* as "the one capable of apprehending religious laws (*darak aḥkām al-shar'*) independently (*istiqlāl*[an]) without following another without evidence (*taqlīd ghayrihi*)." After affirming the obligation that a judge be a *mujtahid*, al-Ghazālī then stated that if no independent *mujtahid* can be found, then a *mujtahid* labouring within the interpretative framework of a *madhhab* (*mujtahid fī al-madhhab*) can be appointed. Al-'Imrānī would later characterize al-Ghazālī's position as that of "the Khurasanians"; al-'Imrānī, *al-Bayān*, 13:19. This should not be understood as encompassing all Khurasanians: In the early 11th century, the Khurasanian jurist al-Baghawī still maintained the prohibition of *taqlīd* for the judge; al-Baghawī, *al-Tahdhīb*, 8:168.
57. Ṣāliḥ b. Sirāj al-Dīn al-Bulqīnī, *Tatimmat al-Tadrīb*, in *al-Tadrīb fī al-Fiqh al-Shāfi'ī*, by Sirāj al-Dīn al-Bulqīnī, ed. Abū Ya'qūb b. Kamāl al-Miṣrī, 4 vols. (Riyadh: Dār al-Qiblatayn, 2012), 4:319–320; Jamāl al-Dīn al-Isnawī, *al-Muhimmāt fī Sharḥ al-Rawḍā wa'l-Rāfi'ī*, ed. Abū al-Faḍl Aḥmad b. 'Alī, 10 vols. (Beirut: Dār Ibn Ḥazm, 2009), 9:215. Ibn al-Mulaqqin, *'Ujālat al-Muḥtāj ilā Tawjīh al-Minhāj*, ed. 'Izz al-Dīn al-Badrānī (Jordan: Dār al-Kitāb, 2001), 1799.
58. Al-Māwardī, *al-Ḥāwī*, 16:24
59. The position that lay Muslims needed to follow the *fatwā*s of a *mujtahid* was maintained by al-Ghazālī's student, Ibn Barhān; see Ibn Barhān, *al-Wuṣūl ilā al-Uṣūl*, ed. 'Abd al-Ḥamīd Abū Zunayd, 2 vols. (Riyadh: Maktabat al-Ma'ārif, 1984), 2:358–362.
60. Al-Āmidī, *al-Iḥkām*, 4:287. Al-Āmidī contends that the transmission of legal doctrine is only permissible for one who has reached the status of *mujtahid fī al-madhhab*. Al-Āmidī adds that if the jurist is a scholar-in-training (*muta'allim*) but does not reach the level of *ijtihād*, he must perform *taqlīd*, 4:278. See also Badr al-Dīn al-Zarkashī, *al-Baḥr al-Muḥīṭ fī Uṣūl al-Fiqh*, ed. 'Abd al-Sattār Abū Ghudda, 6 vols., 2nd ed. (Kuwait: Wizārat al-Awqāf wa'l-Shu'ūn Islāmiyya, 1992), 6:305; Al-Subkī, *al-Ibhāj fī Sharḥ al-Minhāj*, 3 vols. (Beirut: Dār al-Kutub al-'Ilmiyya, 1995), 3:268–270.
61. Sirāj al-Dīn al-Urmawī himself disagreed with this position; Sirāj al-Dīn al-Urmawī, *al-Taḥṣīl min al-Maḥṣūl*, ed. 'Abd al-Ḥamīd Abū Zunayd, 2. vols. (Mu'assasat al-Risāla, 1998), 2:301. See al-Rāzī, *al-Maḥṣūl*, 2:457.
62. Al-Bayḍāwī, *Minhāj al-Wuṣūl ilā 'Ilm al-Uṣūl*, ed. Sha'bān Ismā'īl (Beirut: Dār Ibn Ḥazm, 2008), 255. Al-Bayḍāwī allows lay-Muslims to engage in the *taqlīd* of a dead

*mujtahid* in his times because he claims there is a need. See also al-Isnawī, *Nihāyat al-Sūl*, ed. ʿAbd al-Qādir ʿAlī (Beirut: Dār al-Kutub al-ʿIlmiyya), 402–403.

63. On the changes in the requirement of *ijtihād* for the giving of *fatwās*, see Wael Hallaq "Ifta' and Ijtihad in Sunni Legal Theory," in *Islamic Legal Interpretation: Muftis and Their Fatwas*, ed. M.K. Masud et al. (Cambridge, MA: Harvard University Press, 1996), 42.
64. Hallaq, *Origins*, 155–167.
65. The Shāfiʿīs also defended the authority of their school by noting the *ḥadīth* that "Imāms are from Quraysh." Since al-Shāfiʿī was a Qurayshite, they found textual evidence for his superiority over the leaders of other legal schools. See al-Samʿānī, *Qawāṭiʿ*, 2:378; al-Rāzī, *Manāqib*, 375. Al-ʿAbbādī (*Ṭabaqāt*, 6) notes that this textual evidence is only relevant for lay Muslims who cannot understand legal argumentation.
66. Ibn ʿAqīl, *Kitāb al-Funūn*, 602; see also Hallaq, "Was the Gate," 18.
67. Ibn ʿAqīl washed al-Shīrāzī's body; al-Subkī, *Ṭabaqāt*, 4:229.
68. Ibn ʿAqīl, *Kitāb al-Funūn*, 645.
69. Al-Māwardī, *al-Ḥāwī*, 16:24; See also al-Shīrāzī, *al-Muhadhdhab*, 5:474; al-Ṭabarī, *al-Taʿlīqa al-Kubrā: min al-Ḍaḥāya ilā Adab al-Qāḍī*, ed. Aḥmad b. Nāṣir b. Saʿīd al-Ghāmidī (PhD diss., Islamic University of Madina, 2005), 884–894. On judicial autonomy under the early ʿAbbasids, see Mathieu Tillier, "Judicial Authority and *Qāḍīs*' Autonomy under the ʿAbbāsids," *Al-Masaq* 26, no. 2 (2014): 127.
70. al-ʿAbbādī, *Ṭabaqāt*, 6; al-Nawawī, *al-Majmūʿ*, 37–38; al-Suyūṭī, *al-Radd*, 67–69.
71. al-Ghazālī, *Iḥyā'*, 1:62.
72. A century after al-Ghazālī, al-Āmidī believed that to qualify as a *mujtahid* of the *madhhab*, one needed to be competent in disputations. Al-Āmidī's position resembles al-Ghazālī's insofar as both see a role for disputations among jurists of a lesser rank than the independent *mujtahid*. Al-Āmidī, *al-Iḥkām*, 4:287.
73. Al-Nawawī, *al-Majmūʿ*, 1:10.
74. Ibid., 1:12.
75. Al-Nawawī, *Rawḍat*, 5.
76. Al-Nawawī, *Minhāj al-Ṭālibīn*, Muḥammad Shaʿbān (Beirut: Dār al-Minhāj, 2005), 64.
77. See the introduction to al-Shīrāzī's *Ṭabaqāt*, 31, where the study of the multiplicity of views of jurists are seen as necessary so as not to overstep the limits of *ijmāʿ*.
78. Al-Nawawī, *al-Majmūʿ*, 1:10.
79. Other Mamluk texts of substantive law also show a commitment to studying the vastness of the Shāfiʿī tradition; see Ibn al-Rifʿa, *Kifāyat*, 1:99. Al-Isnawī, *al-Muhimmāt*, 1:94
80. Al-Subkī, *Ṭabaqāt*, 10:235
81. Al-Isnawī, *al-Muhimmāt*, 1:93–94.
82. Al-Subkī, *Ṭabaqāt*, 10:235.
83. Al-Isnawī, *al-Muhimmāt*, 1:101.
84. For an example of the post-classical reformulation of school doctrine in the Ḥanafī school, see Samy Ayoub, *Law, Empire, and the Sultan: Ottoman Imperial Authority and Late Ḥanafī Jurisprudence* (New York: Oxford University Press, 2019), 8–13, 27–28.

85. Al-Āmidī, *al-Iḥkām*, 4:287.
86. On the Niẓāmiyya college of Baghdad, see Asad Talas, *L'Enseignement chez les arabes: La madrasa niẓāmiyya et son histoire* (Paris: P. Geuthner, 1939).
87. Of note, many Iraqi Shāfiʿīs trained elsewhere before settling down in Baghdad. For instance, al-Ṭabarī trained under Khurasanian Shāfiʿīs before continuing his studies in Baghdad; al-Shīrāzī, *Ṭabaqāt*, 127.
88. Al-Subkī, *Ṭabaqāt*, 4:357; 5:106.
89. Ibid., 5:124; Ibn Khallikān, *Wafayāt*, 1:29. See Omid Safi, *The Politics of Knowledge in Premodern Islam: Negotiating Ideology and Religious Inquiry* (Chapel Hill: University of North Carolina Press, 2006), 103, who interprets al-Shīrāzī's refusal to teach in the Niẓāmiyya as a political stance against government-sponsored institutions.
90. Ibn Khallikān, *Wafayāt*, 1:31.
91. Ibn Khallikān notes that al-Mutawallī was appointed by Niẓām al-Mulk's son without Niẓām al-Mulk's knowledge. When Niẓām al-Mulk discovered that al-Mutawallī had been appointed, he expressed disapproval, stating that the school should have closed for a year out of respect for al-Shīrāzī. Nonetheless, shortly after appointing Ibn al-Ṣabbāgh, Niẓām al-Mulk reinstated al-Mutawallī; *Wafayāt*: 3:133.
92. Ibn Khallikān identifies the following authors of commentaries on the *Muhadhdhab*, the *Tanbīh*, or the *Wasīṭ*: Fakhr al-Islām al-Shāshī (d. 507/1113 CE) (*al-Tanbīh*), Sharaf al-Dīn al-Irbīlī (d. 622/1225 CE) (*al-Tanbīh*), Ḍiyā' al-Dīn al-Hadbānī (d. 605/1209 CE) (*al-Muhadhdhab*), Muḥammad b. Yaḥyā b. Abī Manṣūr (d. 548/1153 CE) (*al-Wasīṭ*), ʿImād al-Dīn b. Yūnus (d. 608/1211 CE), (*al-Muhadhdhab* and *al-Wasīt* in a combined text), Ibn Barhūn al-Fāriqī (d. 528/1133 CE) (*al-Muhadhdhab*), Ibn al-Bazrī (d. 560/1165 CE) (*Muhadhdhab*), Ibn al-Khill (*al-Tanbīh*) (d. 552/1157 CE), Ibn al-Ṣalāḥ (*al-Wasīṭ*), Abū al-Futūḥ al-ʿIjlī (d. 600/1203CE ) (*al-Wasīṭ*); Ibn Khallikān, *Wafayāt*, 1:108, 4:227, 1:33, 2:77, 2:541, 3:243, 3:445, 4:253, 4:256, 3:262, 4:223. Quoting from Muḥammad Hītū's biography of al-Shīrāzī, Chaumont identifies seventy five commentaries of the *Tanbīh* and twenty-five commentaries of the *Muhadhdhab*, highlighting the popularity of both texts in the period between al-Shīrāzī and al-Nawawī; Éric Chaumont, "L'autorité des textes au sein du šāfiʿisme ancien: Du *Muḫtaṣar* d'al-Muzanī (m. 264/878) au *Tanbīh* d'al-Šīrāzī (m. 476/1083) et du *Tanbīh* d'al-Šīrāzī au *Minhāǧ al-ṭālibīn* d'al-Nawawī (m. 676/1277)," *Mélanges de l'Institut dominicain d'études Orientales*, 32 (2017), 53–62.
93. Al-Shīrāzī, *Ṭabaqāt*, 121.
94. Éric Chaumont, "L'autorité," 53–62.
95. Al-Subkī mentions proficiency in disputation in 37/216 biographies of jurists of the the 4th/10th century (al-Subkī, *Ṭabaqāt*, 4:28, 62, 71, 91,94, 114, 119 120, 121, 124, 134, 158, 176, 200, 261, 333, 376, 383, 387, 395; 5:14, 24, 53, 72, 74, 95, 99, 151, 167, 240, 246, 297, 313, 336, 351); for the 5th/11th century: 59/478 entries (al-Subkī, *Ṭabaqāt*, 6:49, 63, 116, 134, 205, 390, 95, 164, 167, 89, 395, 94, 154; 7:29, 66, 72, 95, 138, 298, 305, 233, 101, 49, 177, 249, 256, 286, 304, 307, 309, 190, 294, 155, 240, 256, 127, 337, 156, 323); for the 7th/13th century: 22/350 entries (al-Subkī, *Ṭabaqāt*, 8:31, 108, 394, 60, 377, 317, 146, 134, 156, 158, 317, 373, 374, 16, 108, 34, 100, 343,

110, 346, 318, 87); for the 8th/14th century: 13/128 (al-Subkī, *Ṭabaqāt*, 9:25, 355, 203, 378, 97, 7, 61; 10:75, 140, 339, 203, 166, 378, 203, 61).

96. Ibn Kathīr, *Ṭabaqāt al-Shāfi'iyyīn*, ed. Aḥmad 'Umar Hāshim (Maktabat al-Thaqāfa al-Dīniyya, 1993), 949; Shams al-Dīn al-Sakhāwī, *al-Ḍaw' al-Lāmi' li-Ahl al-Qarn al-Tāsi'*, 12 vols. (Beirut: Dār Maktabat al-Ḥayāt, 1966), 2:189, 2:272, 5:93, 5:139, 5:227, 5:330, 6:188, 8:129, 9:291, 10:266; 'Abd al-Qādir al-Nu'aymī, *al-Dāris fī Tārīkh al-Madāris*, ed. Ibrāhīm Shams al-Dīn, 2 vols. (Beirut: Dār al-Kutub al-'Ilmiyya, 1990), 1:215, 1:402, 2:27, 2:86, 2:92; Ṣalāḥ al-Dīn al-Ṣafadī, *A'yān al-'Aṣr wa-A'wān al-Naṣr*, ed. 'Alī Abū Zayd et al., 6 vols. (Beirut: Dār al-Fikr al-Mu'āṣir, 1998), 1:729, 3:46, 3:484, 4:619, 5:13, 5:34, 5:673. On court patronage of disputations, see Christian Mauder, *In the Sultan's Salon: Learning, Religion, and Rulership at the Mamluk Court of Qāniṣawh al-Ghawrī (r. 1501–1516)*, 2 vols (Leiden: Brill, 2021), 1:251.
97. Al-Baghdādī, *Kitāb al-Faqīh*, 353.
98. Ibid., 354.
99. Ibid., 355–356.
100. Ibn Jamā'a, *Tadhkirat al-Sāmi' wa'l-Mutakallim fī Adab al-'Ālim wa'l-Muta'allim*, ed. Muḥammad Mahdī al-'Ajamī (Beirut: Dār al-Bashā'ir al-Islāmiyya, n.d.), 139. On Ibn Jamā'a's treatise, see Jonathan Berkey, *The Transmission of Knowledge in Medieval Cairo: A Social History of Islamic Education* (Princeton, NJ: Princeton University Press, 1992), 22–36.
101. Ibn Jamā'a, *Tadkhirat*, 64
102. While al-Subkī speaks highly of his father's disputations, he also follows al-Ghazālī in criticizing past jurists who delved into disputation to such an extent as to lose all focus on their own spiritual growth; al-Subkī, *Mu'īd al-Ni'am wa-Mubīd al-Niqam* (Beirut: Mu'assasat al-Kutub al-Thaqāfiyya, 1986), 68. For a 13th century, Ḥanafī pedagogical text warning against disputation, see Burhān al-Islām al-Zarnūjī, *Ta'līm al-Muta'allim Ṭarīq al-Ta'allum*, ed. Marwān Qabbānī (Beirut: al-Maktab al-Islāmī, 1981), 71.
103. Al-Subkī, *Ṭabaqāt*, 10:203.
104. Al-Sakhāwī, *al-Manhal*, 43.
105. Al-Subkī, *Ṭabaqāt*, 10:339–366. Like al-Shīrāzī, al-Bājī was called a debating "lion that could not be beat." And like al-Shīrāzī, he was granted primacy of place to contest, exposit, and demonstrate the relevant considerations of legal matters through debate gatherings.
106. Ibid., 8:81, 318. In the next generation, Taqī al-Dīn al-Subkī was also noted for his debating skill. Tāj al-Dīn al-Subkī reports an exchange between himself and his father. Tāj al-Dīn implored his father to engage in a disputation. He explains that his father obliged out of concern for "his education." Taqī al-Dīn asked his son to find a topic with a sufficient number of divergent opinions for his and his classmates to each adopt, study, and defend one of them. The son proposed the topic of the impermissible (*mas'alat al-ḥarām*). When the son and his classmates returned, the elder al-Subkī defended each position in turn. Afterwards, he sought to defend the Shāfi'ī position by critiquing all other positions. Tāj al-Dīn asserts that the event solidified in his mind the vastness of his father's knowledge; al-Subkī, *Ṭabaqāt*, 10:203. See also

Michael Chamberlain, *Knowledge and Social Practice in Medieval Damascus, 1190–1350* (Cambridge: Cambridge University Press, 1994), 174.

107. Al-Subkī, *Ṭabaqāt*, 10:378. Al-Subkī also gives us reason to believe that questions of piety, like the meaning of the word *wara'*, had become important topics of disputation among Mamluk scholars; on the nexus between law and piety, see Megan Reid, *Law and Piety in Medieval Islam* (Cambridge: Cambridge University Press, 2013).
108. Al-Sakhāwī provides the example of jurists seeking to engage in debate with al-Nawawī on the *Waṣīt*. Al-Nawawī, who disliked debating, rebuked them for questioning his knowledge of the *Wasīṭ*; see Al-Sakhāwī, *al-Manhal*, 43.
109. On the increasing consensus that the 13th century marked a turning point in deference to legal schools, see Katz, "The Age of Development," 439.
110. Jackson believes that the triumph of *taqlīd* is the result of the need for authority in the law, but perhaps the reverse is true: perhaps the triumph of *taqlīd* was the cause of an increased reverence of doctrinal authority among jurists; see Jackson's comments on "legal scaffolding"; Jackson, "*Taqlīd*," 167.

# Bibliography

## Arabic Sources


Al-ʿAbbādī, Abū ʿĀṣim. *Ṭabaqāt al-Fuqahāʾ al-Shāfiʿiyya*. Ed. Gösta Vitestam. Leiden: Brill, 1964.

Abū Yūsuf. *Al-Radd ʿalā Siyar al-Awzāʿī*. Ed. Abū al-Wafāʾ al-Afghānī. Hyderabad: Lajnat Iḥyāʾ al-Maʿārif al-Nuʿmāniyya, 2007.

Abū Yūsuf. *Kitāb al-Kharāj*. Beirut: Dār al-Maʿrifa, 1979.

N.A. *Akhbār al-Dawla al-ʿAbbāsiyya wa-fīhi Akhbār al-ʿAbbās wa-Waladihi*. Ed. ʿAbd al-ʿAzīz al-Dūrī and ʿAbd al-Jabbār al-Muṭṭalabī. Beirut: Dār al-Ṭalīʿa, 1971.

Al-Āmidī, Sayf al-Dīn. *Al-Iḥkām fī Uṣūl al-Aḥkām*. Ed.ʿAbd al-Razzāq ʿAfīfī. 4 vols. Riyadh: Dār al-Ṣumayʿī, 2003.

Al-ʿAynī, Badr al-Dīn. *Al-Bināya: Sharḥ al-Hidāya*. Ed. Ayman Shaʿbān. 13 vols. Beirut: Dār al-Kutub al-ʿIlmiyya, 2000.

Al-ʿAẓm, Ṣādiq. *Naqd al-Fikr al-Dīnī*. Beirut: Dār al-Ṭalīʿa, 1977.

Al-Bābartī, Akmal al-Dīn. *Al-ʿInāya: Sharḥ al-Hidāya*. 10 vols. Cairo: Muṣṭafā al-Bābī al-Ḥalabī wa-Awlāduhu, 1970.

Al-Baghawī, Abū Muḥammad. *Al-Tahdhīb fī Fiqh al-Imām al-Shāfiʿī*. Ed. ʿĀdil ʿAbd al-Mawjūd and ʿAlī Muʿawwaḍ. 8 vols. Beirut: Dār al-Kutub al-ʿIlmiyya, 1997.

Al-Baghdādī, al-Khaṭīb. *Kitāb al-Faqīh waʾl-Mutafaqqih*. Beirut: Dār Ibn Ḥazm, 2014.

Al-Baghdādī, al-Khaṭīb. *Tārīkh Madīnat al-Salām*. Ed. Bashshār ʿAwwād Maʿrūf. 21 vols. Beirut: Dār al-Gharb al-Islāmī, 2001.

Al-Bājī, Abū al-Walīd. *Al-Minhāj fī Tartīb al-Ḥijāj*. Ed. ʿAbd al-Majīd Turkī. 3rd ed. Beirut: Dār al-Gharb al-Islāmī, 2001.

Al-Bājī, Abū al-Walīd. *Iḥkām al-Fuṣūl fī Aḥkām al-Uṣūl*. Ed. ʿAbd Allāh Muḥammad al-Jabūrī. Beirut: Muʾassasat al-Risāla, 1989.

Al-Balkhī, Abū al-Qāsim, ʿAbd al-Jabbār, and al-Ḥākim al-Jushamī. *Faḍl al-Iʿtizāl wa-Ṭabaqāt al-Muʿtazila*. Ed. Fuʾād Sayyid. Beirut: al-Maʿhad al-Almānī liʾl-Abḥāth al-Sharqiyya, 2017.

Al-Bāqillānī, Abū Bakr. *Al-Taqrīb waʾl-Irshād (al-Ṣaghīr)*. Ed. ʿAbd al-Ḥamīd Abū Zunayd. 3 vols. 2nd ed. Beirut: Muʾassasat al-Risāla, 1998.

Al-Baṣrī, Abū al-Ḥusayn. *Al-Muʿtamad fī Uṣūl al-Fiqh*. Ed. Khalīl al-Mays. 3rd ed. 2 vols. Beirut: Dār al-Kutub al-ʿIlmiyya, 2005.

Al-Bayḍāwī, Nāṣir al-Dīn. *Minhāj al-Wuṣūl ilā ʿIlm al-Uṣūl*. Ed. Shaʿbān Ismāʿīl. Beirut: Dār Ibn Ḥazm, 2008.

Al-Bayhaqī, Abū Bakr. *Manāqib al-Shāfiʿī*. Ed. Al-Sayyid Aḥmad Ṣaqr. 2 vols. Cairo: Maktaba Dār al-Turāth, 1970.

Al-Bukhārī, ʿAlāʾ al-Dīn. *Kashf al-Asrār: Sharḥ Uṣūl al-Bazdawī*. Ed. ʿAbd Allāh ʿUmar. 4 vols. Beirut: Dār al-Kutub al-ʿIlmiyya, 1997.

Al-Bulqīnī, Ṣāliḥ b. Sirāj al-Dīn. *Tatimmat al-Tadrīb*. In *Al-Tadrīb fī al-Fiqh al-Shāfiʿī*, by Sirāj al-Dīn al-Bulqīnī. Ed. Abū Yaʿqūb Kamāl al-Miṣrī. 4 vols. Riyadh: Dār al-Qiblatayn, 2012.

Al-Būṭī, Muḥammad Saʿīd Ramaḍān. *Muḥāḍarāt fī al-Fiqh al-Muqāran*. Damascus: Dār al-Fikr, 1993.

Al-Dabbūsī, Abū Zayd. *Taqwīm al-Adilla fī Uṣūl al-Fiqh*. Ed. Khalīl al-Mays. Beirut: Dār al-Kutub al-ʿIlmiyya, 2001.

Al-Dhahabī, Shams al-Dīn. *Siyar Aʿlām al-Nubalāʾ*. Ed. Muḥammad b. ʿAbd Allāh al-Shabrāwī. 18 vols. Cairo: Dār al-Ḥadīth, 2006.

Al-Dīb, ʿAbd al-ʿAẓīm. "*Muqaddimāt Nihāyat al-Maṭlab*." In *Nihāyat al-Maṭlab fī Dirāyat al-Madhhab*, Abū al-Maʿālī al-Juwaynī. Ed. ʿAbd al-ʿAẓīm al-Dīb, vol. 1. Jeddah: Dār al-Minhāj, 2007.

Al-Ghazālī, Abū Ḥāmid. *Al-Mustaṣfā min ʿIlm al-Uṣūl*. Ed. Muḥammad al-Murʿashlī. 2 vols. Beirut: Dār al-Nafāʾis, 2011.

Al-Ghazālī, Abū Ḥāmid. *Iḥyāʾ ʿUlūm al-Dīn*. Ed. Muḥammad al-Dālī Balṭa. 5 vols. Beirut: al-Maktaba al-ʿAṣriyya, 2015.

Al-Ghazālī, Abū Ḥāmid. *Al-Wasīṭ fī al-Madhhab*. Ed. Muḥammad Tāmir. 8 vols. Cairo: Dār al-Salām, 1996.

Hītū, Muḥammad Ḥasan. *Al-Imām al-Shīrāzī: Ḥayātuhu wa-Ārāʾuhu al-Uṣūliyya*. Damascus: Dār al-Fikr, 1980.

Ibn Abī Yaʿlā, Abū al-Ḥusayn. *Ṭabaqāt al-Ḥanābila*. Ed. Muḥammad Ḥāmid al-Fiqī. 2 vols. Cairo: Maṭbaʿat al-Sunna al-Muḥammadiyya, n.d.

Ibn ʿAqīl, Abū al-Wafāʾ. *Kitāb al-Funūn*. Ed. George Makdisi. Damhur: Maktabat Līna, 1991.

Ibn ʿAqīl, Abū al-Wafāʾ. *Kitāb al-Jadal ʿalā Ṭarīqat al-Fuqahāʾ*. Port Said: Maktabat al-Thaqāfa al-Dīniyya, n.d.

Ibn ʿAqīl, Abū al-Wafāʾ. *Al-Wāḍiḥ fī Uṣūl al-Fiqh*. Ed. ʿAbd Allāh Al-Turkī. 5 vols. Beirut: Muʾassasat al-Risāla, 1999.

Ibn ʿAsākir. *Tabyīn Kadhib al-Muftarī fī mā Nusiba ilā al-Imām al-Ashʿarī*. 3rd ed. Beirut: Dār al-Kitāb al-ʿArabī, 1984.

Ibn ʿĀshūr, Muḥammad. *Maqāṣid al-Sharīʿa al-Islāmiyya*. Ed. Muḥammad al-Ṭāhir al-Mīsāwī. Amman: al-Bashāʾir liʾl-Intāj al-ʿIlmī, 1998.

Ibn Aʿtham, Abū Muḥammad. *Kitāb al-Futūḥ*. Ed. ʿAlī Shīrī. 8 vols. Beirut: Dār al-Aḍwāʾ, 1991.

Ibn al-Athīr. *Al-Kāmil fī al-Tārīkh*. Ed. Yūsuf al-Daqqāq. 11 vols. Beirut: Dār al-Kutub al-ʿIlmiyya, 1987.

Ibn Barhān. *Al-Wuṣūl ilā al-Uṣūl*. 2 vols. Riyadh: Maktabat al-Maʿārif, 1984.

Ibn Daqīq al-ʿĪd. *Sharḥ al-Arbaʿīn Hadīth$^{an}$ al-Nawawiyya*. Beirut: Dār al-Kutub al-ʿIlmiyya, 1983.

Ibn al-Farrāʾ, Abū Yaʿlā. *Kitāb al-Muʿtamad fī Uṣūl al-Dīn*. Ed. Wadīʿ Ḥaddād. Beirut: Dār al-Mashriq, 1974.

Ibn al-Farrāʾ, Abū Yaʿlā. *Al-ʿUdda fī Uṣūl al-Fiqh*. Ed. Muḥammad ʿAbd al-Qādir ʿAṭā. 2 vols. Beirut: Dār al-Kutub al-ʿIlmiyya, 2002.

Ibn Fūrak, Abū Bakr. *Mujarrad Maqālāt al-Shaykh Abī al-Ḥasan al-Ashʿarī: Min Imlāʾ al-Shaykh al-Imām Abī Bakr Muḥammad b. al-Ḥasan b. Fūrak (T. 406/1015)*. Beirut: al-Maktaba al-Sharqiyya, 1987.

Ibn ʿImād. *Shadharāt al-Dhahab*. Ed. ʿAbd al-Qādir al-Arnaʾūṭ. 10 vols. Damascus: Dār Ibn Kathīr, 1986.

Ibn Jamā'a, Badr al-Dīn. *Tadhkirat al-Sāmi' wa'l-Mutakallim fī Adab al-'Ālim wa'l-Muta'allim*. Ed. Muḥammad Mahdī al-'Ajamī. Beirut: Dār al-Bashā'ir al-Islāmiyya, n.d.

Ibn al-Jawzī, Abū al-Faraj. *Al-Muntaẓam fī al-Mulūk wa'l-Umam*. Ed. F. Krenkow. 8 vols. Hyderabad: Dā'irat al-Ma'ārif, 1938–1940.

Ibn al-Jawzī, Abū al-Faraj. *Manāqib al-Imām Aḥmad*. Ed. 'Abd Allāh al-Turkī. Cairo: Maktabat al-Khānjī, 1979.

Ibn Kathīr. *Qiṣaṣ al-Anbiyā'*. Ed. Muṣṭafā 'Abd al-Wāḥid. 2 vols. 3rd ed. Mecca: Maktabat al-Ṭālib al-Jāmi'ī, 1988.

Ibn Kathīr. *Ṭabaqāt al-Shāfi'iyyīn*. Ed. Aḥmad 'Umar Hāshim. Maktabat al-Thaqāfa al-Dīniyya, 1993.

Ibn Khaldūn. *Dīwān al-Mubtada' wa'l-Khabar fī Tārīkh al-'Arab wa'l-Barbar wa-Man 'Āṣarahum min Dhawī al-Sha'n al-Akbar*. Ed. Khalīl Shaḥāda. 8 vols. Beirut: Dār al-Fikr, 1988.

Ibn Khallikān. *Wafayāt al-A'yān wa-Anbā' Abnā' al-Zamān*. Ed. Iḥsān 'Abbās. 8 vols. Beirut: Dār al-Ṣādir, 1968–1977.

Ibn al-Mulaqqin, 'Umar b.'Alī. *Al-'Aqd al-Mudhhab fī Ṭabaqāt Ḥamalat al-Madhhab*. Ed. Ayman Naṣr al-Dīn al-Azharī. Beirut: Dār al-Kutub al-'Ilmiyya, 1997.

Ibn al-Mulaqqin, 'Umar b.'Alī. *'Ujālat al-Muḥtāj ilā Tawjīh al-Minhāj*. Ed. 'Izz al-Dīn al-Badrānī. Jordan: Dār al-Kitāb, 2001.

Ibn Nujaym, Zayn al-Dīn. *Al-Baḥr al-Rā'iq: Sharḥ Kanz al-Daqā'iq*. Ed. Zakariyya 'Umayrāt. 9 vols. Beirut: Dār al-Kutub al-'Ilmiyya, 1997.

Ibn Nujaym, Sirāj al-Dīn. *Al-Nahr al-Fā'iq*. Ed. Aḥmad 'Ināya. 3 vols. Beirut: Dār al-Kutub al-'Ilmiyya, 2002.

Ibn Qāḍī Shuhba, Badr al-Dīn. *Bidāyat al-Muḥtāj fī Sharḥ al-Minhāj*. Ed. Anwar al-Dāghistānī. 4 vols. Jeddah: Dār al-Minhāj, 2011.

Ibn Qāḍī Shuhba, Taqī al-Dīn. *Ṭabaqāt al-Shāfi'iyya*. Ed. 'Abd al-'Alīm Khān. 2 vols. Beirut: 'Ālam al-Kutub, 1987.

Ibn al-Qāṣṣ. *Al-Talkhīṣ*. Ed. 'Ādil 'Abd al-Mawjūd and 'Alī Mu'awwaḍ. Mecca: Maktabat Nizār Muṣṭafā al-Bāz, n.d.

Ibn al-Qāṣṣ. *Adab al-Qāḍī*. Ed. Ḥusayn al-Jabūrī. Taif: Maktabat al-Ṣadīq, 1989.

Ibn al-Qāṣṣ. *Nuṣrat al-Qawlayn li'l-Imām al-Shāfi'ī*. Ed. Māzin Sa'd al-Zabībī. Damascus: Dār al-Bayrūtī, 2009.

Ibn al-Qaṣṣār. *Muqaddima fī Uṣūl al-Fiqh*. Ed. Muṣṭafā Makhdūm. Riyadh: Dār al-Ma'lima li-Nashr wa-Tawzī', 1999.

Ibn Qudāma. *Al-Mughnī*. Ed. 'Abd Allāh al-Turkī and 'Abd al-Fattāḥ al-Ḥulū. 15 vols. Beirut: Dār 'Ālam al-Kutub, 1997.

Ibn Qudāma. *Ḥikāyat al-Munāẓara fī al-Qur'ān ma'a ba'ḍ Ahl al-Bid'a*. Ed. 'Abd Allāh al-Juday'. Riyadh: Maktabat al-Rushd, 1997.

Ibn al-Rif'a, Najm al-Dīn. *Kifāyat al-Nabīh: Sharḥ al-Tanbīh fī Fiqh al-Imām al-Shāfi'ī*. Ed. Majdī Bāsallūm. 20 vols. Beirut: Dār al-Kutub al-'Ilmiyya, 2009.

Ibn Rushd, *Bidāyat al-Mujtahid wa-Nihāyat al-Muqtaṣid*. Ed. Mājid al-Ḥamawī. 4 vols. 2nd ed. Beirut: Dār Ibn Ḥazm, 2012.

Ibn al-Ṣalāḥ. *Ādāb al-Fatwā wa'l-Muftī wa'l-Mustaftī*. Ed. Muwaffaq 'Abd al-Qādir. Mecca: 'Ālam al-Kutub, 1986.

Ibn al-Ṣalāḥ. *Ṭabaqāt al-Shāfi'iyya*. Ed. Muḥyī al-Dīn 'Alī Najīb. 2 vols. Beirut: Dār al-Bashā'ir al-Islāmiyya, 1992.

Al-ʿImrānī, Abū al-Ḥusayn. *Al-Bayān fī Madhhab al-Imām al-Shāfiʿī*. Ed. Qāsim al-Nūrī. 14 vols. Beirut: Dār al-Minhāj, 2000.

Al-Iṣbahānī, Abū Nuʿaym. *Ḥilyat al-Awliyāʾ wa-Ṭabaqāt al-Aṣfiyāʾ*. 10 vols. Cairo: Khānjī, 1997.

Al-Isnawī, Jamāl al-Dīn. *Al-Muhimmāt fī Sharḥ al-Rawḍā waʾl-Rāfiʿī*. Ed. Abū al-Faḍl Aḥmad b. ʿAlī. 10 vols. Beirut: Dār Ibn Ḥazm, 2009.

Al-Isnawī, Jamāl al-Dīn.*Ṭabaqāt al-Shāfiʿiyya*. Ed. Kamāl Yūsuf Ḥūt. 2 vols. Beirut: Dār al-Kutub al-ʿIlmiyya, 1987.

Al-Isnawī, Jamāl al-Dīn. *Nihāyat al-Sūl*. Ed. ʿAbd al-Qādir ʿAlī. Beirut: Dār al-Kutub al-ʿIlmiyya, 1999.

Al-Jaṣṣāṣ, Abū Bakr. *Al-Fuṣūl fī al-Uṣūl*. Ed. Muḥammad Tāmir. 2 vols. Beirut: Dār al-Kutub al-ʿIlmiyya, 2010.

Al-Jaṣṣāṣ, Abū Bakr. *Sharḥ Mukhtaṣar al-Ṭaḥāwī*. Ed. Muḥammad ʿAbd Allāh Khān. 8 vols. Beirut: Dār al-Sirāj, 2010.

Al-Juwaynī, Abū al-Maʿālī. *Al-Burhān fī Uṣūl al-Fiqh*. Ed. ʿAbd al-ʿAẓīm al-Dīb. 2 vols. N.p., 1979.

Al-Juwaynī, Abū al-Maʿālī. *Al-Kāfiya fī al-Jadal*. Ed. Fawqiyya Maḥmūd. Cairo: Maṭbaʿat ʿĪsā al-Bābī al-Ḥalabī wa- Shurakāʾuhu, 1979.

Al-Juwaynī, Abū al-Maʿālī. *Kitāb al-Ijtihād*. In *al-Burhān fī Uṣūl al-Fiqh*. Ed. ʿAbd al-ʿAẓīm al-Dīb, 2: 1316–1329. N,p., 1979.

Al-Juwaynī, Abū al-Maʿālī. *Kitāb al-Fatwā*. In *al-Burhān fī Uṣūl al-Fiqh*. Ed. ʿAbd al-ʿAẓīm al-Dīb, 2: 1330–1366. N.p. 1979.

Al-Juwaynī, Abū al-Maʿālī. *Nihāyat al-Maṭlab fī Dirāyat al-Madhhab*. Ed. ʿAbd al-ʿAẓīm al-Dīb. 21 vols. Jeddah: Dār al-Minhāj, 2007.

Al-Juwaynī, Abū al-Maʿālī. *Al-Talkhīṣ fī Uṣūl al-Fiqh*. Ed. ʿAbd Allāh al-Nībālī and Shubbayr al-ʿAmarī. 3 vols. Beirut: Dār al-Bashāʾir al-Islāmiyya, 1996.

Al-Juwaynī, Abū al-Maʿālī. *Kitāb al-Irshād ilā Qawāṭiʿ al-Adilla fī Uṣūl al-Iʿtiqād*. Ed. Aḥmad ʿAbd al-Raḥmān Sāyiḥ. Cairo: Maktabat al-Thaqāfa al-Dīniyya, 2009.

Al-Juwaynī, Abū al-Maʿālī. *Al-Ghiyāthī*. Ed. ʿAbd al-ʿAẓīm al-Dīb. 2nd ed. (n.p. and n.d.).

Al-Kalwadhānī, Abū al-Khaṭṭāb. *Al-Tamhīd fī Uṣūl al-Fiqh*. Ed. Mufīd Abū ʿAmsha and Muḥammad b. ʿAlī b. Ibrāhīm. 4 vols. Jedda: Dār al-Madanī, 1985.

Al-Kāsānī, Abū Bakr. *Badāʾiʿ al-Ṣanāʾiʿ fī Tartīb al-Sharāʾiʿ*. Ed. ʿAlī Muḥammad Muʿawwaḍ and ʿĀdil al-Mawjūd. 10 vols. Beirut: Dār al-Kutub al-ʿIlmiyya, 2003.

Al-Maḥāmilī, Aḥmad b. Muḥammad. *Al-Lubāb fī al-Fiqh al-Shāfiʿī*. Ed. ʿAbd al-Karīm al-Ḥarbī. Medina: Dār al-Bukhārī, 1995.

Al-Marghīnānī, Burhān al-Dīn. *Al-Hidāya: Sharḥ Bidāyat al-Mubtadī*. Ed. Muḥammad Tāmir and Ḥāfiẓ ʿĀshūr Ḥāfiẓ. 4 vols. Cairo: Dār al-Salām liʾl-Ṭibaʿa waʾl-Nashr, 2000.

Al-Marwarrūdhī, al-Qāḍī Ḥusayn. *Al-Taʿlīqa*. Ed. ʿAlī Muḥammad Muʿawwaḍ and ʿĀdil ʿAbd al-Mawjūd. 2 vols. Mecca: Maktabat Nizār Muṣṭafā al-Bāz, n.d.

Al-Marwarrūdhī, al-Qāḍī Ḥusayn. *Fatāwā al-Qāḍī Ḥusayn*. Ed. Amal Khaṭṭāb and Jamāl Abū Ḥassān. Amman: Dār al-Fatḥ, 2010.

Al-Masʿūdī, Abū al-Ḥasan. *Murūj al-Dhahab wa-Maʿādin al-Jawhar*. Ed. Kamāl Ḥasan Marʿī. 4 vols. Beirut: al-Maktaba al-ʿAṣriyya, 2005.

Al-Māwardī, Abū al-Ḥasan. *Al-Ḥāwī al-Kabīr fī Fiqh Madhhab al-Imām al-Shāfiʿī, wa-huwa Sharḥ Mukhtaṣar al-Muzanī*. Ed. ʿAlī Muḥammad Muʿawwaḍ and ʿĀdil ʿAbd al-Mawjūd. 19 vols. 3rd ed. Beirut: Dār al-Kutub al-ʿIlmiyya, 2009.

Al-Māwardī, Abū al-Ḥasan. *Kitāb al-Aḥkām al-Sulṭāniyya wa'l-Wilāyāt al-Dīniyya*. Mansoura: Dār al-Wafā', 1989.

Al-Miṣrī, Abū Muḥammad. *Sīrat 'Umar b. 'Abd al-'Azīz 'alā mā Rawāhu Mālik wa-Aṣḥābihi*. Ed. Aḥmad 'Ubayd. Beirut: 'Ālam al-Kutub, 1984.

Al-Mutawallī, Abū Sa'd. *Tatimmat al-Ibāna 'an Furū' al-Diyāna, min Awwal Bāb al-Ṣalāt ilā Nihāyat al-Bāb al-Ḥadī 'Ashar: Fīmā Yaqtaḍī Karāhiyat al-Ṣalat*. Ed. Nisrīn bt. Hilāl Ḥamādī. PhD diss., Umm al-Qurā University, Mecca, 2007.

Al-Mutawallī, Abū Sa'd. *Tatimmat 'an Furū' al-Diyāna, min Awwal Kitāb al-Nikāḥ ilā Nihāyat Bāb Nikāḥ Ḥarā'ir al-Kuffār*. Ed. Taghrīd bt. Muẓahhir al-Bhukhārī. PhD diss., Umm al-Qurā University, Mecca, 2007.

Al-Muzanī, Abū Ibrāhīm. *Mukhtaṣar al-Muzanī*. Ed. Muḥammad Shāhīn. Beirut: Dār al-Kutub al-'Ilmiyya, 1998.

Al-Nasafī, Abū al-Mu'īn. *Tabṣirat al-Adilla*. Ed. Ḥusayn al-Ātāy. Ankara: Diyāneṭ Işleri Başlangi, 1993.

Al-Nasafī, Abū al-Barakāt. *Kanz al-Daqā'iq*. Ed. Sā'id Bakdāsh. Beirut: Dār al-Bashā'ir al-Islāmiyya, 2011.

Al-Nawawī, Muḥyī al-Dīn. *Al-Majmū': Sharḥ al-Muhadhdhab*. Ed. Rā'id b. Abī 'Alfa. 2 vols. Amman: Bayt al-Afkār al-Dawliyya, 2009.

Al-Nawawī, Muḥyī al-Dīn. *Minhāj al-Ṭālibīn*. 2 vols. Beirut: Dār al-Bashā'ir al-Islāmiyya, 2000.

Al-Nawawī, Muḥyī al-Dīn. *Tahdhīb al-Asmā' wa'l-Lughāt*. 4 vols. Cairo: Idārat al-Ṭibā'a al-Munīriyya, 1925–6; reprint, Beirut: Dār al-Kutub al-'Ilmiyya, n.d.

Al-Nu'aymī, 'Abd al-Qādir. *Al-Dāris fī Tārīkh al-Madāris*. Ed. Ibrāhīm Shams al-Dīn. 2 vols. Beirut: Dār al-Kutub al-'Ilmiyya, 1990.

Al-Qāḍī 'Iyāḍ. *Tartīb al-Madārik wa-Taqrīb al-Masālik*. 8 vols. 2nd ed. Rabat: Wizārat al-Awqāf wa'l-Shu'ūn al-Islāmiyya, 1983.

Al-Qārī al-Harawī, 'Alī b. Sulṭān. *Al-Athmār al-Janiyya fī Asmā' al-Ḥanafiyya*. Ed. Muḥammad Jawal. Beirut: Manshūrāt al-Jamāl, 2012.

Al-Qudūrī, Abū al-Ḥusayn. *Mukhtaṣar al-Qudūrī*. Ed. Kāmil 'Awīḍa. Beirut: Dār al-Kutub al-'Ilmiyya, 1997.

Al-Qudūrī, Abū al-Ḥusayn. *Al-Tajrīd*. Ed. Muḥammad Aḥmad Sarāj and 'Alī Jum'a. 12 vols. Cairo: Dār al-Salām, 2006.

Al-Qurashī, Ibn Abī al-Wafā'. *Al-Jawāhir al-Muḍī'a fī Ṭabaqāt al-Ḥanafiyya*. Beirut: Dār al-Kutub al-'Ilmiyya, 2005.

Al-Rāfi'ī, 'Abd al-Karīm b. Muḥammad. *Al-Muḥarrar fī Fiqh al-Imām al-Shāfi'ī*. Ed. Muḥammad Ismā'īl. Dār al-Kutub al-'Ilmiyya, 2013.

Al-Rāfi'ī, 'Abd al-Karīm b. Muḥammad. *Al-'Azīz fī Sharḥ al-Wajīz*. Ed. 'Alī al-Mu'awwaḍ and 'Ādil 'Abd al-Mawjūd. 13 vols. Beirut: Dār al-Kutub al-'Ilmiyya, 1997.

Al-Rāzī, Fakhr al-Dīn. *Manāqib al-Imām al-Shāfi'ī*. Ed. Muḥammad Majāzī al-Saqqā. Cairo: Maktabat al-Kulliyyāt al-Azhariyya, 1986.

Al-Rāzī, Fakhr al-Dīn. *Al-Maḥṣūl fī 'Ilm Uṣūl al-Fiqh*. Ed. Muḥammad 'Aṭā. 2 vols. 2nd ed. Beirut: Dār al-Kutub al-'Ilmiyya, 2015.

Al-Rāzī, Fakhr al-Dīn. *Munāẓarāt Fakhr al-Dīn al-Rāzī fī Bilād Mā Warā' al-Nahr*. Ed. Fatḥ Allāh Khulayf. Beirut: Dār al-Mashriq, 1967.

Al-Rāzī, Ibn Abī Ḥātim. *Ādāb al-Shāfi'ī wa-Manāqibuhu*. Ed. 'Abd al-Ghanī 'Abd al-Khāliq. Beirut: Dār al-Kutub al-'Ilmiyya, 2003.

al-Rāzī, Aḥmad b. Sahl. *Akhbār Fakhkh wa-Khabar Yaḥyā b. 'Abd Allāh wa-Akhīhi Idrīs*. Ed. Māhir Jarrār. Beirut: Dār al-Gharb al-Islāmī, 1995.

Al-Rūyānī, Abū al-Maḥāsin. *Baḥr al-Madhhab fī Furū' al-Madhhab al-Shāfi'ī*. Ed. Ṭāriq Fatḥī al-Sayyid. 14 vols. Beirut: Dār al-Kutub al-'Ilmiyya, 2009.

Al-Ṣafadī, Ṣalāḥ al-Dīn. *A'yān al-'Aṣr wa-A'wān al-Naṣr*. Ed. 'Alī Abū Zayd, Nabīl Abū 'Amsha, Muḥammad Maw'id and Maḥmūd Sālim Muḥammad. 6 vols. Beirut: Dār al-Fikr al-Mu'āsir, 1998.

Saḥnūn (Ibn Sa'īd al-Tanūkhī). *Al-Mudawwana al-Kubrā*. 5 vols. Beirut: Dār al-Kutub al-'Ilmiyya, 1994.

Al-Sakhāwī, Shams al-Dīn. *Al-Manhal al-'Adhb al-Rawī fī Tarjumat Quṭb al-Awliyā' al-Nawawī*. Ed. Aḥmad Farīd al-Mazīdī. Beirut: Dār al-Kutub al-'Ilmiyya, 2005.

Al-Sakhāwī, Shams al-Dīn. *al-Ḍaw' al-Lāmi' li-Ahl al-Qarn al-Tāsi'*, 12 vols. Beirut: Dār Maktabat al-Ḥayāt, 1966.

Al-Sam'ānī, 'Abū al-Muẓaffar. *Qawāṭi' al-Adilla fī al-Uṣūl*. Ed. Muḥammad al-Shāfi'ī. 2 vols. Beirut: Dār al-Kutub al-'Ilmiyya, 1997.

al-Samarqandī, 'Alā' al-Dīn. *Tuḥfat al-Fuqahā'*. 3 vols. Beirut: Dār al-Kutub al-'Ilmiyya, 1984.

al-Samarqandī, 'Alā' al-Dīn. *Mīzān al-Uṣūl fī Natā'ij al-'Uqūl*. Ed. Muḥammad Zakī 'Abd al-Barr. Doha: Maṭābi' al-Dawḥa al-Ḥadītha, 1984.

Al-Sarakhsī, Muḥammad b. Aḥmad. *Sharḥ Kitāb al-Siyar al-Kabīr*. Ed, Abū 'Abd Allāh Ismā'īl al-Shāfi'ī. 5 vols. Beirut: Dār al-Kutub al-'Ilmiyya, 1997.

Al-Sarakhsī, Muḥammad b. Aḥmad. *Al-Mabsū ṭ*. 31 vols. Beirut: Dār al-Ma'rifa, 1989.

Al-Ṣaymarī, Abū 'Abd Allāh. *Kitāb Masā'il al-Khilāf fī Uṣūl al-Fiqh*. In "Les Problèmes de divergences en méthodologie juridique de Ḥusayn B.'Alî al- Ṣaymarî: Présentation, analyze et édition critique." Ed. Abdelouahad Jahdani, vol. 2. 2 vols. PhD diss., Université de Provence, 1991.

Al-Ṣaymarī, Abū 'Abd Allāh. *Akhbār Abī Ḥanīfa wa-Aṣḥābihi*. 3rd ed. Beirut: 'Ālam al-Kutub, 1985.

Al-Shāfi'ī, Muḥammad b. Idrīs. *Kitāb al-Umm*. Ed. Rif'at Fawzī 'Abd al-Muṭṭalib. 11 vols. Mansoura: Dār al-Wafā', 2008.

Al-Shāfi'ī, Muḥammad b. Idrīs. *Al-Risāla*. Ed. Aḥmad Shākir. Beirut: Dār al-Kutub al-'Ilmiyya, n.d.

Al-Shāshī, Al-Qaffāl. *Ḥilyat al-'Ulamā'*. Ed. Sa'īd 'Abd al-Fattāḥ. 3 vols. 2nd ed. Mecca: Nizār Muṣṭafā al-Bāz, 1998.

Al-Shāshī, Al-Qaffāl. *Maḥāsin al-Sharī'a fī furū' al-Shāfi'iyya*. Ed. Abū 'Abd Allāh Samaka. Beirut: Dār al-Kutub al-'Ilmiyya, 2007.

Al-Shaybānī, Muḥammad b. al-Ḥasan. *Kitāb al-Ḥujja 'alā Ahl al-Madīna*. Ed. Mahdī al-Kaylānī al-Qādirī. 4 vols. Beirut: 'Ālam al-Kutub, 1983.

Al-Shaybānī, Muḥammad b. al-Ḥasan. *Kitāb al-Aṣl*. Ed. Muḥammad Būyanūkālin. 12 vols. Beirut: Dār Ibn Ḥazm, n.d.

Al-Shīrāzī, Abū Isḥāq. *Kitāb al-Luma' fī Uṣūl al-Fiqh*. Ed. 'Abd al-Qādir al-Ḥasanī. Tangier: Dār al-Ḥadīth al-Kittāniyya, 2013.

Al-Shīrāzī, Abū Isḥāq. *Kitāb al-Ma'ūna fī al-Jadal*. Ed. 'Abd al-Majīd Turkī. Beirut: Dār al-Gharb al-Islāmī, 1988.

Al-Shīrāzī, Abū Isḥāq. *Al-Muhadhdhab fī Fiqh al-Imām al-Shāfi'ī*. Ed. Muḥammad al-Zuḥaylī. 6 vols. Damascus: Dār al-Qalam, 1992.

Al-Shīrāzī, Abū Isḥāq. *Al-Mulakhkhaṣ fī al-Jadal*. Manuscript. Istanbul: Atif Effendi Library, *copied 590AH/1194CE*.

Al-Shīrāzī, Abū Isḥāq. *Sharḥ al-Luma' fī Uṣūl al-Fiqh*. Ed. 'Abd al-Majīd Turkī. 2 vols. Beirut: Dār al-Gharb al-Islāmī, 1988.

Al-Shīrāzī, Abū Isḥāq. *Ṭabaqāt al-Fuqahā'*. Ed. Iḥsān 'Abbās. Beirut: Dār al-Rā'id al-'Arabī, 1970.

Al-Shīrāzī, Abū Isḥāq. *Al-Tabṣira fī Usūl al-Fiqh*. Ed. Muḥammad Ḥasan Hītū. Damascus: Dār al-Fikr, 1980.

Al-Shīrāzī, Abū Isḥāq. *Al-Tanbīh fī al-Fiqh al-Shāfi'ī*. Beirut: 'Ālam al-Kutub, 1983.

Al-Shīrāzī, Abū Isḥāq. *Mu'taqad Abī Isḥāq al-Fayrūzabādī al-Shīrāzī*. In *Shārḥ al-Luma' fī Uṣūl al-Fiqh*. Ed. Majīd Turkī, 1:91–116. 2 vols. Beirut: Dār al-Gharb al-Islāmī, 1988.

Al-Shīrāzī, Abū Isḥāq. *Al-Nukat fī al-Masā'il al-Mukhtalaf fīhā Bayna al-Shāfi'ī wa Abī Ḥanīfa, min Awwal Kitāb al-Jināyāt ilā Nihāyat al-Kitāb al-Iqrār*. Ed. Ṣabāḥ bt. Akbar Ḥusayn Akbar. MA thesis, Umm al-Qurā University in Mecca, 2003–2004.

Al-Shirbīnī, Muḥammad b. Aḥmad. *Mughnī al-Muḥtāj ilā Ma'rifat Ma'ānī Alfāẓ al-Minhāj*. Ed. 'Alī Mu'awwaḍ and 'Ādil 'Abd al-Mawjūd. 6 vols. Beirut: Dār al-Kutub al-'Ilmiyya, 2000.

Al-Sijistānī, Abū Dāwūd. *Sunan Abī Dāwūd*. Ed. Shu'ayb al-Arna'ūṭ and Muhammad Kāmil Qarah Ballī. 7 vols. Damascus: Dār al-Risāla al-'Ālamiyya, 2009.

Al-Subkī, Tāj al-Dīn. *Al-Ibhāj fī Sharḥ al-Minhāj*. 3 vols. Beirut: Dār al-Kutub al-'Ilmiyya, 1995.

Al-Subkī, Tāj al-Dīn. *Ṭabaqāt al-Shāfi'iyya al-Kubrā*. Ed. 'Abd al-Fattāḥ al-Ḥulū and Maḥmūd al-Ṭanāḥī. 10 vols. Cairo: Maṭba'at 'Īsā al-Bābī al-Ḥalabī, 1964.

Al-Subkī, Tāj al-Dīn. *Mu'īd al-Ni'am wa-Mubīd al-Niqam*. Beirut: Mu'assasat al-Kutub al-Thaqāfiyya, 1986.

Al-Sakūnī, Abū 'Alī 'Umar. *'Uyūn al-Munāẓarāt*. Ed. Sa'd Ghurāb. Tunisia: Manshūrāt al-Jāmi'a al-Tūnisiyya, 1976.

Al-Suyūṭī, Jalāl al-Dīn. *Al-Radd 'alā Man Akhlada ilā al-Arḍ wa-Jahila anna al-Ijtihād fī Kull 'Aṣr Farḍ*. Ed. Khalīl al-Mays. Beirut: Dār al-Kutub al-'Ilmiyya, 1983.

Al-Ṭabarī, Abū al-Ṭayyib. *Al-Ta'līqa al-Kubrā, min al-Ḍaḥāya ilā Adab al-Qāḍī*. Ed. Aḥmad b. Nāṣir b. Sa'īd al-Ghāmidī. PhD diss., Islamic University of Medina, 2005.

Al-Ṭabarī, Abū al-Ṭayyib. *Al-Ta'līqa al-Kubrā, min Bāb mā Yufsid al-Mā' Ḥattā Nihāyat Bāb Istiqbāl al-Qibla*. Ed. 'Ubayd b. Sālim al-'Amarī. MA thesis, Medina University, 1998–1999.

Al-Ṭabarī, al-Abū Ṭayyib. *Al-Ta'līqa al-Kubrā: Kitāb al-Nikāḥ, Kitāb al-Ṣadāq, Kitāb al-Qasm wa'l-Nushūz*. Ed. Yūsuf 'Abd Allāh al-'Aqīl. PhD diss., University of Medina, 2004–2005.

Al-Ṭabarī, Muḥammad b. Jarīr. *Jāmi' al-Bayān*. Ed. Maḥmūd Shākir. 15 vols. Beirut: Dār Ibn Ḥazm, 2013.

Al-Ṭabarī, Muḥammad b. Jarīr. *Tārīkh al-Ṭabarī*. Ed. Muḥammad Abū al-Faḍl Ibrāhīm. 11 vols. 2nd ed. Cairo: Dār al-Ma'ārif, 1967.

Al-Tanūkhī, Abū al-Fahm. *Nishwār al-Muḥāḍara wa-Akhbār al-Mudhākara*. Ed. 'Abūd al-Shālijī. 2nd ed. 8 vols. Beirut: Dār al-Ṣadr, 1995.

Turkī, 'Abd al-Majīd. "*Al-Tamhīd al-Awwal*." In *Sharḥ al-Luma' fī Uṣūl al-Fiqh*, by Abū Isḥāq al-Shīrāzī. Ed. 'Abd al-Majīd Turkī, 1:5–64. Beirut: Dār al-Gharb al-Islāmī, 1988.

Turkī, 'Abd al-Majīd. *Munāẓarāt fī Uṣūl al-Sharī'a al-Islāmiyya bayna Ibn Ḥazm wa'l-Bājī*. Beirut: Dār al-Gharb al-Islāmī, 2008.

Al-'Ukbarī, Abū al-Ḥasan. *Risālat al-'Ukbarī fī Uṣūl al-Fiqh*. Ed. Badr b. Nāṣir al-Subay'ī. Amman: Arwiqa, 2017.

Al-Urmawī, Sirāj al-Dīn. *Al-Taḥṣīl min al-Maḥṣūl*. Ed. 'Abd al-Ḥamīd Abū Zunayd. 2 vols. Mu'assasat al-Risāla, 1998.

Al-Wāqidī, Abū 'Abd Allāh. *Futūḥ al-Shām*. Ed. 'Abd al-Laṭīf 'Abd al-Raḥmān. 2 vols. Beirut: Dār al-Kutub al-'Ilmiyya, 1997.

Al-Zarkashī, Badr al-Dīn. *Al-Baḥr al-Muḥīṭ fī Uṣūl al-Fiqh*. Ed. 'Abd al-Sattār Abū Ghudda. 2nd ed. 6 vols. Kuwait: Wizārat al-Awqāf wa'l-Shu'ūn al-Islāmiyya, 1992.

Al-Zarnūjī, Burhān al-Islām. *Ta'līm al-Muta'allim Ṭarīq al-Ta'allum*. Ed. Marwān Qabānī. Beirut: al-Maktab al-Islāmī, 1981.

Al-Zayla'ī, Jamāl al-Dīn. *Naṣb al-Rāya li-Aḥādīth al-Hidāya*. Ed. Aḥmad Shams al-Dīn. 5 vols. Beirut: Dār al-Kutub al-'Ilmiyya, 2010.

Al-Zayla'ī, Fakhr al-Dīn. *Tabyīn al-Ḥaqā'iq: Sharḥ Kanz al-Daqā'iq*. 6 vols. Cairo: al-Maṭba'a al-Kubrā al-Amīriyya, 1895.

## Non-Arabic Sources

Abbas, Shemeem. *Pakistan's Blasphemy Laws: From Islamic Empires to the Taliban*. Austin: University of Texas Press, 2013.

Abou El Fadl, Khaled. *Speaking in God's Name: Islamic Law, Authority and Women*. Oxford: Oneworld, 2001.

Abou El Fadl, Khaled. *The Search for Beauty in Islam: A Conference of the Books*. Lanham, MD: Rowman and Littlefield Publishers, Inc., 2006.

Abū Yūsuf. *Abū Yūsuf's Kitāb al-Kharāj*. Trans. A. Ben Shemesh. Leiden: Brill, 1969.

Adanali, Ahmet. "Dialectical Methodology and Its Critique: al-Ghazālī as a Case Study." PhD diss., University of Chicago, 1995.

Agrama, Hussein Ali. *Questioning Secularism: Islam, Sovereignty, and the Rule of Law in Modern Egypt*. Chicago: University of Chicago Press, 2012.

Ahmad, Atif Ahmad. *The Fatigue of the Shari'a*. New York: Palgrave Macmillan, 2012.

Ahmad, Irfan. *Religion as Critique: Islamic Critical Thinking from Mecca to the Marketplace*. Chapel Hill: University of North Carolina Press, 2017.

Ahmad, Ziauddin. "The Concept of Jizya in Early Islam." *Islamic Studies* 14, no. 4 (1975): 293–305.

Ahmed, Leila. *A Border Passage*. New York: Farrar, Straus and Giroux, 1999.

Ahmed, Rumee. *Narratives of Islamic Legal Theory*. Oxford: Oxford University Press, 2012.

Al-Alwani, Taha Jabir. *The Ethics of Disagreement in Islam*. Trans. Abdul Wahid Hamid. London: International Institute of Islamic Thought, 2011.

Al-Azem, Talal. *Rule-Formulation and Binding Precedent in the* Madhhab-*Law Tradition: Ibn Quṭlūbughā's Commentary on* The Compendium *of Qudūrī*. Leiden: Brill, 2017.

Al-Ghazālī, Abū Ḥāmid. *The Remembrance of Death and the Afterlife*. Trans. T.J. Winter. Cambridge: Islamic Texts Society, 1989.

Al-Hibri, Azizah. "An Introduction to Muslim Women's Rights." In *Windows of Faith: Muslim Women Scholar-Activists in North America*. Ed. Gisela Webb, 51–71. Syracuse, NY: Syracuse University Press, 2000.

Ali, Kecia. *Sexual Ethics in Islam: Feminist Reflections on Qur'an, Hadith, and Jurisprudence*. Oxford: Oneworld, 2006.

Ali, Kecia. *Marriage and Slavery in Early Islam*. Cambridge, MA: Harvard University Press, 2010.

Ali, Kecia. "Marriage in Classical Islamic Jurisprudence: A Survey of Doctrines." In *The Islamic Marriage Contract: Case Studies in Islamic Family Law*. Ed. Asifa Quraishi and Frank E Vogel, 11–45. Cambridge, MA: Harvard University Press, 2009.

Ali, Muhammad Yunis. *Medieval Islamic Pragmatics*. Richmond: Routledge, 2000.

Ali-Karamali, Shaista P., and Fiona Dunne. "The Ijtihad Controversy." *Arab Law Quarterly* 9, no. 3 (1994): 238–257.

Al-Shīrāzī, Abū Isḥāq. *Kitāb al-Luma' fī Uṣūl al-Fiqh*. Trans. Eric Chaumont. Berkeley, CA: Robbins Collection, 1999.

Allen, Roger. *An Introduction to Arabic Literature*. Cambridge: Cambridge University Press, 2000.

Anderson, Benedict R. *Imagined Communities: Reflections on the Origin and Spread of Nationalism*. Revised ed. London: Verso, 2006.

Antilla, Jaako Hämeen. "The Essay and the Debate (*Al-Risāla* and *Al-Munāẓara*)." In *Arabic Literature in the Post-Classical Period*. Ed. Roger Allen and D.S. Richards, 134–144. Cambridge: Cambridge University Press, 2006.

Arberry, A.J. *Shiraz: Persian City of Saints and Poets*. Norman: University of Oklahoma Press, 1960.

Asad, Talal. *Genealogies of Religion*. Baltimore: The Johns Hopkins University Press, 1993.

Asad, Talal. *Formations of the Secular: Christianity, Islam, Modernity*. Stanford, CA: Stanford University Press, 2003.

Asad, Talal. "Free Speech, Blasphemy, and Secular Criticism." In *Is Critique Secular?: Blasphemy, Injury, and Free Speech*. Ed. Talal Asad, Wendy Brown, Judith Butler, and Saba Mahmood, 20–63. Berkeley, CA: The Townsend Center for the Humanities, 2009.

Asad, Talal. *The Idea of an Anthropology of Islam*. Washington, DC: Center for Contemporary Arab Studies at Georgetown University, 1986.

Asad, Talal. "Remarks on the Anthropology of the Body." In *Religion and the Body*. Ed. Sarah Coakley, 42–52. Cambridge: Cambridge University Press, 2000.

Asad, Talal. "Thinking about Religion, Belief, and Politics." In *The Cambridge Companion of Religious Studies*. Ed. Robert Orsi, 36–57. Cambridge: Cambridge University Press, 2011.

Auda, Jasser. *Maqāṣid al-Sharī'ah: A Beginner's Guide*. London: International Institute of Islamic Thought, 2008.

Ayoub, Samy. *Law, Empire, and the Sultan: Ottoman Imperial Authority and Late Ḥanafī Jurisprudence*. New York: Oxford University Press, 2019.

Azam, Hina. *Sexual Violation in Islamic Law: Substance, Evidence, and Procedure*. New York: Cambridge University Press, 2015.

Balibar, Etienne. "Marxism and the Idea of Revolution: The Messianic Moment in Marx." In *Historical Telelogies in the Modern World*. Ed. Henning Trüper, Dipesh Chakrabarty, and Sanjay Subrahmanyam, 235–250. London: Bloomsbury, 2015.

Barlas, Asma. *Believing Women in Islam*. Austin: University of Texas Press, 2002.

Bashir, Shahzad. "The Living Dead of Tabriz: Explorations in Chronotopic Imagination." *History of Religions* 59, no. 3 (2020): 169–192.

Baugh, Carolyn. *Minor Marriage in Early Islam*. Leiden: Brill, 2017.

Bedir, Murteza. "An Early Response to Shāfi'ī: 'Īsā b. Abān on the Prophetic Report (*Khabar*)." *Islamic Law and Society* 9, no. 3 (2002): 285–311.

Belhaj, Abdessamad. *Argumentation et dialectique en islam: Formes et séquences de la munāẓara*. Bruxelles: Presses universitaires de Louvain, 2010.

Belhaj, Abdessamad. "*Ādāb al-Baḥth wa'l-Munāẓara*: The Neglected Art of Disputation in Later Medieval Islam." *Arabic Sciences and Philosophy* 26, (2016): 291–307.

Berkey, Jonathan. *The Transmission of Knowledge in Medieval Cairo: A Social History of Islamic Education*. Princeton, NJ: Princeton University Press, 1992.

Bernand, Marie. *Le problème de la connaissance d'après le Muġnī du cadi 'Abd al-Ǧabbār*. Alger: Société nationale d'édition et de diffusion, 1982.

Brunschvig, Robert. "Problème de la décadence." In *Classicisme et déclin culturel dans l'histoire de l'Islam*. Ed. R. Brunschvig and G. von Grunebaum, 29–51. Paris: Besson et Chantemerle, 1957.

Brunschvig, Robert. "Polémiques médiévales autour du rite de Mālik." *Al-Andalus* 15 (1950): 377–413.

Brunschvig, R. and G. von Grunebaum, eds. *Classicisme et declin culturel dans l'histoire de l'Islam*. Paris: Besson et Chantemerle, 1957.

Bosworth, C. E. "The Concept of *Dhimma* in Early Islam." In *Christians and Jews in the Ottoman Empire: The Functioning of a Plural Society*. Ed. Benjamin Braude and Bernard Lewis, 37–51. New York: Holmes and Meier Publishers, 1982.

Bulliet, Richard. *Conversion to Islam in the Medieval Period: An Essay in Quantitative History*. Cambridge, MA: Harvard University Press, 1979.

Bulliet, Richard. *The Patricians of Nishapur: A Study in Medieval Islamic Social History*. Cambridge, MA: Harvard University Press, 1972.

Brown, Johnathan. "Scripture in the Modern Muslim World: The Quran and Hadith." In *Islam in the Modern World*. Ed. Jeffrey Kenney and Ebrahim Moosa, 13–34. New York: Routledge, 2014.

Brown, Wendy. "Introduction." In *Is Critique Secular?* Ed. Talal Asad, Wendy Brown, Judith Butler, and Saba Mahmood, 7–19. Berkeley, CA: The Townsend Center for the Humanities, 2009.

Calasso, Giovanna and Giulano Lancioni, eds. *Dār al-Islām/Dār al-Ḥarb: Territories, People, Identities*. Leiden: Brill, 2017.

Calder, Norman. *Islamic Jurisprudence in the Classical Era*. New York: Cambridge University Press, 2010.

Calder, Norman. "Al-Nawawī's Typology of *Muftī*s and Its Significance for a General Theory of Islamic Law." *Islamic Law and Society* 3, no. 2 (1996): 137–164.

Calhoun, Craig J., ed. *Habermas and the Public Sphere*. Cambridge, MA: MIT Press, 1992.

Calmard. J. "Kāzarūn." *Encyclopaedia of Islam, Second Edition*. Ed. P. Bearman, Th. Bianquis, C.E. Bosworth, E. van Donzel, and W.P. Heinrichs. Leiden: Brill, 2012. Consulted online September 4, 2018, http://dx.doi.org.myaccess.library.utoronto.ca/10.1163/1573-3912_islam_SIM_4079

Chakrabarty, Dipesh. *Provincializing Europe: Postcolonial Thought and Historical Difference*. Princeton, NJ: Princeton University Press, 2000.

Chamberlain, Michael. *Knowledge and Social Practice in Medieval Damascus, 1190–1350*. Cambridge: Cambridge University Press, 1994.

Chaudhry, Ayesha S. *Domestic Violence and the Islamic Tradition: Ethics, Law and the Muslim Discourse on Gender*. Oxford: Oxford University Press, 2013.

Chaumont, Eric. "Al-Shīrāzī." *Encyclopaedia of Islam, Second Edition*. Ed. P. Bearman, Th. Bianquis, C.E. Bosworth, and E. van Donzel. Leiden: Brill, 2012. Accessed February 1, 2017, http://dx.doi.org.myaccess.library.utoronto.ca/10.1163/15733912_islam_COM_1060

Chaumont, Eric. "Encore au sujet de l'ash'arisme d'Abû Ishâq Ash-Shîrâzî." *Studia Islamica* 74 (1991): 167–177.

Chaumont, Eric. L'autorité des textes au sein du šāfi'isme ancien: Du *Muḫtaṣar* d'al-Muzanī (m. 264/878) au *Tanbīh* d'al-Šīrāzī (m. 476/1083) et du *Tanbīh* d'al-Šīrāzī au *Minhāğ al-ṭālibīn* d'al-Nawawī (m. 676/1277). *Mideo: Mélanges de L'Institut dominicain d'études orientales* 32 (2017): 53–62.

Collins, Ronald K. L., and David M. Skover. *On Dissent: Its Meaning in America*. Cambridge: Cambridge University Press, 2013.

Conrad, Lawrence I. "Ibn A'tham and His History." *Al-'Uṣūr al-Wusṭā* 23, no. 1 (2015): 87–125.

Connolly, William. *Why I Am Not a Secularist*. Minneapolis: University of Minnesota Press, 2003.

Cook, Michael. "Ibn Qutayba and the Monkeys." *Studia Islamica* 89 (1999): 43–74.

Coulson, NJ. *A History of Islamic Law*. Reprint. Edinburgh: Edinburgh University Press, 1978.

Crone, Patricia. *The Nativist Prophets of Early Islamic Iran: Rural Revolt and Local Zoroastrianism*. New York: Cambridge University Press, 2012.

Deeb, Lara. *An Enchanted Modern: Gender and Public Piety in Shi'i Lebanon*. Princeton, NJ: Princeton University Press, 2006.

Dennett, Daniel Clement. *Conversion and the Poll Tax in Early Islam*. Cambridge, MA: Harvard University Press, 1950.

Duderja, Adis. "Contemporary Reformist Muslim Thought and Maqāṣid cum Maṣlaḥa Approaches to Islamic Law: An Introduction." In *Maqāṣid al-Sharī'a and Contemporary Reformist Thought*. Ed. Adis Duderja, 1–12. New York: Palgrave Macmillan, 2014.

Donner, Fred McGraw. *Muhammad and the Believers: At the Origins of Islam*. Cambridge, MA: The Belknap Press of Harvard University Press, 2010.

Donner, Fred McGraw. *The Early Islamic Conquests*. Princeton, NJ: Princeton University Press, 1981.

El Omari, Racha. *The Theology of Abū l-Qāsim al-Balkhī/al-Ka'bī (d. 319/931)*. Leiden: Brill, 2016.

El Shakry, Hoda. *The Literary Qur'an*. New York: Fordham University Press, 2020.

El Shamsy, Ahmed. "Rethinking '*Taqlīd*' in the Early Shāfi'ī School." *Journal of the American Oriental Society* 128, no. 1 (2008): 1–23.

El Shamsy, Ahmed. *The Canonization of Islamic Law: A Social and Intellectual History*. New York: Cambridge University Press, 2013.

El Shamsy, Ahmed. "Bridging the Gap: Two Early Texts of Islamic Legal Theory." *Journal of American Oriental Society* 137, no.3 (2017): 505–536.

El Shamsy, Ahmed. "Al-Shāfi'ī's Written Corpus: A Source-Critical Study." *Journal of the American Oriental Society* 132, no. 2 (2012): 199–220.

Emon, Anver. "Ijtihad." In *The Oxford Handbook of Islamic Law*. Ed. Anver Emon and Rumee Ahmed, 181–206. Oxford: Oxford University Press, 2018.

Emon, Anver. *Islamic Natural Law Theories*. New York: Oxford University Press, 2010.

Emon, Anver. *Religious Pluralism in Islamic Law: Dhimmīs and Others in the Empire of Law*. Oxford: Oxford University Press, 2012.

Emon, Anver. "To Most Likely Know the Law: Objectivity, Authority, and Interpretation in Islamic Law." *Hebraic Political Studies* 4, no. 4 (2009): 415–440.

Ephrat, Daphna. *A Learned Society in a Period of Transition: The Sunni 'Ulama' of Eleventh-Century Baghdad*. Albany: State University of New York Press, 2000.

Fadel, Mohammad. "Reinterpreting the Guardian's Role in the Islamic Contract of Marriage: The Case of the Maliki School." *The Journal of Islamic Law* 3 (1998): 1–26.

Fadel, Mohammad. "The Social Logic of *Taqlid* and the Rise of the *Mukhtaṣar*." *Islamic Law and Society* 3, no. 2 (1996): 193–233.

Fadel, Mohammad. "*Istiḥsān* Is Nine-Tenths of the *Furu'*: The Puzzling Relationship of *Usūl* to *Furū'* in the Mālikī *Madhhab*." In *Studies in Islamic Legal Theory*. Ed. Bernard Weiss, 161–177. Leiden: Brill, 2002.

Farahat, Omar. *The Foundation of Norms in Islamic Jurisprudence and Theology*. Cambridge: Cambridge University Press, 2019.

Fattal, Antoine. *Le statut légal des non-musulmans en pays d'islam*. Beirut: Imprimerie catholique, 1958.

Foucault, Michel. *Fearless Speech*. Ed. Joseph Pearson. Los Angeles: Semiotext, 2001.

Foucault, Michel. *Hermeneutics of the Subject: Lectures at the Collège de France, 1981–82*. Trans. Graham Burchell. Ed. Frederic Gros. New York: Palgrave Macmillan, 2005.

Foucault, Michel. "What is Critique?" Trans. Kevin Paul Geiman. In *What Is Enlightenment? Eighteenth-Century Answers and Twentieth-Century Questions*. Ed. James Schmidt, 382–388. Berkeley: University of California Press, 1996.

Foucault, Michel. "What is Enlightenment?" In *The Foucault Reader*. Ed. P. Rabinow, 32–50. New York: Pantheon Books, 1984.

Fraser, Nancy. "Rethinking the Public Sphere: A Contribution to Actually Existing Democracy." In *Habermas and the Public Sphere*. Ed. Craig J. Calhoun, 109–142. Cambridge, MA: MIT Press, 1992.

Fromherz, Allen James. *Ibn Khaldun: Life and Times*. Edinburgh: Edinburgh University Press, 2011.

Gadamer, Hans-Georg. *Truth and Method*. Trans. Joel Weinsheimer. Wiltshire: Continuum, 2004.

Gibb, H.A.R. *Modern Trends in Islam*. Chicago: University of Chicago Press, 1947.

Goldziher, Ignaz. *The Ẓāhirīs: Their Doctrine and Their History: A Contribution to the History of Islamic Theology*. Ed. and trans. Wolfgang Behn. Reprint. Leiden: Brill, 2008.

Gould, Rebecca. "Beyond the *Taqlīd/Ijtihād* Dichotomy: Daghestani Legal Thought under Russian Rule." *Islamic law and Society* 24, no. 1–2 (2017): 142–169.

Gutas, Dimitri. *Greek Thought, Arabic Culture: The Graeco-Arabic Translation Movement in Baghdad and Early 'Abbasid Society (2nd–4th/8th–10th Centuries)*. London: Routledge, 1998.

Habermas, Jürgen. *The Structural Transformation of the Public Sphere: An Inquiry into a Category of Bourgeois Society*. Trans. Thomas Burger. Cambridge, MA: MIT Press, 1989.

Habermas, Jürgen. "*Between Facts and Norms: Contributions to a Discourse Theory of Law and Democracy*. Trans. William Rehg. Cambridge, MA: MIT Press, 1996.

Haj, Samira. *Reconfiguring Islamic Tradition: Reform, Rationality, and Modernity*. Stanford, CA: Stanford University Press, 2008.

Halim, Fachrizal A. *Legal Authority in Premodern Islam: Yaḥyā b. Sharaf al-Nawawī in the Shāfi'ī School of Law*. New York: Routledge, 2015.

Hanif, Sohail. "A Tale of Two Kufans: Abū Yūsuf's *Ikhtilāf* Abī Ḥanīfa wa-Ibn Abī Laylā and Schacht's Ancient Schools." *Islamic Law and Society* 25, no.3 (2018): 173–211.

Hallaq, Wael B. *A History of Islamic Legal Theories: An Introduction to Sunnī Uṣūl al-Fiqh*. New York: Cambridge University Press, 1997.

Hallaq, Wael B. "A Tenth-Eleventh Century Treatise on Juridical Dialectic." *The Muslim World* 77, no. 3–4 (1987): 197–206.

Hallaq, Wael B. *The Impossible State: Islam, Politics, and Modernity's Moral Predicament*. New York: Columbia University Press, 2013.

Hallaq, Wael B. *The Origins and Evolution of Islamic Law*. Cambridge: Cambridge University Press, 2005.

Hallaq, Wael B. "Was al-Shafi'i the Master Architect of Islamic Jurisprudence?" *International Journal of Middle East Studies* 25, no. 4 (1993): 587–605.

Hallaq, Wael B. "Was the Gate of Ijtihad Closed?" *International Journal of Middle East Studies* 16, no.1 (1984): 3–41.

Hallaq, Wael B. "Ifta' and Ijtihad in Sunni Legal Theory." In *Islamic Legal Interpretation: Muftis and their Fatwas*. M.K. Masud, B. Messick, and D. Powers, 33–43. Cambridge, MA: Harvard University Press, 1996.

Hallaq, Wael B. "On the Origins of the Controversy about the Existence of Mujtahids and the Gate of Ijtihad." *Studia Islamica* 63 (1986): 129–141.

Harding, Susan, ed. *Feminist Standpoint Theory Reader: Intellectual and Political Controversies*. New York: Routledge, 2004.

Heinrichs, Wolfart. "*Qawā'id* as a Genre of Legal Literature." In *Studies in Islamic Legal Theory*, 365–384. Ed. Bernard Weiss. Leiden: Brill, 2002.

Hernandez, Rebecca. *The Legal Thought of Jalāl al-Dīn al-Suyūṭī*. Oxford: Oxford University Press, 2017.

Hirschkind, Charles. *The Ethical Soundscape: Cassette Sermons and Islamic Counterpublics*. New York: Columbia University Press, 2006.

Holder, Cindy. "Debating the Danish Cartoons: Civil Rights or Civil Power?" *University of New Brunswick Law Journal* 55 (2006): 179–185.

Hijri, Zulfika Amir. *Diversity and Pluralism in Islam: Historical and Contemporary Discourses amongst Muslims*. New York: I.B. Tauris, 2010.

Ibrahim, Ahmed Fekry. "Rethinking the *Taqlīd–Ijtihād* Dichotomy: A Conceptual-Historical Approach." *Journal of the American Oriental Society* 136, no. 2 (2016): 285.

Ibrahim, Ahmed Fekry. "Rethinking the *Taqlīd* Hegemony: An Institutional, Longue-Durée Approach." *Journal of the American-Oriental Society* 136, no. 4 (2016): 801–816.

Jackson, Sherman. *Islamic Law and the State: The Constitutional Jurisprudence of Shihāb al-Dīn al-Qarāfī*. Leiden: Brill, 1996.

Jackson, Sherman. "Fiction and Formalism: Towards a Functional Analysis of *Uṣūl al-Fiqh*." In *Studies in Islamic Legal Theory*. Ed. Bernard Weiss, 177–204. Leiden: Brill, 2002.

Jackson, Sherman. "Setting the Record Straight: Ibn al-Labbād's Refutation of al-Shāfi'ī." *Journal of Islamic Studies* 11, no. 2 (2000): 121–146.

Jackson, Sherman. "*Ijtihād* and *Taqlīd*: Between the Islamic Legal Tradition and Autonomous Western Reason." In *The Routledge Handbook of Islamic Law*. Ed. Khaled Abou El Fadl, Ahmad Atif Ahmad, and Said Fares Hassan, 255–272. Abingdon: Routledge, 2019.

Johansen, Baber. *Contingency in a Sacred Law: Legal and Ethical Norms in the Muslim Fiqh*. Leiden: Brill, 1999.

Johansen, Baber. *The Islamic Law on Land Tax and Rent*. London: Croom Helm, 1988.

Kaddouri, Samir. "Refutations of Ibn Ḥazm by Mālikī Authors of al-Andalus and North Africa." In *Ibn Ḥazm of Cordoba: The Life and Works of a Controversial Thinker*. Ed. Camilla Adang, Maribel Fierro, and Sabine Schmidtke, 539–600. Leiden: Brill, 2012.

Kamali, Mohammad Hashim. *Islamic Commercial Law: An Analysis of Futures and Options*. Cambridge: Islamic Texts Society, 2000.

Kamali, Mohammad Hashim. "Goals and Purposes *Maqāṣid al-Sharīʿa*: Methodological Perspectives." In *The Higher Objectives of Islamic Law: The Promises and Challenges of Maqāṣid al-Sharīʿa*. Ed. Idris Nassery, Rumee Ahmed, and Muna Tatari, 7–34. Lanham, MD: Lexington Books, 2018.

Kant, Immanuel. *Prolegomena to Any Future Metaphysics*. Ed. and trans. Gary Hatfield. Revised ed. Cambridge: Cambridge University Press, 2004.

Kant, Immanuel. "*An Answer to the Question: What is Enlightenment?*" In *Practical Philosophy*. Ed. and trans. Mary J. Gregor, 11–22. Cambridge: Cambridge University Press, 1996.

Karabela, Mehmet. "The Development of Dialectic and Argumentation Theory in Post-Classical Islamic Intellectual History." PhD diss., McGill University, 2010.

Katz, Marion. "The Age of Development and Continuity, 12th–15th Centuries CE." In *The Oxford Handbook of Islamic Law*. Ed. Anver Emon and Rumee Ahmed, 437–458. Oxford: Oxford University Press, 2018.

Kaya, Eyyüp Said. "Continuity and Change in Islamic Law: The Concept of Madhhab and the Dimensions of Legal Disagreement in Hanafi Scholarship of the Tenth Century." In *The Islamic School of Law: Evolution, Devolution, and Progress*. Ed. P.J. Bearman, Rudolph Peters, and Frank E. Vogel, 26–40. Cambridge, MA: Harvard Law School, 2005.

Kennedy, Hugh. *The Court of the Caliphs: The Rise and Fall of Islam's Greatest Dynasty*. London: Weidenfeld & Nicolson, 2004.

Khadduri, Majid. *War and Peace in the Law of Islam*. Baltimore: The Johns Hopkins University Press, 1962.

Kraemer, Joel L. *Humanism in the Renaissance of Islam: The Cultural Revival During the Buyid Age*. Leiden: Brill, 1986.

Lambton, Ann. "Shiraz" *Encyclopaedia of Islam, Second Edition*. Ed. P. Bearman, Th. Bianquis, C.E. Bosworth, and E. van Donzel. Leiden: Brill, 2012. Consulted online January, 18 2023, <http://dx.doi.org/10.1163/1573-3912_islam_SIM_6958>

Landes, Joan. *Women and the Public Sphere in the Age of the French Revolution*. Ithaca, NY: Cornell University Press, 1988.

Lassner, Jacob. *The Topography of Baghdad in the Early Middle Ages: Text and Studies*. Detroit: Wayne State University Press, 1970.

Limbert, John. *Shiraz in the Age of Hafez: The Glory of a Medieval Persian City*. Seattle: University of Washington Press, 2004.

Lazarus-Yafeh, Hava, Mark Cohen, Sasson Somekh, and Sidney Griffith, eds. *The Majlis: Interreligious Encounters in Medieval Islam*. Wiesbaden: Harrassowitz, 1999.

Lee, Susanna. "American Animus: Dissent and Disapproval in *Bowers v. Hardwick*, *Romer v. Evans*, and *Lawrence v. Texas*." In *Dissenting Voices in American Society: The Role of Judges, Lawyers, and Citizens*. Ed. Austin Sarat, 56–91. Cambridge: Cambridge University Press, 2012.

Le Strange, Guy. *Baghdad during the Abbasid Caliphate: From Contemporary Arabic and Persian Sources*. Oxford: Clarendon Press, 1900.

Levy-Rubin, Milka. *Non-Muslims in the Early Islamic Empire: From Surrender to Coexistence*. New York: Cambridge University Press, 2011.

Lowry, Joseph E. *Early Islamic Legal Theory: The Risāla of Muḥammad ibn Idrīs al-Shāfiʿī*. Leiden: Brill, 2007.

Luz, Nimrod. *The Mamluk City in the Middle East: History, Culture, and the Urban Landscape*. Cambridge: Cambridge University Press, 2014.

Khan, Naveeda. *Muslim Becoming: Aspiration and Skepticism in Pakistan*. Durham, NC: Duke University Press, 2012.

Koselleck, Reinhart. *Critique and Crisis: Enlightenment and the Pathogenesis of Modern Society* Cambridge, MA: MIT Press, 1998.

Kraus, Paul. "The Controversies of Fakhr al-Din Razi." *Islamic Culture* 12, no. 2 (1938): 131–150.

MacIntyre, Alasdair. *After Virtue: A Study in Moral Theory*. 3rd ed. Notre Dame, IN: University of Notre Dame Press, 2007.

Madelung, Wilferd. *Religious Trends in Early Islamic Iran*. Albany, NY: Persian Heritage Foundation, 1988.

Masud, Muhammad Khaled, Brinkley Messick, and David Powers. "Muftis, Fatwas, and Islamic Legal Interpretation." In *Islamic Legal Interpretation: Muftis and their Fatwas*. Ed. M.K. Masud, Brinkley Messick, and David Powers, 3–32. Cambridge, MA: Harvard University Press, 1996.

Mauder, Christian. *In the Sultan's Salon: Learning, Religion, and Rulership at the Mamluk Court of Qāniṣawh al-Ghawrī (r. 1501–1516)*. 2 vols. Leiden: Brill, 2021.

Mahmood, Saba. *The Politics of Piety: The Islamic Revival and the Feminist Subject*. Princeton, NJ: Princeton University Press, 2005.

Makdisi, George. "Dialectic and Disputation: The Relation between the Texts of Qirqisani and Ibn ʿAqil." In *Mélanges d'islamologie: Volume dédié à la mémoire d'Armand Abel par ses collègues, ses élèves et ses amis*. Ed. P. Salmon, 201–206. Leiden: Brill, 1974.

Makdisi, George. "Muslim Institutions of Learning in Eleventh-Century Baghdad." *Bulletin of the School of Oriental and African Studies* 24, no. 1 (1961): 1–56.

Makdisi, George. "The Juridical Theology of Shâfiʿî: Origins and Significance of *Uṣûl al-Fiqh*." *Studia Islamica* 59 (1984): 5–47.

Makdisi, George. *The Rise of Colleges: Institutions of Learning in Islam and the West*. Edinburgh: Edinburgh University Press, 1984.

Makdisi, George. "The Scholastic Method in Medieval Education: An Inquiry into Its Origins in Law and Theology." *Speculum: A Journal of Medieval Studies* 49, no. 4 (1974): 640–661.

Makdisi, George. "The Significance of the Sunni Schools of Law in Islamic Religious History." *International Journal of Middle East Studies* 10, no. 1 (1979): 1–8.

Makdisi, George. *Ibn ʿAqīl et la resurgence de l'Islam traditionaliste au XI e siècle*. Damascus: Institut français de Damas, 1963.

Makdisi, George. "Freedom in Islamic Jurisprudence: Ijtihad, Taqlid, and Academic Freedom." In *La notion de liberté au Moyen Age: Islàm, Byzance, Occident*. Ed. G. Makdisi, Dominique Sourdel, and Janine Sourdel-Thomine, 79–88. Paris: Les Belles Lettres, 1985.

Makdisi, George. "Authority in the Islamic Community." In *La notion d'autorité au Moyen Âge: Islam, Byzance, Occident*. Ed. G. Makdisi, Dominique Sourdel, and Janine Sourdel-Thomine, 117–126. Paris: Presses Universitaires de France, 1982.

Marx, Karl. "For a Ruthless Critique of Everything in Existence." In *The Marx-Engels Reader*. Ed. Robert Tucker, 12–15. 2nd ed. New York: WW Norton and Company, 1978.

Marx, Karl. "Contribution to the Critique of Hegel's *Philosophy of Right*." In *The Marx-Engels Reader*. Ed. Robert Tucker, 16–25. 2nd ed. New York: WW Norton and Company, 1978.

Masuzawa, Tomoko. *The Invention of World Religions: Or, How European Universalism Was Preserved in the Language of Pluralism*. Chicago: University of Chicago Press, 2005.

Mattson, Ingrid. *The Story of the Qur'an*. 2nd ed. West Sussex: John Wiley & Sons, Ltd, 1993.

Mernissi, Fatema. *Le Harem politique: Le prophète et les femmes*. Paris: A. Michel, 1987.

Melchert, Christopher. *The Formation of the Sunni Schools of Law, 9th–10th Centuries C.E.* Leiden; New York: Brill, 1997.

Melchert, Christopher. "The Early Ḥanafiyya and Kufa." *Journal of 'Abbasid Studies* 5, no.1 (2014): 23–45.

Melchert, Christopher. "Basra and Kufa as the Earliest Centers of Islamic Legal Controversy." In *Islamic Cultures, Islamic Contexts: Essays in Honor of Professor Patricia Crone*. Ed. Asad Q. Ahmed, Behnam Sadeghi, Robert G. Hoyland, and Adam Silverstein, 173–194. Leiden: Brill, 2014.

Metcalf, Barbara Daly. *Islamic Revival in British India: Deoband, 1860–1900*. Princeton, NJ: Princeton University Press, 1982.

Miller, Larry Benjamin. *Islamic Disputation Theory: The Uses & Rules of Argument in Medieval Islam*. Cham: Springer, 2020.

Mitchell, Timothy. "The Stage of Modernity." In *Questions of Modernity*. Ed. T. Mitchell, 1–34. Minneapolis: University of Minnesota Press, 2000.

Moosa, Ebrahim. "Ethical Landscape: Laws, Norms, and Morality." In *Islam and the Modern World*. Ed. Jeffrey Kenney and Ebrahim Moosa, 35–56. London: Routledge, 2014.

Moumtaz, Nada. "Critique, *Naqd*, Orthodoxy." *Critical Research on Religion* 7, no.2 (2019): 194–198.

Mustawfī, Hamd-Allāh. *The Geographical Part of the* Nuzhat-al-Qulūb. Trans. G. Le Strange. Leiden: Brill. 1915.

Naaman, Erez. *Literature and the Islamic Court*. London: Routledge, 2016.

Osti, Letizia. "Culture, Education and the Court." In *Crisis and Continuity in the Abbasid Court*. Ed. Maaike van Berkel, Nadia Maria El Cheikh, Hugh Kennedy, and Letizia Osti, 187–214. Leiden: Brill, 2013.

Ostroróg, Leon. *The Angora Reforms*. London: University of London Press, 1927.

Opwis, Felicitas. *Maṣlaḥa and the Purpose of the Law: Islamic Discourse on Legal Change from the 4th/10th to 8th/14th Century*. Leiden: Brill, 2010.

Opwis, Felicitas. "Shifting Legal Authority from the Ruler to the '*Ulamā*': Rationalizing the Punishment for Drinking Wine During the Saljuq Period." *Der Islam* 86, no. 1 (2011): 65–92.

Opwis, Felicitas. "The Role of the Biographer in Constructing Identity and Doctrine: Al-'Abbādī and His *Kitāb Ṭabaqāt al-Fuqahā' al-Shāfi'iyya*." *Journal of Arabic and Islamic Studies* 11 (2011):1–35.

Osman, Amr. *The Ẓāhirī* Madhhab *(3rd/9th–10th/16th Century)*. Leiden: Brill 2014.

Pellat, Charles. "Les Étapes de la décadence culturelle dans les pays Arabes d'Orient." In *Classicisme et déclin culturel dans l'histoire de l'Islam*. Ed. R. Brunschvig and G. von Grunebaum, 81–91. Paris: Besson et Chantemerle, 1957.

Peacock, A.C.S. *The Great Seljuk Empire*. Edinburgh: Edinburgh University Press, 2015.

Peters, Rudolph. "*Idjtihād* and *Taqlīd* in 18th and 19th Century Islam." *Die Welt des Islams* 20, no. 3–4 (1980): 131–145.

Powers, David Stephan. *Law, Society, and Culture in the Maghrib, 1300–1500*. New York: Cambridge University Press, 2002.

Powers, Paul R. *Intent in Islamic Law: Motive and Meaning in Medieval Sunnī Fiqh*. Boston: Brill, 2006.

Quraishi-Landes, Asifa. "What Is Sharia and Is It Creepy?" *The Islamic Monthly*, June 18, 2012. Accessed November 16, 2021, http://onlinedigeditions.com/article/What+is+Sharia+and+is+it+Creepy%3F/1006292/104350/article.html.

Quadri, Junaid. Transformations of Tradition: Islamic Law in Colonial Modernity. Oxford: Oxford University Press, 2021.

Rabb, Intisar. "Islamic Legal Minimalism: Legal Maxims and Lawmaking when Jurists Disappear." In *Law and Tradition in Classical Thought: Studies in Honor of Professor Hossein Modaressi*. Ed. Michael Cook, Najam Haider, and Intisar Rabb, 145–166. New York: Palgrave, 2013.

Rahemtullah, Shadaab. *Qur'an of the Oppressed*. Oxford: Oxford University Press, 2017.

Rahman, Shahid, Muhammad Iqbal, and Youcef Soufi. *Inference by Parallel Reasoning in Islamic Jurisprudence: Al-Shīrāzī's Insights into the Dialectical Constitution of Meaning and Knowledge*. Cham: Springer, 2020.

Reid, Megan. *Law and Piety in Medieval Islam*. Cambridge: Cambridge University Press, 2013.

Reinhart, A. Kevin. *Before Revelation: The Boundaries of Muslim Moral Thought*. Albany, NY: State University of New York Press, 1995.

Saba, Elias. Harmonizing Similarities: A History of Distinctions Literature in Islamic Law. Berlin: De Gruyter, 2019.

Sadeghi, Behnam. *The Logic of Law-Making in Islam: Women and Prayer in the Legal Tradition*. New York: Cambridge University Press, 2013.

Safi, Omid. *The Politics of Knowledge in Premodern Islam: Negotiating Ideology and Religious Inquiry*. Chapel Hill: University of North Carolina Press, 2006.

Said, Edward. *The World, the Text, and the Critic*. Cambridge MA: Harvard University Press, 1983.

Savant, Sarah Bowen. *The New Muslims of Post-Conquest Iran: Tradition, Memory, and Conversion*. New York: Cambridge University Press, 2013.

Schacht, Joseph. *Introduction to Islamic Law*. Reprint. Oxford: Clarendon Press, 1982.

Schacht, Joseph. "The Schools of Law and Other Developments of Jurisprudence." In *Origin and Development of Islamic Law*. Ed. Majid Khadduri and Herbert J. Liebesny, 57–84. Clark: The Lawbook Exchange, 2008.

Schacht, Joseph. "Classicisme, traditionalisme et ankylose dans la loi religieuse de l'Islam." In *Classicisme et déclin culturel dans l'histoire de l'Islam*. Ed. R. Brunschvig and G. von Grunebaum, 141–161. Paris: Besson et Chantemerle, 1957.

Sheibani, Mariam. "Innovation, Influence, and Borrowing in Mamluk-Era Legal Maxim Collections: The Case of Ibn 'Abd al-Salām and al-Qarāfī." *Journal of the American Oriental Society* 140, no. 4 (2021): 927–954.

Siddiqui, Mona. "Law and the Desire for Social Control: An Insight into the Hanafi Concept of *Kafa'a* with Reference to the Fatawa 'Alamgiri." In *Feminism in Islam: Legal and Literary*. Ed. Mai Yamani, 49–68. New York: New York University Press, 1996.

Siddiqui, Sohaira. *Law and Politics under the 'Abbasids: An Intellectual Portrait of al-Juwaynī*. Cambridge: Cambridge University Press, 2019.

Siddiqui, Sohaira. "*Jadal* and *Qiyās* in the Fifth/Eleventh Century: Two Debates between al-Juwaynī and al-Shīrāzī." *Journal of American Oriental Society* 139, no. 4 (2019): 923–44.

Soufi, Youcef L. "The Lost Oral Genesis of Islamic Law: The Case of an Eleventh-Century Disputation (*munāẓara*) on Broken Oaths." *Journal of the American-Oriental Society* 141, no. 4 (2021): 823–846.

Soufi, Youcef. "Why Study *Uṣūl al-Fiqh*?: The Problem of *Taqlīd* and Tough Cases in in 4th–5th/10th–11th Century Iraq." *Islamic Law and Society* 28, no.1–2 (2021): 1–31.

Soufi, Youcef. "Pious Critique: Abū Isḥāq al-Shīrāzī and the 11th Century Practice of Juristic Disputation (*Munāẓara*)." PhD diss., University of Toronto, 2017.

Spectorsky, Susan. *Women in Classical Islamic Law: A Survey of the Sources.* Leiden: Brill, 2011.

Star, S. Frederick. *Lost Enlightenment: Central Asia's Golden Age from the Arab Conquest to Tamerlane*. Princeton, NJ: Princeton University Press, 2013.

Stroumsa, Sarah. *Freethinkers of Medieval Islam: Ibn al-Rāwandī, Abū Bakr al-Rāzī and Their Impact on Islamic Thought*. Leiden: Brill, 1999.

Stroumsa, Sarah. "Ibn Rāwandī's *sū' adab al-mujādala*: The Role of Bad Manners in Medieval Disputations." In *The Majlis: Interreligious Encounters in Medieval Islam*. Ed. Hava Lazarus-Yafeh, Mark Cohen, Sasson Somekh, and Sidney Griffith, 60–76. Wiesbaden: Harrassowitz, 1999.

Syed, Mairaj. *Coercion and Responsibility in Islam: A Study in Ethics and Law*. Oxford: Oxford University Press, 2017.

Talas, Asad. *L'Enseignement chez les arabes: La madrasa niẓāmiyya et son histoire*. Paris: P. Geuthner, 1939.

Tillier, Mathieu. "Judicial Authority and *Qāḍīs*' Autonomy under the 'Abbāsids." *Al-Masaq* 26, no. 2 (2014): 119–131.

Toorawa, Shawkat. "The Dhimmī in Medieval Islamic Society: Non-Muslim Physicians of Iraq in Ibn Abī Uṣaybi'ah's 'Uyūn al-Anbā' fī Ṭabaḳāt al-Aṭibba'." *Fides et Historia: Official Publication of the Conference on Faith and History* 26, no. 1 (1994): 10–21.

Tritton, A. S. *The Caliphs and Their Non-Muslim Subjects: A Critical Study of the Covenant of 'Umar*. London: Oxford University Press, 1930.

Tsafrir, Nurit. *The History of an Islamic School of Law: The Early Spread of Hanafism*. Cambridge, MA: Harvard University Press, 2004.

Tully, James. *Public Philosophy in a New Key*. 2 vols. Cambridge: Cambridge University Press, 2008.

Urban, Elizabeth. *Conquered Populations in Early Islam: Non-Arabs, Slaves and the Sons of Slave Mothers*. Edinburgh: Edinburgh University Press, 2020.

Van Ess, Josef. "Disputationspraxis in der Islamischen Theologie. Eine Vorläufige Skizze," *Revue des études islamiques* 44 (1976): 23–60.

Vajda, Georges. "Études sur Qirqisānī, les règles de la controverse dialectique." *Revue des études juives* 122 (1963): 7–74.

Van Gelder, Geert. "The Conceit of Pen and Sword: On an Arabic Literary Debate." *Journal of Semitic Studies* 32, no. 2 (1987): 329–335.

Vidal-Castro, Francisco. "Al-Bājī, Abū al-Walīd." *Encyclopaedia of Islam, Third Edition*. Ed. Kate Fleet, Gudrun Kramer, Denis Matringue, John Nawas, and Everett Rowson. Leiden: Brill, 2011. Accessed February 1, 2017, <http://dx.doi.org.myaccess.library.utoronto.ca/10.1163/1573-3912_ei3_COM_24281>.

Vishanoff, David. *The Formation of Islamic Hermeneutics: How Sunni Legal Theorists Imagined a Revealed Law*. New Haven, CT: American Oriental Society, 2011.

Wadud, Amina. *Qur'an and Woman: Rereading the Sacred Text from a Woman's Perspective*. New York: Oxford University Press, 1999.

Watt, Montgomery. *The Formative Period of Islamic Thought*. Reprint. Oxford: Oneworld Publications, 1998.

Watt, Montgomery. *Islamic Philosophy and Theology*. 2nd ed. Edinburgh: Edinburgh University Press, 1985.

Watt, Montgomery. "The Closing of the Door of Iğtihād." *Orientalia Hispanica 1*. Ed. J.M. Barral, 675–678. Leiden: Brill, 1974.

Weiss, Bernard. *The Search for God's Law: Islamic Jurisprudence in the Writings of Sayf al-Dīn al-Āmidī*. Revised ed. Salt Lake City: University of Utah Press, 2010.

Weiss, Bernard. *The Spirit of Islamic Law*. Athens: University of Georgia Press, 1998.

Wiederhold, Lutz. "Legal Doctrines in Conflict the Relevance of *Madhhab* Boundaries to Legal Reasoning in the Light of an Unpublished Treatise on *Taqlīd* and *Ijtihād*." *Islamic Law and Society* 3, no. 2 (1996): 234–304.

Widigdo, Mohammad Syifa Amin. "Imām al-Ḥaramayn al-Juwaynī on *Jadal*: Juridical and Theological Dialectic in the Fifth/Eleventh Century." PhD diss., Indiana University, 2016.

Widigdo, Mohammad Syifa Amin. "Arab-Islamic or Greek Dialectics? Revisiting the Origins and Development of *Jadal*." *Islam and Christian–Muslim Relations* 32, no. 2 (2021): 203–222.

Widigdo, Mohammad Syifa Amin. "Aristotelian Dialectic, Medieval *Jadal*, and Medieval Scholastic Disputation." *The American Journal of Islamic Social Sciences* 34, no. 4 (2018): 1–24.

Wittgenstein, Ludwig. *The Philosophical Investigations*. Trans. G.E.M. Anscombe. Cambridge: Cambridge University Press, 1986.

Yacoob, Saadia. "Islamic Law and Gender." In *The Oxford Handbook of Islamic Law*. Ed. Anver Emon and Rumee Ahmed, 75–104. Oxford: Oxford University Press, 2018.

Yarbrough, Luke. *Friends of the Emir: Non-Muslim State Officials in Premodern Islamic Thought*. Cambridge: Cambridge University Press, 2019.

Young, Iris Marion. "Impartiality and the Civic Public: Some Implications of Feminist Critiques of Moral and Political Theory." In *Feminism as Critique: On the Politics of Gender*. Ed. Drucilla Cornell and Seyla Benhabib, 56–76. Minneapolis: University of Minnesota Press, 1987.

Young, Walter Edward. *The Dialectical Forge: Juridical Disputation and the Evolution of Islamic Law*. Cham: Springer, 2017.

Young, Walter. "*Mulāzama* in Action in the Early *Ādāb al-Baḥth*." *Oriens* 44, no. 3–4 (2016): 332–385.

Zaman, Muhammad Qasim. *Religion and Politics under the Early ʿAbbāsids: The Emergence of the Proto-Sunnī Elite*. Leiden: Brill, 1997.

Zysow, Aron. "Muʿtazilism and Māturīdism in Ḥanafī Legal Theory." In *Studies in Islamic Legal Theory*. Ed. Bernard Weiss, 235–265. Leiden: Brill, 2002.

Zysow, Aron. *The Economy of Certainty: An Introduction to the Typology of Islamic Legal Theory*. Atlanta: Lockwood Press, 2013.

# Index

*For the benefit of digital users, indexed terms that span two pages (e.g., 52–53) may, on occasion, appear on only one of those pages.*


'Abbasids, 23–24, 52–53, 54–55, 57–59, 74
'Abd al-Salām, 'Izz al-Dīn, 188–89
Abū Ḥanīfa, 46, 54–55, 56–57, 58–59, 62–64, 68–69, 83, 106, 169, 175
Abū Yūsuf, 54–58, 83
Ahmed, Leila, 140
'Alī, Fourth caliph, 42, 53–54
Ali, Kecia, 41
al-Āmidī, Sayf al-Dīn, 177–78, 183
analogical argument (*qiyās*), 39, 41, 43, 45–46, 47, 86, 108–9, 110, 137–38, 148, 149–50, 170–72, 176–77
Asad, Talal, 19, 23, 34–35, 96–97, 160–61
al-Ash'arī, Abū al-Ḥasan, 90
Ash'arī theological school, 10–11, 82, 137–38, 139

al-Bājī, Abū al-Walīd, 12–13, 29–31, 32–35, 39, 40, 48–49, 55–56, 96, 122–23, 188–89
al-Baghdādī, al-Khaṭīb, 30–31, 64–66, 67, 96, 183–85, 187–88
al-Bājī, 'Alā' al-Dīn, 188–89
al-Balkhī al-Ka'bī, Abū al-Qāsim, 72–73
al-Bāqillānī, Abū Bakr, 55–56, 59, 82, 83–84, 86–87
Basra, 8–9, 87–88, 90, 106–7
al-Baṣrī, Abū al-Ḥusayn, 82, 86–87, 90
al-Bayḍāwī, Nāṣir al-Dīn, 177–78
Belhaj, Abdessamad, 73
al-Bulqinī, Ṣāliḥ b. Sirāj al-Dīn, 177–78

Calder, Norman, 172–73, 182
Chaudhry, Ayesha, 140–41
critique, across cultures, 18–20

al-Dāmaghānī, Abū 'Abd Allāh, 12–13, 29–30, 33, 36, 37, 40, 43–46, 77, 84, 94–95, 103–5, 106–7, 109, 110, 111–12, 113, 114, 115, 116–17, 118, 119–20, 121–24
Damascus, 12–13, 17–18, 166, 167, 170–71
Danish Cartoons, 1, 22–23
disagreement (*khilāf*), 4, 11, 18–19, 69–70, 77–78, 79–80, 90–91, 106–7, 183
  *khilāf/ikhtilāf*, 2–3

El Shamsy, Ahmed, 16, 92–93
Emon, Anver, 104–5

Fadel, Mohammad, 15, 17, 179, 190–91
Fars, 106–7, 144–45, 158
*fatwā* (responsa), 8, 14, 36–37, 80, 81, 86–87, 152, 175, 177–78
financial maintenance (*nafaqa*), 12, 40–41, 46–47
Firuzabad, 7–8, 94, 144–45
forced marriage, 24
  contemporary context, 125–26
  and guardianship, 127–30, 134
  and *maṣlaḥa* (benefit), 137–38
  and minority age, 130–31
  and rational capacity, 136–37
Foucault, Michel, 19, 20–21

al-Ghazālī, Abū Ḥāmid, on the Muṣawwiba, 90–92
  on *ijtihād*, 21, 37, 57–58, 73–74, 95–97, 122–23, 137–38, 160, 166, 175–80, 183–86, 189, 190

Habermas, Jürgen, 20–21

Hallaq, Wael, 14–15, 16, 69, 73, 77–78, 89–91, 152, 170–71, 172–73, 177–79
Hārūn al-Rashīd, Caliph, 55–56, 57–58, 59
humiliation (*ṣaghār*), 20–21, 118–21, 123, 129–30

Ibn Abī Laylā, 54–55
Ibn A'tham, 53–54
Ibn 'Aqīl, 22–23, 59, 65, 96, 122–23, 170, 178–79
Ibn Bint al-A'azz, 188–89
Ibn Dāwūd al-Ẓāhirī, 70–72, 82
Ibn al-Farrā', Abū Ya'lā, 82, 86–87, 88, 89
Ibn Ḥanbal, Aḥmad, 60, 61–62, 66–67, 82, 89
Ibn Jamā'a 188–89
Ibn Kathīr, 186–87
Ibn Khaldūn, 165, 173, 183, 188–89
Ibn al-Mulaqqin, 157–58, 177–78
Ibn al-Qāṣṣ, 122–23, 185
Ibn al-Qaṣṣār, 82
Ibn Rāhawayh, 60–64, 69–70, 74
Ibn al-Rāwandī, 72–73
Ibn al-Rif'a 177–78
Ibn al-Ṣabbāgh, Abū Naṣr, 10, 122–23, 159–60, 183–85
Ibn al-Ṣalāḥ, 12–13, 16, 94–95, 166, 170–71, 172–73, 176–77
Ibn Surayj, 68–75, 81–82, 145–46, 154, 161–62, 169, 170
*ijtihād*, and school belonging, as an obligation, Independent *ijtihād*, 4–5, 11, 14–18, 23–25, 29–30, 78, 79–85, 86–90, 91–95, 97–98, 99, 103–4, 106–7, 109–10, 111, 121–22, 123–24, 147–48, 153–54, 155–57, 160, 161–62, 165–67, 169–73, 174–80, 181–82, 183, 185–86, 190–91
*ijtihād* in the *madhhab*, 16–17, 94–95, 177–78
al-'Imrānī, Abū al-Ḥusayn, 123
infallibilism (*taṣwīb*), 87–92
Iraq, 63–64, 67
  beginning of disputations, 40, 54–59, 64
  culture of critique, 4–5, 13, 165–66
  decaying time, 166, 170, 176–77, 178–79, 190–91
  and the discursive foundations of disputation, 78, 79, 82, 88, 90, 99
  jurists, 16–17, 51–52, 66–67, 69, 74–75
  makeup of scholarly community, 8–9
  Mongol invasion, 17–18, 166–67, 177–78
  scholarship, 29–30
  Seljuks, 10
  Shāfi'īs, 104, 144–47, 153–54, 157–62, 178–79, 183–85
  theological circles, 72–73
al-Isfarāyinī, Abū Ḥāmid, 9, 95–96, 104, 146, 158, 159–60, 168–69, 170
al-Isfarāyinī, Abū Isḥāq, 137–38, 179–80
al-Isnawī, Jamāl al-Dīn, 177–78, 182–83
al-Iṣṭakhrī, Abū Sa'īd, 70–71, 157

Jackson, Sherman, 15, 17, 106, 190–91
*jadal*, as dialectic, 5–6, 51–52, 118
  and Aristotle, 73
  beginnings of dialectical science, 68–75
  *jadal al-madhmūm*, 65–68
  *jadal al-maḥmūd* (praiseworthy disputation), 51–52, 66
  as a synonym for *munāẓara*, 51–52, 64–65
al-Jaṣṣāṣ, Abū Bakr, 6–7, 73–74, 90
al-Jubbā'ī, Abū 'Alī, 87–88, 90
juristic elite (*al-khāṣṣ*), 29–30, 140, 161–62
al-Juwaynī, Abū al-Ma'ālī, 10–11, 145
al-Juwaynī, Abū Muḥammad, 146
*jizya* (poll-tax), 12, 103–9, 110–13, 114–24, 157

al-Karkhī, Abū al-Ḥasan, 73–74, 83
Khan, Syed Ahmed, 1
*Khiyār*, definition, 40–43, 46–47, 77, 84, 94–95, 103–4, 157
Khurasan, 4, 10–11, 17–18, 57–58, 60–61, 63–64, 69–70, 74, 110–11, 128–29, 144, 145–46, 148, 152–53, 157–59, 160, 161–62, 166, 170–71, 176, 177–78, 179–80, 183–85

land-*kharāj*, 109, 110, 111–13, 114–15, 116–18, 121–22, 123–24

lay Muslims (*al-'āmm*), 4, 14, 17, 21, 23–24, 29–30, 35–40, 42–43, 45–46, 47–48, 49, 81–82, 92–93, 96–97, 128–29, 152, 154, 155–56, 159–60, 169–72, 173–75, 176–77
legal school (*madhhab*), training of jurists, 4, 155–56
  consolidation of doctrine, 143–44, 152, 154, 156, 157
  defense of school doctrine, 92–95, 96–97, 153–54
  finality and canonization, 24–25, 154–55, 156–57, 182, 185–86
  hierarchies, 5–6, 31–33, 170–72
  and *ijtihād*, 1–5, 17–18, 79–84, 103–4, 106–7, 109–11, 115, 119, 123–24, 154, 155–56, 159–60, 165–66, 175, 180–81
  inter-*madhhabic* disputation, 32
  intra-*madhhabic* disputation, 127, 131, 134, 139, 140–41
  as a tradition, 153–54, 160–61, 169–70
  legal theory, 118
al-Lu'lu'ī, al-Ḥasan b. Ziyād, 63–64

MacIntyre, Alasdair, 160–61
Al-Mahdī, Caliph, 73
Makdisi, George, 5–6, 69–70, 77–78, 90–91, 103, 152
Mālik b. Anas, 55–58, 66–67, 169
Malikshāh, 126
Mamluk, 166–67, 173, 177–78, 183, 186–87, 189
al-Manṣūr, caliph, 58–59
al-Marghīnānī, Burhān al-Dīn, 119
al-Marwarrūdhī, al-Qāḍī al-Ḥusayn, 146
al-Marwazī, Abū Zayd, 145–46
al-Marwazī, Abū Isḥāq, 145–46
al-Marwazī, al-Qaffāl, 145–46, 158–60, 185
Marx, Karl, 21–22
*maṣlaḥa* (benefit), 137–38
al-Māwardī, Abū al-Ḥasan, 6–7, 8–9, 92–93, 104, 107, 109, 110–11, 119–20, 122–23, 128–29, 159, 173–74, 177–78, 179, 185
Melchert, Christopher, 66–67, 69, 73–74
Mernissi, Fatema, 140
Miller, Larry, 72–73
Mongols, 17–18, 166–67, 177–78
Moosa, Ebrahim, 137
*munāẓara* (Disputation), meaning, 5, 52–53
  al-Shāfi'ī's disputations, 59–64
  and the caliph's court, 34, 51–52, 53, 57–59
  discursive foundations, 175
  early legal *munāẓara*, 54–59
  ethics of, 18, 22–23, 32–34, 51, 57–58, 69–75, 187
  as a form of critique, 18–20
  genealogy of, 23–24, 51–52, 74–75
  and Ibn Surayj, 68–72
  inter-school polemics, 73–74
  and *jadal*, 64–68
  in the Mamluk era, 165, 179–80, 188, 189
  occasions for, 5, 30–32, 126
  as pious critique, 4, 30–31, 32–33, 34–40, 54, 66, 74–75, 77
  socio-legal impact, 21, 23–24
  theological, 72–73
  theo-political, 53–54
al-Mutawallī, Abū Sa'd 183–85
al-Mu'tazila, 72–73, 82, 87–88, 90, 96–97
al-Muṭṭawwi'ī, Abū Ḥafṣ, 68–69
al-Muzanī, Abū Ibrāhīm, 81–82, 152–53, 155, 167, 170, 185–86

al-Nawawī, Muḥyī al-Dīn, 157–58, 166–74, 175–78, 179–83, 185, 188–89, 190–91
Nishapur, 10–11, 12–13, 69–70, 126, 145–46, 159, 160–61, 183–85
Niẓām al-Mulk, 10–11, 126, 173–74, 183–85
Niẓāmiyya college, 10–11, 126, 183–85
al-Nu'aymī, 'Abd al-Qādir, 186–87

prayer direction (*qibla*)
  abandoning, 148–49, 151, 157
  as a metaphor for *ijtihād*, 92–93
  mistaken, 146, 147, 152–54, 156–57, 159–60

al-Qāḍī 'Iyāḍ, 55–56

al-Qudūrī, Abū al-Ḥusayn, 135, 168–69
questioner (*sā'il*), 5, 37–38, 40, 52–53, 62, 66–67, 68–69, 73–74, 103–4, 126, 147

al-Rāfi'ī, 'Abd al-Karīm b. Muḥammad, 122–23, 176–77, 181, 182–83
al-Rāzī, Fakhr al-Dīn, 87–88, 169, 177–78
respondent (*mujīb*), 5, 37–38, 52–53, 62, 68–69, 103–4, 147
Rushdie Affair, 1, 22–23

al-Ṣafadī, Ṣalāḥ al-Dīn, 186–87
al-Safāḥ, Abū al-'Abbās, 52–53
al-Sakhāwī, Shams al-Dīn, 187, 188–89
al-Sakūnī, Abū 'Alī, 53, 57–58
al-Samarqandī, 'Alā' al-Dīn, 83
al-Ṣaymarī, Abū 'Abd Allāh, 31–32, 33, 36–37, 48–49, 77, 83, 86–87
al-Ṣayrafī, Abū Bakr, 122–23
secularism, 2–3, 21–22
Schacht, Joseph, 14–16, 92, 103, 172–73
al-Shāfi'ī, Muḥammad b. Idrīs, disputations, 56–57, 59–64, 67–68, 72–73, 77, 81–82, 106, 115, 168–69, 171–73
al-Shāshī, al-Qaffāl, 69–70, 72–73
al-Shaybānī, Muḥammad b. al-Ḥasan, 42, 55–58, 77, 82, 83, 84
Shiraz, 8–9, 59, 94
al-Shīrāzī, Abū Isḥāq
  biography, 7–11
  on certainty, 84–86, 96–97
  definition of *munāẓara*, 53, 65
  disputation transcripts, 11–13
  on *ijtihād*, 37, 38, 79–82, 94–95
  influence on the *madhhab*, 121–23
  and the Niẓāmiyya, 11, 126, 183–85
  rivalry with Ibn al-Ṣabbāgh, 10, 159–60
  trip to Khurasan, 10–11, 126, 144–45
al-Sinjī, Abū 'Alī, 146, 157–58, 179–80
al-Subkī, Tāj al-Dīn, 7–8, 12–13, 70–72, 103–4, 123, 157–58, 182
al-Subkī, Taqī al-Dīn, 182–83, 186–87, 189, 190
suitability in marriage law (*kafā'a*), 128–30
al-Ṣu'lūkī, Abū al-Ṭayyib, 159

al-Ṭabarī, Abū 'Alī, 69–70
al-Ṭabarī, Abū al-Ṭayyib, 9–10, 12–13, 30, 31–32, 33, 36–37, 40–41, 47–49, 77, 89, 92, 122–23, 152–53, 155–56, 159–60, 170, 177–79, 183–85
al-Ṭabarī, Muḥammad b. Jarīr, 54
*taqlīd*, 4–5, 14, 15–18, 80–84, 92–93, 172–73, 174, 176–77, 178–79, 186, 190–92
*taslīm* (transferring), 43–44
Temporal Decay, 17–18, 166, 167–69, 170–71, 173–74, 178–80, 183, 190–92
al-Thawrī, Sufyān, 54–55

'Umar, Second caliph, 89
*umm al-walad*, 45–46, 47
uncertainty in the law, 4–5, 23–24, 78, 79, 84–87, 89–90, 91–92, 95–98, 99, 161–62, 165–66
al-Urmawī, Sirāj al-Dīn, 177–78
*'ushr*, 117–18, 123–24
*uṣūl al-fiqh* (legal theory), 23–24, 69, 75, 78–79, 82, 83–84, 86–88, 90, 92–93, 118, 139, 146–47, 170, 173–74, 177–78

Wittgenstein, Ludwig, 20–21, 51

Yacoob, Saadia, 140
Young, Walter, 59–60, 73–74

al-Ẓāhirī, Dāwūd, 70–71, 82
*zakāt* (alms-tax), 85–86, 112–15, 116–18, 122, 123–24, 131–32
al-Zayla'ī, Jamāl al-Dīn, 132–33, 134
Zufar b. al-Hudhayl, 55